NOTEBOOK OF AN AGITATOR

NOTEBOOK OF AN Agitator

James P. Cannon

PATHFINDER
New York London Montreal Sydney

ISBN 978-0-87348-770-2
Library of Congress Catalog Card Number 93-84144
Manufactured in Canada

First edition, 1958
Second edition, 1973
Third edition, 1993
Twelfth printing, 2026

COVER DESIGN: Toni Gorton

COVER: Top, 1927 demonstration in New York organized by International Labor Defense following execution of Sacco and Vanzetti. Bottom, steelworkers in Gary, Indiana, picket United States Steel during 1952 strike (UPI/Bettman).

PATHFINDER
pathfinderpress.com
Email: pathfinder@pathfinderpress.com

For

Rose Karsner

who was there

all the

time

Contents

Preface to the first edition

This book consists of a selection of articles written for various publications in various places over a stretch of thirty years. They begin with the campaign to save Sacco and Vanzetti from the electric chair in Massachusetts and end in 1956 with a memorial tribute to an attractive intellectual figure, a friend and collaborator of the author, who gave his best years to the socialist movement.

As the title of the book indicates, the articles are definitely partisan. James P. Cannon has been in the thick of the fight for socialism since 1910. His apprenticeship was served in the IWW under Vincent St. John. With the Russian Revolution of 1917 he became a Leninist, participated in the founding of the American Communist party, and was soon recognized as one of its top leaders. Along with others of like view, he was summarily expelled in 1928 at the Kremlin's insistence when, in the struggle against the then new phenomenon of Stalinism, he defended the position of Leon Trotsky. The expelled grouping, continuing to defend the program of revolutionary socialism, developed eventually into the Socialist Workers Party.

In 1941 Cannon was one of the defendants in the Minneapolis labor case. For opposition to imperialist war and advocacy of socialism, he and seventeen others, including prominent Minneapolis union officials, were sentenced to Federal prison for terms varying from a year and a day to sixteen months. The case attracted nation-wide attention, as the victims were the first ones under the notorious Smith Act.

Notebook of an Agitator is a sampling of socialist journalism at its best. Objective, factual reporting in the light of Marxist analysis is inspired with the insistence upon action that a participant in the class struggle is bound to feel. For one of Cannon's outlook, this, of course, means action calculated as to its effectiveness. That is why we see, for example, in the articles on Sacco and Vanzetti scathing indictment of the frame-up of these two anarchist workers combined with cool political consideration as to the best course to take in winning their freedom. Cannon, it should be mentioned, was not speaking as a side-line commentator but as the National Secretary of the International Labor Defense and a key figure in arousing the nation-wide protest movement that sought to save the two famous victims of capitalist "justice."

Of the many strike struggles in which Cannon has been involved, two are represented here. In the 1934 battles that converted Minneapolis from an open-shop to a union town, he writes as a spokesman of the union forces that successfully stood off the strikebreaking combination of employers, police, national guard, government officials and top union bureaucrats. In the 1936–37 West Coast maritime strike, as editor of the San Francisco socialist newspaper *Labor Action,* he takes a hard look at the Stalinist-influenced strategy that endangered one of the most powerful, but quietest, strikes the country has ever seen.

The final two sections, covering the longest period, are the most varied. The prize fighters, the intellectuals, the movies, the Korean war, the Catholic Church, Stalinist ideology, American fascism, visiting preachers, crime and criminals, a blood transfusion, the Fourth of July . . . these are typical topics.

What do such disparate subjects have in common from the viewpoint of a socialist agitator? Or, putting it another way, what's different about the socialist approach to them? If these questions interest you, try the *Notebook of an Agitator* for the answers. I can recommend the search as both stimulating and rewarding.

Joseph Hansen

James P. Cannon

James Patrick Cannon was born in Rosedale, Kansas, on February 11, 1890, into a working-class family. He joined the Socialist Party in 1908 and the Industrial Workers of the World in 1911. In the IWW Cannon worked with Vincent St. John, William "Big Bill" Haywood, and Frank Little, organizing, writing, and speaking in defense of striking workers. A leader of the Socialist Party left wing after the Russian Revolution, he became a founder of the communist movement in the United States in September 1919 and was elected to the Central Committee of the United Communist Party in 1920. When the Workers Party was founded in 1921 as the legal arm of the communist movement, Cannon was elected its national chairman. One of the key leaders of the CP during its first decade, he served on the Presidium of the Communist International in Moscow (1922–23) and was executive secretary of the International Labor Defense (1925–28).

While attending the Sixth World Congress of the Comintern in 1928, Cannon was won over to the fight, led by Leon Trotsky, to continue Lenin's battle against the counterrevolutionary policies of a growing privileged social layer headed by Joseph Stalin. Expelled from the CP later that year he became, with Max Shachtman and Martin Abern, a founding leader of the Communist League of America and served as editor of its newspaper, the *Militant*.

Cannon was a founder of the Socialist Workers Party in January 1938 and a participant in the founding conference of the Fourth International held in France later that year, where he was elected to its International Executive

Committee. Convicted in 1941 with seventeen other leaders of the SWP and of the Midwest Teamster strikes and organizing drives for opposing the imperialist aims of the U.S. government in World War II, Cannon served thirteen months at Sandstone penitentiary in 1944–45.

Cannon was the national secretary of the SWP from 1938 until 1953. Thereafter he was the party's national chairman, and later national chairman emeritus until his death on August 21, 1974.

1

International Labor Defense 1926–1928

Vanzetti (left) and Sacco.

Introductory note

From 1925 to 1928 James P. Cannon served as executive secretary of the International Labor Defense. At the time, he was also a central leader of the Communist Party.

The ILD was formed in 1925 to defend working-class fighters being victimized by the capitalists' courts and cops. It raised money for imprisoned workers and their families, organized speaking tours to publicize their cases, and published the monthly magazine *Labor Defender*. Non-partisan to the core, the ILD included in its ranks members of the Communist Party, Socialist Party, and Industrial Workers of the World. Its national committee included such prominent figures as Eugene V. Debs, Upton Sinclair, and Clarence Darrow.

Under Cannon's leadership, the ILD built a reputation for integrity through its unwavering adherence to the principle that an injury to one is an injury to all. After Cannon's expulsion from the Communist Party in October 1928, the organization was transformed into a factional instrument of the CP.

The period during and after World War I was one of stepped-up victimization of working-class militants, as Washington, fearing the example set by the October 1917 revolution in Russia, used its drive to war and its victory over the Central Powers to strike at labor militants and defenders of democratic rights. Hundreds were jailed for opposing the war and engaging in union activity. In 1919 the FBI organized the notorious Palmer Raids, in which thousands of foreign-born militants were rounded up and 700 deported. Prominent frame-up victims during these years included Tom Mooney and Warren Billings; Eugene V. Debs; and William ("Big Bill") Haywood. The most famous case, however, involved anarchist immigrant workers Nicola Sacco and Bartolomeo Vanzetti.

Sacco and Vanzetti were framed up in 1920 on charges of robbery and murder and sentenced to the electric chair. For the next seven years, workers around the world rallied to their cause, making their names synonymous with the fight against capitalist injustice. Despite the protests, Sacco and Vanzetti were executed in August 1927.

The articles in this section were originally published in the ILD's *Labor Defender* and the *Daily Worker,* newspaper of the Communist Party.

For Sacco and Vanzetti

With all our strength for Sacco and Vanzetti!

DAILY WORKER, MAY 20, 1926

The fatal hour draws near for our beloved comrades, Sacco and Vanzetti. The frame-up witnesses and perjurers have finished their testimony. The lawyers have finished their arguments. The august courts have rendered their verdict. After six years of suspense and torture the ghastly conspiracy is scheduled to culminate very soon by a cruel death in the electric chair.

Sacco and Vanzetti remain undaunted after their long ordeal. They look into the face of death without fear. How heroic and inspiring they are, and what an example they set before the labor movement! After the Supreme Court rendered its decision refusing them a new trial, Comrade Vanzetti wrote to the International Labor Defense: "I am and will remain to the death for the emancipation of the working class!"

The two Italian rebel workers know the issues involved in their case better than all the clever lawyers. They know it is for the crime of solidarity that their lives are to be sacrificed. Comrade Vanzetti says in the same letter: "It is a long time that I wanted to write to you to tell you that I appreciate your solidarity. I am one of the old guard who appreciate and approve the solidarity and have been solidarity with all." Our brave comrade in his own manner of expression puts the idea clear and straight.

Our brothers in prison have no illusions. They know the bloodthirsty master class of Massachusetts intends to do them finally to death. Vanzetti says in his letter: "They are preparing the fire on which to burn us alive."

Not only do they understand the reason for their long suffering and sacrifice, with the death chair at the end of it. They know also where the power lies that can save them. In the hour of their desperate need they turn to the labor movement with their appeal. "Only the revolutionary workers, the people, can give us life and freedom," writes Comrade Vanzetti.

Let us make these words of our imprisoned comrades ring around the world. Let us make them a clarion call to the workers everywhere to raise their voices in such a mighty protest that the monstrous conspiracy will be defeated and our comrades brought back to "life and freedom."

Time is pressing!

Precious lives are in danger!

Swell the protest!

Sacco and Vanzetti must not die!

Who can save Sacco and Vanzetti?

LABOR DEFENDER, JANUARY 1927

The Sacco-Vanzetti case is at a turning point. Legally speaking, it now rests on another appeal to the Massachusetts State Supreme Court from the latest decision of Judge Thayer refusing a new trial. But speaking from a more fundamental standpoint; that is, from the standpoint of the class struggle, the issue really hangs on developments taking place within the Sacco-Vanzetti movement which embraces workers of various views.

Within this movement lately a certain indecision and hesitation has been noticeable. This by no means signifies a change in the attitude of the masses toward Sacco and Vanzetti. Their faith and solidarity remain unshaken. The waiting and uncertainty which characterize the movement at the present time are merely the reflection of a serious conflict over policy and methods of conducting the fight.

The Sacco-Vanzetti case is no private monopoly, but an issue of the class struggle in which the decisive word will be spoken by the masses who have made this fight their own. It is, therefore, necessary to discuss openly the conflicting policies which are bound up with different objectives.

One policy is the policy of the class struggle. It puts the center of gravity in the protest movement of the workers of America and the world. It puts all faith in the power of the masses and no faith whatever in the justice of the courts. While favoring all possible legal proceedings, it calls for agitation, publicity, demonstrations—organized protest on a national and international scale. It calls for unity and solidarity of all workers on this burning issue, regardless of conflicting views on other questions. This is what has prevented the execution of Sacco and Vanzetti so far. Its goal is nothing less than their triumphant vindication and liberation.

The other policy is the policy of "respectability," of the "soft pedal" and of ridiculous illusions about "justice" from the courts of the enemy. It relies mainly on legal proceedings. It seeks to blur the issue of the class struggle. It shrinks from the "vulgar and noisy" demonstrations of the militant workers and throws the mud of slander on them. It tries to represent the martyrdom of Sacco and Vanzetti as an "unfortunate" error which can be rectified by the "right" people proceeding in the "right" way. The objective of this policy is a whitewash of the courts of Massachusetts and "clemency" for Sacco and Vanzetti, in the form of a commutation to life imprisonment for a crime of which the world knows they are innocent.

The conscious proletarian elements with whom we identify ourselves unconditionally, are for the first policy. The bourgeois elements, and those influenced by them, are for the second.

The corruption and class bias of the courts of Massachusetts are already proved to the hilt. A division of the proletarian forces will only facilitate their murderous plans. They are determined to have the blood of Sacco and Vanzetti.

Only the organized and united protest movement of the masses can save them. In this movement the class conscious workers—the militants—are the driving force. Let those who hamper this movement or endanger its unity pause lest they unconsciously become the executioners of Sacco and Vanzetti.

The international campaign for Sacco and Vanzetti

LABOR DEFENDER, FEBRUARY 1927

Rarely has the vital importance of international solidarity of the working class been so decisively shown as in the world campaign for Sacco and Vanzetti. Had there not from the very beginning been demonstrated that unbreakable determination of the workers everywhere to make the fight of the two Italian agitators their fight; had there not been that splendid series of labor demonstrations in the capitals of the world; the incessant flow of resolutions and protests against this hideous conspiracy to murder two innocent workers—then the judicial vultures of Massachusetts might long ago have seized and demolished their prey.

Realizing this essential fact, as soon as the verdict against a new trial was rendered by the Massachusetts court, International Labor Defense appealed to labor defense organizations throughout the world to renew their agitation for Sacco and Vanzetti. The need was desperate, for the Massachusetts Bourbons had—as they still have—every intention to apply as swiftly as possible the electrodes of death to their long-suffering victims.

Those who have observed even superficially the development of the case from that time on, know that it was this new campaign of protest and demonstration of solidarity that halted the hand of the executioner. The workers of this country, and of Latin America and Europe, by their tireless solidarity, placed an unbroken wall between Sacco and Vanzetti and the death chair that is being held vacant for them and gained for them a new respite.

The campaign that was conducted in the United States is well known to all workers. At the request of the I.L.D., Congressman Victor Berger introduced his resolution in Congress calling for an investigation of the case. Hundreds of labor organizations and men and women prominent in the labor and progressive movements, reiterated their belief in the innocence of Sacco and Vanzetti and pledged themselves to a renewed drive for their final vindication and release.

Mass meetings were held in every large city. In New York City alone some 18,000 workers came to Madison Square Garden to protest against the proposed legal assassination. Resolutions poured into the office of Governor Alvan T. Fuller of Massachusetts. Hundreds of thousands of leaflets, an appeal by International Labor Defense, and a stirring call to action by Eugene V. Debs, were distributed everywhere. Posters, buttons, articles for the press, the *Labor Defender*—every means of publicity and agitation was utilized in the campaign. The Sacco-Vanzetti Conferences, into which hundreds of thousands of workers were organized, made the names of the two Italian workers the symbol of solidarity and united efforts.

In Europe the campaign received its greatest support from Germany, Italy and England. In the German Reichstag, a large group of members of various parties combined to send a telegram of protest to Governor Fuller. The president of the Reichstag, Paul Loebe, also cabled his protest. Dozens of the prominent leaders of the German trade unions aligned themselves with the movement. Leading publicists, scientists, artists and public officials, including the former ambassador to the United States, Von Bernstorff, Maximilian Harden, Rudolf Breitscheid, Professor Liebermann, General Music Director Kreisler, Georg Brandes, added their voices. Deputations from labor bodies were sent to protest to the American ambassador in Berlin. Scores of meetings were held in every German center, and to list the organizations which adopted resolutions of protest would require an issue of the *Labor Defender.*

From England came the protests of the Trade Union Congress, from the British Labour Party, the Independent Labour Party, the Communist Party and the "Minority Movement." A telegram signed by members of parliament which included George Lansbury, Ellen Wilkinson, Robert Smillie, Sullivan and many others was sent to the now deluged Governor of Massachusetts. The International Class War Prisoners' Aid (the British counterpart of the I.L.D.) did some remarkable work in agitating for Sacco and Vanzetti, and literally hundreds of local labor organizations throughout England were listed by the I.C.W.P.A.

as having adopted protest resolutions.

In Italy, despite the incredibly difficult situation, meetings were held wherever possible to protest against the conviction of Sacco and Vanzetti. The labor representatives in the Chamber of Deputies demanded the interference of the Italian government in the case. Constant interpellations to the government were made by the radicals in the Chamber.

Since the May decision of the court, demonstrations were held in front of the American embassies at Paris, Sofia, Lisbon, Buenos Aires, Berlin, Montevideo and Mexico. Everywhere the demand of the workers was for the immediate cessation of this hounding of two innocent labor fighters.

Governor Fuller, who fled from America to France, was pursued there by the international solidarity of the workers. The *Secours International Rouge* (International Red Aid) of France announced its intention of interviewing him by means of a workers' demonstration, and Fuller was forced into hiding in France. To escape the demonstration he even saw to it that his name was omitted from the list of American arrivals which is regularly given in the Paris edition of the *Chicago Tribune.*

In the Union of Soviet Socialist Republics, literally millions of workers and peasants have recorded their opposition to the planned execution of the two American radicals.

The same story can be told of the work in a dozen other countries, and a great debt is owed by us to the International Red Aid, to which the I.L.D. appealed at the crucial moment, and which organized and centralized the protest movement in many countries.

It was this campaign for international solidarity that has so far saved Sacco and Vanzetti from the death chair, and not the reliance solely upon the good intentions and judicial honesty of the Massachusetts courts. So long as Sacco and Vanzetti remain in the shadow of danger the workers of the world will stand guard. They will continue to make the cause of the two Italian radicals their cause, until their liberation has brought a successful end to the Sacco-Vanzetti case.

From the Supreme Court of the capitalists to the supreme court of the laboring masses

LABOR DEFENDER, MAY 1927

The news of the decision of the Supreme Court of Massachusetts comes to hand just as this number of the *Labor Defender* goes to press.

The black-robed judges have pronounced the doom of Sacco and Vanzetti. Evidence of frame-up and conspiracy was piled high enough for the whole world to see, but the judges would not look at it. The New England Bourbons want the blood of innocent men. This was decided from the first. Only fools expected otherwise. Only fools put faith in the courts of the enemy.

It is all planned and decided. The two Italian workers have been taken into the Dedham courtroom, where they were falsely convicted of murder six years ago this summer, and there sentenced by Judge Webster Thayer of the Superior Court to die in the electric chair at Charlestown on July 10 for the crime of rebellion against the capitalists.

They will take them from their cells and strap them securely in the chair. They will turn on the switch with the hope that when the deadly current burns and sears the warm flesh of the two rebel workmen, there will also be consumed within these flames the cause they symbolize.

So they have decreed and so they hope. But the game is not over. There is another power yet to be considered. There is a higher court than that of the solemn reprobates who decreed the death of Sacco and Vanzetti. The laboring masses of America and the world have faith in Sacco and Vanzetti. It is time now to appeal finally to the masses. It is time for the workers to say their word.

Such slender legal resources as yet remain must be utilized. This goes without saying. But the real hope for Sacco and Vanzetti must now be placed in the protest movement of the workers. Only the united protest movement of the workers can save Sacco and Vanzetti from the hands of the executioners.

The defense of Sacco and Vanzetti is an issue of the class struggle. They are not criminals but the symbols and standard bearers of the militant labor movement. The fight for Sacco and Vanzetti is the fight of the working class.

The need of the hour is an organized, united movement of protest and solidarity on a national and international scale. The great world-wide movement which has stayed the hands of the executioners up till now must be revived and infused with new strength and militancy. In this movement unity must be the watchword. All partisan aims, all differences of opinion and all controversial questions must be put aside. All forces must be united without delay on the broadest possible basis for the struggle to free Sacco and Vanzetti.

The agitation must be conducted with concrete aims. The first big objective is the concentration of the indignation and protest of the workers in a gigantic National Sacco and Vanzetti Conference. Only through a National Conference can the forces be united and the resources gathered for further struggle. We must go forward with the organization of this National Conference at all costs, in spite of all difficulties and without delay.

A speech for Sacco and Vanzetti

At the Sacco-Vanzetti mass meeting in Chicago, May 13, 1927

LABOR DEFENDER, JUNE 1927

The Sacco-Vanzetti case has been a part of American labor history in the making. It is seven years now since Sacco and Vanzetti have been in the shadow of the electric chair. I do not believe that history knows of a similar case. I do not believe that we could find anywhere a case of such prolonged torture as the holding of the sentence of death over the heads of men for seven years. At the end of that time we come together for a meeting and do not know yet whether that sentence is to be executed or not.

The cause of Sacco and Vanzetti demands of us, of the entire labor movement, militant, unhesitating and united support. We may have different opinions on many problems; but there is one thing we have become sure of in these seven years in which we have said our word for Sacco and Vanzetti. We have become absolutely convinced that the case of Sacco and Vanzetti, the case of these two Italian workers in Massachusetts, is not the case of two hold-up men or bandits. We have become convinced that it is the working class against the capitalists. We have become convinced that Sacco and Vanzetti are not only innocent of this specific crime which they are charged with, but that they are innocent of any crime except that of being rebels against capitalist exploitation of the masses.

Their case has gone so far that we do not need to discuss it any longer from a legal standpoint. But for those who are interested, it has been set forth by Mr. Holly. And we can say for others, that recently a book was published by Professor Felix Frankfurter in which he comes to the conclusion that there is no legal case against Sacco and Vanzetti.

But the case of Sacco and Vanzetti has a far bigger significance than any legal procedure. Sacco and Vanzetti began in this case as two employees, obscure fighters of the working class. But they have grown in these years until their personalities have made their impression not only in Massachusetts, not only in the United States, but all over Europe and America.

Sacco and Vanzetti have grown as the great symbols of the whole labor movement. They stand for the upward struggle against oppression and exploitation, for that fearless defiance of the enemies of labor with which the best representatives of the working class are instinct.

Everyone today knows why the Bourbons of Massachusetts arrested, imprisoned and tried Sacco and Vanzetti. Had they not been scrupulously loyal to the cause of the working class, they would not now be faced with the grim march to the death chair. Had they remained silent while their brothers and comrades around them suffered persecution and oppression, had they not made the ideal of the liberation of the working class their own ideal, there would not today be a Sacco-Vanzetti case. Had they, in court, begged for mercy and renounced their cause and their past, they would have been freed to achieve obloquy.

But they did none of this. Despite the hundreds of interminable nights and days of imprisonment, with the ghastly thought of execution constantly in their minds, they have remained as simply true to the workers' cause as they were before this infamous frame-up was conceived in the minds of the Massachusetts reaction. Yes, their persecution has even steeled their convictions, and has already bound them inseparably with the history of the American labor movement.

After seven years they came to court for sentence. I wish every worker in America could read the speech that Vanzetti made there. After seven years of torture, with the death sentence hanging over him, this man stood up in court, not as one guilty, not as one afraid. He turned to the judge on the bench and said to him:

> You are the one that is afraid. You are the one that is shrinking with fear, because you are the one that is guilty of attempt to murder.

Vanzetti called his witnesses there, and not merely legal witnesses. He marshalled before Judge Thayer's attention the thousands who have decided to hold mass meetings such as ours; and public men of our period like Anatole France, Maxim Gorky, Bernard Shaw, Henri Barbusse, Albert Einstein. He pointed to the many millions who have protested against the frame-up.

He turned to Eugene Victor Debs and other men in America. Let us not forget that we should measure guilt and innocence not by formal evidence in court alone, but by higher values than that. Let us not forget that the last thing that Eugene Debs wrote publicly was an appeal to the workers of America for Sacco and Vanzetti, an appeal whose stirring language aroused with renewed vigor the protest of hundreds of thousands in this country, and brought again the million-voiced demand for life and freedom for these two valiant fighters, and condemnation of their persecutors.

It is hard to speak with restraint. I, like Comrade Chaplin, also had the honor of talking with Vanzetti. Everyone that has seen and talked with him comes away with the feeling that he has stood in the presence of one of the greatest spirits of our time.

It is hard to speak with restraint when one is pressed by the thought that the vengeful executioners of Massachusetts are consummating their hideous plan to press the switch that will forever remove from our ranks the persons of these two men who we feel are so much a part of labor and its cause. Our impassioned determination to mobilize all of our strength and power to rescue Sacco and Vanzetti from their blood-lusting jailers must be communicated throughout the land, if we are to save them from the fate that has been prepared for them.

While I agree with the statements of Fitzpatrick that our meeting should dissociate itself from irresponsible people, let us not forget the year 1915 when Joe Hill was killed in Utah. We must remember that when the wave of working-class protest began to rise in protection of Joe Hill, gangs of detectives began to fake threatening letters. After the heart of Joe Hill had been pierced by the bullets of the death squad, it was exposed that frame-up letters had been used. This must be a lesson for us and for those who are the friends of Sacco and Vanzetti.

There is no need to threaten the governor or anyone else because the protection of Sacco and Vanzetti is far stronger than any personal act. The protection of Sacco and Vanzetti is the job of the working class of the world, which is knocking on the door, not with the hands of irresponsible individuals, but with the titanic fist of the workers of the wide world, because they believe in the innocence of Sacco and Vanzetti. We say to you, our friends and our chairman, before they turn on the switch, that the real aim is not only to burn Sacco and Vanzetti in the electric chair but to burn the labor movement in America.

If the workers of America and the workers of the world

are determined enough and encouraged enough, we can yet save Sacco and Vanzetti. And it is in that spirit that we meet here tonight. We do not meet here to resign ourselves to their fate. We meet as another stage in the fight for Sacco and Vanzetti. We believe that the workers assembled here will go back to their organizations and their jobs and raise again the battle cry for Sacco and Vanzetti.

Let us demand not only the liberation of Sacco and Vanzetti. Let us demand also the impeachment of the monstrous judge who tried and sentenced them. Let us consider ways and means of making our protest more effective. From this great movement, from the words of Sacco and Vanzetti, let us draw inspiration.

We have hope, and we have faith in the workers of America, and in the workers of the rest of the world, who have so often and readily responded to the calls for solidarity and aid for Sacco and Vanzetti. Every worker in the land must be made to realize the monstrosity and significance to the whole labor movement of this crime. Every worker must stand shoulder to shoulder with his brothers to build a solid wall of defense for the victims of the Massachusetts Bourbons who are bent on their bestial revenge. Only the great and inspiring solidarity of the whole working class will succeed in snatching Sacco and Vanzetti from the chair of death.

Death, commutation or freedom?

LABOR DEFENDER, JULY 1927

The great movement of solidarity in the campaign to save Sacco and Vanzetti for the working class, which has developed to such splendid proportions, may be confronted with a new danger by the time these words appear in the *Labor Defender*. It is the same danger that sapped the strength, resoluteness and militancy of the movement to rescue Tom Mooney and Warren Billings from the hangman's noose. It arises out of the diabolical cunning and fear of the vultures of capitalism who see their prey staunchly defended and seek to hold it with new snares.

This is known to us from the history of the past. We remember the movement for Mooney and Billings; how it enlisted the support of the entire labor movement in this country and in others, of prominent men and women, writers and thinkers; how the cry for a general strike to free the two frame-up victims found an echo among hundreds of thousands of workers. We know that with a whole world convinced of their innocence, the executioners were forced to forego murdering Mooney and Billings. Then they cheated the movement for the two labor fighters out of its victory by putting them in prison for life.

The change of the death sentence to one of life imprisonment was the clever evasion of the consequences of the powerful and swiftly growing movement to vindicate Mooney and Billings. But although they were saved from the death of the sprung trap, they were condemned to the living death of life imprisonment, and the movement for their release was virtually destroyed.

The workers who had rallied to Mooney and Billings were soothed by the sinister argument that imprisonment for life was, in any event, better than execution. They were told that we would have to be satisfied for the while with one victory, and that the final release of the two fighters would be won later. But after ten years there remain only a few who still keep alive the memory of these buried men and who are pledged to continue the work for their freedom.

The great movement for Sacco and Vanzetti, which now embraces millions of workers, must not allow itself to be dissolved by a similar subterfuge. It is not a fantastic possibility that is projected here, but a probability that may rapidly develop into a fact.

Already the rumor is being cautiously spread that the governor of Massachusetts, in whose hands the final decision on Sacco and Vanzetti is placed, may commute the sentence of death to one of life imprisonment. It is being spread so that the enemies of Sacco and Vanzetti may feel out the reaction to this prospect among the defenders of the two Italian rebels. They want to know if this splendid movement of solidarity, which has time and again struck heavy blows at the Massachusetts reaction, will allow itself to be dissolved with the bait of a commutation. They want to know if, since some retreat must be made, they can wreak their revenge upon these rebels, who have not feared to defy them, *by burying them alive and at the same time liquidating the movement which must free them!*

We declare that these "kind" gentlemen, who are so ready to grant a commutation of sentence to life imprisonment, and those who are so ready to greet such a commutation, are not the friends of Sacco and Vanzetti. For these fighters, who have so bravely withstood the tortures and nightmares of seven years of being constantly confronted with the frightful prospect of death in the electric chair; who have been borne up only by their own bravery and the knowledge of the support and solidarity of the millions of the world—a sentence of life imprisonment is in many respects worse than death. It is at best a living death, a death by the spirit-crushing torture of cold walls and bars.

We repeat the warning to the friends of Sacco and Vanzetti which Bartolomeo Vanzetti addressed to his friends almost a year ago, in the pages of the *Labor Defender,* when the decision on the case had been postponed and illusions on its outcome were being created:

> We see evil, not good, in this delay. Look out, friends and comrades, let no unfounded optimism lure you in a restful slumbering of confidence that could be awakened only by a shameful and deadly, new and final vanquishment.

The millions of workers in every part of the world who have not ceased to fight for the cause of Sacco and Vanzetti, which has become the cause of the whole working class, must not be deluded by talk of commutation of sentence. The workers who have thus far, by their power and solidarity, prevented the execution of the two rebels must continue their great fight with more consciousness and determination. The workers who have snatched Sacco and Vanzetti from the chair of death must snatch them from the cell of death by slow torture. No unfounded joy must dull the sharp edge of the movement. It must continue to fight forward with its million-armed power until this great issue is settled with a great victory.

The hearts of the Massachusetts executioners have not softened with kindness, and their desire to murder our comrades has not changed. On the contrary, they seek for new methods of torment. The working class must reply:

Not the chair of death, but life for Sacco and Vanzetti!

Not imprisonment of death, but freedom for Sacco and Vanzetti!

No illusions!

DAILY WORKER, AUGUST 18, 1927

The lives of Sacco and Vanzetti still hang in the balance and they are in greater danger now than ever before. Every mention of the case should begin with this warning to the working masses not to be fooled with false hopes and false security.

What has happened, and what are the conclusions to be drawn for our guidance in the struggle during the remaining days of suspense? Some people, no doubt, have seen in the eleventh-hour reprieve a sign of a change of heart of the Massachusetts Bourbons who have been moving, with such refined and deliberate cruelty, to blot out the lives of the Italian rebel workers. Such ideas are the most dangerous illusions. It was just to create these illusions and thereby to get some relief from the thundering clamor of the world's millions, that this latest action in the "cat and mouse" game was taken.

❖

There is not a hint or promise in any aspect of this new development of any design except to gain time, to maneuver for the demoralization of the protest movement of the masses and to organize a counter-campaign against it. The foremost problem of the workers, who see in Sacco and Vanzetti the symbols and banner bearers of their own class and cause, is to understand clearly the new turn of events and to shape their course along the right line.

The militant protest movement has halted the executioners up till now. As the final hour drew near, the movement assumed such proportions and militancy and expressed itself in mass demonstrations and strikes on such a scale, as to shake the world. It was especially the last phase of mass demonstrations and strikes which threw the real power of the masses into the scale against the murder plans of the Massachusetts hangmen. Those who emphasized this line of action, who understood and pointed out at every turn the fundamental class issues involved in the case, and who appealed to the mass power of the workers, were entirely correct. This line is the decisive line. The greatest hope now lies in a further development and energetic promotion of this class-struggle policy.

❖

The case is again before the black-gowned judges on another appeal by the defense against flagrant errors in the trial. It is, of course, absolutely right to exhaust every legal possibility and technicality in the fight, provided—that the workers have no illusions. We must remember that the case has been before these same judges many times before, and that they have again and again put their seal of approval on the criminally false verdict. We must remember that the appointment of Governor Fuller's Commission revealed itself as a ghastly trick to disarm the protest movement and fortify the verdict with more dignified sanctions. The latest move should be suspected as another maneuver of the same sort, designed to give the outward appearance of still more scrupulous "fairness" in the process by which the two labor fighters are to be burned alive.

Remember, also, that powerful influences of the exploiting class are being brought to bear for the carrying out of the death sentence, and that the final issue, just because it is an issue of the class struggle, and not merely an isolated instance of the miscarriage of their so-called "justice," will depend upon the power and might of the class forces set into motion on each side.

The great task, therefore, in the few fateful days remaining, up to the last minute of the last hour, is to put all energy, courage and militancy into the organization of mass demonstrations and protest strikes. All brakes upon this movement must be regarded as the greatest danger. All illusions which paralyze the movement must be overcome. All agents of the bosses who try to sabotage and discredit the protest and strike movement must be given their proper name.

❖

While the judges of the Supreme Court prepare their decision on the case again, we must appeal at the same time to the laboring masses of America and the whole world who are the highest court of all. The workers have a deep conviction for Sacco and Vanzetti, and they have the power to compel their release. We must help the workers to understand this power, to organize it and to use it. The protest strikes already carried out, in spite of and against the misleaders of labor, are opening up a new page in the development of the American working class. The unparalleled heroic example of Sacco and Vanzetti has inspired and called forth new resources of courage, class solidarity and sacrifice.

The tireless work of the militants has already been responsible for the organization of this spirit on an astounding scale. Concentration of all forces and energies along this line, will succeed in harnessing the mood of the masses to an organized demonstration of such intensity and power that it will compel the liberation of Sacco and Vanzetti.

IT WILL DEAL A POWERFUL BLOW TO THE WHOLE INFAMOUS FRAME-UP SYSTEM.

IT WILL PUT THE CASES OF MOONEY AND BILLINGS, AND OTHER MILITANT WORKERS LONG BURIED IN THE PRISONS, AGAIN ON THE AGENDA OF THE LABOR

MOVEMENT, AND WILL INFUSE THAT MOVEMENT WITH A NEW CONSCIOUSNESS OF POWER.

New developments—new dangers

DAILY WORKER, AUGUST 19, 1927

The Sacco-Vanzetti case is moving to its final issue with express-train speed. Events in this mighty drama are transpiring now as though some unseen elemental force were driving them on. These events are fraught with significance and danger for Sacco and Vanzetti, and for the cause of labor which they represent and symbolize. The laboring masses must penetrate the haze of these developments, interpret them truly and draw the right conclusion from them. Only on this condition will they be able to strengthen the iron ring of solidarity and protection around Sacco and Vanzetti.

The main developments are the following:

(1) A few days' delay of execution ostensibly to provide opportunity for further legal deliberation (after seven years!), but in reality to maneuver against the protest movement and gather more strength and courage to go through with their plans.

(2) A revival of the old game of bomb "plants" in order to create the impression that friends of the prisoners are irresponsible terrorists.

(3) Governor Fuller promptly issues a statement expressing horror at a bomb explosion that injured no one—the same governor who felt no horror at all in condemning innocent men to death on the basis of an "investigation" framed-up in secret session.

(4) Attempts of the police to prevent and break up protest meetings and demonstrations and to suppress the expression of the workers against the execution. At least

several hundred workers were arrested in the different cities in which demonstrations of protest were held prior to August 10.

(5) A number of capitalistic and "liberal" elements, who "joined" the movement for a time and even tried to lead it, begin to desert, to get cold feet and to find excuses to justify the legal murder or life imprisonment. The suppression of the Heywood Broun articles by the *New York World* and the changed tone of other capitalist papers are cases in point.

(6) Along with these happenings go the outspoken threats of a new drive against the foreign-born workers.

Thus we see the forces of reaction mobilizing along the whole front with a strategy which represents a combination of trickery and force. They are organizing their forces for the counter-campaign against the mass movement of the workers, the power which stands between Sacco and Vanzetti and the electric chair. They are conspiring and working with feverish speed. There is no ground for the belief that they have changed their plans.

The new developments bring out more than ever, and with crystal clearness, the class basis of this famous case. They show that it is a case of workers against exploiters—with Sacco and Vanzetti, the victims elected for the holocaust, standing out before the whole world as the representatives of the exploited class. The class-struggle policy in the fight for Sacco and Vanzetti was right from the beginning and is a thousand times right now. The power that can save Sacco and Vanzetti is the power of the masses.

The short reprieve was not an act of mercy or justice. It was a trick to create illusions and false hopes. It would be criminally foolish to regard it in any other way.

The bomb "plants" are part of the same strategy and are designed to demoralize and discredit the protest movement, to split its ranks and above all to isolate and discredit the militants who are the organizing and driving force in the entire movement the world over.

Bomb-throwing and other futile acts of individual terror are not the weapons of class-conscious workers. We base ourselves on the masses and rely on the power of the masses in the fight for the liberation of Sacco and Vanzetti.

The police violence and suppression against the protest meetings and the threatened drive against the foreign-born are bound up together with the other developments noted above. There is no contradiction between them. The exploiters are operating as a class and on a class basis, combining the tactics of fraud and maneuver with direct attacks and violence.

In all this there is nothing new for those who understand the class struggle and have no illusions about the possibility of "justice" and "fair play" from the courts and other institutions of the class enemy. The Sacco-Vanzetti case must be considered from this point of view. The power of the workers is the court of last resort to which our appeal must be made.

Only to the extent that we understand this elementary fact will our work in the remaining days have the possibility of success.

Put no faith in capitalist justice!

Organize the protest movement on a wider scale and with a more determined spirit!

Demonstrate and strike for Sacco and Vanzetti!

Class against class in the Sacco and Vanzetti case

LABOR DEFENDER, SEPTEMBER 1927

As this number of the *Labor Defender* goes to press (August 16, 1927) the final issue in the Sacco-Vanzetti case is impending. The danger appears greater than ever before and the lives of the heroic labor fighters hang in the balance. This warning against false hopes and illusions and a call to new work and struggles must be the keynote of every word addressed to the masses in these fateful days.

There is nothing in the new developments, in the short respite, to warrant their being taken as anything but a maneuver to quiet the protest movement and, by taking advantage of the paralysis in the movement created by false hopes and groundless illusions, to carry out the murderous designs of the enemies of the two fighters. The workers who have fought so well for Sacco and Vanzetti must understand the danger and guard against it.

The most important thing now is to examine the situation and to draw the necessary conclusions. Unless this is done, the movement will not be able to steer clearly between the rocks of illusion and passivity.

The eleventh-hour reprieve for Sacco and Vanzetti was brought about by the thunderous clamor of the laboring masses of the world who demonstrated their international working class solidarity in an imposing manner. It did not for a moment mean, as some naive people believe, that the Massachusetts Bourbons whose whole energy is bent on continuing their horrible torture of Sacco and Vanzetti until they can safely destroy them in the electric chair, have experienced any change of heart. On the contrary, the reprieve only enabled them to create most dangerous illusions and to gain *for themselves* some relief from the aroused world's millions.

To believe otherwise is to fall victim to just those illusions that the reactionaries are anxious to spread. Not to realize that this latest action is a maneuver to gain time, during which to demoralize and split and weaken the protest movement, is to fail to see the fundamental question involved. Those who from the beginning had seen the class issue in the case, and based their activities and confidence on the mass movement of the workers, were entirely correct, and all events have proved this.

The strike movement, in which millions everywhere participated, has opened a new page in the development of the American working class. Even the sporadic beginnings made in the use of this great weapon in a political cause, in spite of and against the opposition or indifference of the official labor leaders in most cases, is fraught with profound significance. It demonstrates the irresistible power that lies in the organized working class, spurred on by the spirit of solidarity.

The case has always been an issue of the class struggle and not merely one of an exceptional miscarriage of so-called justice. The Massachusetts Bourbons know this well, and they recognize the magnificent protest movement as a distinctly class movement against which there must be, and is being, organized a counter-campaign.

First there is a new delay of a few days ostensibly for the purpose of providing for further legal deliberations (after seven years!) but in reality to instil the masses with the illusion of hopes from the courts that have prejudged the case. It is a delay calculated to sap the strength of the protest movement and make it more easy for the executioners to carry out their plans of death.

Then there is a worn-out trick of "bomb" plants, which of course never hurt anyone, and which gives Governor Fuller the opportunity to express "indignation" and "regret" at such "horrible deeds"—the same Governor Fuller who coldly and deliberately already put the seal of approval on the burning alive of Sacco and Vanzetti. This old game of "plants" is well known in the labor movement. It is being played now with the aim of discrediting the movement for Sacco and Vanzetti by creating the impression that the friends of the two rebels are irresponsible terrorists. More cunningly, it is hoped to isolate the militant elements of the movement in this manner, and leave the field to those groups who put all their cards on the illusion of Sacco and Vanzetti's chance of obtaining justice from the courts.

The mass movement of the workers, which relies upon its organized strength, has no use for the methods of individual terror, and does not agree with them. Moreover, the history of the labor movement in this country is rich with incidents of the work of provocateurs and we know how to correctly estimate such transparent fakes.

Together with this are the attempts everywhere to suppress meetings in order to prevent the expression of the demand of the workers for the liberation of Sacco and Vanzetti. Thousands of police, armed with clubs, riot and machine guns, and tear-gas bombs, were mobilized for these meetings, and hundreds of workers were arrested throughout the country. In Chicago alone, a score of meetings was broken up in one evening. The capitalists fear the protest of the workers for they realize that therein lies the strength of Sacco and Vanzetti.

If we add to these developments the attempt of a number of the capitalist-liberal elements who joined the movement only to betray it at the critical moment—shown by the suppression of Heywood Broun's articles in the *New York World* and the change of tone in other capitalist papers; and the threats of Congressman Johnson and Secretary of Labor Davis against all foreign-born workers for participation in the Sacco and Vanzetti movement—we can see that the whole machinery of reaction is being mobilized for the counter-campaign which is a combination of trickery and force, illusion and coercion. The new developments bring out with crystal clearness the class issue in the case, the fact that the exploiters are launching all their forces against the movement of the workers which alone stands between Sacco and Vanzetti and the chair of death.

We have no grounds for the belief that there has been the slightest change of plan by the executioners. On the contrary they are conspiring against our comrades with the same malice and working with feverish speed to consummate the assassination. It is true that the case is now before the judges of the Supreme Court. But this gives us no hopes, for it has been there before and we know what to expect from that source.

The working masses have a deep conviction of solidarity toward Sacco and Vanzetti, and they know that even the illusory respite was granted only because of the menacing protest of the workers. We must therefore confidently proceed at all costs to still further arouse and organize the anger of the working men and women against the slaughter of the two labor fighters, and assist it to take the form of huge mass demonstrations and effective strikes.

That is the great task in the coming days: to put all our energy, militancy and courage up to the last minute into the strike movement and the mass demonstrations. We depend for this on the work of the men in the ranks, those class-conscious militants who have been working steadily and quietly, often in the face of calumny, to organize and build the magnificent protest movement. We must work swiftly. All brakes on the movement must be regarded as the greatest danger. All illusions which paralyze the movement must be overcome. All agents of the bosses who try to sabotage and discredit the protest and strike movement must be given their proper names and exposed.

Only a few fateful days remain. But there is still time,

if we are able to disperse the illusions that have been created, to mobilize the power of the workers which is for us the court of last resort to which our appeal must be made. Only to the extent that we understand this elementary fact will our work in the remaining days have the possibility of success.

No faith in capitalist justice and institutions! That is the lesson of history confirmed by every development in the Sacco and Vanzetti case.

Organize the protest movement on a wider scale and with more determined spirit!

Remember the Haymarket martyrs! Remember Mooney and Billings! Remember the other class-war prisoners!

Demonstrate for Sacco and Vanzetti! Strike a blow for freedom!

The murder of Sacco and Vanzetti

DAILY WORKER, AUGUST 24, 1927

Sacco and Vanzetti are dead but their names will live forever and become a shining banner for the upward striving toilers of the world. They have been murdered by the assassins of the capitalist class. Their execution was a cynically brutal defiance of the worldwide demand of the millions of people that they be liberated or at least be given a new trial to prove again their innocence. It was a legal lynching, a fiendish act of class vengeance, cunningly prepared and planned and violently consummated by the willing tools of the capitalist class.

Sacco and Vanzetti died for the working class. Like their immortal comrades of Chicago's Haymarket they died as martyrs to the cause of labor. This was known or felt by tens of millions of workers in every corner of the globe who fought bitterly to the very last moment to vindicate the two martyred labor fighters. Their admirable loyalty and devotion to labor was the only crime they were guilty of; they were innocent of the crime charged against them by their executioners.

The last words of Vanzetti uttered a minute before the current of death silenced his voice were the echo of the deep convictions of the people:

> I wish to tell you that I am innocent and have never committed a crime, but perhaps some sins. I am innocent of all crimes, not only of this one but of all. I am an innocent man.

The Massachusetts executioners have put to death two glorious spirits. These two fighters, living for seven years in the shadow of the electric chair, unceasingly tortured by their suspension between delay and death, calmly watching the relentless net of the capitalist lynchers closing about them, showed by their heroic conduct how the revolutionary fighters of the working class can die at the hands of their class enemy.

The noble dignity and courage which sustained them throughout the seven years remained with them to the end. They went to death calmly and bravely without fear or embarrassment. It was their murderers, the governors and the judges who hid their faces in fear and shame.

Yes, their names will live forever, for the electric current that killed them has burned their names permanently into the hearts of the toilers of the world. Their miserable executioners will be buried in oblivion while the names and struggles of Sacco and Vanzetti still remain a shining guide to the masses, an inspiration to the oppressed everywhere.

They are our noble and heroic martyrs. Their conduct

up to the very last moment was in that spirit. Their voices are stilled but their silence thunders around the world. The workers of America who fought to free Sacco and Vanzetti must pay tribute to their heroic memory in every section of the country. The workers must gather at memorial meetings to pledge themselves to keep alive the memory of Sacco and Vanzetti and their fight; to pour their hatred upon the heads of the murderers; to build their strength to prevent new Sacco-Vanzetti cases and to obtain freedom for the class fighters who are also victims of the frame-up and still in prison.

The International Labor Defense will continue its work for that cause in the spirit of Sacco and Vanzetti.

Honor and respect to our fallen comrades! Remember Sacco and Vanzetti! Remember labor's deathless martyrs!

A living monument to Sacco and Vanzetti

LABOR DEFENDER, OCTOBER 1927

After seven years of delay the electric chair has finally claimed its victims. In defiance of the civilized world, in the face of the protest of the world's millions, Sacco and Vanzetti have been executed. This foul murder is the cynical answer of the American capitalists to the people of other countries who appealed to America in the name of humanity and justice. At the same time it is their warning to the protesting workers of America that they are prepared to go to any length to beat down the labor movement, and that legal murder is one of their established weapons.

In this act of assassination the ruling class of America shows its real face to the world. The mask of "democracy" is thrown aside. Judge Thayer and Governor Fuller stand forth not as exceptional officials, apart from all others, but as the authentic spokesmen of American capitalism. The face of Governor Fuller is the face of the American capitalist class. It is the vengeful, cruel and murderous class which the workers must fight and conquer before the regime of imprisonment, torture and murder can be ended. This is the message from the chair of death. This is the lesson of the Sacco-Vanzetti case.

Sacco and Vanzetti were victims of the frame-up system which is an established part of American police methods, insofar as labor prisoners are concerned. The case against them was a transparent fake from start to finish, as everybody who has investigated the facts knows. Faked evidence, perjured witnesses, prejudiced judges and jurors, dynamite "plants" and newspaper lies and misrepresentations—all the paraphernalia of the frame-up against the Haymarket martyrs, against Mooney and Billings, and in other labor cases were repeated here. The Sacco-Vanzetti case, in addition, however, was characterized by such monstrous cruelty and long-drawn-out torture of the victims as to call for the indignant protest of the entire civilized world.

But in all of its main features, the Sacco-Vanzetti case was a repetition of the many legal lynchings of labor leaders that have taken place in the past and a forerunner of others which will inevitably follow in the future. It was not simply an extraordinary "miscarriage of justice," as many apologists of the capitalist order attempt to maintain.

Sacco and Vanzetti were labor agitators and foreign-born radicals, arrested at the instigation of the Federal government in the midst of their activities on behalf of other victims of the Palmer reign of terror. It was neither a "criminal" case nor a "Massachusetts" case, but a class frame-up with the United States government behind the prosecution all the time.

It was clear from the beginning that the stage was being set for another Haymarket. This was understood by the militant and conscious workers, and their insistence on a policy based on this point of view brought them into constant conflict with those elements who sought to blur the class character of the case and conduct it in an orderly and "respectable" manner, which would not offend the judge and the governor and other executioners of the capitalists. The infamous slander regarding funds—hurled against the I.L.D. by the Boston committee, in the columns of the capitalist press—was a reflection of this basic conflict over policy and was in reality an attempt to demoralize and break up the protest movement.

In spite of the bourgeois-liberal influences that dominated the official Defense Committee at Boston, the militants would not allow the defense to be confined merely to the narrow groove of Massachusetts legal technicalities. With indefatigable work and sweeping vision they painted the whole monstrous frame-up on a canvas big enough for the workers of all the world to see.

The I.L.D. devoted much of its resources and energies to the work of organizing the protest mass movement in America and throughout the world. It was due to the work of the militants that the crucifixion of Sacco and Vanzetti was not prepared and carried out in a quiet and "orderly" way in whispered consultations behind closed doors, but became a tumultuous issue, storming through the streets and factories of the world.

The industrial masters of America, through their legal hirelings, plotted and carried out the execution of Sacco and Vanzetti with the aim of dealing thereby a blow to the labor movement. But in summing up the case now, and drawing the lessons for the future, it must be plainly said that they were not without allies, both conscious and unconscious, in the camp of the workers themselves.

We will only do justice to the memory of Sacco and

Vanzetti, and to the cause of labor which they lived and died for, if we speak openly about all these questions. Sacco and Vanzetti will have died in vain if the real meaning and the causes of their martyrdom are not understood in all their implications.

In the front ranks of the allies of the executioners of the heroic rebel workers, the official leaders of the American labor movement, Messrs. Green, Woll and Company, took their place. Their role was to hush up the protest movement of the workers and to frown upon all talk of demonstrations or strikes. Under cover of an appeal for "clemency" Mr. Green proposed to the governor that Sacco and Vanzetti, who were innocent of any crime, should be imprisoned for life in the Massachusetts penitentiary. Never have these black-hearted traitors exposed themselves more clearly than in the Sacco-Vanzetti case.

Unlike Debs, who played his part in the fight nobly till the day of his death, certain elements of the Socialist Party were behind Mr. Green and Company only to the extent that their influence was smaller. First, by refusing to participate in any kind of united-front action with the left wing and the Communist workers; and, second, by trying to discredit and sabotage all protest activities undertaken independently by the left wing—these office boys for the big labor fakers did their bit to hamper and demoralize the organization of the mass protest movement of the workers, which was the only possible salvation for Sacco and Vanzetti. The baseless attacks on the International Labor Defense, the organizer of the protest movement, on the ground of "misuse of funds," were merely a part of the game of demoralization.

In appealing to the workers for solidarity with Sacco and Vanzetti, and in organizing the protest movement in their behalf, the I.L.D. never considered the case as simply that of two individuals involved in a trial at law. We always pointed out its direct connection with the general issues of the struggle between the classes. We endeavoured to link up the fight for Sacco and Vanzetti with the general defense of the scores of labor prisoners confined in the penitentiaries today, and with the broader fight of the toiling masses for liberation from the yoke of capitalism.

Viewing the case always as an issue of the class struggle, we had no illusions about the possibilities of "justice" from the judges or the governor. Time and again we warned against these illusions, against confining the defense to the task of collecting money for lawyers whose vision did not extend beyond Judge Thayer's courtroom.

The best defense for Sacco and Vanzetti was to concentrate all energies in arousing the protest movement of the masses. Sacco and Vanzetti themselves understood this. These humble workers saw with clear-eyed vision that their hope lay in the masses and not in the courts or the governor's commission. The contemptuous refusal of Sacco to sign the legal papers brought to him was a gesture more eloquent than all the arguments of all the lawyers. Every utterance that came from them was infused with this spirit. Sacco and Vanzetti were blood brothers to all labor militants, bound by a thousand ties to the labor fighters in the front ranks of the class struggle, and to those languishing in the prisons today for the cause of labor. The deathless heritage of the two great martyrs belongs to the militants, and they need no one's permission to carry on their work in the name and spirit of Sacco and Vanzetti.

For those who saw the long torture and cruel death of the two heroic workmen as a personal affair, or as an isolated miscarriage of justice, the case of Sacco and Vanzetti is ended. For some people who connected themselves with the case in one way or another without really knowing what it was all about, the whole affair is a piece of business which is to be wound up now, the books closed and a "final" statement rendered.

But for the labor militants who fought with and for them, the light of Sacco and Vanzetti burns more brightly and fiercely than before. For us the last word has not yet been spoken. We have work to do and we must be about it. The great movement of the working masses for Sacco and Vanzetti must not be allowed to dissolve. The first and foremost task in honor of the memory of the martyrs is to bind this movement more closely together; and to infuse it with a stronger spirit, and a broader vision and understanding of the manifold questions which were involved in the Sacco-Vanzetti case.

We must especially endeavor now to turn the attention of this entire movement to the many other labor prisoners and create a new reservoir of strength and power for a determined nation-wide fight against the frame-up system.

The experiences of the Sacco-Vanzetti case have demonstrated more clearly than ever before the real role of the International Labor Defense as an arm of the labor movement, and the necessity for strengthening its effectiveness and of enrolling tens of thousands more of the sympathizing workers into its ranks. The fight against the frame-up system will acquire significance and power to the extent that those who oppose this system take part in the organized movement against it. Such an organization is the I.L.D. Its position as the leading and organizing center of the movement has been established not by words but by deeds, in the course of the fight. To strengthen the I.L.D. is to strengthen the fighting capacity of the labor movement.

The electric flames that consumed the bodies of Sacco and Vanzetti illuminated for tens of thousands of workers, in all its stark brutality, the essential nature of capitalist justice in America. The imprisonment, torture and murder of workers is seen more clearly now as part of an organized system of class persecution.

Against this system—the system of labor frame-ups—we must deliver our heaviest blows. The defense of individual workers, the material support of their families and our general work of defense agitation must be carried on as a part of the fight to build a wall of labor defense against the frame-up system.

The Third Annual Conference of International Labor Defense will organize its work around this slogan. The Conference will meet in New York City on the fortieth anniversary of the Haymarket martyrs and will bear testimony to the fact that their memory, like the memory of Sacco and Vanzetti, remains a powerful inspiring force for the movement of the labor militants.

From the Conference a stronger, more united and determined movement for labor defense on a class basis will emerge—a movement which will incorporate in its work and achievements the spirit of Sacco and Vanzetti and thus become a living monument to their memory.

Frank Little

On the ninth anniversary of his death

LABOR DEFENDER, AUGUST 1926

It is nine years, this month, since they hanged Frank Little to the trestle's beam in Butte. They put Frank out of the way and thought they were through with him, but they made a mistake. The things Frank Little stood for—and that was the real Frank Little—are still alive. The things Frank Little did in his lifetime are not forgotten, and the memory of them is not without influence even today.

Indeed, Frank Little is beginning, after the interval of nine years, to loom bigger and bigger against the background of the events of his living days. The revolutionary youth of America, especially, with a wisdom of appraisal that belongs exclusively to the young, are beginning to manifest a great interest in the story of this daring rebel who threw his life away so carelessly for the revolution. And with an unerring instinct, they are picking him out from the American personalities of his day as one of their own.

Here was a real American—so much American that he was part Indian—who, no less than Liebknecht in time of storm and stress was capable of scorning all personal hazards and remaining true to revolutionary duty. The rebel youth see him as a hero. His soul is marching on.

It is known by all that Frank Little died a heroic death. It must also become generally known that he lived the same kind of a life, and that the final sacrifice he made at the rope's end in Butte, fighting to the last for the cause of the workers and against the capitalist war, was of one piece with his life-long record of activity and struggle as a revolutionary worker.

Frank belonged to the "Old Guard" of the I.W.W. He was one of its founders. Before that, he was one of the militants of the Western Federation of Miners. With a singleness of purpose possessed by few, he molded his whole life's activities around one central idea—the idea of the revolutionary struggle of the workers for the overthrow of capitalism and the establishment of the workers' society. Year after year, through storm and conflict, through jails and prisons, he held resolutely to his chosen course to the end.

In his prime he had been a man of sturdy physical make-up, fitted for his hard and hazardous trade as a metal miner. But the hardships he endured, especially the body-breaking jails, took a heavy toll. In his later years the tortures of rheumatism and other physical ailments were with him constantly. But he bore these burdens uncomplainingly and never shirked any duties or obligations on that account. Even the accident which crippled him shortly before his death did not turn him aside from active work.

Frank was a warm human, hating and fighting the exploiting class and all its personal representatives savagely and bitterly. But for the workers, especially for the rebel workers, he always had a soft and friendly mood. He was inclined to look upon their shortcomings and weaknesses with an indulgent eye. For his personal friends he had a strange and wonderful kindness and considerateness, and he was greatly beloved by them.

Frank Little had many personal characteristics of a truly admirable kind. His honesty, courage and selfless devotion to the cause of the workers stood out so strongly and impressed itself so deeply on all who crossed his path, that no one could forget them. But the central feature of the whole personality of Frank Little, the one that it is most important for the coming generation of labor fighters to know about and to strive to emulate, was his dauntless rebel spirit.

His hatred of exploitation and oppression, and of all those who profited by it, was irreconcilable. He was always for the revolt, for the struggle, for the fight. Wherever he went he "stirred up trouble" and organized the workers to rebel. Bosses, policemen, stool pigeons, jailers, priests and preachers—these were the constant targets of his bitter tongue. He was a blood brother to all insurgents, "to every rebel and revolutionist the world over."

Frank Little had faith in the working class. He verily believed in the coming workers' society and he lived and died for it. His scorn for cynics, pessimists, dilettantes and phrasemongering "philosophers" knew no bounds. He believed and acted out the creed of action and inspired all around him with the same attitude.

He was not a "swivel chair" leader, but a man of the field and the firing line. He was always on the trail, in the thick of the open fight. He was well known in all the active centers from Chicago, west. He had a habit of always turning up in the place where the fight was on, or of "starting something"—a strike, a free-speech fight or an agitation, wherever he might be.

Frank Little's influence was very great amongst the type of workers with whom he mixed all his life—miners, migratory workers, railroad builders, and the like. Amongst this type of workers, the first virtue is physical courage, and Frank Little possessed it to a superlative degree. One of the first remarks I ever heard about Frank Little was to the effect that he did not understand the meaning of the word "fear." Later acquaintance and association with him confirmed my own opinion to the same effect, and I never heard anyone who knew him dispute that judgment.

I remember a characteristic instance. During the ore-docks strike in Duluth and Superior in 1913, after he had been kidnapped and held under armed guard in a deserted farm house for several days; after several meetings of the strikers had been broken up by uniformed armed thugs of the steel company—he invited me one morning to take a walk with him down to the docks. With a pistol in his pocket and his hand on it, we walked for an hour or two around the docks, directly past all the places swarming with gunmen, till we had completed the entire rounds, crossing and re-crossing company property many times.

It was a rather dangerous trip to undertake, but he insisted on it, so there was no alternative. He considered it necessary, he said, "to show the gunmen that we are not afraid of them, and also to show the strikers that we're not afraid, so they won't be afraid."

Jail was double hell for Frank. The wild Indian strain in him, combined with his rebel worker spirit, rendered confinement particularly odious to him, and he used to chafe in jail like a tiger caught in a trap. Yet he never flinched from it, and—so great were his inner resources—he knew how to contain himself, to hold his rage in hand and to bear himself with a quiet dignity in jail, which jailers as well as jailmates could not but be affected by.

I remember vividly to this day the quieting effect of his entrance into the jail in Peoria, Illinois, during the strike and free speech fight there in 1913; and the rebuke he gave, in the tone of a father talking to a child (he was about 35 then and was already recognized as a veteran), as he sat on the bunk, calmly chewing his tobacco, to an impulsive lad who wanted to start a "battleship" prematurely.

He also possessed moral courage, never fearing to take an unpopular stand in the organization, never hesitating for a moment to identify himself, positively and aggressively, with any proposal or tendency he thought was right, regardless of how many stood with him or against. "Decentralization" was a quite popular movement in the I.W.W. at that time. The migratory workers, with their individualistic spirit, responded quite readily to the idea of doing away with leaders and centralized authority and letting each local run affairs as it saw fit. Frank Little stood like a rock against this. He was one of the strongest pillars in the camp of the so-called "centralizers."

His sound organizational instincts, fortified by wide experience, enabled him to recognize quickly the disintegrating tendencies of the "decentralization" movement. He poured out the most withering invective on the heads of those who wanted to change officers every year, etc. In the faction fight over this issue his energetic and determined struggle against decentralization was one of the most decisive factors in the defeat of the movement in 1913.

Frank Little's last speech, for which he paid with his life, was directed against the capitalist war. In that speech he set up his own doctrine against that of the warmongers. His philosophy, compressed into a single sentence, was picked up and carried all over the country on the telegraph wires with the news of his assassination: "I stand for the solidarity of labor." This was the final message from that tongue of fire.

Labor leaders on every side, in this and other countries, were fooled, bullied, or bribed into supporting the capitalist slaughter-fest. Frank Little was not one of them. And with a wisdom never learned in books, he seemed to sense the great historical significance of the stand he was taking. His speech at Butte, his letter to Haywood, his resolution introduced in the General Executive Board of the I.W.W. on the subject of the war, will influence the rising young generation of the labor movement much more than that of his own day.

Frank Little sensed this. His letter to Haywood indicates clearly that he expected he would have to pay with his life for the stand he was taking against the war, but he considered it worth the sacrifice. He knew the great power of example, and always considered that in the last resort all philosophies are tested by deeds.

The memory of Frank Little seemed to be obscured for a time. Months and even years passed by, and we did not see it mentioned anywhere. But that is passing now. The rising revolutionary movement of today is learning to see past events in truer perspective and the name of Frank

Little, and his fame also, are beginning to grow bigger. The life and deeds of Frank Little are beginning to stand out as those of a hero of the American revolution, who has left a priceless heritage to the coming generation.

Frank Little will become a tradition, one of the greatest traditions of the American movement. A study of his life will become part of the revolutionary education of the American revolutionary youth. His personal characteristics of courage, honesty, straightforwardness, self-sacrifice and rebel spirit will exert a strong influence, which is much needed, on the new fighters.

The fragmentary notes which a few of us are putting into this special number of the *Labor Defender* to keep his memory green, will not be the last words said about Frank Little by any means. It will not be long till more systematic work is done, and the accounts of his manifold activities and struggles will be gathered together and woven into a story of his life and work which will become a textbook for the movement.

The Frank Little tradition is one of the best traditions of America. It is a tradition of the American revolution.

The cause that passes through a prison

For the second annual conference of International Labor Defense

LABOR DEFENDER, SEPTEMBER 1926

The path to freedom leads through a prison. The door swings in and out and through that door passes a steady procession of "those fools too stubborn-willed to bend," who will not turn aside from the path because prisons obstruct it here and there.

The doors of San Quentin penitentiary swung outward the other day and three men stepped forth and drank in their first breath of freedom for several years. They were workers, members of the I.W.W., who had just finished a sentence under the criminal syndicalism law. On almost the same day, at the other end of the country, in Massachusetts, John Merrick began to serve his sentence imposed for activity in a shoe-workers' strike several years before. A week or so later, George Papcun, a young man who distinguished himself in the struggle to organize the coal miners of Pennsylvania, was convicted of sedition and took his first steps in the long tortuous path which leads through technical motions and appeals to the prison.

In the state penitentiary in Massachusetts, Sacco and Vanzetti wait for the final judgment to be passed upon them because they are rebels and foreigners. The United States Supreme Court will decide the Ruthenberg appeal in the October term. The warden of the Michigan state penitentiary is ready.

The mills of capitalist justice grind out victims for the penitentiary. If you put your finger on any corner of the map of America, whether Texas, California, Washington, Pennsylvania, Maine, Massachusetts, West Virginia, New York—you can say with certainty: "In this state is a penitentiary which confines labor prisoners."

In one sense of the word the whole of capitalist society is a prison. For the great mass of people who do the hard, useful work there is no such word as freedom. They come and go at the order of a few. Their lives are regulated according to the needs and wishes of a few. A censorship is put upon their words and deeds. The fruits of their labor are taken from them. And if, by chance, they have the instinct and spirit to rebel, if they take their place in the vanguard of the fight for justice, the prisons are waiting.

The procession that goes in and out of the prison doors is not a new one. It is the result of an old struggle under new forms and under new conditions. All through history those who have fought against oppression have constantly been faced with the dungeons of a ruling class. The greater the cause has been, and the deeper it has been rooted in the needs and sufferings of the masses, the more it has been menaced by the tortures of prison cells. The number of victims taken from among the ranks of those who have fought for a cause has been the measure of its greatness. No cause is a great one which has not produced fighters in its ranks who have dared to face arrest and trial and imprisonment. The fear of a ruling class, and the effectiveness of those who struggle against them, can always be measured by the number upon whom they wreak revenge in this way.

The class-war prisoners of today, just as those in previous periods of history, are representatives of the most courageous and advanced section of the oppressed but upward-striving class. As a rule they are individuals of particular audacity and ability who have stood out conspicuously in their environment as leaders and militants, and have thereby incurred the hatred of the oppressors.

Even in prison they continue to serve their class. Read the prisoners' letters which appear every month in the *Labor Defender.* See their dauntless spirit reflected there. See how little confinement has been able to tame their spirit or to weaken their faith in the eventual triumph of their class.

The fortitude with which they bear their ignominious punishment and the fidelity to principle which they show in almost every case, gives them a power, as an inspiring and forward-driving force in the labor movement as a whole, which cannot be overestimated. The service they render is as great as their sacrifice is heavy.

The class-conscious worker accords to the class-war prisoners a place of singular honor and esteem. The class-war prisoners are stronger than all the jails and jailers and judges. They rise triumphant over all their enemies and oppressors. Confined in prison, covered with ignominy, branded as criminals, they are not defeated. They are destined to triumph. They are the representatives of an idea that will crack the walls of every prison and crumble them into dust.

There is a way of saying that the class-war prisoners are victorious, which smacks of superficial optimism and which offers little consolation to men who spend long, almost forgotten years behind the gray walls of the jail. We do not mean to speak in this sense, as though it were an automatic process. The victory of the class-war prisoners is possible only when they are inseparably united with the living labor movement and when that movement claims them for its own, takes up their battle cry and carries on their work.

The matter-of-fact attitude which shrugs its shoulders lightly at the procession of rebel workers passing through the prison doors, passes it off as "part of the game," lets the prisoners lie there year after year neglected and forgotten, and lets the prisoners' helpless dependents shift for themselves—is a poisonous and dangerous attitude indeed. That way spells defeat for the class-war prisoners and for the things they stand for. There has been too much of this in the past, as many a prisoner could tell with bitter words if he wished to speak about it.

We believe it is one of the great tasks of the movement

to make war upon this attitude and to eliminate it entirely. There are plenty of signs already that our efforts are meeting with success and that the claim of the class-war prisoners is beginning to occupy a prominent place on the agenda of the labor movement.

The never-to-be-forgotten conference of earnest militants held on June 28 last year to launch the International Labor Defense, marked a turning point in the struggle to unite the imprisoned fighters with the militant labor movement. The conference which founded International Labor Defense set before the organization a number of serious and difficult tasks. In the year which has intervened, substantial progress has been made in all directions.

The burning issue of labor defense has been raised more insistently and in a more organized fashion than ever before in America. The assistance given to prisoners and their dependents during the last year, though pitifully small when measured in comparison to their sacrifice, still is something—a sign of remembrance and an act of practical solidarity. The legal defense of persecuted workers has been put on an organized basis and not a single one has appealed to us in vain.

Our development of publicity for labor defense, the crowning achievement of which is the solid establishment of the *Labor Defender,* which represents an entirely new departure in American labor journalism, has been a fruitful and substantial work indeed.

The I.L.D. way, which is the way of brotherly solidarity and unity, has made its impression deep and indelible on all sections of the conscious and militant labor movement. And most important of all, a solid organization has been built up, embracing many thousands of militant workers of diverse views who are uniting in practical solidarity under the banner of the I.L.D. This is exerting a powerful influence for unity in other activities in the class struggle.

International Labor Defense is not a separate and independent movement of itself; it is a part of the whole labor movement. It is a shield for the workers as a whole in their daily struggle in their battle for liberation. It keeps the issue of the liberation of the imprisoned labor fighters constantly before the eyes of labor.

The work of International Labor Defense is by its very nature work for the class struggle and for solidarity. Thousands of workers who are going into activity for I.L.D. are being led by degrees into the main stream of the class struggle itself, not only as sympathizers but as participants, as active soldiers. By its work and organization I.L.D. draws greater numbers of workers into the movement and reveals to them, with the aid of their own experiences, more and more the role of our class government.

I.L.D. has a great work to perform in building and rebuilding the revolutionary traditions of America, some of the most valuable inheritances of the working class. The Frank Little number of our *Labor Defender* contributed to this side of our work and we plan, in November, to organize a revival, more widespread and profound than ever before, of the militant traditions of the Haymarket martyrs of 1887.

International Labor Defense is only in the initial stages of its development, but its power and potentialities have already been demonstrated. Our great campaign for Sacco and Vanzetti reached almost every corner of the American labor movement and resounded throughout the world. The reports from our local secretaries show that the Sacco-Vanzetti conferences which were organized everywhere on the initiative and inspiration of I.L.D. units have embraced more than a million workers.

The Second Annual Conference of the International

Labor Defense which meets in Chicago on September 5 will mark another milestone along the road we travel. The leading spirits of the I.L.D. from all sections of the country will assemble there to review the year's work and to lay out the lines for the future. It will be a gathering of historical significance, permeated through and through with the I.L.D. spirit and the I.L.D. way, made up of men and women who are bound for life and death with the cause of the class-war prisoners and the movement they represent.

The second annual conference of the International Labor Defense

LABOR DEFENDER, OCTOBER 1926

In many respects the conference we have just held was different from the one we held a year ago, at which we founded International Labor Defense. Last year at the conference there were only a few cities represented outside of Chicago. One delegate from here and there; one from Pittsburgh, and a few from the outlying districts of Illinois. This year there were 248 delegates from 38 cities in all parts of the country—and this speaks volumes for the extent to which the organization has taken root.

Last year the keynote of the conference was to call again to mind the many fellow workers and fighters in the class struggle who had been behind prison walls for many years. We took it upon ourselves to make their names better known throughout the labor movement and to dedicate ourselves and our activities and efforts to their liberation.

Eugene V. Debs peering out of "Red Special." Tom Mooney (right) and his brother John stand in front.

Frank Little

Max Eastman, James P. Cannon, and Big Bill Haywood in Moscow, 1922.

We carried out that pledge to the best of our ability during the year that intervened. And the second conference formulated plans for a big organization drive to strengthen the work for the fight to release all the labor prisoners.

June 28, last year, represented a turning point in the labor defense movement in America. We met and took stock of the general situation, analyzed the experience of the past and laid out a new path to follow. We made a program for the guidance of our work. The second conference was able to record substantial progress during the past year in the task of unifying on a non-partisan basis the forces for labor defense. We built an organization not on the personal basis of defense for this or that individual or group, but on the class basis of extending aid and defense to all workers who were in need of it.

The conference had to record the defense of scores of cases in one year. There were the miners of Zeigler, Illinois, whose defense we are still conducting; the cases of the Pittsburgh Communists held under the Anti-Sedition Act of the state; the three Portuguese anarchist workers in Fall River, Massachusetts; the striking taxi drivers of Boston; the I.W.W. deportees in New York; the Passaic textile workers; the campaign for Sacco and Vanzetti in which the I.L.D. really reached its full stride. Anarchists, Socialists, Communists, I.W.Ws, members of the A.F. of L. and workers without affiliation have found the hand of the I.L.D. ready and able to aid them at all times.

The important work of systematic prison relief was quickly begun and has been maintained ever since, and a long step was taken in the equally important work of systematizing the relief of the dependents of class war prisoners. The valuable publication of the *Labor Defender* which was enthusiastically received by all active workers, and the maintenance in its pages of the non-partisan spirit of the organization, was the fulfilment of another decision of the first conference.

The second conference recorded the growth of the organization from little more than an idea last year to a functioning, active body of some 20,000 individual members and a collective, affiliated membership of 75,000 workers. With 156 branches throughout the country, I.L.D. had developed in one year to be able to play an effective and sometimes a decisive role in the class struggle in connection with labor defense.

It was an open secret that at the first conference the organization had to contend with a certain skepticism, a feeling that the I.L.D. did not have a place in the labor movement, or else that it would not be able to fill that place. Those who heard the reports of the delegates at the second conference know that this skepticism was overcome by the deeds and acts of the I.L.D., which spoke louder and with more effectiveness than any declarations. A new faith had been generated in many sections of the labor movement and the increased popularity of International Labor Defense was an indication of this. The entry of the organization into the struggle of labor, with the intention of giving fraternal aid to those workers captured by the capitalist class, to give it without pursuing any sectional advantage, had built the I.L.D. into an arm of the labor movement.

The line of the first year of work was proved correct by the deeds and by the results. For the first time in years there were gathered into one organization workers of all political and economic affiliations and opinions, held together by the unifying chain of non-partisan united defense of class-war fighters whose freedom was endangered.

The main line of the second conference was a reaffirmation

of the decisions of the first conference, with special emphasis on the necessity for organization. The small group which had founded International Labor Defense last year was now a large conference of delegates who had come to review their experiences of months of work and formulate concrete tasks for the future. The spirit and enthusiasm of the conference was an inspiration for the more intensive work which I.L.D. will conduct in the next year.

Animated with this spirit and enthusiasm, the conference adopted as its main slogan that of "Organization!" The whole activity of the conference was organized around this watchword. Especially during the second day of the conference, which was devoted entirely to organizational problems, the delegates discussed to the smallest detail the practical, everyday tasks of their work. Every phase of labor defense activity, from the problem of branch accounts, the organization of united-front conferences, to the distribution of literature and the organization of campaigns, was thoroughly gone into and elaborated upon in the discussion.

The problem of organization is a very significant one for labor defense as a school for the class struggle. We must not get the idea that we are merely "defense workers" collecting money for lawyers. That is only a part of what we are doing. We are organizing workers on issues which are directly related to the class struggle. The workers who take part in the work of the I.L.D. are drawn, step by step, into the main stream of the class struggle. The workers participating begin to learn the ABC of the labor struggle.

There are big struggles ahead for us. The conference considered especially the question of the approaching sessions of the Supreme Court. In the October term of the Supreme Court, the criminal syndicalist laws of three states are coming up for review on the appeal of Ruthenberg in Michigan, Anita Whitney in California, and Fiske, the I.W.W., in the state of Kansas.

In the event of an unfavorable decision, the I.L.D. should be in a position to see to it that there is no such thing as Ruthenberg, Anita Whitney and Fiske just quietly saying "Good-by" and going to the penitentiary, and then sitting there year after year, being forgotten by the labor movement. The I.L.D. must be prepared to make this occasion, if it comes, the starting point of a real campaign of agitation which will reach the proportions of the old Mooney case and the Haywood case. This task can be accomplished only with the aid of a real organization.

The conference had material progress to record in the maintenance of the international obligations of the I.L.D. which were pledged at the first conference. The campaigns we conducted for Rakosi in Hungary, for the Polish and Lithuanian workers, were amply compensated for by the generous help given us by the workers in Europe and Latin America, through the cooperation of the International Red Aid, in our campaign here for Sacco and Vanzetti. In this reciprocal work the principle of internationalism was taught by deeds.

The second annual conference of International Labor Defense will be remembered as the beginning of a real knitting together of defense forces into a mighty organization. The coming year of its activity must be devoted to the forging of an invincible shield of the working class. The spirit and enthusiasm of the members of the I.L.D., which have built the organization in the past year, will translate into living reality the slogan of "Organization" raised at the second conference. Fifty thousand individual members and a quarter of a million collective membership was the goal set by the conference. The spirit of devotion and sacrifice of the I.L.D. will in the coming year give body and form to this aim.

Eugene V. Debs

LABOR DEFENDER, DECEMBER 1926

Eugene Victor Debs lived and did his work in the years which marked the rise and development of American imperialism, when American industry expanded on a gigantic scale and when the working class, which holds the future in its hands, went through a series of stormy struggles which were the harbinger of far greater ones to come.

In 1894, after a record of successful activity in building the railroad brotherhoods, he led the first great strike of an industrial union, the American Railway Union strike against the Pullman Company. It was in this strike that the injunction was first used against workers combined in struggle, and it was Debs who led the fight against it. This fight led him into Woodstock jail and it set his feet on the road of the revolutionary movement. Debs came out of jail firm in the belief he held to the last that the emancipation of the workers could be achieved only by the unity of their political and economic power and that socialism was the goal of their struggle.

He aided in the foundation of the Socialist Party, which reached the apex of its revolutionary spirit and power when the United States entered the imperialist World War. In his party, he was never identified with those who sought to smooth the road with respectability and base compromise. To the contrary, his voice was always raised with those in his party who stood for a revolutionary policy.

Debs was one of the most active spirits in organizing the Industrial Workers of the World. In it he hoped to embody and vitalize the idea of industrial unionism which he cherished so passionately and defended to the last. Even in later years, when he had ceased to belong to the I.W.W., he continued to defend it and its members. There were those, particularly in the period before and after the war, who anxiously protested their disagreement with and disassociation from the despised and hunted "Wobblies;" but Debs was not among them. In the greatest speech of his life at Canton, in the midst of the lynching campaign against the I.W.W., he extended his great spirit of solidarity to them. He defended Haywood and the others on trial at Chicago, just as strongly as he denounced Gompers hobnobbing with the warmongers at Washington.

Debs did not fear to align himself with unpopular causes. When Moyer, Haywood and Pettibone faced legal assassination by the servile courts of Idaho, Debs rallied to their cause with unforgettable revolutionary fervor. He poured his entire rebel body and mind into a rousing call to the workers of America. In the *Appeal to Reason,* to which he contributed at that time, he issued his appeal "Arouse, Ye Slaves."

"If they attempt to murder Moyer, Haywood and their brothers, a million revolutionists, at least, will meet them with guns. . . . Let them dare to execute their devilish plot and every state in this Union will resound with the tramp of revolution. . . .

"Get ready, comrades, for action! . . . A special revolutionary convention of the proletariat at Chicago, or some other central point, would be in order, and, if extreme measures are required, a general strike could be ordered and industry paralyzed as a preliminary to a general uprising.

"If the plutocrats begin the program, we will end it."

The revolutionary activity of Comrade Debs reached its highest point at Canton, Ohio, and at the trial which followed in the courtroom in Cleveland. When the imperialists of this country entered the World War, when the masses were armed to shoot down their brothers in other lands for the profit of the master class, when the workers found themselves dragooned and betrayed on every hand, their organizations debauched and suppressed; when the traitors and cowards—the Spargos and Wallings and Bensons—went over openly to the side of the enemy; when the masses listened for an authentic voice of opposition, they heard it from the lips of Eugene Debs.

The speech of Debs at Canton was a call to action for the class-conscious workers of America. It was a courageous and revolutionary defiance of the warmongers and of the Judases in the ranks of labor, Debs realized the consequences of his word and deed. Just as proudly therefore did he bear himself during the trial at Cleveland. Just as staunchly did he refuse to crave the pardon of the ruling class while he served his term of imprisonment at Atlanta. He left the prison with shattered health, but his revolutionary spirit was stronger than ever, supported by the greetings of solidarity sent him by workers from all parts of the world.

In the closing years of his life Debs took a different path from that followed by many of those who had stood closest to him in the times of trial and stress. The World War and the Russian Revolution had changed the face of the world in which Debs had formed his conceptions and done his work. In drawing the conclusions from these world-shaking events, many of us parted company politically with the Socialist Party. Debs did not go with us in this. In many respects we found ourselves in serious disagreement with him, but at the same time we always drew a sharp distinction between Debs and those who, while wearing the cloak of socialism, actually forsook the cause to which Debs sincerely and honestly devoted all his life.

Debs always stood for unity in the struggle. He made his word a deed in many instances, especially by his persistent support of the International Labor Defense, upon whose national committee he served from the very beginning. The old class-war prisoner knew the value of a unified movement to batter down the walls and bars that hold our comrades confined. How different was his sincere and untiring support of this work from the malicious attacks of the *Jewish Daily Forward*! No one could more sharply mark the distinction between two differing spirits and traditions in the movement than did Debs, by his actions and work for the I.L.D., in comparison with those of the *Forward* who, without basis, claim him as their own. It is not to them that Debs belongs.

Debs was no colorless saint standing above the battle. He was a warm and passionate partisan, and his whole life's activity is a record of unceasing devotion to the cause of the workers in the class struggle. His great love for the masses cannot be understood if it is separated from the movement whose struggles and ideals he incarnated. He was such a superior personality that he was able, while fighting in the sordid environment of capitalism, to keep a clear vision of the goal of the struggle. He saw always the golden future which will follow the final victory of the workers and he was able, in the fight for that future, to conduct his personal life according to its nobler and higher standards.

In honoring the memory of Comrade Debs we should strive to emulate some of his attributes, to show some little part at least of his dauntless courage, his uncalculating generosity and his marvelous comrade spirit. Debs was not only a tireless agitator against capitalism and a champion of the workers in the revolutionary struggle. He was also a herald of the comrade-world which will be organized after the final conflict and victory, when classes and class exploitation will have been abolished, when culture will become universal, and the finer and nobler aspects of the human character become not merely the possession of rare individuals but the attributes of the entire race.

Capitalism, with its hypocrisy and cynicism, its injustice and oppression, makes it difficult to visualize the society which the regenerated human race will construct upon the ruins of capitalism. But the personality of Comrade Debs has given us a glimpse of it.

Debs left to the American workers a great tradition of persistent revolutionary struggle. The great fighter was our elder brother, and he remains ours, in spite of the differences that we may have had with him. We know that he grew to the full stature of his greatness in the storm of struggle, that he was identified prominently with every outstanding movement and battle of the American workers since the last part of the nineteenth century.

The influence of Eugene V. Debs has not ended with his death. The modern militant labor movement, which is the heir and successor of that movement of revolt which took shape in the years preceding the World War, has taken to heart the death of Debs, the most authentic spokesman of the earlier movement. It is to this movement, inheriting the best of the traditions of the past, that Debs belongs. It is the best representative of the revolutionary spirit and work of the dead leader.

The death of Eugene V. Debs has called forth the most profound sorrow from the ranks of the American workers. At his grave we greet him as a great warrior and pay our tribute to him by pledging ourselves to the continuation of his work.

The "Debs' Enrollment" which has been initiated by International Labor Defense is intended as a tribute to Debs and as a memorial to him. Those who enter the ranks and march with them will continue the work of the prisoner of Atlanta and Woodstock, who, having overcome both of these prisons, continued to the end to fight for the release of the whole working class from the greater prison which is capitalism.

C.E. Ruthenberg

LABOR DEFENDER, APRIL 1927

The great outpouring of the masses for the memorial meeting bears testimony to the fact that the name of Ruthenberg is highly honored already today. It is quite probable that much greater honor will be given to his memory in the future. For Ruthenberg was a pioneer in a great social movement which has the future on its side, and history deals generously with pioneers.

Most of us who had the opportunity of working hand in hand with Comrade Ruthenberg through many stormy years can pay an ungrudging tribute to those personal qualities which made him such an outstanding figure in the ranks of the American revolutionaries. He was steeled and strengthened by every test imposed upon him and remained a dauntless, unwavering fighter to the end. He died at his post in the prime of his powers, as befits a soldier.

We will not deny the shock of grief that his untimely

death brought to every one of us, but just the same we could stand at his funeral with heads uplifted in pride that this man, who embodied so many of the highest qualities of soldier manhood, belonged to us.

We honor Ruthenberg for his long and valiant revolutionary record. I first met him in 1913 when he came to Akron to speak to the striking rubber workers. He was already then a prominent figure in the Socialist Party and his speech had the ring of militancy which denotes the irreconcilable enemy of capitalism. We sized him up then as a fighter; and later knowledge of his character, born of the closest association in common work, only strengthened and confirmed the first impression and estimate. "He was a fighter." These words came spontaneously to the lips of his comrades-in-arms in the first moment we heard of his passing. What tribute can be higher?

He was no fly-by-night dabbler with the idea of revolution. His record goes back for many years. The proletarian revolutionaries who fought on the side of Haywood remember with gratitude his support in the great battle in the Socialist Party which came to a climax in 1912. A consistent advocate of political action, he, nevertheless, even in those days fought against the current of reformist corruption in the Socialist Party and interpreted "politics" in the proletarian and revolutionary sense.

He fought the capitalist war. He carried the St. Louis Resolution out into the public streets of Cleveland and attempted to organize the laboring masses around it. The most prized picture of him which adorns this page shows Ruthenberg, the fighter, in action, speaking against the war on the public square of Cleveland. He paid the price for his courage with a year's imprisonment in the Canton Workhouse, that same workhouse within whose shadow Debs made his historic speech. Ruthenberg, Wagenknecht and Baker, prisoners there at the time, were the inspiration of that speech which rang 'round the world.

On his release from prison, Ruthenberg identified himself with the left wing of the Socialist Party which was taking shape under the influence of the Russian Revolution. He was the only one of the nationally prominent leaders of the party to come with the left wing and remain with it consistently through all the vicissitudes of the struggle. He was a follower of the Communist International since the first day its banner was raised. His vision of a great revolutionary organization on an international scale unfolded his powers and raised him far above the petty men whose conception of socialism was distorted by narrow national provincialism.

Ruthenberg, the fighter, stood up in the capitalist court in New York in 1920, facing a ten-year sentence, and hurled the scorn and defiance of a revolutionary class in the face of the judge and prosecutor. The young Communist Party was outlawed and driven underground; the reaction was everywhere triumphant, but this man arose from his seat in the courtroom and calmly informed all present that the cause which they sought to imprison would emerge triumphant and put its heel on all class oppression.

As one of the founders of the I.L.D. and a member of its national committee from the first, Ruthenberg was a great believer in the idea of non-partisan labor defense on the basis of the class struggle. Himself a class-war prisoner, he felt a close kinship with all workers who languish in the prison-hells of the masters. He was an enthusiastic supporter of the work of the I.L.D. in helping and defending all persecuted workers regardless of their views or affiliations.

Those who knew him best know him as, above all, a party man. He was all for the party. He regarded the revolutionary party of the workers as the highest instrument history creates for the liberation of the enslaved masses of the world. He attached the greatest significance to every action or decision of the party and set an example of discipline and responsibility in all his work.

He was a tireless worker for the party. His great energies were given unsparingly to its service. In the literal sense of the word it can be said he lived for the party. Yes, and died for it too. For if he had spared himself a little and devoted even the minimum attention to his own health, there is no doubt that the fatal illness could have been warded off.

Ruthenberg was a soldier. He saw the cause for which he labored as a fight to which one must bring the discipline and devotion of an army that never knows retreat. He was a soldier who had faith in his cause and gave his life for it.

The America of today reeks with cynicism and corruption. The Americans of energy and talent are in the service of the oppressors. America is money-mad. Brains and ability are bought and sold—nothing is given away. Those who see higher values than personal material gain are regarded as fools in our insane America. Corruption is the hallmark of our country.

Ruthenberg was an American who did not go that way. Money meant nothing to him and the "honors" which capitalism bestows upon its lackeys meant even less. His vision was a social one; the world was his country and the oppressed masses were his people. To the service of the oppressed masses he gave all his energies and talents without calculation or price. He lived a full and fruitful life of struggle and sacrifice for an imperishable ideal and died a soldier's death.

The America of today had no time for Ruthenberg. For this splendid character, this valiant soldier of the revolution, the masters of America had no praise. They covered him with ignominy. They hounded him from one prison to another. At the time of his death, the Honorable Judges of the Supreme Court had his latest conviction under review. Capitalist America made Ruthenberg an outlaw and a convict.

The America of tomorrow will revise that judgment. That is already indicated by the attitude of the militant workers who are the vanguard of the future. Ruthenberg was a pioneer who broke a new path. The Americans of tomorrow will travel that path and give its highest honors to the pioneers who broke it. The name of Ruthenberg will have a distinguished place in the list of heroes and pioneers of the American Revolution.

The ranks of the revolutionary working-class movement in America are small, and able and tested leaders are very few indeed. It would be foolish to deny that the death of a leader of the caliber of Ruthenberg represents a great loss to the proletarian cause. A recognition of the great role played by outstanding individuals of his type is no contradiction to the social theory upon which the whole activity of Ruthenberg as a revolutionary agitator was based.

But the revolutionary labor movement is driven forward by social forces which arise out of the very conditions of capitalism and make for its destruction. The men who inspire and lead the movement of working-class revolt are themselves products of the conditions which bring the movement into existence. The loss of leaders may shake and weaken the ranks for a time, but the irrepressible needs of the movement call new forces from the ranks to fill the gap.

The work that Ruthenberg performed with such fidelity in his lifetime remains behind him. His example of courage, devotion and self-sacrifice remains as an asset of the movement as a whole. His tradition as a revolutionary fighter will be treasured by every section of the militant labor movement. The new generation of militants will be influenced by that tradition and will carefully safeguard it.

Let the corrupt and decaying capitalist society have those heroes who typify it—the dollar-chasing exploiters, the blood-smeared generals, the lying, treacherous statesmen. Our movement, which is the herald of the new social order, claims proudly for its own the men of a different and immeasurably better type—the type of Ruthenberg.

The cause of the martyrs

DAILY WORKER MAGAZINE SECTION, OCTOBER 8, 1927

Standing on the scaffold 40 years ago the Haymarket martyrs warned the hangmen that their case was by no means ended. "The day will come," said August Spies, "when our silence will be more powerful than the voices you strangle today." Events are bearing testimony to the truth of this assertion.

The fortieth anniversary of their martyrdom shows their memory greener than ever before. Their spirit was alive in the great movement for Sacco and Vanzetti; and the militant workers generally, especially the rising generation, are learning to esteem more highly than ever before the priceless heritage of the pioneers who died for the cause of labor on November 11, 1887. Their very names have become a battle cry to stir the blood of the revolutionaries of today, and we dare assert they will be heard in the triumphant shouts of the final victory of the working class tomorrow.

The holding of the Third Annual Conference of the

I.L.D. on the fortieth anniversary of the Haymarket martyrs gives to that occasion an exceptional significance and importance. "Third Annual Conference of International Labor Defense—Fortieth Anniversary of the Haymarket Martyrs." The very words ring like a slogan, and indeed they are a slogan, for they signify the binding together of the fight of the living workers with the imperishable memory of the illustrious dead. A true commemoration of the men of Haymarket could not be a funeral affair—their tradition and spirit are a call to battle.

The memory of Parsons, Spies and their comrades in life and death, was very dear to those two who followed them on the path of martyrdom a few weeks ago in Boston. Sacco wrote with great warmth of "the celebration day of the martyrs of Chicago, that in the mind of humanity oppressed will never be forgot." In our estimate we put Sacco and Vanzetti beside the giants of 1887, and properly so, for they were of the same heroic stature and they died in the same fight, which was not an individual nor an isolated one in either case. The rope which strangled the Haymarket martyrs, the chair which snuffed out the lives of Sacco and Vanzetti, the prison walls which confined them all—these instruments of torture and death are weapons in the class war, employed against prisoners taken on the field of battle.

The martyrs of 1887 understood this well and used the courtroom and the scaffold as a forum from which to proclaim it to the world. Sacco and Vanzetti understood it no less, as all their utterances testify, and they knew and understood also—what so many around them did not know and understand—the indissoluble bonds which united them, their cause and their fate, to the other militants of the labor vanguard who languish in the prison cells of capitalism today or await trial before the courts of the class enemy.

"See if you cannot do something for Tom Mooney," Vanzetti used to entreat those who came to see him in Charlestown prison. "Tom is a sick man. He will die in prison soon if something is not done for him," he told a writer who visited him during his last days.

These great and noble spirits who died in the electric chair felt themselves to be, as they were in fact, blood brothers to all the persecuted, imprisoned and tortured fighters of the liberation struggle of the workers. They saw the great movement of the masses which was set into motion in their behalf as a class awakening, and they wished it to become a liberating force for others as well as for themselves.

Sacco told Judge Thayer on the day the death sentence was pronounced: "I know the sentence will be between two classes, the oppressed class and the rich class. . . . That is why I am here today on this bench, for having been of the oppressed class."

Shall the Sacco-Vanzetti case be "wound up" now? Shall the record be closed and the fight be stopped and the magnificent movement dissolved?

The other side has proposed this. They have agreed to a conspiracy of silence in the papers about the case; they have burned the films and they want us to "forget." Having killed Sacco and Vanzetti they want also to kill the Sacco-Vanzetti movement or, at least, to reduce it to a sterile cult, separate and apart from the burning issue of the others who suffer in prison or face trial in the same cause.

Our task as militants is to defeat these aims, and the Third Annual Conference of the I.L.D. will be the concentration point for the higher development of our fight. We will not allow the Sacco-Vanzetti movement, called into life by their examples and by the untiring energy and sacrifices of the class-conscious workers, to be dissipated. The memory of Sacco and Vanzetti, like the memory of the Haymarket martyrs, must become an inspiring force in the living struggle of today and tomorrow. The various elements which compose it must be bound more closely together, and the full class significance of the martyrdom of Sacco and Vanzetti made clear to all the workers who participated in the fight.

The Sacco-Vanzetti movement as a whole, enriched and broadened in its outlook by its merger with the glorious memory and tradition of the Haymarket fighters, shines with brighter luster than ever before on the fortieth anniversary of their martyrdom. It must be directed, with all its driving power, into a new fight for the liberation of the class fighters, many of them obscure, some of them all but forgotten, who suffer in the prison hells of capitalism today.

The basis of this fight which we take up anew in the name of the martyred dead, is the united front of all workers, regardless of party or viewpoint, who stand on the platform of the class struggle. This was the line and policy of the men of Haymarket. The guiding lines of Parsons, Spies and their comrades harmonized with our united front conceptions and can very well illuminate our pathway in the common fight today. For they were men of the broad movement and the open fight; all sectarian and clique tendencies were alien to them.

The Boston martyrs likewise stood for common action and united struggle, despite the stupidly sectarian and even reactionary influences which surrounded them. Vanzetti told me with his own lips that he believed in the intrinsic worth of all demonstrations and protests, and the necessity of united action of all forces when the issue to be fought for is a common one. In a letter to me dated April 11, 1927, signed jointly by Sacco and Vanzetti, they said: "When free and in solidarity with others, we have believed that there are circumstances under which a unity of efforts is desirable. . . . What is essential is good faith in each and all, for that would harmonize and direct to the common good all the different elements, characters and actions."

There is power in heroic example to stir the imagination of the masses and inspire them with the courage and solidarity and faith without which there can be no fight and no victory. The martyrs of 1887 and those of August of this year have alike set before the present and the coming generation an example of noble dignity and selfless daring unsurpassed in the history of all times and all classes.

And when these qualities of personal conduct are combined—as they are combined in both instances—with clear-eyed vision and practical wisdom for the regulation of the common fight, then the story of their life and death becomes indeed a heritage of immeasurable value. The class movement of the workers proudly claims that heritage as its own and draws upon it for strength and inspiration in its struggle for a better and higher life.

The Third Annual Conference of International Labor Defense will mark a milepost in the development of the American working class. The class-conscious elements meeting there will organize their forces for new battles against the lynch-law and frame-up system of the exploiters and will bind together, more closely and indissolubly than before, the issues and struggles of today with the undying tradition of the martyrs of the past.

The Third Annual Conference of the I.L.D., meeting on the fortieth anniversary of the Haymarket martyrs, and animated in its work by their spirit and the spirit of Sacco and Vanzetti, will demonstrate before the world that the aims of the executioners have been defeated. The cause of the martyrs is alive and is fighting on to victory.

A Christmas fund of our own

DAILY WORKER, OCTOBER 17, 1927

The *New York Times,* the organ of big business, is making its annual plea for contributions for Christmas to the "100 Neediest Cases." Other capitalist papers and organizations are conducting similar drives. The men, women and children of the working class, who have been on the rack of capitalist exploitation and are now dropped into the abyss of misery and poverty, are chosen and classified by these arch hypocrites—so their sanctimonious appeal can be made to the comfortable capitalists, to soften the bitterness of these few workers with the insult of charity, and to salve their own conscience by acts of "generosity."

This horrible farce is annually repeated in scores of other cities.

The militant workers have nothing but hatred and contempt for such appeals and drives. This year, therefore, they are again following the world-wide custom that has developed in the ranks of the working class for many years. It is the custom of raising a special fund for the men in prison for the labor cause and their wives and children, of transforming the hypocritical spirit of Christmas into the spirit of solidarity with the class-war fighters behind bars.

The International Labor Defense has already started a campaign for a Christmas Fund for the men in prison, and their dependents who suffer on the outside. The labor militants throughout the entire country are working to collect this fund. Nowhere has the appeal or the response been made on the basis of charity. Everywhere has been emphasized the duty of those who are outside toward the men on the inside.

The imprisoned fighters know the value of the money that is sent to them regularly by the International Labor Defense, and especially the Christmas gift of $25 to each prisoner, $50 to each family, and $5 to each child. And they appreciate even more the feeling of solidarity they get in the knowledge that the movement outside is still interested and is still determined to fight for their liberation.

The workers belonging to the I.L.D. and supporting its work have not forgotten them and their dependent families.

The men in prison are still a part of the living class movement. The Christmas Fund drive of International Labor Defense is a means of informing them that the workers of America have not forgotten their duty toward the men to whom we are all linked by bonds of solidarity. It is the Christmas drive of Labor and must have its generous support!

William D. Haywood

DAILY WORKER, MAY 22, 1928

The death of Haywood was not unexpected. The declining health of the old fighter was known to his friends for a long time. On each visit to Moscow in recent years we noted the progressive weakening of his physical powers and learned of the repeated attacks of the fatal disease which finally brought him down. Our anxious inquiries during the past month, occasioned by the newspaper reports of his illness, only brought the response that his recovery this time could not be expected. Nevertheless we could not abandon the hope that his fighting spirit and his will to live would pull him through again, and the news that death had triumphed in the unequal struggle brought a shock of grief.

The death of Haywood is a double blow to those who were at once his comrades in the fight and his personal friends, for his character was such as to invest personal relations with an extraordinary dignity and importance. His great significance for the American and world labor movement was also fully appreciated, I think, both by our party and by the Communist International, in the ranks of which he ended his career, a soldier to the last.

An outstanding personality and leader of the pre-war revolutionary labor movement in America, and also a member and leader of the modern communist movement which grew up on its foundation, Bill Haywood represented a connecting link which helped to establish continuity between the old movement and the new. Growing out of the soil of America, or better, hewn out of its rocks, he first entered the labor movement as a pioneer unionist of the formative days of the Western Federation of Miners 30 years ago. From that starting point he bent his course toward the conscious class struggle and marched consistently on that path to the end of his life. He died a Communist and a soldier of the Communist International.

It is a great fortune for our party that he finished his memoirs and that they are soon to be published. They constitute a record of the class struggle and of the labor movement in America of priceless value for the present generation of labor militants. The career of Haywood is bound up with the stormy events which have marked the course of working-class development in America for 30 years and out of which the basic nucleus of the modern movement has come.

He grew up in the hardship and struggle of the mining camps of the West. Gifted with the careless physical courage of a giant and an eloquence of speech, Bill soon became a recognized leader of the metal miners. He developed with them through epic struggles toward a militancy of action combined with a socialistic understanding, even in that early day, which soon placed the Western Federation of Miners, which Haywood said "was born in a Bull Pen," in the vanguard of the American labor movement.

It was the merger of these industrial proletarian militants of the West with the socialist political elements represented by Debs and De Leon, which brought about the formation of the I.W.W. in 1905. The fame and outstanding prominence of Haywood as a labor leader even in that day is illustrated by the fact that he was chosen chairman of the historic First Convention of the I.W.W. in 1905.

The brief, simple speech he delivered there, as recorded in the stenographic minutes of the convention, stands out in many respects as a charter of labor of that day. His plea for the principle of the class struggle, for industrial unionism, for special emphasis on the unskilled workers, for solidarity of black and white workers, and for a revolutionary goal of the labor struggle, anticipated many established principles of the modern revolutionary labor movement.

The attempt to railroad him to the gallows on framed-up murder charges in 1906 was thwarted by the colossal protest movement of the workers who saw in this frame-up against him a tribute to his talent and power as a labor leader, and to his incorruptibility. His name became a battle cry of the socialist and labor movement and he emerged from the trial a national and international figure.

He rose magnificently to the new demands placed upon him by this position and soon became recognized far and wide as the authentic voice of the proletarian militants of America. The schemes of the reformist leaders of the Socialist Party to use his great name and popularity as a shield for them were frustrated by the bold and resolute course he pursued. Through the maze of intrigue and machinations of the reformist imposters in the Socialist Party, he shouldered his way with the doctrine of class struggle and the tactics of militant action.

The proletarian and revolutionary elements gathered around him and formed the powerful "left wing" of the party which made its bid for power in the convention of 1912. The "Reds" were defeated there, and the party took a decisive step along the pathway which led to its present position of reformist bankruptcy and open betrayal. The subsequent expulsion of Haywood from the National Executive Committee was at once a proof of the opportunist degeneration of the party and of his own revolutionary integrity.

Haywood's syndicalism was the outcome of his reaction against the reformist policies and parliamentary cretinism of the middle-class leaders of the Socialist Party—Hillquit, Berger and Company. But syndicalism, which in its final analysis, is "the twin brother of reformism," as Lenin has characterized it, was only a transient theory in Haywood's career. He passed beyond it and thus escaped that degeneration and sterility which overtook the syndicalist movement throughout the world during and after the war. The World War and the Russian Revolution did not pass by Haywood unnoticed, as they passed by many leaders of the I.W.W. who had encased themselves in a shell of dogma to shut out the realities of life.

These world-shaking events, combined with the hounding and dragooning of the I.W.W. by the United States government—the "political state" which syndicalism wanted to "ignore"—wrought a profound change in the outlook of Bill Haywood. He emerged from Leavenworth Penitentiary in 1919 in a receptive and studious mood. He was already 50 years old, but he conquered the mental rigidity which afflicts so many at that age. He began, slowly and painfully, to assimilate the new and universal lessons of the war and the Russian Revolution.

First taking his stand with that group in the I.W.W. which favored adherence to the Red International of Labor Unions, he gradually developed his thought further and finally came to the point where he proclaimed himself a communist and a disciple of Lenin. He became a member of the Communist Party of America before his departure for Russia. There he was transferred to the Russian Communist Party and, in recognition of his lifetime of revolutionary work, he was given the status of "an old party member"—the highest honor anyone can enjoy in the land of workers' triumph.

As everyone knows, Haywood in his time had been a prisoner in many jails and, like all men who have smelt iron, he was keenly sensitive to the interests of revolutionaries who suffer this crucifixion. He attached the utmost importance to the work of labor defense and was one of the founders of the I.L.D. He contributed many ideas to its formation and remained an enthusiastic supporter right up to his death. What is very probably his last message to the workers of America, written just before he was stricken the last time, is contained in a letter which is being published in the June number of the *Labor Defender* now on the press.

As a leader of the workers in open struggle Haywood

was a fighter, the like of which is all too seldom seen. He loved the laboring masses and was remarkably free from all prejudices of craft or race or nationality. In battle with the class enemies of the workers he was a raging lion, relentless and irreconcilable. His field was the open fight, and in mass strikes his powers unfolded and multiplied themselves. Endowed with a giant's physique and an absolute disregard of personal hazards, he pulled the striking workers to him as to a magnet and imparted to them his own courage and spirit.

I remember especially his arrival at Akron during the great rubber-workers' strike of 1913, when 10,000 strikers met him at the station and marched behind him to the Hall. His speech that morning has always stood out in my mind as a model of working-class oratory. With his commanding presence and his great mellow voice he held the vast crowd in his power from the moment that he rose to speak. He had that gift, all too rare, of using only the necessary words and of compressing his thoughts into short, epigrammatic sentences. He clarified his points with homely illustrations and pungent witticisms which rocked the audience with understanding laughter. He poured out sarcasm, ridicule and denunciation upon the employers and their pretensions, and made the workers feel with him that they, the workers, were the important and necessary people. He closed, as he always did, on a note of hope and struggle, with a picture of the final victory of the workers. Every word from beginning to end, simple, clear and effective. That is Haywood, the proletarian orator, as I remember him.

There was another side to Bill Haywood which was an essential side of his character, revealed to those who knew him well as personal friends. He had a warmth of personality that drew men to him like a bonfire on a winter's day. His considerateness and indulgence toward his friends, and his generous impulsiveness in human relations, were just as much a part of Bill Haywood as his iron will and intransigence in battle.

"Bill's room," in the Lux Hotel at Moscow, was always the central gathering place for the English-speaking delegates. Bill was "good company." He liked to have people around him, and visitors came to his room in a steady stream; many went to pour out their troubles, certain of a sympathetic hearing and a word of wise advice.

The American ruling class hounded Haywood with the most vindictive hatred. They could not tolerate the idea that he, an American of old revolutionary stock, a talented organizer and eloquent speaker, should be on the side of the exploited masses, a champion of the doubly persecuted foreigners and Negroes.

With a 20-year prison sentence hanging over him he was compelled to leave America in the closing years of his life and to seek refuge in workers' Russia. He died there in the Kremlin, the capitol of his and our socialist fatherland with the red flag of his class floating triumphantly overhead.

Capitalist America made him an outlaw and he died expatriated from his native land. But in the ranks of the militant workers of America, who owe so much to his example, he remains a citizen of the first rank. He represented in his rugged personality all that was best of the pre-war socialist and labor movement, and by his adhesion to communism he helped to transmit that inheritance to us. His memory will remain a blazing torch of inspiration for the workers of America in the great struggles which lie before them.

His life was a credit and an honor to our class and to our movement. Those who pick up the battle flag which has fallen from his lifeless hands will do well to emulate the bigness and vision, the courage and the devotion which were characteristics of our beloved comrade and friend, Bill Haywood.

Tom Mooney's appeal

DAILY WORKER, APRIL 12, 1928

San Francisco, April 11—Tom Mooney today appealed through the International Labor Defense to the workers of America and the world to raise their voices again in his behalf and bring about the liberation of himself and Warren Billings from the California prisons, where they have been confined for nearly 12 years on framed-up charges.

I talked to him for two hours today in San Quentin Penitentiary, and he asked me to make it clear that he has not given up the fight for his freedom or the hope that, with the help of the working class, it will be gained.

"Our hope is in a new protest movement," he said. "Every possible legal and technical move has been made to prove our innocence and our right to an unconditional pardon, but without success. The years go by until nearly 12 have elapsed, and still we are held in prison for a crime of which the world knows we are not guilty. Our crime was loyalty to the workers. Now, let the workers speak again in our behalf. I have confidence that our friends will find the way to make our appeal heard throughout the world."

Twelve years of prison have made their mark on Tom Mooney. It has grayed his hair and impaired his once robust health; but his indomitable spirit, which was the marvel of all who knew him, remains unshaken. His mind is as keen as ever and his eyes flash with the old fire of the fighter who never admits defeat. He still believes in the power of labor solidarity, and is full of hope that the power of the workers will yet bring about his vindication and his freedom from San Quentin Prison.

"I have been fortified all through these years of prison," he said, "by my faith in the movement which I serve and by the consciousness that, even though confined here, I am an instrument of the workers' cause and a symbol of their struggle. I have not forgotten the protest of the Russian workers which saved us from the gallows, and I have not lost my confidence that the workers of America, and the world, will again make their mighty voices heard in our behalf."

I brought him greetings from the mass meetings I have addressed throughout the country; particularly from the Colorado miners, who, in the midst of their own desperate struggle, have not forgotten the names of Mooney and Billings and who asked me to take a special message of cheer and encouragement to them.

His face lighted up with satisfaction and he enquired eagerly regarding the latest developments in the labor movement and the miners' strike. Tom Mooney is a labor man through and through. The cause of the workers for which he has already suffered 12 years in prison is uppermost in his mind and heart, and he looks forward eagerly for the day of liberation which will bring him back to active work in the ranks.

There has been talk of efforts to secure his release on parole; but Tom Mooney doesn't want to come out that way. "I am not guilty of any crime, so why should I be paroled and have all my movements mortgaged and restricted? I want to be free to take up my work where I left it off 12 years ago."

We discussed various methods and plans of reviving the public interest in the case and of putting the names of Mooney and Billings again on the agenda of the labor movement. An aggressive campaign to rebuild the protest movement for the unconditional release of Mooney and Billings was the center of the understanding arrived at.

As we shook hands at parting, he said, "Go ahead! You have my full approval and authorization for the work in our behalf."

A visit with Billings at Folsom Prison

LABOR DEFENDER, JUNE 1928

To get to Folsom Prison you take the train to Sacramento and then transfer to the stage for Represa. The journey from San Francisco kills a whole day. They call Folsom "the Rock Pile"—a God-forsaken out-of-the-way place, inconvenient for visitors, and few go there. The day I went to see Warren Billings, I was the only visitor to ride the stage on that desolate journey over the winding road, through beautiful green hills and hollows, that ends in the Folsom rock quarry—California's dread prison for second-term convicts.

I left the stage and walked towards the main gate with a depressing feeling of loneliness. The stone prison rises from the ground like a massive boulder within the gray enclosing walls with their machine gun turrets at the vantage points. The rock quarries deface the lovely hillside like ugly scars. The green sward of the lawn, close-cropped and smooth and well attended like the frontyards of all prisons, was resplendent in the California sunshine.

I was given a seat in the warden's office to wait for Billings—there appeared to be no special visiting room. The warden's secretary went out of his way to make me comfortable. Made a little conversation about the weather. Offered me a copy of the *Saturday Evening Post,* or perhaps it was *Liberty.* I didn't read it.

The warden returned soon. Billings was with him. A rather slight man, somewhat less than medium height. Reddish hair and sandy complexion. A friendly, boyish countenance with lines carved in it which seemed strangely out of place. I had never met him before, but I am sure I know him now. His character is all written in his face and manner and his ready, engaging smile. A warm personable fellow, without guile or subtlety. The kind that mixes well and makes friends easily.

He is 35 years old now. There are lines in his face that usually come only to later years, but his manner and appearance on the whole are those of a younger man. He was only 23 when he was caught with Tom Mooney in the frame-up trap and he has been in prison the whole intervening 12 years—all his years of flush young manhood and ripening maturity. In many ways he suggested a youth of 23, as though the characteristics which belonged to him at that age, when he was first imprisoned, had frozen in him and become a permanent part of his personality.

He works hard at manual labor and has done more than his bit in the prison quarries, the chief "industry" of Folsom. He is one of 2,200 men imprisoned there under the California system which segregates men who have been convicted more than once—"the two-time losers"—in a separate penitentiary. Billings did a short "jolt" before from the Pacific Gas and Electric strike.

The regime at Folsom is a rigorous one. There is no pampering of convicts serving their second term in California. The inexhaustible quarries, which are the pride of Folsom, not only provide work for their idle hands, but turn a pretty penny of profits also. The Folsom prisoners quarried the rock to build their own jail and the frowning walls around it; and enormous quantities of rock for road building come from there. The paved roads of California, interweaving and running in all directions, are justly famous. The stones of Folsom, hewn out of the prison quarries by the heart-breaking labor of the convicts, pave many a mile over which the autos skim.

It was on the twenty-second day of July, 1916, that a bomb was thrown into a Preparedness Parade, killing a number of people. Five days later Billings was arrested and he has been imprisoned ever since. He had nothing to do with the crime as everybody now knows. But the open-shop interests were out to "get" some labor men, and Tom Mooney and the militants associated with him, who had organized a strike on the street railways of San Francisco two weeks before, were the group selected. They were arrested, "framed" and railroaded.

If you and I had been compelled to spend our entire adult lives in prison for a crime we didn't commit, that fact would very likely be burning uppermost in our minds all the time. So it is with Warren Billings. But he has not given way to self-centered sourness. He is awake and receptive to the big things transpiring in the world and talks about them. He was in the movement since he was 16 years old and was active all the time even before 1913, when, at the age of 20, he told me, he "became class conscious."

Thereafter class consciousness was the determining

factor in all his work and thought, as it still is today.

He told me some details of his case. They tried him with a "professional jury"—that is a jury composed of members who serve on juries all the time and make a living from the fees. They play in with the District Attorney and are selected for their reliability in bringing in convictions.

"They fixed me good and plenty with the jury," Billings told me. "One of my jurymen was an old man named Fraser who had been a professional juryman continuously for 10 years and during that entire time, found every defendant guilty!"

I gasped, and started to speak but he checked me with an ironical laugh. "I guess he didn't want to break his record in my case," he said.

It was the testimony of John McDonald, the dope fiend and degenerate, that constituted the principal evidence against him. It is well known that McDonald repudiated his entire testimony five years later. But the horror of the whole business struck me with a special intensity as Billings spoke about the effect of his testimony at the trial—because I, with Robert Minor and others, had heard McDonald in New York in 1921 tell in great detail how the whole thing had been cooked up and how he knew no more about the case than we did.

Warren Billings was born in New York State of New England German stock. He is a shoe worker by trade and joined the Boot and Shoe Workers Union at the age of 16. He was president of Local 220 at San Francisco when he was arrested in 1916. He was an active "union man" while yet a boy in his teens. Association with radicals and militants in San Francisco broadened his outlook and gave him a social vision. That was in 1913; and from that time onward he plunged into the movement, giving all his thought and energy to it.

Those were days of boundless enthusiasm and soaring dreams. He told me about the work he did as "undercover man" for the union. "When the bosses tried to operate their shops during a strike I used to go and get a job there to get information for the union as to the exact state of affairs. I also worked to demoralize the strikebreakers and tried to get them to organize a second strike, and sometimes I succeeded."

General radical activities claimed his attention. He took an active part in the work of the old International Workers Defense League of San Francisco. This historic body, one of the forerunners of the I.L.D., had been formed originally during the Moyer-Haywood case. It was a delegate body and was held together for other defense cases. It took up the fight for Rangel and Cline in 1913 and for Ford and Suhr the following year, and many others.

Tom Mooney and Warren Billings were both delegates from their unions to the International Workers Defense League and active participants in its activities in behalf of persecuted workers. There, unknowingly, they were building the structure of an organization which was to be their strongest support in the time of their own distress. For it was this League which first took up their defense and blazoned their story to the world. The International Workers Defense League, which Mooney and Billings helped to build, later made the Mooney-Billings case a world issue and thoroughly and completely exposed the frame-up against them.

The diabolical conspiracy against Mooney and Billings has been thoroughly exposed and is an old story now. We will tell it over again in the July number of the *Labor Defender* as the starting point of a new movement in their behalf on the twelfth anniversary of their imprisonment.

Let us hope that the observance of this twelfth anniversary will witness the awakening of the workers to a new interest in the case of Mooney and Billings and the beginning of a new resolute fight in their behalf.

A talk with the Centralia prisoners

LABOR DEFENDER, JUNE 1928

Over 300 workers' halls were raided by inspired mobs of "patriots" during the war and the year that followed it. When an armed mob attacked the lumber workers' hall in Centralia, Washington, on Armistice Day 1919, it met a group of workers who resisted and fought back. In the fight which ensued, three of the raiders were killed, one of the lumber workers, Wesley Everest, was lynched and seven others were sentenced to terms of 25 to 40 years in the State Penitentiary at Walla Walla, after a trial which was a legal lynching conducted in an atmosphere of terror and intimidation. The eighth man, Loren Roberts, was adjudged insane without definite sentence, although his sanity now is obvious.

I went to see them on my western trip. I had been in correspondence with several of the men and they had invited me to come.

A visit with them is not soon to be forgotten. They belong to that wholesale western breed of rebel outdoor workers—freedom-lovers and wholehearted fighters; idealistic men who stake their heads on the things they believe in. Confinement bears heavily upon such men as they, who are used to the forests and the open field.

Three of them have families waiting for them and dependent on them, with children growing up without the father's steadying hand over them. The Centralia prisoners have borne their martyrdom with a soldier spirit, but after nearly eight years in prison they are now beginning to put the question of a real effort to get them out in the most direct and pertinent manner.

"We are a part of the price paid for better conditions for the lumber workers," said Eugene Barnett, a fine type of American rebel worker, whose life of poverty, hardship and struggle has been interestingly told in "The Autobiography of a Class War Prisoner," which was published serially in the *Labor Defender.*

"We are here as an example to other workers. There is not a criminal amongst us. We are here in the cause of labor and we want a united movement of all the workers for our release. We do not see why all elements who are honestly devoted to the working class cannot unite on such an issue, even though they have differences on other questions. Those who take a different attitude do not represent our views or wishes."

The others whom I talked to echoed these sentiments. They spoke—these men with nearly eight years of imprisonment behind them—with bitter indignation about the factional wrangling over their case, the paralysis it has brought about and the failure to organize a united movement in their behalf.

We talked of many things in a crowded, hurried way. Did you ever visit men in prison? It is like a meeting between people from different worlds. There is so much to say, so many questions to discuss, and it must all be done within a time limit. The guard is waiting and every minute you expect the notice "time's up!" Then the hurried words of parting, the hand clasps and the horrible clangor of iron doors slamming shut and the harsh, grating noise of the bars sliding back into the slots.

"We belong to the working class," said James McInerney, "and we want all the workers to know about our case and take part in the fight for us." I was especially anxious to see McInerney, as I had heard much in praise of his character by those who know him. "When you see McInerney, you'll see a man," a former prisoner of Walla Walla told me at Portland.

I suggested an attempt to get support from the trade unions and farmers in the state and also from some liberal and humanitarian elements, and they agreed with that. There is no sectarianism in their attitude.

"The thing that burns a man up in a place like this," said McInerney, "is to see your own kind who are supposed to be closest to you, doing absolutely nothing for you and acting as though you were a bone to fight over.

"Eight years of another man's life in prison is a mere trifle for some people, but for the man who serves the time it is a very important matter. These eight years have been the best eight years of our lives. It was our service to the cause of the workers that brought us here, not any selfish purpose, and we don't want anybody to stand in the way of a united movement of the workers to get us out."

I told them I had talked with Elmer Smith, and at the mention of his name, the conversation switched around to him. He has first place in their hearts, and for good reasons.

The tireless work and selfless devotion of this Centralia lawyer in behalf of the eight lumber workers at Walla Walla is a big story in itself. He was a young lawyer in Centralia with bright "prospects," but he had antagonized the moneyed interests by his friendship for the workers and his attempt to defend their legal rights. When the Armistice Day tragedy occurred, the lumber interests set out to "get" him and he was indicted and brought to trial along with others.

Since the day of his acquittal, nearly eight years ago, he has worked and fought unceasingly for the release of the men who were convicted. He has made a national speaking tour on the case and he has carried the issue into the most remote rural corners of the state of Washington in long campaigns. Moreover he stuck it out in Centralia, the scene of the fight, facing the ostracism boycott and threats of the whole crowd of lynchers and farmers, and finally winning over the great majority of the people of Centralia to the cause of the prisoners.

Serious illnesses and several operations have only been interludes between his strenuous campaigns. When I saw him at Centralia he was hard at it again, although still weak from a recent operation. He is working now on a petition of Centralia citizens for release of the men. It is the work of Elmer Smith more than anything else which has kept the Centralia case alive.

This has been especially true since the split in the I.W.W. The Centralia case was dragged into the controversy, and activities in their behalf were paralyzed to a large extent. The prisoners were the football in that football game, and their wishes for unity of action got scant consideration. The rank and file of the I.W.W. have always been loyal to the Centralia martyrs; but for many little office holders in both factions, the case ceased to be an issue of the class struggle and became a private business.

The only activity of any consequence I could discover on my trip west was that conducted by the Centralia Publicity Committee, with which Elmer Smith is connected. Its work is concentrated at present on securing a petition of Centralia people. This is good, but a broader and bigger fight must be organized.

"Nothing but a general strike will free the class-war prisoners"—is a remark one hears quite frequently. There is no doubt that a general strike is a powerful weapon; but in the period when the conditions for the strike are lacking, this slogan can easily become a cloak for passivity and for neglect of those forms of protest action which are possible under the circumstances. It is the task of conscious workers to organize those small actions which are now possible—meetings, petitions, pamphlets, conferences, etc.—and to strive to develop them into higher forms of class action. Passivity in these forms of class action under present circumstances amounts to betrayal of the class-war prisoners.

The "labor jury" selected by the trade unions of the state, which sat at the trial, voted "not guilty" unanimously. Seven of the jurymen who convicted the Centralia men have since admitted they have appealed to the Governor to pardon them. Elmer Smith told me 85 percent of the people of Centralia would sign the petition for pardon. A well organized campaign, uniting all forces, would gain tremendous support which could not be disposed of easily.

The prisoners themselves, who are the final determining factor, have said their word very decisively. Their open letter to the International Labor Defense, which is being published in the press, appeals clearly for a united movement in their behalf. It is the duty of all labor militants to see that this appeal has not been made in vain.

2

Minneapolis 1934

Police attempt to get a scab truck through during 1934 strikes in Minneapolis.

Introductory note

In October 1928 Cannon was expelled from the Communist Party for supporting the fight led by Leon Trotsky to continue Lenin's battle against the counterrevolutionary policies of growing petty-bourgeois social layers headed by Joseph Stalin. While in Moscow as a delegate to the Sixth Congress of the Communist International, Cannon and Canadian CP leader Maurice Spector had come across a document by Trotsky (then in exile in Soviet central Asia) criticizing the efforts of the Stalin-led Comintern to seek accommodation with world capitalism. Under the name "socialism in one country," this subordination of the world working-class struggle to the diplomatic needs of the Soviet bureaucratic caste had led to the defeat of a revolutionary upsurge in China the previous year.

Convinced by Trotsky's views, which were officially banned, Cannon smuggled the document out of Russia and passed it along to other party members in the United States. When the CP leadership learned of Cannon's support for Trotsky's position, he was summarily expelled, together with Max Shachtman and Martin Abern. Within a week, the first issue of the *Militant* was published, with Cannon as editor.

All members of the party were asked to endorse the expulsions. Those refusing to do so were themselves kicked out. In early 1929 the expelled members formed the Communist League of America. Its strongest branch, in Minneapolis, was led by Vincent R. Dunne and Carl Skoglund, who had long experience in the communist and labor movements.

In 1934 Minneapolis CLA members helped lead a series of strikes by truck drivers and helpers, which eventually emerged victorious despite the combined efforts of the antilabor Citizens' Alliance, the state and federal governments, and the police and national guard. An account of this battle by Farrell Dobbs, a CLA member and leader of the strike, has been published in *Teamster Rebellion* (Pathfinder, 1972).

The Minneapolis victory, coming in the fifth year of the Great Depression and on the heels of victorious strikes in Toledo and San Francisco, electrified the labor movement and helped prepare the massive upsurge that led to the establishment of the Congress of Industrial Organizations (CIO).

The CLA assigned Cannon to Minneapolis to assist the strike leadership. Among his contributions were a series of articles for the *Organizer,* the first daily strike newspaper in the United States.

Strike call of Local 574

Unanimously adopted at general membership meeting, Wednesday, July 11

THE ORGANIZER—DAILY STRIKE BULLETIN
MINNEAPOLIS, JULY 16, 1934

Since the settlement of the strike on May 25, Local 574, through its duly authorized representatives, has been attempting to negotiate wage scales with the employers in accordance with the agreement which brought about the ending of the strike. We have attempted to settle with the employers all other matters left for negotiation. All these attempts to settle the dispute by negotiation, conducted with the greatest patience and persistence, have met with failure. The employers, egged on by the union-hating Citizens' Alliance, behind which stand the banks and the sinister financial interests of Wall Street, have violated the agreement. They have set out to break our union and rob us of the fruits of our victory.

All the efforts of our union, over a period of six weeks since the ending of the strike, to establish living wages and hours have been frustrated by the arrogant attitude of the employers. The Regional Labor Board by its action, or rather by its failure to act, has aided in every case in upholding the hands of these employers. Every attempt of the union to negotiate and secure satisfaction for the just demands of its members has been met with evasions, tricks and subterfuges. Every approach for practical discussions of our grievances has been answered by columns of paid newspaper advertisements filled with misrepresentations, lies and slanders against the union and its leadership.

The vital questions of wages and hours, which are of life-and-death concern to our members and their families, have been callously ignored. The right of the union to represent all its members, which was explicitly agreed to in the strike settlement, has been denied. Seniority rules, provided for in the agreement, have been violated by a majority of the firms.

In this unscrupulous course, the Citizens' Alliance and the employers are seeking to shift the issue. They cloak their campaign to wreck the trade-union movement and deprive the workers of decent human lives behind personal attacks on the leaders of the union. The bosses want to dictate to the union what leaders it should have. We reject this dictation. We have the right to be represented by leaders of our own choosing and we intend to assert this right. We reject the insolent demand of the Citizens' Alliance and the bosses to choose our leaders for us. Local 574 is a democratic trade-union organization. Its membership is fully capable of deciding this question for itself without any advice from the exploiters of labor.

The general membership meeting declares that the leaders of our union have faithfully served the interests of the membership. They have conducted themselves as responsible trade-union officials and have not imposed on the union any issues, political or otherwise, contrary to the interests of the union and its members. They have shown their efficiency as organizers in the building of our union. They have demonstrated their loyalty and courage under fire.

The "red scare" of the Citizens' Alliance is nothing but a fraudulent maneuver to distract our attention from the struggle for decent living conditions and demoralize our ranks.

They will not succeed. The conditions of our lives are too bitter. Nobody can divert us from the fight to better them.

We note with the greatest indignation that D.J. Tobin, president of our international organization, has associated himself with this diabolical game of the bosses by publishing a slanderous attack on our leadership in the official magazine. The fact that this attack has become part of the "ammunition" of the bosses in their campaign to wreck our union, is enough for any intelligent worker to estimate it for what it really is. We say plainly to D.J. Tobin: "If you can't act like a union man and help us, instead of helping the bosses, then at least have the decency to stand aside and let us fight our battle alone. We did it in the organization campaign and in the previous strike, and we can do it again. We received absolutely no help of any kind from you. Our leadership and guidance has come from our own local leaders, and them alone. We put our confidence in them and will not support any attack on them under any circumstances."

We are fighting for more wages, for better hours and working conditions, and for the right of union organization. The conditions under which we work are intolerable for men who want to live as human beings and who aspire to provide a decent existence and a future for their families in this, the richest country in the world. That is our right. We have worked for it, and we intend to fight for it to the bitter end.

In doing so we feel deeply convinced that we are fighters for the preservation of the trade-union movement and for the rights and interests of all workers. Our strength and confidence is multiplied by the conviction that our fellow workers and brother unionists in other trades, who helped us so nobly before, will rally to our aid again. We rely on the sympathy and solidarity of the other unions and workers' organizations, who endorsed our demands by their presence in the great labor demonstration Friday,

July 6. We appeal for the support also of the organizations of farmers and gardeners, of the unemployed workers, of the rank and file of small business and professional people—of all who are cheated and oppressed by the financial tyrants who have turned our great, rich country into a land of privation and misery for the masses.

We are confident that our appeal will not be in vain. Therefore, convinced of the justice of our cause, relying on our own strength and the sympathetic aid of the great majority of the population, the general membership meeting solemnly declares:

1. All members of Local No. 574 will go on strike for the enforcement of the union demands on Monday, July 16, at 12 o'clock midnight.

2. We call upon our sister Local No. 120 in St. Paul to take similar action at its general membership meeting Thursday night, and we pledge to Local 120 our solidarity and cooperation in a joint struggle to a successful conclusion.

3. We call upon all other trade unions in the Twin Cities to rally to our support with moral and financial aid, and to hold themselves in readiness to take sympathetic strike action if such becomes necessary to secure our victory and smash the union-wrecking campaign of the Citizens' Alliance.

'. . . If it takes all summer'

THE ORGANIZER—DAILY STRIKE BULLETIN
MINNEAPOLIS, JULY 29, 1934

The most successful commander of the Civil War was General Ulysses S. Grant, the man of whom Roscoe B. Conkling said:

"If you ask what state he came from, our answer then will be: 'He came from Appomattox and its famous apple tree!'" By that he meant to say that he was a fighter who scored victories, and that it didn't make any difference what state he came from.

We too are in a war. We may well study the secrets of the success of General Grant.

How did Grant win his battles and drive the enemy to surrender? Not by "slick" maneuvers, not by oversubtle "cleverness," not by fine tricks. No, the secret of Grant's driving power was bullheaded persistence.

Whenever they had him in a tight corner and put the squeeze on him, he only bowed his neck and declared: "We will fight it out on these lines if it takes all summer!"

We take this example from military history on purpose. We take it because we regard this fight as a battle in a great war—the war between predatory capital and exploited labor, the war between the classes.

The hour has now struck when we are to be put to a new test. Local 574 has shown the world that it has a body of courageous fighters. They are not afraid. They can exchange blows with anybody. They can give it, and they can take it too. The labor movement of America, yes, of the whole world, admirably acknowledges the battle-courage of the men of Fighting 574 and their allies of the Minneapolis working class.

The world admits that we can fight. Now the question arises: Can we stick?

And our answer must be: We'll bow our necks and stick it out if it takes all summer!

But it won't take all summer. Our lines are solid. It is the bosses who are cracking under the pressure of the fight. They are losing millions of dollars and the strain is telling on them.

We are able to state on reliable authority that more than a third of the market firms are clamoring for a settlement in the employers' meetings.

The bandits of the Citizens' Alliance are finding themselves compelled to yield to this pressure from the ranks of the market bosses.

Take the employers' statements printed in the Saturday papers. The haughty expressions barely conceal the fact that you are listening to people who are in retreat and looking for a way out. A few days ago they said that they wouldn't deal with the "Communist leaders of Local 574"—anybody who wants more than $12 a week and is ready to fight for it to the end, is a Communist in their eyes.

In their last statement, however, they say: "We will not negotiate with that leadership unless compelled to do so."

Well, this strike is being carried on for the specific purpose of "compelling them to do so," and we will succeed in this aim if we fight it out to the end.

The strike is a test of strength, of persistence, of endurance. The employers have vast resources and great power: their money, the kept press, the police, the militia—all these forces are against our strike, and we do not fool ourselves about it.

But 574 has even greater resources to draw upon: the inexhaustible energy of the working class, its capacity for endurance and sacrifice, the solidarity of our fellow workers in other trades, the sympathy of the great majority of the population, an honest and courageous leadership and—*our own daily paper!* If we marshal all these resources and utilize them to the full, there can be no question of the outcome.

We must, furthermore, assert all our rights, and let nobody take them away from us.

The employers can foregather in the dark of the moon, in secret session. They can pull strings behind the scenes to make their puppets dance for them.

The workers, whose strength lies in the mass movement, can fight only in the open. Not through secret agents but in their own person. That is why they are so insistent upon the right to free assemblage, so that they may speak freely. The right to free speech, so that they may organize. The right to organize, so that they may strike freely. The right to strike, so that they may picket freely. The right to picket, so that they may win swiftly!

Whoever limits or seeks to limit these rights to the slightest degree, is striking a blow at the workers. The resolution of the Strike Committee of 100, which demands the withdrawal of the troops, the right to hold public meetings in front of our headquarters, and the right to picket, shows how determined Local 574 is to allow no infringement upon its rights.

We shall not allow ourselves to be cut slowly to pieces. We shall not allow ourselves to be delivered, bound hand and foot, to the employers. Instead, we shall resist every effort to strip us of our fighting strength. Instead, we shall bring the employers to terms which make it possible for us to live like human beings.

Those who think that we can be worn down in the battle, that our ranks and spirit can be broken, will be taught a lesson that will not soon be forgotten. We are imbued not only with an unshakable conviction in the justice of our cause, but with an iron resolve to fight to the last ditch.

We will not go back as beaten dogs! We will go back only as union men on union conditions!

The eyes of the labor movement of the whole country are upon us today. Financial support is coming in. Pledges of aid have been received from all parts of the land. The workers everywhere are looking to us. We shall not fail them.

We will fight it out on the picket line if it takes all summer!

Eternal vigilance

THE ORGANIZER—DAILY STRIKE BULLETIN
MINNEAPOLIS, AUGUST 6, 1934

Various sources, including direct statements of individual employers themselves, indicate a widespread revolt during recent days in the ranks of the firms affected by the strike. The staggering financial losses incurred as a result of the strike already far exceed what the cost of the modest wage increases demanded by the union would amount to over a long period of time. A settlement has become a practical necessity for the employers. The real force that has stood in the way of a settlement long ago has been the financial dictatorship of the Citizens' Alliance.

It has been disclosed that this gang of financial pirates, which howls so loudly and piously for "democracy" and "secret ballots" in the union, does not allow the employers who want to settle with the union the right even to attend the sessions of the committee which speaks in their name, to say nothing of having a voice as to what the decisions of this committee should be. The financial Hitlers who want to smash every labor union in town, even though the attempt in the single case of Local 574 is driving half the firms involved to the point of bankruptcy, have confronted these firms with the alternative of a ruination of their business in further attempts to break the strike, or a settlement with the union and the resumption of normal business. The result has been a revolt against the strangulating grip of the Citizens' Alliance clique.

In these new developments all workers can see the tangible results of militant struggle combined with a reasonable attitude toward settlement terms.

The whole country knows and marvels at the unparalleled militancy of our union. Every worker worth his salt has been inspired by the heroic example of the men of 574 who boldly fought for their rights in the face of Bloody Johannes' murderous police terror and Olson's military tyranny. Many a poor slave of this infamous social system, beaten down into the dust and deprived of the benefit of organization, has witnessed this example and felt his own heart beat with aspiration to follow it. The story of our magnificent struggle is first-page news everywhere. Our fellow workers throughout the country are watching our fight with sympathy and hope. Local 574 stands in the very vanguard of the American labor movement today. By our will to battle and our sacrifices we have put it there. And by that fact we have taken upon ourselves an obligation to fight to the end in the same spirit. We shall not fail in that obligation, come what may.

And who can deny the justice of our cause, or the reasonableness of our demands? Even the *Minneapolis Journal,* mouthpiece of the Citizens' Alliance, had to admit in its Sunday editorial that it could not undertake "to say that the strikers are wrong and the employers right." Yes, indeed, it is impossible for anyone, even the *Journal,* to say that we are wrong. For, in the present struggle, we are demanding no more than the right to organize, without which we are slaves; a piece of bread, without which our families cannot live. That is our minimum. All hell shall not beat us down or make us agree to less.

They can't say that we are wrong. But this has not stopped them from trying to beat us out of our just demands by every means of violence and tyrannical oppression; to cheat us out of them by every trick and subterfuge. They shot 50 pickets down and killed two of them in cold blood. They whitewashed the murderers and defamed the victims. They raided our headquarters, with full military force and equipment, as though it were an enemy fortress in time of war. They imprisoned our leaders whom they couldn't buy and couldn't terrorize. They even confined our union doctor in their stockade for the crime of attending to our sick and wounded free of charge.

They try to trick us in the negotiations. They lie about us. And—worst of all—they give us lectures about "violence" and want us to agree to a blacklist against the best members of our union, the leading spirits of our picket line!

Do they want to talk about violence? Do they want to speak of bodily injuries and intolerable indignities to the human spirit? Do they want an accounting of the dead? Let Henry Ness and John Belor answer them from their martyr graves. Let the scores who were shot in the back, who were arrested and imprisoned and persecuted—let them be called as witnesses.

At this present moment, while negotiations for a settlement are pending, we do not allow ourselves for one moment to forget that 130 members of our union, our pickets—the best men in the labor movement of Minneapolis—are penned like wild animals in the stockade at the Fair Grounds for no crime but the courageous exercise of their constitutional rights. They have been put there by military force under the direction of the Farmer-Labor Governor, Floyd B. Olson. What a shame! What an outrage! The 130 pickets in the military stockade are 130 silent witnesses who accuse Floyd B. Olson of treachery to the labor movement. If there is to be a hearing about "violence" be sure to take their testimony!

It is our stubborn resistance to all this violence, this tyranny, oppression and murder, that has brought us to the point where a settlement on favorable terms is in sight. Without this resistance our union would have been smashed long ago and our members would have been driven back to work like beaten slaves, without organization and without even a prospect of gains. Let us not forget that, especially now, as they are trying the last desperate trick to get us to agree to a blacklist against the most active pickets under cover of a "violence" clause in the settlement.

They want to discriminate against those "known" to have used violence. They, who shot and killed two members of our union; they, who flung 130 of our members into the military stockade; they, whose hands are still wet and still red with the blood of our martyrs—they dare to ask us to agree to a blacklist against the victims of this violence, that is, against those who are still alive. Never! We shall not make the peace of slaves! Rather a thousand times the peace of Henry Ness and John Belor! Rather the peace of dead men than such a shameful truce!

Guarding ourselves against the tricks and crooked maneuvers of our enemies in this crucial hour, let us also beware of illusions. Our strength is in ourselves—nowhere else. The most fatal illusion that could seize us now would be the idea that the new military orders of Governor Olson, limiting truck permits, can win the strike for us and that we can passively rely on such aid. It was Olson and his military force that started the truck movement in the first place. There is no guarantee that he will not turn about and do the same tomorrow. The federal injunction sought by the employers may very well serve as the ground for such a shift. There is no power upon which we can rely except the independent power of the union. Trust in that, and that only.

"Eternal Vigilance" is the motto of the hour.

Spilling the dirt—a bughouse fable

THE ORGANIZER—DAILY STRIKE BULLETIN
MINNEAPOLIS, AUGUST 8, 1934

By a lucky combination of circumstances the real issues of the strike have at last been brought out into the open. The dirty dogs at the head of Local 574 have been exposed. The federal mediators, too. Here's the lowdown. Watch closely, and remember that the hand is quicker than the eye.

First: Joseph R. Cochran, chairman of the Employers Advisory Committee, spilled the beans in a statement issued last night. He put this here Father Haas and Mr. Dunnigan on the spot and showed them up as Communist agents "boring from within" the United States Government. He said: "If the Haas-Dunnigan proposals were accepted by the employers, it would enable Local 574 to claim a victory for Communist leadership . . . Thus communism, after all, is still the real issue in this strike."

Second: The editor of the *Organizer* was picked up and taken before the kangaroo court for questioning. The examining officer had been eating onions and drinking scab beer, and his breath was so strong that it overcame the editor and he broke down and confessed everything.

Since reports of this confession will most likely be printed in the other papers in garbled form, we publish it here verbatim as it was really made. (A secret agent of Local 574, working as court stenographer, smuggled out a carbon copy of the original confession.) Here it is:

OFFICER: You might as well come clean now. Give us the whole dope.

EDITOR: O.K., officer, I'm willing to tell everything. But, would you mind turning your breath the other way for a minute. I'm a little bit sick.

OFFICER: Who's dis guy called Father Haas? What's the tie-up between him and Governor Olson and youse guys?

EDITOR: His real name is Haasky. He's a Russian Bolshevik, brought over here by the Brain Trust to put across a modified form of communism through the NRA. Cochran got the goods on him, all right. His proposal of 42 ½ cents an hour is practically the same thing as communism. He writes editorials for the *Militant* under an assumed name.

OFFICER: Spill the rest of it. What about Dunnigan, Olson, Brown and the Dunne brothers—how many of these here Dunne brothers is there all told?

EDITOR: Their real name is Dunnskovitsky. They are Irish Jews from County Cork, smuggled into the country about six months ago disguised as sacks of Irish potatoes. There are 17 of them in Minneapolis, all the same age, and they all holler for 42 ½ cents an hour. They say that's the beginning of communism, and they are all strong for it. They have a brother in New York who is a famous acrobat. He inspired the popular ballad, "The Man on the Flying Trapeze." Mr. Dunnigan's right name is Dunnigansky—a cousin of the Dunne boys and hand in glove with them on the 42 ½ cents an hour racket.

OFFICER: What about Brown?

EDITOR: He's a Jew named Bronstein, a fish peddler from the east side of New York. He came here a few weeks ago and tried to sell Bismark herring down at the market. Then he lined up with the Dunnskovitskys and muscled into the union racket, and got himself elected president of Local 574. He's sitting pretty now and doesn't have to peddle herring any more. By the way, he is a son of Leon Bronstein—that's the original name of this guy Trotsky that started all the trouble over in Russia.

OFFICER: How about Governor Olson? He's in wit youse guys in the communist racket, ain't he?

EDITOR: Sure! That's the slickest part of the whole game. That guy's a card. His right name is not Olson, and he's not a Swede either—that's just a gag to get the Scandinavian vote. He's a Russian importation—direct from Moscow—and his real name is Olsonovich. He's been a big help to the strike. That raid he pulled off at the union headquarters, and the throwing of the pickets into the stockade, was all a trick to get sympathy for the strikers.

OFFICER: This is gettin' too deep for me. Who cooked up this whole scheme, anyway?

EDITOR: Well, to tell the truth, it was all planned out in Constantinople a few months ago. Some of the boys worked a week driving trucks and saved up enough money to take a trip to Europe. They went over to Constantinople to see Trotsky and get instructions for their next move. Trotsky said: "Boys, I want a revolution in Minneapolis before snow flies." They said "O.K." and started to leave.

Just as they were about to take the boat, Vincent Dunne stepped up to old man Trotsky and said, "What's your last word of advice before we go?"

OFFICER: What did Trotsky say?

EDITOR: He said, "Boys, keep your eye on Olsonovich. He is liable to double cross you any minute."

Drivers' strike reveals workers' great resources

THE ORGANIZER—DAILY STRIKE BULLETIN
MINNEAPOLIS, AUGUST 11, 1934

The strike of Local 574 is a marvelous illustration of the initiative and resources of the workers, when they awaken to the necessity of organizing and fighting for their own interests. The bosses have been having their own way so long, without any serious opposition from the workers, that they got into the habit of thinking they are just so much raw material that goes into the process of production. That the workers have feelings, ambitions, yes, and brains, too—that, they cannot understand.

If the workers organize and put up a fight the bosses are always sure that some "outside agitator" is responsible. It never occurs to them that the workers who run the industries of the world have also got sense enough to run their own organizations and run them effectively. When they confront a real example of this working class ability they get blue in the face. It is costing the Minneapolis bosses millions of dollars to learn that the drivers, help ers and inside men of Local 574 mean business, and are not being fooled by anybody.

Local 574's strike is the best example of organization and efficiency I have ever seen—and I have seen a lot in my lifetime as a union man. A movement like this could never be built by a few individual leaders, as the bosses maintain, no matter how capable these leaders might be. The one thing that stands out in the strike is that here is a living monument of determined people. Hundreds and thousands of men and women have to combine their energy, their intelligence and their enthusiasm to make such a strike. That is what we have in Local 574 and its Women's Auxiliary.

The leaders don't have to worry about going too far ahead of this bunch; the problem is to keep pace with it. Almost every day we get some new proof that the workers—once they make up their minds—can give the wise bosses cards and spades when it comes to organizing things and making a group of people pull together for the common interest.

It would take a story long enough to fill a book to describe all the details of organization that fit together to make up the strike machine. And one of the most important chapters should be devoted to an account of the wonderful support and help we get from other unions and the unemployed workers, and also from the farmers and small-business and professional men.

It certainly warms the heart to see a poor farmer, who is run pretty ragged himself and cheated out of practically everything he works for, come into strike headquarters with a supply of food which he donates free to the commissary. And compare the work of our doctor and nurses, working all hours for nothing to tend the sick and care for the wounded—compare examples of humanity like that with the bosses and money-sharks who never have a thought for anything but their own personal profits.

When you see things like that you have to ask yourself

where these chiselers who live on the labor of others get the nerve to lecture the common run of people about anything. But they have the nerve. They want to hog everything for themselves and then tell us that is the best and most moral arrangement that could be made.

Every strike nowadays brings out proof of the fact that not only the workers directly involved, but also the great mass of the population in general, are fed up with the small clique of financial highbinders who run the country for their own exclusive benefit. The masses—and this includes the small-business and professional people and the farmers as well as the wage workers—are anxious to show their sympathy for the strikers and take a sock at the arrogant money-hogs who begrudge a worker a decent wage for his labor. The Citizens' Alliance gang in Minneapolis, like similar cliques in other cities, are playing with dynamite in trying to override this sentiment of the masses. Some day they are going to make us all mad. Then it will be too late to settle for 42 ½ and 52 ½ cents an hour, or anything like it. The workers are just beginning to realize their power. They can make over this old world to suit themselves—if they really make up their minds to do it.

Thanks to Pine County farmers

THE ORGANIZER—DAILY STRIKE BULLETIN
MINNEAPOLIS, AUGUST 13, 1934

Chicken dinner was served to 3,000 by the commissary department at strike headquarters yesterday, the twenty-eighth day of the greatest strike Minneapolis ever saw.

The fraternal alliance of the farmers and the workers in a struggle against a common enemy was vividly demonstrated as the embattled workers lined up at the commissary for the sumptuous banquet prepared for them today through the generosity of the farmers supporting the strike.

The luscious young chickens, which constituted the *pièce de résistance* of the banquet, were donated by Pine County farmers, members of the Pine County Farm Holiday Association, at whose picnic President Brown was the invited guest speaker Sunday.

It was a meal fit for a king—or a union man. Besides the chicken the menu consisted of mashed potatoes, chicken gravy, radishes, celery, bread, butter and milk, coffee or buttermilk. Even the truck drivers, helpers and inside men—all fat and overfed from the high living they have enjoyed on the big wages the bosses paid before the strike—had to admit that this feed was just a little better than even they are used to.

A few pickets, recently released from the military stockade, never said a word but just quietly concentrated on the job of stowing away the chow, like men whose dream had come true.

It was one of the "high" days of the strike. A festive spirit prevailed around strike headquarters. Everybody was happy, well-fed and confident of victory. Even the union mascot, the little white pig with the number "574" painted in red on his sides, scampered around more frisky than ever, in honor of the day.

The strikers of Local 574 warmly appreciate the generosity of the farmers and their fine solidarity in this struggle. Thanks. Brothers! The bosses give us baloney when we are working; you give us chicken when we are out on strike!

The secret of Local 574

THE ORGANIZER—DAILY STRIKE BULLETIN
MINNEAPOLIS, AUGUST 18, 1934

The amazing vitality of the strike of Local 574, and its ability to survive the heaviest blows and come back fighting, are evoking continued amazement and admiration in the ranks of the general labor movement. The prestige of Local 574 extends far beyond the borders of Minneapolis.

This was strikingly demonstrated by the enthusiasm of the International Convention of the Hotel and Restaurant Workers International Alliance and Bartenders International League, and its generous donation of $1,000. This is a lot of money to donate to the strike of a local union in another trade, and could not have been possible if the delegates, coming from all parts of the country, had not been deeply stirred by the magnificent fight of our union.

Trade unionists, including many labor leaders of a more or less conservative tendency, have paid tribute to the fighting abilities of Local 574 and its methods of conducting the struggle against the heaviest odds. Even those who have taken part in important labor struggles and studied the history of others, recognize something new and different in Local 574's way of doing things, something which enables it to stand its ground and keep on fighting where an ordinary trade union would have folded up long ago.

What is the secret of this remarkable vitality and resourcefulness? What is "different" about Local 574?

The answer is, that almost everything is different. By its constitution and affiliation, Local 574 is an ordinary trade union, indistinguishable from thousands of others. But within the framework of the old-line trade-union movement, represented by the A.F. of L., our Local has evolved methods of organization and forms of activity which go far beyond the traditional craft-union methods and ideas.

The outward form is old-fashioned and "regular," but the inner content is modern and pulsating with new vigorous life. In one sense of the word it can be said that Local 574 represents a fusion of the new and the old at the moment when the American labor movement as a whole stands before the prospect of great changes to meet the modern needs of the workers. No single one of the distinct features of our strike can explain the full significance of Local 574 as the herald of this new movement evolving within the formal framework of the old. The new features and methods of work fit and supplement each other. They are combined by a unifying idea, and it is this *combination* that gives Local 574 its power and fighting capacity.

Nevertheless, each of the distinct features brought out in this strike has its own separate importance and deserves special study. Trade unionists who want to get at the heart of the whole method of 574, and learn its secret, ought to devote attentive study to each of these features separately.

One of the many distinct contributions made by Local 574 to the labor movement is the organization of the womenfolk of the strikers and their direct participation in the strike through the Ladies' Auxiliary. Even if this organization doesn't function perfectly, and still suffers from the weakness that always goes with inexperience, it has shown itself to be a real power in this strike, as it already did in the May strike to a lesser extent. The Ladies' Auxiliary is so much a part of the strike and carries such heavy burdens, that it is taken for granted as an indispensable part of the union. Nobody even thinks of going on without it.

It is hard to realize that other unions go into struggle

without such a valuable ally. Yet this is what happens in nearly every case. Local 574 is one of the very few local unions that have understood the necessity of organizing the women and making their organization a vital part of the strike machinery.

There is an *idea* behind this, also. Local 574 doesn't take any stock in the theory that capital and labor are brothers, and that the way for little brother labor to get a few crumbs is to be a good boy and appeal to the good nature of big brother capital. We see the issue between capital and labor as an unceasing struggle between the class of exploited workers and the class of exploiting parasites. It is a war. What decides in this war, as in all others, is power. The exploiters are organized to grind us down into the dust. We must organize our class to fight back. *And the women are half of the working class.* Their interests are the same as ours and they are ready to fight for them. Therefore: Organize them to take part in the class battle. This is the idea behind the wonderful organization of the Ladies' Auxiliary, and its effective cooperation with the union in the struggle.

Of course, Local 574 cannot claim to be the pioneer in grasping this idea and carrying it into practice. There have been numerous examples of attempts along this line on the part of other organizations, although seldom has it been done as effectively. The greatest example of effective organization of women—one that did much to inspire us—belongs to the Progressive Miners of Illinois.

This organization carried on some heroic struggles during 1932–1933 and needed extraordinary resources to survive. One of these resources, which played a decisive part in keeping the union alive and beating back its enemies, was the Women's Auxiliary of the Progressive Miners. The great importance of organizing the women, even where they are not directly employed in industry, was brought out very clearly in this experience. The Women's Auxiliary of the Progressive Miners set the pace for the whole labor movement and by right holds first place as the real pioneer.

Local 574 learned from this example and was influenced by it to encourage and assist the organization of our women. That, by the way, is another merit of our union and its leadership—they watch what is going on in the world of labor, and they study the experiences of other workers and learn from them.

What the union means

THE ORGANIZER—DAILY STRIKE BULLETIN
MINNEAPOLIS, AUGUST 23, 1934

The victory of unionism in our industry has already been won. In two great battles which stirred the whole country—first in the May strike and then in the strike just concluded—the drivers, helpers and inside workers of Minneapolis showed their determination to have a union of their own, free from the influence or coercion of the employers. Now there is to be an election to see if the workers really meant it. Very well. We shall have the election and go through the formality. Our big task now is to get ready for it, and to roll up such an overwhelming vote for the union that the question cannot be raised again.

There hasn't been a free and honest election held anywhere to our knowledge that did not result in a majority of the workers voting for a union of their own. Even on those railroads where trade unions have been outlawed and "company unionism" has been forced on the workers, the elections now taking place, under the auspices of the National Mediation Board, are resulting in sweeping victories for the bona fide unions, according to the report in *Labor,* the national weekly organ of the railroad unions.

The awakening workers of America, in every trade and industry, are moved by one common, overpowering impulse which can be expressed in a single word: UNIONISM! Every intelligent worker understands that that is the first step on the road to a better and freer life. "In almost every case," says *Labor,* "the paramount issue is the right of the workers to organize." Once that is accomplished, the worker, weak and helpless as an individual, becomes strong and independent. He has the confidence to demand improved conditions and better wages. And—united with his fellow workers—he has the strength to get them.

And that is just the point. In clinging to the idea of unionism, and fighting so doggedly for it, the workers are inspired by the thought of *what the union means!*

The union means bread and butter. The union is the weapon by which the workers wrest better wages from the profit-mad bosses. It means more and better food for the workingman's kids and a decent dress for his wife to wear. It means a few nickels in his own pocket to pay for a glass of beer or two if he feels that way. In fighting for a union, the worker in reality is fighting to improve his standard of life and to give his family a chance to live like human beings.

The union means protection and a certain degree of security in employment. Once a strong union appears on the scene the arbitrary powers of the employers over the lives of the workers are limited. The old system of hiring and firing according to the whim of the bosses gives way to seniority rights. The union is a protection to the individual worker against discrimination. In fighting for a union the worker is fighting for certain rights of "citizenship" in industry. He is fighting for the right to have something to say about his job. Without a union this is impossible.

The union means the beginning of independence. The unorganized worker has no rights whatever which the boss is obliged to respect. No matter how proud and sensitive the individual may be, he has to take what is offered and keep his mouth shut. Long hours, miserable wages, all kinds of abuse—the worker has to put up with all of that and has no comeback, no means of redress. The unorganized worker is as helpless as a slave.

The union man stands up on his feet and looks the world in the face. He has something behind him, a power to which he can appeal. The individual "bargain" between the worker and the boss, in which the worker is licked before he starts, is replaced by "collective bargaining" when the union is organized. That doesn't apply only to the question of wages. The union is the "collective" representative of the worker in any dispute he may have with the employer. Feeling that strength behind him, the worker gets more confidence in himself, more self respect, more of the sense of human dignity that befits a useful and productive member of society.

It is because the union means so much in the daily life of the workers that the movement for unionism is rising like a tidal wave. The workers want a new life and a better one, and the first step on this path is organization.

All Minneapolis workers will watch the election with sympathy and hope for 574.

We are sure of victory if our members remain alert and active from now till Tuesday under the great slogans:

Vote for Local 574

Make Minneapolis a Union Town!

3

San Francisco
1936–1937

Introductory note

In late 1934, the CLA fused with the American Workers Party—which had played a leading role in the Toledo Auto-Lite strike earlier that year—to form the Workers Party of the U.S. Two years later the new organization entered the Socialist Party to fuse with revolutionary-minded workers and youth streaming into that organization. The SP was growing under the impact of Hitler's rise to power in Germany, a wave of sit-down strikes in France, and the beginning of the Spanish civil war. The depression had already extended more than half a decade, and the CIO-led labor battles were organizing tens of thousands of unskilled workers in the auto, steel, rubber, electrical, and other industries into unions for the first time. Cannon was sent to California to assist the left-wing forces, and helped found and edit the weekly *Labor Action*. Several of his articles are published in this section.

Among the subjects dealt with by Cannon were the activities of the Communist Party in the trade union movement, in particular the West Coast longshoremen's union. (The union's president, Harry Bridges, is caricatured by Cannon in "The Champion from Far Away.") The CP—along with other union officials, including social democrats—took a position of firm support to President Franklin Roosevelt and the "New Deal" reforms with which U.S. capitalism sought to sidetrack rising social discontent. Because the revolutionary forces were badly outnumbered, the trade union misleaders were able to blunt the combat momentum of the labor movement, tying it firmly to Roosevelt's banner. By so doing, they cut short the possibility that labor would act increasingly in its own name and helped pave the way for U.S. entry into World War II.

Is everybody happy?

LABOR ACTION, SAN FRANCISCO, NOVEMBER 28, 1936

The tumult and the shouting dies and the smoke—to say nothing of the fog—of the election clears away and leaves the bright sun shining down on a free, happy and prosperous America. It was a famous victory for progress.

The well-known friend of labor rolled up an imposing majority and sailed away for South America with a smile. The stock market is booming. The crestfallen economic royalists took their beating like good sports and, by way of self-consolation, are distributing profits and extra dividends among themselves on the biggest scale since 1929. Farley's multitude of postmasters, fixers, ward heelers and bunco steerers are as happy and as fat as pigs in clover, and we mean clover.

Even Hearst hails the election results as a vindication of the American system of government, which he prizes so highly. They say in Washington that a new "Era of Good Feeling" is upon us. In short, everything is lovely and the goose hangs high. Everybody's happy. That is, nearly everybody.

Of course, the thousands of WPA workers who got lay-off slips in their envelopes in the past two weeks are not taking a conspicuous part in the general jubilation. That, however, is hardly to be expected. The kick in the pants they have received is too much like an echo of the vote they cast in the election. Nor can the maritime workers, forced out on strike to defend their organization, be blamed if they are singing "Hold the Fort" on the picket line instead of the Democratic theme song, "Happy Days Are Here Again."

And when, in the coming months, wages lag behind price increases while profits mount sky high again, when the million-headed standing army of the unemployed remains stationary despite increasing production, when military and naval expenditures grow ever larger in preparation for foreign war, and strikers are attacked at home with clubs and guns and gas—when all this happens, as it inevitably will, a fairly sizeable mass of working people are quite apt to stop short and ask themselves: "What are we cheering for, anyway?"

That question will have point and meaning and may spell the beginning of a great awakening if it is directed to the right place—to the false advisers and misleaders in the labor ranks who told the workers that salvation lay in supporting the candidate of a capitalist political party who swore allegiance to the system of "private enterprise, private ownership and private profit." It is precisely this system that breeds poverty, unemployment and war and is inseparable from them.

When this irrefutable idea begins to dawn in the minds of the masses it will be an unhappy day for the labor lieutenants of the Democratic Party, for Green, Lewis, Dubinsky and Co., not forgetting their poor relations, the Old Guard socialists and the Roosevelt communists. By the same token it will be a day of opportunity and revival for a workers' political party that told the truth and keeps on telling it.

The maritime strike

LABOR ACTION, SAN FRANCISCO, NOVEMBER 28, 1936

The maritime strike of the Pacific Coast, now four weeks old, is still stalemated and is clearly becoming a test of strength and endurance. A good deal is said about strike "strategy"—and that has its uses within certain clearly defined limits—but when you get down to cases this strike, like every other strike, is simply a bullheaded struggle between two forces whose interests are in constant and irreconcilable conflict. The partnership of capital and labor is a lie. The immediate issue in every case is decided by the relative strength of the opposing forces at the moment. The only strike strategy worth a tinker's dam is the strategy that begins with this conception.

The problem of the strikers consists in estimating what their strength is, and then mobilizing it in full force and pressing against the enemy until something cracks and a settlement is achieved in consonance with the relation of forces between the unions and the organizations of the bosses. That's all there is to strike strategy. You cannot maneuver over the head of the class struggle.

We pass over entirely the question of who is "right" in the maritime strike, for we believe with Ben Hanford that the working class is always right. From our point of view the workers have a perfect right to the full control of industry and all the fruits thereof. The employers on the other hand—not merely the shipowners; all bosses are alike—would like a situation where the workers are deprived of all organization and all say about their work and are paid only enough to keep body and soul together and raise a new generation of slaves to take their places when they drop in their tracks.

Any settlement in between these two extremes is only a temporary truce and the nature of such a settlement is decided by power; "justice" has nothing to do with it. The workers will not have justice until they take over the world. The demands of the workers in a strike are to be judged solely by their timeliness and the way they fit realistically into the actual relation of forces at the time.

The demands of the maritime workers in the present strike are perfectly reasonable from this standpoint. In standing pat for the union hiring hall they are only asserting their determination to safeguard the organizations which they have already won in struggle and maintained in struggle. The fight for the hiring hall is in essence the old familiar fight for union recognition; when the unions supply workers from the union hall they have union recognition in its best form. The demand of the bosses for the re-establishment of the practice of hiring and firing whom they please, is a proposal to substitute individual bargaining and the black-list system for collective bargaining and a reasonable protection to the worker against discrimination.

This issue is perfectly clear to every unionist. The maritime workers are strong enough—as they have demonstrated in the past and in the present strike—to assert this demand and to refuse to "arbitrate" it, that is, to let some supposedly "neutral" body decide the question whether they should have unions or not. The other demands of the unions, such as the demand for the eight-hour day for cooks and stewards, are surely modest and realistic enough in this age when even a section of the most far-sighted capitalists are advocating the universal six-hour day.

The resources of the workers in the present struggle are far superior to those with which they entered the historic strike of 1934. They have strong organizations forged in the battle of two years ago and continually tested in the running fight with the shipowners ever since. In the meantime they have bound the various craft organizations together into a federation pledged to the common action of all crafts on the old principle of the Knights of Labor that an injury to one is the concern of all. The

Maritime Federation of the Pacific is a new and most formidable weapon in the hands of the strikers, even if it falls far short of the effectiveness and power of one industrial union in the industry, the most modern instrument of struggle. The increased self confidence that has come with the experiences of the past two years, and the habit of cooperation in the Federation, all spell the same thing—greater strength and greater solidarity in the labor camp and better chances for success.

The strikers have other resources also. The organized labor movement in the West is on the upgrade. This is due in no small degree to the influence of the maritime example. The upsurge of militancy on the waterfront, and the tangible proofs that this policy pays big dividends in the form of strengthened organization and better conditions, have inspired unorganized workers to organize and fight and older unions to grow and to gain. Throughout the labor movement there is a feeling of deep gratitude to the maritime workers and a warm sympathy for them in their present fight. This is a real asset which might easily be the deciding factor to tip the scale in favor of the strikers in the final show down.

In addition, the Maritime Federation has in the *Voice of the Federation* an admirable organ of publicity and propaganda—one of the very best trade union papers in the entire labor movement in fact—which can, and in our opinion should, be converted into a daily for the duration of the strike. The art of strike publicity consists primarily in getting the facts and the union side of the story daily to the strikers and to the working class public.

The experience of the Minneapolis truck drivers with their strike daily in 1934 shows that strikers who are on to their business don't have to worry much about what the daily capitalist press prints—they can't control or influence that anyway. If they publish their own daily paper the workers will read it and believe it and hold a solid wall of sympathy and support around the strike. For publicity that counts, that is, keeps the strikers themselves and their sympathizers informed from day to day, the daily strike paper is the thing. A publicity program in a modern strike that does not include a daily paper is like a knife without a blade.

The maritime workers are fighting against a powerful enemy and their victory is by no means assured. The strikers can quite easily defeat themselves if they make a miscalculation as to the strength and resources of the enemy, and particularly if they rely on the support of factors which are in reality lined up on the other side. Here we refer directly to the government and the reactionary labor leaders of the type of Ryan, Hunter and Green. The first duty of militant leadership is to tell the strikers the truth in this respect so that they will not entertain dangerous illusions and be taken by surprise at a critical moment.

The bosses are powerful, in the first place, because they own the ships and the docks, and the workers have not yet challenged their fraudulent claim to such ownership. And because they own the ships the bosses own the government. And the same holds true in regard to such labor leaders as those mentioned above. The slightest misunderstanding on these two points can easily prove fatal.

The strikers have to battle the shipowners, plus the government, plus the labor lieutenants of the capitalist class. That's the score. Ryan and Hunter have already shown their hands on the East Coast. Green and Co. backed them up by denouncing the East Coast strike as "outlaw." And it ought to be painfully apparent to all that the administration at Washington, which was sold to the workers as a "friend of labor" in one of the biggest skin games ever put over, hasn't made a move to help the strikers get their extremely modest demands. "Expectations" in this regard have been cruelly disappointed. And the worst is yet to come.

But in spite of all these powerful forces arrayed against them, the embattled maritime workers have better than a fighting chance to win. As a matter of fact, once the actual line-up is clearly understood and this understanding is consciously incorporated into the strike policy of the unions, the victory is two-thirds won. For that will mean that the strikers see the real issue clearly, rely solely on themselves and the support of their fellow workers in other trades and dig in for a bitter-end struggle.

A victory in the maritime strike under the banner of the Federation will affect profoundly the lives of all the workers involved, for the better. It will prove in life the superiority of common action through federation over the old craft isolation and stimulate the movement for thoroughgoing industrial unionism, the next step. And it will encourage the whole labor movement of the West to press forward.

These are big stakes. They are worth fighting for. Every worker in the West has a vital interest in the success of the fight.

In the spirit of the pioneers

LABOR ACTION, SAN FRANCISCO, NOVEMBER 28, 1936

At the Thomas meeting in Los Angeles during the campaign, William Velarde, leader of the agricultural workers' union in southern California, out on bail furnished by the Non-Partisan Labor Defense, made a speech in which he frankly stated: "The Socialist Party and the Young People's Socialist League were the backbone of our strike." In San Francisco, two months before the waterfront tie-up, the Socialist Local held a public mass meeting under its own auspices, with prominent leaders of the maritime unions on the platform, to popularize the labor side of the controversy with the shipowners and state the position of the party; and newly recruited young socialist activists were in the forefront of the Salinas battle and won a secure place for themselves and their party in the hearts of the militants there.

Throughout this period the party in California found time to conduct a fairly active general agitation—the writer alone spoke at 19 meetings through the state; Glen Trimble and other party leaders were on the firing line—and the YPSL conducted a successful summer school at which the weighty problems of revolutionary theory and practice were elucidated by young Marxists who know what they are talking about. On top of this the Workers Defense League has been firmly established as a bona fide non-partisan defense organization mainly through the initiative and participation of socialists.

These variegated activities, this combination of energetic agitation, theoretical inquiry and resolute, courageous participation in the mass struggles of the workers was organized and conducted under the general head of what the revitalized party in California understands as an election campaign. Net results: It didn't succeed in stemming the Roosevelt landslide when it came to votes—the socialist campaign lacked the forces and resources, and the Roosevelt movement was too strong and too deep, for such a result—but the party and the

YPSL increased their membership, strengthened and tempered their organizations and telescoped the closing of the election campaign into a drive to launch a weekly socialist paper.

And that's what counts. Short-sighted people, snivellers and vote-catchers can talk all they want to about socialist "defeat and disintegration" in the elections. We haven't noticed it here. We don't know yet how matters stand in other parts of the country, but here in California the party is not groggy, but up and on its toes and fighting. Our election campaign was only a training school of all-round socialist activity and a prelude to deeper and broader struggles. That's primarily what election campaigns are for anyway.

I've been around and seen a lot since I first joined the I.W.W. in 1911 and, soon afterward, became one of the "voluntary organizers" who got their training in Vincent St. John's school of learning by doing; but it seems to me that the California socialists, especially the YPSL, have as much of the militant crusading spirit of the old movement as any group I have worked with throughout that fairly long stretch of years.

"The Saint," of affectionate memory, was a wonderful man to learn from. He was short on palaver and had some gaps in his theory, but he was long on action and he was firmly convinced that the water is the only place where a man can learn to swim. His way of testing, and also developing, the young militants who grew up under his tutelage was to give them responsibility and shove them into action and see what happened. Those who acquired self-confidence and the capacity to make decisions under fire on the spot, which are about 90 percent of the distinctive quality of leaders and organizers, eventually received credentials as voluntary organizers. Thereafter they enjoyed a semi-official status in the strikes and other actions which marked the career of the I.W.W. in its glorious heyday. The shock troops of the movement were the foot-loose militants who moved around the country as the scene of action shifted.

As is more or less chronically the case in revolutionary organizations, which are historically fated to be poor until they win the final victory and have no need of money, there was very little cash in the treasury in those days. That's why the organizers' credentials as a rule were marked "voluntary"—so that they would not get ridiculous ideas into their heads about the responsibility of the organization for their food and shelter from wind and rain. True, St. John's first thought was always for the man in the field, and he had a marvelous and unfailing ability to dig up a couple of dollars in a pinch. But for the most part, the voluntary organizers foraged, producing activity wherever they went and finding sustenance one way or another, preaching the gospel in the manner of the early Christians and, like them, living by the gospel. By and large this was the story also of the pioneer socialist agitators of the time.

I think to this day that the spirit, method and technique of the pre-war socialist and I.W.W. movements belong naturally and of necessity to a genuine proletarian movement growing indigenously in the soil of America. This tradition is a rich heritage which the new generation of revolutionary militants must make their own.

It is imperative, of course, that our youth deeply ponder the great lessons to be derived from the world experience of the working class since 1914. Then they will be able to see clearer, and work with a better sense of direction, than the pioneers of an earlier day upon whose shoulders they stand. But the makers of the new movement, if they really want to make it move, must be fired with the spirit of the pioneers, with the courage, self-sacrifice and purposeful activism for which the names of Bill Haywood and Gene Debs and Ben Hanford and Vincent St. John are unforgettable and inspiring symbols.

The socialist movement, if it is really socialist, is a poor man's movement, which operates every day in defiance of the rules of bookkeeping and the bankruptcy laws and cannot hire high-priced experts to bring about the socialist society. Those who have gone before us have shown how to make out in spite of all that. Debs campaigned for the presidency for the party wage of $3 a day, and in 1917 they had to take up a collection in New York to send Trotsky to Russia to organize a revolution.

We have no subsidy to draw on, and that is very probably a good thing. Subsidy is all too easily converted into a corrupting influence, as the sorry degeneration of Stalin's jumping-jack parties so eloquently testifies. Better for the movement to stand on its own feet and pay its own way as best it can. Better to draw on the hidden and financially intangible resources of enthusiasm, conviction and self-sacrifice of party militants who dare to "storm the heavens."

These are the main resources which have sustained the party in California during the recent months and finally nerved it to undertake such a heroic enterprise as the launching of a weekly paper on the heels of an election campaign. If the party, a numerically small organization, weakened by the mass exodus of Epic utopians, and still further attenuated by new desertions since the Old Guard split, could develop a healthier and more rounded activity during the election campaign than ever before, and grow stronger and more cohesive in the process, then we have a right to conclude that we are on the right track and to calculate that the coming months will bring new successes and increased strength.

Deeper into the unions

LABOR ACTION, SAN FRANCISCO, DECEMBER 5, 1936

Not the least of the reasons for the renewed vitality and firm, healthy growth of the socialist movement in California, is the newly developed activity of many of its members in trade unions and the increased attention the party as a whole is devoting to this field.

The turn toward trade-union work means the turn toward new life for the Socialist Party in the West. It means reconstructing the organization on a proletarian foundation. And that is what is needed first of all, if we are to be a real force in the class struggle and not a mere club of well-meaning people which never offends anybody, and which nobody ever thinks of taking seriously.

It takes a fighting organization to make a revolution, and the place to build it is inside, not outside, the broad labor movement. That means, primarily, the trade unions. We still have a long way to go to complete this necessary transformation of the party. What has been done so far—and it is all to the good—is, after all, merely dabbling. We will not really get down to business until we devote nine-tenths of our time and attention to trade-union work.

The trade unions are the elementary and basic organizations of the workers and the main medium through which the socialist idea can penetrate the masses and thus become a real force. The masses do not come to the party; the party must go to the masses. The militant activist who carries the banner into the mass organization and takes his place on the firing line in their struggle is the true representative of resurgent socialism.

And it is not enough by any means to have a few "specialists" attending to this function while the others occupy the cheering section in the grandstand. Nothing is more absurd and futile than such a party. Auxiliary organizations can and should be formed to enlist the support of sympathizers and fellow-travelers. But the party of the proletariat, to my notion, should be conceived as an organization of activists with the bulk of its members—everyone eligible, in fact—rooted in the trade unions and other mass organizations of the workers.

At this point we always come to the old moth-eaten and utterly ridiculous contrast of theory and practice. There is neither sense nor profit in such a debate, for the theory of Marxism, as Engels explained many times, is a guide to action. Let muddleheads argue which comes first and which is more important. As an all-around nuisance and futilitarian the misnamed "Marxist" who mulls over theory in a vacuum is tied by the vulgar activist who is "all motion and no direction." Effective revolutionists unite theory with practice in all their activity.

Engels fought on the barricades in his youth. Marx, the formulator of the theory of the proletariat, devoted an enormous amount of time to the practical work of organization in the First International, and he remained a revolutionary war horse till the day of his death, sniffing the battle from afar. Lenin was a thinker and a doer. And Trotsky, the greatest revolutionary man of action the world has ever seen, elucidated problems of theory on a military train in the heat of civil war.

The purposeful activism of the educated socialists must be directed primarily into the trade unions precisely because they are the immediate connecting link with a broader circle of workers and therefore the most fruitful field of activity. When the socialist idea is carried into the workers' mass organizations by the militant activists, and takes root there, a profound influence is exerted upon these organizations. They become more aware of their class interest and their historic mission, and grow in militancy and solidarity and effectiveness in their struggle against the exploiters.

At the same time, the party gains strength from the live mass contact, finds a constant corrective for tactical errors under the impact of the class struggle and steadily draws new proletarian recruits into its ranks. In the trade-union struggle the party tests and corrects itself in action. It hardens and grows up to the level of its historic task as the workers' vanguard in the coming revolution.

The trail-blazing work of the socialist activists in the California unions has opened a path for the party as a whole. There can be no doubt that the near future holds great successes for the party if it follows that path.

The color of arsenic—and just as poisonous

LABOR ACTION, SAN FRANCISCO, DECEMBER 12, 1936

It is common knowledge among informed union men on the water front that a factional clique operating in the maritime unions exerts an influence in committees and other delegated bodies out of all proportion to its real strength in the membership. The name of this clique is the Communist Party—and that is no secret either.

But what is puzzling and confusing quite a few maritime unionists, who understand communism as extreme radicalism, is the increasingly evident fact that the Communist Party is putting forward and trying to put over a line of policy in the unions which Sam Gompers would have attacked from the left. These misnamed radicals appear more and more in close alliance with people who are notorious for their conservatism in theory and practice, today and yesterday. At the same time, despite the indubitable militancy and class-struggle spirit of the rank and file, the most militant and progressive elements in the unions and in the leadership find themselves victims of well-organized and all-too-often successful "campaigns."

They are undermined, slandered, shoved aside and jockeyed out of positions by this new conservative combination engineered by the Communist Party. And, since people are important mainly as symbols and representatives of policies and programs, it must be understood that the attempt to "gang up" on the genuine militants has something behind it. What is really involved is a deliberate purpose to switch the maritime unions from the line of class struggle militancy to the line of class collaboration—that is, conciliation with the bosses and craven subordination to the government.

Of course, these ideas and these attempts are not new. What is new is the organizer and director of the enterprise, the erstwhile radical, and even revolutionary, Communist Party. There was a time when the Communist Party was called radical and revolutionary with a certain justice; and that was to the credit of the party. But this description is decidedly out of date. Things have changed since Stalin began to imprison and kill the revolutionary Bolsheviks in the Soviet Union and to rely on pacts with capitalist governments abroad. The wisest capitalists caught the drift of things long ago. Ignorant "red-baiters" who still attack the Communists, are entirely out of date. Red is not their color any more.

To give the devil his due, it must be acknowledged that the Stalinite Communists are experts in their line. They are almost as good at "capturing" unsuspecting organizations as they are at wrecking them. Almost, but not quite; for when it comes to wrecking unions under their control their batting average up to date is 1,000 percent—a home run, or at least a two-base hit every time they came to bat. If anyone tries to refute this by saying: "The Communists control such-and-such a union and it isn't ruined yet"—my statement still stands. Just give them time. Rome wasn't destroyed in a day.

The Stalinist technique in "taking over" a union is not confined to manipulation at the top, although that is their long suit, especially since they have taken a position in the right wing of the labor movement and the left wing of liberalism. Like the cynical gentry who play the people for suckers in the prize fight and wrestling rackets, they take care of all the angles. All experienced confidence men, fixers and bunco steerers proceed according to one central theory enunciated by the illustrious Barnum: A sucker is born every minute. But the successful disciples of Barnum all know that it is not enough to cheat the people; the thing is to make them like it. This is the function of ballyhoo or, if you prefer, propaganda.

In addition to the numerous organs of general circulation published by the Communist Party and its stooge organizations, the business of misrepresenting, falsifying and befuddling the situation in the maritime unions requires special publications. These are the *Maritime Worker* and the *Beacon*—the mimeographed green sheets, of the color and also the quality of arsenic.

They are supposed to be deucedly clever, using the intimate, you-and-me, hello pal! style of approach which every confidence man has adopted since the first gold brick was sold to the first farmer. The latest issue of the green *Beacon* undertakes to sell the strikers the idea of voluntarily moving "perishable" cargo, and if that isn't a gold brick the man who bought Brooklyn Bridge at a bargain made a shrewd business deal. The arguments of the green *Beacon* on this point are revealing and instructive, both as to the real policy of the communo-democrats and their estimate of the intelligence and class understanding of the strikers.

You may have the old-fashioned idea that strikes are for the purpose of stopping the production or distribution of the commodities or services affected, until the bosses feel the pressure enough to accede to the demands of the union. But you don't know the trade-union policy that emanates from 121 Haight Street and spreads out over the waterfront like a San Francisco fog. Here is the real dope from the *Beacon:* "A working class housewife goes to the store and asks for a certain article. She is informed that due to the strike she cannot get it. She goes home and reads in the paper that the strikers are permitting perishable cargo to rot aboard the ships. You can see what effect this has on the average family."

Isn't that argument clear, pal? You are probably one of those dumb clucks who would think that a shortage of "certain articles" shows the strike is effective and is all to the good. But you are all wrong, and you probably have "syndicalist tendencies" besides. The central aim of "strike strategy" is to win over the well-known "public" and to see that nobody is inconvenienced, for doesn't everybody belong to the public?

Look what saps the Minneapolis teamsters were to call

a coal strike in the dead of a bitter winter, making exemptions only for hospitals. True, they won the strike in three days by taking such unfair advantage. But at what a cost! The "public" will never think the same of them again. And think of the political immaturity of streetcar men in the past who have gone on strike and obliged the public to walk or take a jitney bus. "You can see what effect this has on the average family."

If you answer that in every effective streetcar strike on record the "average family" has proudly refused to ride streetcars during a strike, and that quite a few of them have cheerfully tossed cobble stones at the scab motormen, the green sheet has another argument for you.

The *Beacon* points out that if "perishable" cargo is not moved forthwith the shipowners "can act very indignant and demand that the unions furnish 'safety crews' to keep the perishables from rotting." And, "what could be more demoralizing than 'safety crews' working day in and day out behind the picketlines."

Of course, if the shipowners "demand" that the unions furnish safety crews there is nothing to do but accede to the demand forthwith. Do you think this is a class struggle you are conducting? The bosses may get real sore some of these days and "demand" that all the strikers go back to work without any more stalling around. You will have to agree that that would be very "demoralizing."

And, here is another argument from the *Beacon* if you are still not convinced: "It's not impossible for a federal marshal to deputize some men for this work, or have the coast guards and marines unload the perishables." There's an angle, pal, which you probably never thought of. You wouldn't think of interfering with deputy marshals going through your picket lines, would you? And you surely wouldn't object if the coast guard and marines stepped in to do strikebreaking work.

The green *Beacon* is just suggesting this angle to you. Better think it over. The *Beacon* says finally: "The smart thing to do is to get rid of this issue." You surely want to be smart, don't you?

Keep cool, pal. Keep your head. Don't fly off the handle and talk about the class struggle and the Russian Revolution and Lenin's Communist Party. The class struggle is out of date, Lenin is dead and so is his party, and this is not 1917, my boy.

Take a shot of arsenic and pull yourself together.

Four days that shook the waterfront

LABOR ACTION, SAN FRANCISCO, JANUARY 2, 1937

The four days beginning on the afternoon of Thursday, the day before Christmas, and ending abruptly on the afternoon of Monday, December 28, deserve to go down in the history of San Francisco alongside the famous earthquake. And as the earthquake is never mentioned by native sons without a certain embarrassment, so it is very likely that the sailors who sail the ships will not want to talk about what happened on December 24.

For on that date the sailors who sail the sailors—in other words the water-front "fraction" of the Communist Party—"captured" the Sailors' Union of the Pacific. And that was a boat ride the offshore sailors will not soon forget and will never want to talk about. To be sure it only lasted for four days. But many a rugged seaman, who has sailed windjammers and kept his spirits up and sung a merry song through perilous seas and hurricanes galore, grew sick and faint on the voyage. They quaked with fear and never smiled until the lookout sighted land, two points off the starboard bow.

The famous imaginative picture of Christopher Columbus and his hardy crew, kneeling in thanksgiving for a safe arrival after storms at sea, would not do justice to the jubilant feelings of the West Coast sailors Monday afternoon when they walked down the gangplank, off the C.P. ship and safe at last. The ship is moored fast to the dock, hatches battened and gear squared up, and all hands accounted for. So now the story can be told.

It happened this way. All athletes must keep in training, and the Communist Party, which holds the all-time record for capturing and wrecking unions, is, in a way, an athlete. A prize fighter, as they say, has to get a fight under his belt every now and then or he goes stale; and the Stalinist party has to "take over" a union every so often in order to keep in shape to fulfill its historic mission. They marked "next" after the name of the Sailors' Union of the Pacific sometime ago, and have been reconnoitering, or "casing," the job ever since.

Three things stood in their way: (1) The conservative class-collaborationist policies of the so-called Communists do not square with the militant traditions and sentiments of the sailors. (2) The rank and file don't want to be "captured." (3) The leaders of the union know what the score is and do not want any part of C.P. policy or C.P. "control."

Last week the athletic commissars decided to hurdle all these obstacles in one leap. A special combination of circumstances arose which seemed to present the opportunity. Some of the special circumstances were accidental. The others were created, or, to speak plainer English, framed. Things happened rapidly and rather hectically, and some of the sailors, like rescued victims of a shipwreck, are still a little dizzy and hazy in their recollections. But here is about the way the story they tell pieces together:

Harry Lundeberg, secretary of the Sailors' Union, negotiated an agreement with the shipowners for submission to the membership. There was nothing wrong about that; it has been the practice of all the unions in the Maritime Federation to negotiate separately; three other unions were actually negotiating at the same time. The solidarity obligation of the Federation is for no union to *sign* an agreement until a settlement is made with all.

There was nothing wrong about the agreement, either. It secured concessions which the people who wanted to stall off, postpone and finally prevent the strike—and they were not Lundeberg and his friends—never dreamed of getting when they were denouncing the sailors as "strike crazy" and "the obstacle to settlement." As a matter of fact the agreement negotiated by Lundeberg contains the best and clearest provisions for union recognition and control of hiring ever put on paper, and every informed unionist knows it.

But the Communist Party, which opposed and tried to prevent the strike and fought the militant class-struggle line of Lundeberg, couldn't get any credit from a good agreement secured by strike action and negotiated by Lundeberg. Consequently they launched a hue and cry against it.

That is the real reason behind all their ballyhoo of the past week. They put insinuations into circulation about "one-man negotiations" and broadcast the infamous lie that the sailors were planning to make a separate settlement, although the union had made a public statement that it would not sign any agreement until all the unions had negotiated satisfactory settlements.

The sailors, who are too well-known for their patience

and good-natured tolerance, finally got mad and put out a bulletin in reply to the slanders. This famous "Bulletin No. 32" stated the facts in forthright language and expressed the true sentiments of the sea-going sailors. That put the fat in the fire. What's this? These damn sailors are beginning to talk back! Don't they know the "party" has a monopoly of the publicity business? Hell began to pop in earnest. The frame-up machine went into action and the stage was set for the "raid" on the Sailors' Union.

What was the game? The game was to represent the sailors as strikebreakers in a deal with the bosses and to frame Lundeberg as a betrayer of the workers' trust. That was the dirty game, no less. And for this nefarious business the trustworthy *San Francisco Chronicle,* which has dealt the sailors many a blow below the belt in the past, was pressed into service again.

The *Chronicle* was "accidentally" supplied a copy of the sailors' bulletin. Then it came out in its first edition early in the evening of December 23 with the screaming headline: "LUNDEBERG FOLLOWERS JOIN SHIP-OWNERS IN ATTACK ON BRIDGES."

That *Chronicle* headline was not an honest headline written by a disinterested editor honestly reporting the news. The *Chronicle* headline was framed! It was framed to put Lundeberg and the sailors in a false light before the workers, create demoralization in their ranks and prepare the way for the "raid" on the Sailors' Union. Lundeberg was out of town—on a train to the northern ports to report to the membership. The "party fraction" was mobilized. A special meeting of the Sailors' Union was hastily engineered in an atmosphere of panic. An attorney, who is as handy in a union as a sailor in a law office, misrepresented the position of the absent Lundeberg. The militants were caught off guard, disorganized and thrown into confusion.

By four o'clock of the afternoon of December 24 the following results emerged to confront the groggy sailors: "Bulletin No. 32" had been repudiated; a resolution had been adopted in which the proud Sailors' Union of the Pacific humbly apologized for answering the slanders against it; and a new publicity committee had been elected to convey to the world at large the excuses of the sailors for living. It was a field day for the dry-land sailors, the meddling lawyers and the framers of crooked headlines. The Sailors' Union of the Pacific had been "captured."

And it remained captured for four days—four days that shook the waterfront and brought the noses of the humiliated militants down to their knees in a sort of circle. The new "publicity committee" began issuing press releases and bulletins, apologizing on behalf of the Sailors' Union to all and sundry and rubbing it in on the chagrined and embarrassed militants who built the union in bitter struggle and love it as their life. The fog hung heavy over the Embarcadero. As one old-timer expressed it: "The Sailors' Union was lower than a whale's belly."

But the sun is persistent, and along about Sunday afternoon the fog began to clear. One militant after another began to come to, and to ask: "What happened? Where am I?" That was a bad sign for the people who had slipped them the Mickey Finns. Lundeberg came back to town roaring like a bull about the dirty tricks played in his absence and the misrepresentation of his position. The framed *Chronicle* headline began to appear in its true light and purpose. The hour for the regular Monday afternoon meeting drew near—and with it the reckoning.

When the minutes of the special meeting with their shameful record were read at the regular meeting, Lundeberg took the floor to present a resolution. It carried the signatures of about 30 union members whose names are the militant banner of the union. Lundeberg spoke. Others followed him. The organized "booing squad" of the Communist Party was silent—the sailors, sobered up and on their guard, were in no mood for monkey business.

Then the vote. Lundeberg's resolution was carried with a mighty roar. The opposition—who had been in "control" of the union for four days—mustered only 66 votes out of more than 1,000 present. The proceedings of the special meeting, were declared null and void. The new four-day "publicity committee" was fired. "Bulletin No. 32" reaffirmed. The union was "uncaptured," the real militants were back at the helm and the surroundings began once more to appear the same to the sailors who had just returned from wild and unfamiliar seas which they had never wanted to sail in the first place.

It was a wild ride while it lasted. And it is a warning to the sailors that it is still possible in these days to get shanghaied, and that it is better to be on guard in the future.

As for the four-day "publicity committee" of the raiding party, they deserve a break—at least a quotation in recognition of their literary endeavors. In the *West Coast Sailor,* Bulletin No. 36, issued under date of December 28—the day they ceased to be—they published an overture that turned out to be a swan song. They said: "We know that our efforts in the issuance of future strike bulletins shall be successful only to the extent which the rank and file cooperate with us."

That's a fine sentiment, pals. But, as the saying goes:

> Why worry about the future?
> The first will soon be last;
> The future will soon be present
> And the present will soon be past.

In the meantime, I notice that the latest number of the *Maritime Worker* is changed from arsenical green paper to white. They haven't got the right color yet.

The champion from far away

LABOR ACTION, SAN FRANCISCO, JANUARY 16, 1937

Since coming to San Francisco I have been watching at close range the "build-up" of a new Stalinite labor leader—a transparent mediocrity who was unknown yesterday and will be forgotten tomorrow—and I keep thinking of a fine story Ben Hecht once wrote about the wrestling racket and the way its phony "champions" are made. The story, if I remember correctly, was called, "The Champion From Far Away," and it had to do with a palooka who became a champion for a while without ceasing to be a palooka at heart.

The champion from far away, a muscle-bound lout, was originally a gravedigger in a metropolitan cemetery. There, equipped with the tools of his trade—a "sharp-shooter" and a pick and a No. 2 shovel—he performed his not-too-complicated tasks and, in his own sub-human way, was happy in his work and satisfied with his lot in life. Day in and day out he went through his practiced one-two-three motions like a natural-born muck-stick artist, with never a thought in his thick, hard head of any possible change in the routine until, in the normal course of events, surviving fellow-craftsmen would one day dig a grave for him and plant him underneath the daisies.

But God proposes—and the promoters of the wrestling racket fix things to suit themselves. One day of destiny a couple of these weisenheimers happened in on the cemetery where our hero worked. It seems that one of the outstanding figures in the racket had stopped a score or so machine-gun slugs in a private dispute among the boys, and the two promoters had turned out to the funeral to pay their last respects to the fallen comrade, and to make sure at the same time that he was put away for keeps.

They spotted the big gravedigger swinging his shovel in the cemetery and, needing a new champion, decided then and there that he was it. He appeared to meet all the specifications they required. He came from a distant land—that gave him novelty, mystery and color. He was big and powerful looking—what the public expects in a champion. And he was dumb—which would make him easy to handle. All in all, he looked like a "natural" to the promoters. They signed him up on the spot while his loose mouth was still open in wonderment, and led him away like a captive ox to a new short life of manufactured glory as the greatest wrestler the world had ever seen.

It was all very simple and easy. The promoters gave the gravedigger the "build-up." His non-existent merits were ballyhooed far and wide. Sports writers, secretly on the payroll of the promoters, wrote learnedly and objectively about his new and strange technique, his "color" and his mysterious origin in a far-off land. Fixed matches were arranged and the erstwhile shovel stiff marched triumphantly across the country, sports commentators fell for the general ballyhoo and the clodhopper's impressive string of arranged victories, and they also began to beat the drums for the Champion From Far Away. The wrestling public was worked up into a lather of admiration for the unbeaten and unbeatable phenomenon.

Even the gravedigger himself—and that's the saddest part of the story—began to believe the phony build-up.

He began to think he was really out-wrestling the trained setups who rolled over on their backs and played dead at the appointed moments. The poor sap took the counterfeit publicity of the promoters for real coin.

That was too bad, for it wasn't long afterward that the house of cards collapsed. Through some slip-up in the arrangements, the Champion From Far Away got into the ring one night with an opponent who knew how to wrestle and hadn't been fixed to fall down, and he was mean and tough besides. He put the manufactured champion through an agony of real hammer locks, half nelsons and toe holds which made him long for the old simple life in the graveyard and to wonder why his own highly touted "technique" didn't seem to work any more. The tough mug kept after him, scowling viciously, gouging and biting when he got a chance and squeezing the made-to-order champion until he began to have a real fear that he was coming apart. He became utterly convinced that the wrestling racket had aspects which were not so good.

Finally, when the referee was looking the other way, the rough wrestler who hadn't been fixed, shoved his elbow with a vicious, trip-hammer thrust into the belly of the Champion From Far Away. Then it was his turn to roll over and play dead, like so many of the set-ups had done for him—only he was sincere about it. The referee slapped "the winner and new champion" on the back and our hero was done, finished, his trail of glory ended. It had taken a long time to build him up, but one mean elbow-jab in the belly brought him down. In a single night the champ became a chump.

The promoters who had built him up surveyed the human wreckage of their hand-made champion sadly, but philosophically. And then they calmly went about the business of hunting for another palooka who might be made to look like a champion. They weren't discouraged by the catastrophic result of their failure to fix the match securely, and they never thought for a minute of changing their ways and going straight in the future. For the entrepreneurs of the wrestling racket disagree with Lincoln, and will bet even money any time on the proposition that you can fool all the people all the time.

That is likewise the basic assumption of the cynical gentry who comprise the general staff of the Communist Party, whose operations in the labor movement are far more on the order of a racket than a principled struggle. From old habits, or by way of camouflage, they still occasionally mention Marx and Lenin as their sources of inspiration, but you will never find a clue to their methods and psychology in the books of these great-hearted rebels and honest men. The real model of the Stalinites is the American advertising game which has been developed to its fullest flower by the racketeering promoters of the world of commercial sports.

The rules of this game are few and simple, and are considered sure-fire by the people who think the world is divided into two classes—wise guys and suckers. Rule No. 1 says you can make people believe anything if you repeat it often enough; and Rule No. 2 says Mark Twain was right when he remarked that "a lie can travel half way around the earth while truth is putting its shoes on." That in a nutshell, is the credo of the Stalinites and the essence of their technique in advertising and "building up" labor leaders.

Nowhere has this technique been more crudely employed than in the present campaign to build up the new champion Labor Leader From Far Away, the Great Whoosis who is touted and advertised as though he were a combination of Christ and Buddha and the Sacred Cow. As for Debs and Haywood and Vincent St. John and Albert

Parsons—such real men and real leaders of the great tradition, whose memory might truly inspire the new generation of labor militants if they but knew the simple truth about their rich abilities, so nobly and generously devoted to the workers' cause—as for them, the Stalinite School of Ballyhoo can find no place at all beside the new divinity, the Johnnie-come-lately who just arrived from nowhere. Indeed, in this part of the country, at least, you would think, if you took the ballyhoo seriously, that the history of the labor movement only began with the discovery of the Great Whoosis a short time ago.

One of the tricks—and not exactly a new one—for putting this four-flushing false alarm across is to represent him as super-human, beyond comparison with ordinary mortals, above criticism, not to be touched or pinched to see whether he is real or a motion picture, and, above all, not to have the elbows of inconsiderate opponents shoved into his belly.

As remarked above, this trick is not new. They used it to bamboozle the ignorant long before the Great Whoosis came down to survey the situation on our planet, like God on a vacation. "The King can do no wrong," was the original formula for the trick. In the prize-fighting and wrestling rackets they translate the same principle: "Don't knock the champ—because he's the champ." Out here they hang a tin halo around the ears of a two-spot and say in effect: "Don't throw tomatoes at the Great Whoosis, you might smear his halo."

Everybody is supposed to rise to his feet when the Great Whoosis enters the room and when he starts to speak. I had heard about this crude stunt, but being from Missouri, had to see it myself at a public meeting before I would believe that even Stalinites would attempt to introduce such a degrading slave-minded practice, and in the West of all places!

I saw the Great Whoosis finally get his "rising ovation," but the whole thing was too transparent a fake to impress me. There was an organized claque down front, rising in unison as though in response to a signal, and waving and motioning to others to get up. Then one could see individuals milling around at strategic points in the crowd, like cowboys around a herd of cattle, motioning for everybody to get up. Finally, as though anxious to get the thing over with, about half of the crowd slowly stood up and quickly sat down again.

It was all organized, perfunctory, like taking off your hat in a court room when his honor, the judge, comes in. There was nothing spontaneous about it—and what is a demonstration worth to a self-respecting man, if it isn't spontaneous? The very fact that a "leader" will stand for such a shoddy tribute earmarks him as a base pretender.

In my time I have heard Debs speak; and I can remember yet the hearty, joyous shouts of affection and comradeship with which the great agitator was greeted as he entered the hall. But there was no formal rising when he began to speak. For one thing, Debs was too eager to plunge into his speech and always deprecated unnecessary demonstrations.

I have heard Haywood speak in the heat of bitter struggle to strikers who adored him, but there was none of this formal, organized rising, like serfs greeting the feudal lord. Big Bill would have been mortally offended by such cut-and-dried horseplay. When Haywood was on the platform he made the workers feel that here was a comrade and fellow-worker, one of their very own. That was one of the secrets of the real power of real leaders of the workers like Debs and Haywood.

I have even heard Lenin speak—at the Fourth Congress

of the Communist International in 1922. I must confess that I really wanted to rise to my feet on that memorable occasion. The whole Congress rose as one man, in spontaneous, heart-felt acclaim for the leader of the Russian Revolution, and we didn't need any claque down front to set the example, nor any cowboys running through the aisles to whip us into line. There were ushers and "inside people" in the aisles, but they served another purpose. They asked us to please sit down because the "Old Man" was not feeling very well, and he didn't like formal demonstrations anyway!

The real leaders of the working class could dispense with all the empty fakery of capitalist advertising, ballyhoo and "build-up" because their merits were genuine and they honestly and truly represented the cause of the workers. They were tried and tested over a long period of time. Their deeds spoke for them and they had no need of press agents, lackeys, sycophants and organized handclappers. They grew, with deep roots in the workers' movement, and did not require artificial props.

It is precisely because they lack these qualities, because they play a game of deception and fraud under a hypocritical pretense of radicalism, that the Stalinites require entirely different methods borrowed from the shadiest fringes of the capitalist world. The system of Stalinism has no use or place for honest militants of tested character and ability and independent opinions. It needs pliable nonentities, parvenus and careerists on the make. Against the former it employs the frame-up; for the latter it provides the build-up. This is the whole sum and substance of the attitude of Stalinism to leaders of the labor movement, the real and the counterfeit.

But the whole strategy of the Stalinites, like that of their prototypes in the wrestling racket, is founded on an illusion and is doomed to explode. Lincoln was right: You can't fool all the people all the time. And the truth, slow-moving at the start, will eventually catch up with the lie. And built-up Champions From Far Away, in the labor movement as well as in the ring, eventually encounter opponents who don't believe the ballyhoo. This is bad news for the Great Whoosis, who like the ill-starred hero of Ben Hecht's story, is beginning to take his own phony build-up seriously and is beginning to strut and pose like a real champion. But it's the truth just the same, and the truth never hurt anybody that was on the level.

After the maritime strike

LABOR ACTION, SAN FRANCISCO, FEBRUARY 20, 1937

The more thoroughly the result of the 99-day maritime strike is considered the more convincingly does the victory of the unions stand out. The gains of the workers have two aspects. The immediate material benefits in the form of increased wages and cash payment for overtime are worth the struggle and suffering which the workers had to pay for them. The shortening of the working day of the Cooks and Stewards—even if it fell short of the eight-hour objective—is a benefit which the workers involved will enjoy every day they are at sea. The general movement of labor for better wages and shorter hours is greatly stimulated by the tangible concessions won by the maritime workers in these respects.

But, in my opinion, the outstanding and most important result of the strike was the unquestionable strengthening of the individual unions, and of the Maritime Federation as a whole. That is the safeguard and the promise of better things to come.

The 1934 strike, with all its heavy cost of struggle and sacrifice, laid the foundation for all the advances of maritime labor in the past two and a half years. But it left the question of the stability of the unions still undetermined. The seafaring crafts had to fight every inch of the way by means of job action—the only recourse left to them—to wrest the recognition and the consideration denied them in formal agreement. The attempt to wreck the Sailors Union in connection with the revocation of its charter showed that the stability and strength of this militant organization was doubted by labor fakers as well as by shipowners. Finally, the arrogance of the shipowners last fall only demonstrated their underestimation of the stability of the Federation as a whole. They had to be convinced by the strike that maritime unionism is no passing phenomenon.

The unions survived this test of a drawn-out struggle and came out of it stronger than before—and consequently with more confidence in themselves.

The results of the strike are the vindication of the strike. Who could argue now—in the face of the results—that the strike should have been postponed and stalled off indefinitely until Washington came to the rescue of the workers? All the Roosevelt administration ever offered to the maritime workers is the Copeland Book. It is clear now, or ought to be, that the strike was a necessity.

The prevailing policy in the strike was, in the main, a policy of militancy. That accounts for the victory. But this policy made its way and prevailed at times in a peculiar indirect way—from the bottom upward rather than from the top down. The maritime rank and file are fighters. They are strongly influenced by militant traditions. That is the real secret, if there is a secret, of the strength of the

Federation and its affiliated unions, not some new inventions in the line of strategy. The maritime workers FEEL the class struggle, and instinctively act accordingly. That is why they were right every time they blocked policies inspired by a different conception of capital-labor relations.

Some very erroneous conceptions were entertained in some of the leading circles of the Federation. At times they were even put forward as official decisions, but fortunately they were not carried out and therefore were not so harmful as they might have been.

Among them the following stand out most prominently: (1) The policy of stalling off the strike so as "not to embarrass President Roosevelt;" (2) The decision to move "perishable cargo" from the strike-bound ships; (3) The tendency to make a fetish of the "public;" (4) The conciliatory attitude toward government interference; (5) Most dangerous of all—the proposals to "accept the Copeland fink book and protest afterward."

There was really nothing new in any or all of these erroneous proposals. The argument against them is not new either. It consists simply in an explanation that a conflict between workers and employers is not a mere misunderstanding between two elements who have a common general interest. On the contrary it springs from an irreconcilable conflict of interest; it is an expression of a ruthless class struggle wherein power alone decides the issue.

Viewed in this light, a dispute between workers and employers cannot be settled fairly by the government; the government is an instrument of one of the parties to the dispute—in this case the capitalists. The class conflict cannot be handed over to the "public" to decide; the "public" is itself divided into classes with different interests and different sympathies regulated primarily by these interests. The polemics of Karl Marx against the conservative labor leaders of his day answered all these questions. All the experience of the labor movement since that time, including the recent west coast strike, speaks for the position of Marx and against all conceptions which overlook the class struggle.

In the strike the Maritime Federation of the Pacific went through its first real test. The results show that this formation was an aid to solidarity. The Federation proved its superiority over the system of every craft for itself. The habit of cooperation between the crafts and the practice of solidarity, through the Federation, tested in the strike, will undoubtedly bind the Federation together more cohesively.

But for all its unquestionable superiority to the isolated system, the Federation should be regarded as a transitional form of organization. The organizational goal of militant labor is industrial unionism. The militants should begin to consider this problem more concretely and to devise steps to advance its solution.

4

New York City
1940–1952

Introductory note

The Socialist Workers Party was formed at a convention in Chicago on January 1, 1938. Its members had been in the revolutionary faction in the Socialist Party, which was expelled for refusing to be gagged on political questions, such as the SP's position on the Spanish civil war. Many of the revolutionary-minded youth and workers in the SP had been won to the faction and became members of the new party. Cannon was elected national secretary at its founding meeting.

With the approach of World War II, the SWP faced weighty challenges. An important goal of the rulers in Washington was to stifle opposition within the labor movement to its drive toward war. Targeted for attack was the Minnesota Teamsters movement, which was campaigning against the war within the labor movement in the Midwest.

In 1941 Cannon and other leaders of the SWP and Minnesota truck drivers' union were tried and convicted under the federal government's thought-control Smith Act. Sentenced on December 8, 1941, the day after the bombing of Pearl Harbor, Cannon and seventeen others received terms of twelve to eighteen months in prison.

As the war came to a close, a mighty upsurge in labor battles broke out, combined with a massive movement by GIs particularly in the Pacific, demanding demobilization of the armed forces. Members of the SWP took part in these battles and the party grew rapidly.

Within two years, however, the union movement was in retreat in face of a counteroffensive by the employers and the onset of postwar "prosperity." In 1947 the antilabor Taft-Hartley Act was imposed. That same year President Truman signed an executive order launching a loyalty-oath program, initiating what became known as the witch-hunt.

Internationally, Washington was at the center of efforts to shore up capitalism in Europe, to counter the advance of anticapitalist revolutions in eastern and central Europe, and to slow the rising anticolonial revolution in Asia and Africa. In the wake of the victory of the Chinese revolution in 1949, U.S. troops invaded Korea in June 1950 and began a three-year war that took three million lives.

During these years Cannon was a regular contributor to the *Militant*, where he wrote on a variety of themes ranging from efforts to censor Charlie Chaplin to the witch-hunt case against Alger Hiss.

Bandiera Rossa

SOCIALIST APPEAL, NOVEMBER 30, 1940

The biggest and most important news that has yet come out of the bloody and destructive war of the imperialists is contained in a little news item tucked away in the corner of the paper last Friday. A United Press dispatch from Athens, dated November 22, says:

> News of Koritza's fall, given to several thousand Italian prisoners in camps here, started off a spontaneous demonstration. Anti-Fascist Italians sang "Bandiera Rossa," the Italian revolutionary song.

What a message of hope and promise for tomorrow that brief item contains! And what testimony to the real feelings of the Italian soldiers which found tumultuous expression at the first opportunity. Now the world can know the real meaning of the defeats of the Italian army. The brave soldiers who sang that song to celebrate Mussolini's defeat at Koritza were saying for all the world to hear that they have no interest in the tyrant's war of conquest; and that for them, as for the oppressed masses in all imperialist countries, the main enemy is at home.

Above the sound of the biggest guns that message resounds throughout the world today. For 18 long and terrible years now the Italian masses have known the yoke of fascist tyranny. But deep in the hearts of the enslaved abides the memory of their song of freedom. At the first opportunity it came spontaneously to the lips of the imprisoned Italian soldiers in Greece.

When the journalists and commentators speculate about the further progress of the war, they are in the habit of considering only the pronouncements and plans and schemes of the statesmen and generals in the rival camps. They leave out the people. It is customary also for cynics, capitulators and renegades to rule out the people—the workers—in the fascist countries as an independent factor in coming events. The people haven't spoken yet but they are going to say the final and decisive word. The revolutionary song of the Italian soldiers in the Greek prison camp is a signal. The explosive which will blow the fascist tyrants to hell is located in their own countries.

The heroic Italian proletariat showed its mettle in 1921. The workers occupied the factories and were ready for the next decisive steps. Betrayed by pusillanimous leaders, and lacking a strong party of Bolshevism which alone could lead the resolute struggle for power to the very end, the great movement of the Italian workers suffered defeat. In the reaction from that defeat they fell under the iron heel of fascism. But we must believe that they have lived all these terrible years on the memory of their great hope that the people will yet go forward ("Avanti o popolo") under the scarlet banner ("Bandiera Rossa").

The brief dispatch from Athens recalled to me the poignant memory of the departure of the Italian delegation from the Fourth Congress of the Comintern in Moscow, at the end of 1922. The news of the fascist *coup d'état* had arrived and the delegates were returning home to take up the underground fight. The great hall in the Kremlin resounded to their song, "Bandiera Rossa," in which the delegates of all the other countries joined. Many of those communist fighters went to their death and so did thousands and tens of thousands of others of the flower of the Italian proletariat, in the course of these 18 tragic years.

But the blood of these martyrs is the seed of the coming revolution. It flowered spontaneously in Greece the other day for the first time, at the first opportunity. We have ground to believe that those Italian soldiers in the Greek prison camp expressed the profoundest sentiments of the enslaved masses at home and the equally enslaved soldiers in Mussolini's army of conquest. In that sentiment in the hearts of the workers in all the warring countries—and in that alone—resides the hope and the confidence that the bloody and terrible war into which the imperialists have plunged the world will be brought to an end by a victory of the people. "Avanti o popolo"—go forward, people, under the scarlet banner! "Bandiera Rossa trionfera!"

Union boy gets raise

SOCIALIST APPEAL, DECEMBER 7, 1940

Under the heading of "Trade Union Progress" or "Benefits of Organized Labor" we record the news that Brother William Green was granted a wage increase by the AFL Convention from $12,000 to $20,000 per annum—and it is not Confederate money, either. Twenty grand is a nice piece of change any way you look at it, and the action of the Convention shows what organized labor can do for a man who works neither with hand nor brain but only with the larynx.

Brother Green is not the only union boy who got

something in his stocking a month before Christmas. Brother Meany, secretary-treasurer of the AFL, got raised from $10,000 to $18,000. And that, as the saying goes, ain't hay. Green and Meany are still trailing behind John L. Lewis who is sacrificing his life for $25,000 per year from the coal miners. Lewis swears by the Bible, especially that page where it says: "The laborer is worthy of his hire." And he is also strong for the other scriptural injunction: "Thou shalt not muzzle the ox that treadeth out the corn." Lewis treads heavily, has a big muzzle and needs a lot of corn. But even he has been nosed out in the race for big money by Tobin, who got raised from $20,000 to $30,000 per year at the recent convention of the bighearted Teamsters.

Topping them all, is Brother Jimmy Petrillo, head of the Musicians, who doubles up on two jobs, drawing down $20,000 as president of the Chicago local and $15,000 as International President—a total of 35 grand, and this of course, doesn't include expenses and birthday presents. These are only a few who stand out conspicuously by the extraordinary size of their honoraria. The unions are lousy with run-of-the-mill labor skates who struggle along on ten grand or so in regular salaries. Sidney Hillman, for example, puts up a poor mouth and does the best he can on $12,500 per annum.

Who's against these wage scales which enable the labor leaders to keep body and soul together and have a little spending money in their pockets at all times? Many appealing arguments can be made and have been made for providing the labor leaders with a standard of living to which the rank and file are not accustomed:

(1) It gives the workers a sense of vicarious satisfaction to see their servants living on the fat of the land—they

feel rich by proxy.

(2) It is a form of insurance to the unions against their representatives keeling over from malnutrition in the very midst of a conference with the bosses.

(3) It puts them on the same social plane as the bosses and frees them from inferiority complexes.

(4) It keeps them—or ought to keep them—from stealing from the union treasury.

Another important thing to remember is that Green got his raise without striking for it. In fact on the very day (or the day before) he opened his pay envelope and discovered 8,000 extra dollars peeping out at him, he was sounding off against strikes in "defense" industries in general, and the Vultee strike in particular.

On the same day (or the day after) he got the raise, our hero pinned his ears back, oiled up his throat and gave out an oratorical and oracular pronouncement in favor of the "capitalist system." And no doubt he meant it sincerely, insofar as he knew what he was talking about. He was speaking from a practical and personal standpoint. Green, of course, is hardly a profound student of the history and anatomy of social systems, their origins, development, decline and replacement by others. This couldn't be expected of him. Since he quit coal mining 50-odd years ago his time has been pretty well taken up with preaching, praying, orating and drawing his pay check.

Green may not know much about the historical, philosophical and theoretical aspects of "the capitalist system," but he has got a damn good hunch about the practical side of the question. What he lacks in knowledge of the law of value and the automatic regulation of prices, he makes up in mother wit and good old-fashioned horse sense; and he figures that a system which makes it possible for a man to simply open his mouth, lean back on his haunches and bellow at regular intervals "that all is well," and then find an annual check for $20,000 in his hand—that is a first-class system no matter what you call it.

So far, so good. The workers who pay the bill are not stingy; they might as well be broke as the way they are; the fat salaries make the labor leaders happy and may keep them from stealing, so what the hell?

The main hitch is that the 10–20–30 thousand a year salaries for the labor leaders provide them a standard of living far removed from that of the rank and file of the workers. The leaders live like the petty-bourgeoisie, and not so petty at that, and soon cease to think like the poverty-stricken masses who have the dubious blessing of capitalism interpreted to them in the shape of inadequate diet, restricted educational possibilities for their children, unemployment, eviction notices and the policeman's club on the picket line.

Every once in a while this glaring contrast between the over-fed leaders and the under-fed masses is expressed in the most dramatic form. The concurrence of Green's raise of salary to $20,000 per year and the strike of the Vultee workers against a wage scale of 50 cents per hour was such an occasion. The workers went on strike, said nuts to the threats and pleas that they keep slaving at the old rate "in the interests of national defense," and inched up their pitiful wages to 62½ cents. Green denounced the strike, praised the system which exploits and enslaves the masses, and calmly drew down a hike on his pay check from $12,000 to $20,000 per year.

They were both right—in their way. Only, they were each speaking from opposite sides of the picket line.

The Vultee strikers spoke for themselves—and for their oppressed class for whom all is not well by a long shot. Green spoke for himself—as an agent of the exploiting class operating in the labor movement. That is why they could not find a common language on the question of strikes.

There is a lesson in this coincidence. No doubt, Green deserves his 20 grand. But why should the workers pay it? That's where the swindle comes in.

Finland and Greece

SOCIALIST APPEAL, DECEMBER 14, 1940

Public opinion—that melange of sentiments and moods which are set in motion by bourgeois pressure and propaganda—is reacting rather calmly to the Italian attack on Greece. A year ago this same public opinion was all in a lather over Finland, then under attack by the Soviet bear. Why is there no hue and cry for Greece? Isn't poor little Greece as noble as poor little Finland, and isn't Mussolini just as big a bullying scoundrel as Stalin? Evidently there is something different somewhere.

In many respects, the Italo-Greek war appears to be a duplicate of the Soviet invasion of Finland; the points of resemblance strike the eye. In each case a strong military power attacked a smaller and weaker opponent. The Soviet invasion of last year appeared to be poorly prepared. The victim of aggression fought back and scored initial victories. The press dispatches pictured David putting Goliath to rout while thousands cheered. So today, in the modern war of the Greeks and the Romans. The first attacks are repelled and followed by what appear to be successful counterattacks which push the invaders back in retreat.

Nevertheless, the sheer military preponderance of Italy over Greece would seem to assure eventual victory unless powerful new forces are brought to play in favor of Greece. Why, then, is the far-flung anti-Soviet mob of last year not in action? Why are they resting in their dugouts with such maddening nonchalance while the armies of Mussolini and Metaxas fight it out? Where are the sermons thundering from the pulpit? Where is the Hoover Fund Raising Committee? Where are the special theatrical benefits for the victim of aggression? Where are the trade-union relief committees?

The sympathy of the American ruling class is indubitably on the side of Greece, since Greece is the ally of Britain, and thereby also of the United States in the developing and expanding world struggle of the rival imperialist powers. But this sympathy is lukewarm and restrained. There is no drum-beating campaign; we see no hysteria, no unbridled fury, such as that which swelled in a mighty tide against the Soviet Union during the Soviet-Finnish war.

Is this because the rulers and makers of public opinion perceive a fundamental difference between the regime in Greece and that of Finland? Not at all. The bloody work of exterminating the flower of the proletariat, which was carried through to completion under Mannerheim in Finland, and on the basis of which Finnish "democracy" was stabilized, is still in process in Greece under the dictatorship of Metaxas. But this is a factor of secondary importance which does not even interest the class rulers, to say nothing of determining their policy.

The difference from their point of view is the difference between the class nature of the Soviet Union and fascist Italy. A victory of fascist Italy over Greece would be a military episode in a drawn-out world war. The masters of America, because of the international alignment, have an interest in preventing such a victory. But they do not permit themselves to get unduly excited about the prospect. The military domination of Greece by fascist Italy would not change anything fundamentally in the class structure of the latter. It would not spread the infection of expropriation and nationalization which the masters of property fear and dread above everything else.

The difference which the ruling bourgeoisie perceives, and which motivates their instinctive reaction, is the fundamental difference between the property relations in the Soviet Union and those of fascist Italy. They do not delude themselves for one moment by a vulgar identification of the two countries because of the superficial similarity in the political regimes. They know the difference between a fascist regime which reinforces the rule of private property and a soviet regime which signifies its annihilation, and they have great respect for this difference. The preservation of the system of private property is the one thing that really concerns them.

It was the threat to private property, implicit in a Soviet victory over bourgeois Finland, which determined the unrestrained violence of the bourgeois anti-Soviet campaign during the Soviet-Finnish war. They gave the workers an instructive lesson in class politics! The motivation of the bourgeoisie in this case was graphically summarized in the Manifesto of the Fourth International on *The Imperialist War and the Proletarian Revolution,* adopted by the Emergency Conference of the Fourth International last spring.

This manifesto, the last great programmatic document written by Comrade Trotsky, says:

> Extremely eloquent in its unanimity and fury was the campaign which the world bourgeoisie launched over the Soviet-Finnish war. Neither the perfidy nor the violence of the Kremlin prior to this had aroused the indignation of the bourgeoisie, for the entire history of world politics is written in perfidy and violence. Their fear and indignation arose over the prospect of a social overturn in Finland upon the pattern of the one engendered by the Red Army in Eastern Poland. What was involved was a fresh threat to capitalist property. The anti-Soviet campaign, which had a class character through and through, disclosed once again that the USSR, by virtue of the social foundations laid down by the October Revolution, upon which the existence of the bureaucracy itself is dependent in the last analysis, still remains a workers' state, terrifying to the bourgeoisie of the whole world. Episodic agreements between the bourgeoisie and the USSR do not alter the fact that "taken on the historic scale, the contradiction between world imperialism and the Soviet Union is infinitely more profound than the antagonisms which set the individual capitalist countries in opposition to each other." *(War and the Fourth International.)*

From a class point of view, the bourgeoisie were absolutely right in the position they took on the Soviet-Finnish war. So were we right, from the point of view of the fundamental class interests of the proletariat, in firmly maintaining our defense of the Soviet Union in spite of the enormous pressure of bourgeois public opinion, which even found expression at that time in our own ranks. Contemptible was the faction of Burnham and Shachtman which attacked our program in synchronism with the bourgeois anti-Soviet campaign. Pathetic must be the fate of the faction whose "independent" existence stems from that shameful capitulation.

Good-by, Tom Mooney!

THE MILITANT, MARCH 14, 1942

Poor Tom Mooney is dead, the long crucifixion is ended and the martyr is taken down from the cross and laid away in his grave. "The case is closed," said the *New York Times,* in an editorial that was brief and neat and snug and smug. They are through with Tom Mooney and they are glad of it. Ah yes, indeed, the case is closed, and well it is, for it had dragged out an unseemly time; the thread of the story had been lost and the grandeur of the long drama was bogged down in a soggy and pathetic anti-climax.

The Mooney case is closed! The case which mirrored American justice as it really is; the case that broke from the grip of the frame-up gang and shot like a bolt of lightning from San Francisco to Red Petrograd in 1917, and then flashed around the world; the case that moved the hearts of millions—the Mooney case, with all its noble heroism, its unutterable tragedy and its shabby epilogue, is ended now. They buried Tom the other day in San Francisco, where, if you stand on a high hill on a clear afternoon, you can see the sun go down to the sea in blazing glory behind San Quentin across the bay.

Even Tom Mooney's funeral was a frame-up and a tragedy. The dead body of the man who was buried alive because of his opposition to the First World War was held up as a sacrificial offering to the Second. The "united" labor fakers officiated, and the services were patriotically dedicated to "unity for democracy." There was an ironic twist to this dedication which could not have been noticed by the dull-witted authors. God knows Tom Mooney's share of democracy was nothing to brag about. The services were concluded, reports the *Times,* with the singing of the "Star-Spangled Banner"—a tribute, so to speak, to the flag which floated so proudly for 22 years over the prison which confined the rebel who was put there in the first place because he sang another song.

Mooney, in his pamphlet, "Tom Mooney Betrayed by Labor Leaders," referred to himself and Billings as "symbols of American class justice via the frame-up." And he was 100 percent correct. "Organized capital framed us," he said; and he accused "all major labor leaders with a few notable exceptions" of conspiring with his persecutors to keep him in jail. They imprisoned Mooney—as they imprisoned Debs and Haywood and hundreds of others—in order to clear the road of militant labor opposition to the First World War, and they kept him in prison for revenge and for a warning to others.

They are scheming to do the same thing over again, to other militants, in view of the present war, but there was no hint of this, to say nothing of a protest against it, at Mooney's funeral. That funeral service was a sacrilegious defamation of the cause for which Mooney fought and suffered; and a treacherous and hypocritical pretense that everything is rosy now. It was a field day for repudiation of the class struggle and dedication to "unity" of the labor fakers with the oppressors and exploiters of labor.

Naturally, the tone and spirit of the old, long, militant fight of the workers for Mooney's freedom was absent from this macabre ceremony. An unruly "red mob," demonstrating before the American Embassy in Petrograd in 1917, saved Tom Mooney's life. The "labor leaders" deserted and betrayed him, but the "reds" remained his friends. They kept his cause alive and wrote his name on banners carried on every fighting picket line.

The funeral was a repudiation of all this rowdy stuff. "Unity" was the watchword there, says the dispatch of the *New York Times,* "instead of the vitriolic tirades which had marked many Mooney meetings in the past." Everything was nice and tame and circumspect. Russian Bolsheviks shouting "Muni! Muni!" before the American Embassy, and American militants denouncing class justice in turbulent demonstrations, would have been as much out of place on the platform at Mooney's funeral as the unkempt fishermen apostles of Christ at a Christian church service on Fifth Avenue.

The *Times* beams complacently over the happy conclusion of the unpleasant business of the Mooney case. Trouble of this kind belongs to the past. Nobody was to blame. "In 26 years much water has gone over the dam. Labor and the employer are closer to understanding each other." The Mooney case was just one of those things.

It was all a misunderstanding, it seems; perhaps a tragic misunderstanding. Anyway, it was a bit tragic for Mooney, you will have to admit, if you remember back. Twenty-two years in prison is quite a stretch. In fact, when you take them out of the middle of a man's life you don't leave him much. And that is the saddest, the most heart-rending part of the case of Tom Mooney.

When they finally got around to pardoning him three years ago it soon became apparent that they hadn't left him anything of his old self.

The fine strong body of the young ironmolder which they locked up in 1916, was shot to pieces when they finally turned him loose in 1939. All but six months of his three years of freedom were spent, flat on his back, in a hospital bed. Also, his mind, under all the batterings and shocks and disappointments it had suffered, had lost its razor edge and its fine sense of discrimination.

In his confusion he mixed himself up with the Stalinists. From such an association no man, not even Tom Mooney, could emerge wholly clean, for it is written: "He that toucheth pitch shall be defiled therewith." He played ball with the Stalinists and they used him for their purposes. Thus, the magnificent book of Tom Mooney's life closed with a dirty and ugly chapter.

Let us try to forget that, and remember the lion-hearted fighter in his prime, remember him as he so often, and so proudly and so truly described himself, as "a symbol of militant labor." That he was, in fact, throughout the endless years of his martyrdom.

Good-by, Tom. Rest easy. You are entitled to it. In due time everything will be made right. Those who crucified you still sit in the seats of power, more arrogant than ever. They are gaily organizing another slaughter for profit and pelf, and their dirty labor agents at your own funeral mocked the cause for which you suffered. But the day of reckoning will come. The young generation of revolutionary militants, inspired by the memory of Tom Mooney—the rebel Tom Mooney, the real Tom Mooney—who turned away from this ghoulish spectacle with a bitter curse, will avenge your long martyrdom, nobly borne. And they will avenge your funeral too. They will yet dig up your bones and bury them over again properly, with a ceremony—and a song—they deserve.

The tribe of the Philistines

THE MILITANT, JUNE 24, 1944

I see that Joe Hansen's article in the February issue of *Fourth International,* written on the occasion of the departure of the 18 Trotskyist leaders, has elicited comment in *Politics,* the new-thought magazine edited by Dwight Macdonald. In commenting on the comment, I am impelled first of all to congratulate the author on the equanimity with which he is enduring the imprisonment. Evidently he has read and taken to heart the advice Rose Karsner gave to the women in her speech at the farewell dinner: "Don't mope while the men are away."

Macdonald is clearly determined not to let our troubles get him down. From this hard-boiled point of view he takes Joe to task for dwelling on the trivial details of our departure—the leave-takings, the mementos, etc. The doughty Macdonald will have none of this sentimentality. He is a brass-tacks chap—no nonsense, chins up and all that sort of thing. Perhaps he is right on this point. I, at least, can understand and sympathize, to a certain extent, with his matter-of-fact attitude. I am somewhat of a stoic myself—my mother taught me not to cry when I get hurt—and I appreciate the trait in others.

I am ready to admit also that Macdonald is not motivated by personal malice or jealousy, as others who write in the same vein usually are, for I believe that he is sincerely stupid and is only guilty, at most, of indulging his cultivated knack for misunderstanding things and his faunlike impulse to play pranks on inappropriate occasions. In any case, this part of the quarrel between Macdonald and Hansen is not very important. After all, it is a matter of taste and emotion; and as long as freedom and democracy prevail everyone has the right to his own taste and his own emotion.

The other parts of the editorial in *Politics* raise more serious questions. One concerns the attitude of a man of politics toward his own ideas. The other concerns morality. Both are questions of exceptional importance at the present time.

The editorial indicts our party as a "sectarian group" afflicted with "arrogance which verges on paranoia." As evidence he cites Vincent Dunne's statement that "our movement is historic" and Joe Hansen's assertion that "the files of Trotskyist publications" represent more important material for future historians than the Roosevelt minutiae filed away at Hyde Park. These remarks impress Macdonald as the expression of a presumptuousness belonging to the domain of "political pathology."

One cannot make an off-hand decision as to the merits of this dispute, for neither position is right or wrong *per se*. We are confronted here not with facts immediately verifiable but with a conflict of opinions regarding future developments. Consequently, in order to arrive at a reasoned judgment of the respective merits of the contending opinions, one must approach the dispute with a criterion, a point of view of his own, about contemporary society and its prospective future development.

The majority—those who line up with American capitalism and its war program—believe that capitalism has a long and stable future before it. If their assumption is correct, or only half correct, they can very consistently and logically conclude that Dunne and Hansen, and all the rest of us Trotskyists, have fantastic delusions about the way history will some day be written. We, the minority, on the other hand, are completely convinced that capitalism, having outlived its progressive historic role—and a great role it was—is already doomed, is even now in its death agony, and must make way for socialism.

If our assumption is correct, we can with no less logic and consistency conclude that the heralds of the new society, the pioneer militants of the revolutionary party, have far more historic importance than the representatives of the dying system, and that this will be the judgment of the historians of the future. If our assumption is correct, it is the representatives and apologists of the outmoded social system who entertain delusions about the future.

Now, what are the premises, and what are the conclusions of Macdonald and the politico-literary species which he typifies? The magazine *Politics*—as far as one can make out from a cursory reading—is published to inform the world that the editor and his associated independent thinkers are somewhat dubious of the future of capitalism and are committed, more or less, to the socialist alternative. Yet Macdonald says—no, he doesn't say, he takes for granted as self-evident—that the contemporary statesmen of capitalism are the important and the significant men of today and that they will be so regarded in the historical tomorrow. Hansen's idea, for example, that historical research will not center around the personality of Roosevelt, strikes him as too funny for words.

Then, having made his joke, he goes on to say that his convictions—he calls them convictions—are in many respects the same as the Trotskyists' ("The Cannon group stand for many of my own convictions"). In spite of that, he instinctively and automatically brands our party's confidence in the historic vindication of these same convictions as pathologic arrogance.

The significance of this *non sequitur* is quite clear. Macdonald's pen ran away with him. The intended lampoon of the Trotskyists turned out to be an unintended self-revelation. It is the portrait of a man who does not take his own ideas seriously and has no faith in their future. Such people are not worth very much. Their "convictions" are on the side of the proletarian revolution, but all their deep-rooted instincts, feelings and spontaneous reactions—their heart and soul—are in the other camp. Hence their simultaneous "agreement" with the convictions of the Trotskyists and their amazement when we act on these convictions and draw them out to their logical conclusion.

Similarly, when the question of bourgeois and proletarian morality—"their morals and ours"—is mentioned in our press, the jackass ears of the philistine are pointed upward and forward in alarm. And when we calmly assert that our morals are better than theirs, that we are "the only really moral people"—among the conscious, articulate political elements, that is—Macdonald sputters like a society matron who has been insulted by a truckdriver for snarling traffic. Joe Hansen's report of a casual conversation with Cannon about John Dewey and the Moscow Trials causes Macdonald to break out in a moralistic sweat. And "words almost fail him" at Cannon's "nerve" in pointing out a flaw from the standpoint of "strict morality," in Dewey's conduct of the office of chairman of the Commission of Inquiry on the Moscow Trials.

Here also Macdonald mixes up a small matter with a big one. The small point can easily be disposed of. He accuses us of trying to rob the respected Commission of Inquiry chairman of the "credit" due him for his services in that capacity. This is a misapprehension on his part; and we are ready to concede anything he demands in order to set the thing straight, even though we do not attach the same weight as he to the matter of "credit."

His accusation springs from his inability to read our press with an understanding of our standards and our sense of values. When we say that a man was moved to intervene in a great historic case by an appeal to his sense of justice, we have meant to pay him the highest compliment we can possibly pay to a man who is not of our party and class. By his action in heading the Commission of Inquiry, Dewey became the chief instrument in the investigation and exposure of the greatest frame-up in history. We are grateful to him for that, and he will be remembered gratefully by all lovers of truth and justice in time to come.

It makes no difference whether Dewey's action was taken on his own initiative or was suggested to him by others. That is only a small collateral detail of the history of the affair. Dewey's credit flows from the deed itself and we, who believe in giving everyone his just due, would be the last to underrate it in the slightest degree. Dewey must be honored for his courageous action all the more because he might justifiably have asked exemption for reasons of age and ill health. He must be doubly honored because, of all the great public men of present-day America, he alone felt it necessary "to do something for justice."

But when all that is said the fact remains that Dewey, in making public in a radio speech the report of the Commission of Inquiry which found Trotsky not guilty of the crimes alleged against him, took advantage of the occasion to denounce the political doctrines of the defendant. There are no two ways about it, that was "a departure from strict morality," which comes under the heading of *abuse of power.* By our standards of morality that is a serious offense, and we want somebody to tell us by what moral standards it is justifiable.

Macdonald's readiness to defend Dewey's misuse of his office of judge to turn advocate, on the ground that Trotsky, the defendant, also expounded his views before the Commission, will not satisfy anyone who seriously wants to face the moral issue we have raised. Trotsky had been accused of crimes alleged to flow from his doctrines, and was asked by the Commission of Inquiry to give an exposition of these doctrines as evidence in the case. In the same manner the defendants in the Minneapolis Trial were permitted to expound their views in court.

But Dewey, as chairman of the Commission, had assumed the office of *judge,* and with it the obligation, after hearing the evidence, to say truly whether the defendant was guilty or innocent of the *crimes* charged against him. So much and no more is a judge permitted to say when rendering the verdict of his tribunal, according to our standards of morality.

Macdonald's attempt to defend Dewey's moral lapse on this occasion only demonstrates how flexible his own moral standards are. His bad experience should warn all petty-bourgeois critics of the Trotskyists to confine their moralistic sweatings to eternal abstractions and keep away from the discussion of concrete cases. "Morality" is not their strong point—when you get down to cases.

Sandstone Prison
JUNE 1944

A letter to Elizabeth

THE MILITANT, APRIL 19, 1947

It doesn't pay to sell the human race short. Up till now they have successfully resisted every assault on their right to live on this planet and reproduce their kind. Their instinct to survive, and even to make life more bearable and better, is still running strong, reactionary people-haters and weak-willed pessimists to the contrary notwithstanding.

Take this morning's news, for example. American reaction, which has been exceptionally aggressive and truculent of late, has met a formidable challenge from a section of the working population of the country which had hitherto seemed to be the weakest and easiest to push around. We refer, of course, to the 350,000 telephone workers who are standing so valiantly in the breach today; and, in particular, to the all-woman union of 12,000 telephone operators and their women officers, who looked New Jersey Governor Driscoll in the eye and told him to go to hell and take his slave-labor law with him.

The brightest news we have read for many a day was the report in this morning's paper. The three women officers of this all-woman union of telephone operators had appeared in court to answer to the charge that they had openly challenged and violated the slave-labor law. This law was drafted by an agent of the telephone company and rushed through the New Jersey legislature in the record time of two hours. The law was intended to break the telephone strike. But the corporation hirelings, with Driscoll at their head, overlooked a trifling detail. They overlooked the fact that women telephone operators do not want to be slaves; they think they have certain inalienable rights. And they have leaders at their head who dare to assert these rights and flinch not from the consequences, law or no law.

The best touch of all was the report in the paper that the secretary-treasurer of the union, Miss Elizabeth J. Ryan, arrested and taken into court together with her two colleagues, the president and vice-president, had calmly notified the judge that he would have to hold up the proceedings for a while. She explained that she had some important personal business to take care of, to wit: she intended to get married the following Sunday, and she and her husband would need a little time after that, all to themselves, without any intrusion from policemen and officials.

Bless your heart, Elizabeth. I am really sorry that I can't be present at your wedding; and I daresay millions of people who read your story in the papers feel the same way on this bright morning. It would be a real pleasure to see you step out of the picket line, with the consent and goodwill of all your associates, to get married. It would be nice to throw rice and old shoes at you, and wish good luck and happiness, and health and prosperity, and freedom to you and your husband, and your children, when in due time they come along.

I am not acquainted with your husband but he must have plenty of merit to be able to win a girl like you; and plenty of manly courage, too, to step up and claim his bride on the very day that Governor Driscoll hailed you into court and tried to brand you as a criminal.

You make one feel good all over about the prospects of the world. You make one recollect once again what a wonderful country America is, and what fine people are in it; how brave and unselfish and lighthearted they are; and how easily they will be able to fix up everything that is wrong when they get mad enough, and realize that things need fixing. The country is O.K., Elizabeth, and the people are O.K., too. The only trouble is that the country has fallen into the control of a little handful of selfish rascals who think their profits and privileges are more important than human lives and human rights. They have got to be given their come-uppance. They have got to be told off and put in their places. And it is people the likes of you that are going to do it.

You and your worthy associates in the leadership of the union, and the brave girls on the picket line whom you represent and symbolize, have set an example to all America. You are lifting up the hearts of the workers everywhere with new hope and new inspiration.

So good luck, and the top o' the mornin', and thank you kindly, Miss Elizabeth Ryan, soon to be Mrs. Pasquale Siciliano. You and your kind are the real America, the America of Tom Paine and Valley Forge, and the Declaration of Independence, and the Bill of Rights, and John Brown at Harper's Ferry, and Abraham Lincoln and the Battle of Gettysburg. You are the U.S.A. And that ain't hay.

What do they know about Jesus?

THE MILITANT, APRIL 26, 1947

Did you see what I saw in the paper this morning, Thursday, April 17? It took the taste out of my breakfast. The Wall Street money-sharks, pressing their anti-labor drive on all fronts, now claim they have lined up God and Jesus Christ for the open shop. The *New York Times* reports: "Six hundred thirty-seven clergymen attached to various Protestant churches have joined in attacking the closed shop as a violation of basic teachings of the Bible, the American Council of Christian Churches, 15 Park Row, announced today."

What do you know about that? And how do you think it happened? I wasn't present when the deal was cooked up, but knowing whom these theological bunk-shooters serve and from whom they got their orders, I can visualize the proceedings and tell how it happened, in essence if not in precise detail.

The top profit-hogs very probably had a meeting of their board of strategy down in Wall Street the other day and counted up the forces they had mobilized in the grand crusade to break up the unions and beat down the workers who are trying so desperately to make their wages catch up with the increasing cost of living. They checked off Congress, both the House and the Senate. They checked off the President and the courts. They checked off the daily newspapers, from one end of the country to the other, and found a 100 percent score on that front. Then they called the roll of radio commentators, and made a note to put pressure for the firing of the remaining two or three half-liberal "news analysts" on the air who are not going along 100 percent.

On the whole their situation looked pretty good, but they had to acknowledge to themselves that public opinion is not yet responding to the union-busting program with any great enthusiasm. Then one of the union-busters—most probably one of their "idea-men"—got a bright idea. "Let's send somebody around the corner to the American Council of Christian Churches at 15 Park Row," he said, "and tell them to start singing for their supper. Tell them to go out and round up a few hundred preachers and have them sign a statement against the unions. Tell them to put God in the statement, and be sure to ring in Jesus Christ."

No sooner said than done—but good. Now comes the public statement signed by 637 clerical finks who state that the closed shop (they mean the union shop) violates freedom of conscience and the Eighth Commandment, "Thou shalt not steal." They appeal to Christ on the ground that the union shop violates "the individual's responsibility to God" and obliges Christian men to be "yoked together with unbelievers." This, they say, is wrong and not according to Jesus.

Well, I feel like saying to these strikebreaking sky-pilots what Carl Sandburg once said to an anti-labor evangelist 30 years ago: "Here you come tearing your shirt, yelling about Jesus. I want to know what in hell you know about Jesus." I don't know too much myself, but if the only accounts we have of him are true, they called him "the Carpenter;" and he once took a whip and drove the money-changers out of the temple. "Ye have made it a den of thieves," he shouted, in white-hot anger.

And what have you done, you 637 fake-pious pulpit pounders who serve the moneyed interests against the people? You have made it a den of thieves and liars, too. You have the gall to represent the lowly Nazarene as a scab-herder; and to tell the Christian workers, who revere Him as the friend and associate of the publicans and sinners, of all the poor and the lowly, that they should not be "yoked together with unbelievers" in a union to protect their common interests. That's a lie and a defamation. You're simply trying to serve the rich against the poor, to help the rich in their campaign to break up the unions, which are the only protection the poor people have.

And don't try to fool anybody with the statement that you are in favor of unions "properly conducted"—under open-shop conditions. We know what you mean by this mealy-mouthed formulation. Such unions, as Mr. Dooley once said, are unions which have no strikes, no dues and very few members.

And leave Jesus out of your lying propaganda, you scribes and pharisees, full of hypocrisy and iniquity. Every time you mention His name you libel Him, regardless of whether the story of His life and death be taken as literal truth or legend. The Carpenter of Nazareth has been badly misrepresented in many ways for many years, but your attempt to pass Him off as a union-buster goes just a little bit too far. It is just about the dirtiest trick that has ever been played on Jesus Christ since the crucifixion.

Think it over, Mr. Dubinsky

THE MILITANT, MAY 3, 1947

The rights of workers to make a living and speak their minds freely are taking quite a beating these days, and Congress is not the only scene of the crime. A rough job was done this week by Justice E.L. Hammer in New York's Supreme Court. Justice Hammer gave the business to four suspended members of Cutters Union Local 10 of the International Ladies Garment Workers Union.

The four men—Arnold Ames, Charles Nemeroff, Irving Kotler and Emanuel Brownstein—had been suspended from Local 10 for periods of three to five years on charges of circulating defamatory literature against David Dubinsky, the highly touted president, and other officers of the garment union. Their appeal to the court was denied by the judge, who denounced them as "Communists" in a 40-page decision. Emil Schlesinger, attorney for the ILGWU, hailed the decision as a "milestone in the defense of American labor against communist deceit and treachery." Mr. Schlesinger, according to the press reports, expressed certainty that the ruling would serve as a precedent in future cases affecting "communist penetration of trade unions" and applauded "the determination of the courts to prevent totalitarian forces from using democratic institutions as a weapon in their efforts to overthrow democracy."

It seems that the leadership of the ILGWU, which has

been widely advertised as the most progressive and democratic of all unions, is giving us a new definition of this famous "democracy," in cahoots with a friendly Supreme Court Justice. First taking my shoes off, and saving Mr. Dubinsky's presence, I would like to make a few remarks about the matter and pass on a suggestion to Mr. Dubinsky.

I don't for a minute doubt that the four suspended cutters, who were leaders of the Stalinist-backed opposition slate in the union elections in 1944, defamed Mr. Dubinsky and probably also slandered him and other officers of the union—such procedures are in the nature of Stalinism. No one could blame the aggrieved labor leaders for objecting to it and seeking redress. The method employed in this case, however, was not a happy one.

The real authors and inspirers of the defamation and slander are the Stalin-picked bosses of the Communist Party. They escape unscathed, and have been gratuitously handed a democratic issue to exploit, which they do not deserve, while four of their deluded followers, rank-and-file men who work for a living, get the lumps. Suspension from the union in a trade that is 100 percent organized is far too severe a punishment for harsh words—or even false accusations—made in the heat of a union election struggle. And if, as is the general practice in such cases, it is followed by removal from the job and, consequently the denial to the victims of the right to make a living at their trade, it is a brutal injustice, a murderous abuse of power. The whole business makes a mockery of this same "democracy" which Mr. Dubinsky and his fellow Social Democrats seem to preach better than they practice.

The first place where the workers have to win the battle of democracy is in their own organizations. Suspension or expulsion from the union is a penalty fit for strikebreakers or violators of union discipline in struggle against the bosses. But not for dissidents and critics, Mr. Dubinsky. Such a rule reverts to the theory that "the King can do no wrong," and makes *lese majesty* a capital crime. That is not democratic. It is very easy to be agreeable to those who agree with us. Stalin accepts that formula, and so did Hitler in his time. But real democracy begins only when those who disagree and criticize have the right to live and breathe in the union and enjoy full rights of membership, including the right to make a living, as long as they observe the union rules and discipline in the conflicts with the employers.

It may be argued that in spite of everything, a critic gets a much better chance for his white alley in the ILGWU than in any Stalinist-controlled union. That cannot be gainsaid. But in this case under discussion the leaders of the ILGWU are making serious concessions to the Stalinists by imitating the methods they have made notorious.

Of course, this is only one incident resulting from what was doubtless a great provocation, but it points in the wrong direction. It is not only wrong in principle for leaders of workers' organizations and minority groups to encourage, by example, the stultification of democracy. It is also dangerous from a practical point of view. Such actions serve to feed the general trend of reaction in the country, which is running too strong already, and they might be the first victims.

It is an ironical coincidence that the April 4 issue of the *Wage Earner,* the Detroit organ of the Association of Catholic Trade Unionists, files an editorial protest against the Stalinized District Executive Board of the United Electrical Workers of West Michigan for suspending a dissident member named L. Larlton Sanford, and then notifying Sanford's employer to exclude him from the local's bargaining unit. The *Wage Earner* goes on to say: "The UE officials responsible for this blow at a man's livelihood would do well to study the American constitution and try to understand the democracy which protects their rights so generously."

I don't think much of the ACTU and its *Wage Earner,* but in this instance they make a suggestion to the Stalinists which might profitably be accepted by the Social Democrats who denounce the Stalinists so bitterly in the name of democracy. Think it over, Mr. Dubinsky.

The lynching of 'Monsieur Verdoux'

THE MILITANT, MAY 10, 1947

About a year ago I made a firm resolution to boycott all movies unless the picture has a horse for the hero. And I have stuck to it much better than to some other firm resolutions I have made. My heart was in this one. Hollywood double-crossed me once too often. I am no student or critic of cinematic art, but I know what I don't like—and that is the unappetizing and indigestible compound of tripe and syrup which the movie moguls and bankers dish up to the defenseless, amusement-hungry people in the name of art. And I like it still less to come out of a theater, after a three-hour bout with a double-feature, with that let-down, sticky feeling of having been played for a sucker once more.

Dominated by this mood, I was fully prepared to remain indifferent even to the announcement of a new movie by Chaplin, until I noticed the hatchet job most of the critics of the big press were doing on the picture. With almost one voice they denounced Chaplin for introducing social criticism—and deadly serious social criticism at that—into a medium which has become almost universally dedicated to the prettification and falsification of life, and maintained that he wasn't even funny any more. The vicious over-zealousness with which Chaplin and his new film were being attacked, with the obvious design to "kill" the picture before the mass of the people had yet had an opportunity to see it and judge for themselves, aroused suspicions that there might be some ulterior purpose behind the lynching campaign; that the movie critics might be giving a false report of the picture, as most Hollywood pictures give a false report of life.

Word-of-mouth testimony from some friends who had crossed the critics' picket line to examine the picture for themselves gave support to my suspicions, with the result that after more than six months' total abstinence, this reformed movie addict fell off the wagon and went to see *Monsieur Verdoux*. And I thanked my lucky stars for one of the most enjoyable and satisfactory Saturday afternoons I have had in many a day. The critics are definitely misleading the public in their reviews of this picture.

In *Monsieur Verdoux* the supreme master of the screen discards the familiar role of the little tramp with the baggy pants and flopping shoes to play the part of a suavely mannered, impeccably dressed sophisticate. Monsieur Verdoux had been a bank clerk for 25 years or so, and was ruthlessly dismissed from his position when the depression came. He had to make a living somehow, so he went into business for himself—the business of marrying women for their money and then disposing of them. He does it all to support his family to which he is deeply and tenderly attached.

It is this theme of the picture, this merciless satire on

business in general, and the business of war in particular, that has roused up so much antagonism from those who do not want the truth to be told to the people. Deprecation of war and its mass killing is deemed to be out of season by the powers that be. The bland insistence of Monsieur Verdoux that he is only doing on a small scale what others do on a big scale and are acclaimed as heroes for, has set the subservient critics after him like bloodhounds on the trail.

And the justification he gives for his crimes—that he has a dependent family—that is too much like the plea offered in self-defense by all social criminals in our decadent society to be accepted as a joke. It is the truth that hurts. I personally know a man who betrayed his socialist principles and entered the service of the war-propaganda machine, and then excused his action on the ground that he had a wife and child to support.

I don't doubt that he shrugged his shoulders, perhaps a bit regretfully, when the bomb fell on Hiroshima and destroyed a whole city-full of families who also had a right to live and to be supported. That is what Monsieur Verdoux did when the police inspector read him the list of a dozen or so women whom he had done away with in the line of business. "After all, one must make a living." Killing is a recognized business in the world as it is organized today.

From the beginning of the picture up to its supremely tragic denouement, this macabre thesis is sustained. How, then, could comedy be introduced without disintegrating the whole structure into farce? The answer is Chaplin. The comedy in this picture is unsurpassed, even in the movies of the Chaplin of old. But the comedy never runs away with the picture. The somber theme dominates the comedy from beginning to end.

The best comedy parts are those which depict the

numerous and always unsuccessful attempts of Monsieur Verdoux to liquidate one of his numerous wives, a dizzy dame with a raucous, rowdy laugh and a lot of money she had won in a lottery. She simply couldn't be liquidated. Luck was with her every time. The unexpected always happened. This part is played by Martha Raye, and she is terrific. The scene where Chaplin tries to poison her, and the wine glasses get accidentally switched around, and he thinks he has poisoned himself instead, is funny beyond imagining.

Another scene, where Monsieur Verdoux, in the course of business, has finally arranged a wedding with another moneyed widow, after long and arduous preparation, is a masterpiece of comic frustration. It was to be a fashionable wedding. A host of guests were assembled. The preacher had arrived. The bridegroom was nervously waiting, and the bride was descending the staircase. At this point the proceedings were suddenly and violently disrupted by a loud pistol-shot laugh on the edge of the crowd—the unmistakable laugh of Martha Raye. She had been brought to the party by some friends she picked up who were telling her a "rough" story, the kind she dearly appreciated. The expression on the bridegroom's face when he hears that unmistakable explosive laugh of one of his other wives, and his frantic efforts to extricate himself from the impossible situation must be seen, but may not be described. After all, it's Chaplin.

From there the hilarious comedy fades out like a dying echo and the tragic drama mounts in power and suspense to the final catastrophe. There is the stockmarket crash in which all the money Monsieur Verdoux had accumulated in the course of his business is wiped out overnight. Through mortgage foreclosure, he loses the home which he had provided for his family. He loses the family. He is apprehended by the police, tried, convicted and executed.

But never once does Monsieur Verdoux step out of character, never does he bend an inch to comply with the Hollywood formula. In court after his conviction he admits his crimes but denies his guilt. "All business is ruthless. I only did on a small scale what others do on a big scale." Then he receives his death sentence and, with ominous reference to the prospect of an atomic war, ironically bids adieu with the words: "I will be seeing you all very soon."

In the last scene of all, in the death cell awaiting the end, Monsieur Verdoux remains true to himself. The inevitable priest comes to hear his confession and administer spiritual consolation. It is a vain errand. There was no repentant sinner waiting for him. Verdoux rises from his cot to meet the priest with the sprightly manner of a welcoming master of ceremonies. "Father, what can I do for you?"

He is taken aback; no Hollywood priest was ever received that way before.

"I want you to make peace with your God."

"I am at peace with God. My trouble is with my fellow men."

The priest is obviously losing ground, but he tries again.

"May God have mercy on your soul."

"He ought to. It belongs to Him."

After that, there was nothing left for the priest but to start praying aloud in Latin, which he promptly proceeded to do, as the executional squad solemnly surrounded Monsieur Verdoux and marched him, the small-time, unsuccessful murderer, to his doom.

The picture had to end on a note of defeat and despair which was implicitly foreshadowed from the beginning. It is not a call to arms, but only a protest and a warning. The lesson is negative but, for all that, powerful in its indictment of contemporary society. And powerful, too, in its indirect indictment of Hollywood, of its sham and falsity, of its betrayal of the artist's sacred duty to hold the mirror up to life and reflect it truly.

Monsieur Verdoux is dead, but in my opinion, his picture will live; the vindictive and mendacious critics will not succeed in "killing" it. Perhaps they have condemned it to a slow start by their brutal lynching bee. But the truth about *Monsieur Verdoux* will be advertized by word of mouth, and it will make its way. It is a great picture and a brave one, too, hurled in the face of the Truman Doctrine and all the war-mongering. The people will receive it gladly, not only in America, but all over the world.

The mad dog of the labor movement

THE MILITANT, MAY 17, 1947

Among the whole gang of corrupt and contented labor fakers who infest the labor movement to its detriment—especially the AFL unions—and fatten on their crimes against the workers, one in particular is striving, not without success, to distinguish himself as the greatest scoundrel of them all. This is Daniel J. Tobin, the $30,000-a-year president of the International Brotherhood of Teamsters, who has already won for himself the title of The Mad Dog of the Labor Movement, and is demonstrating his right to hold it against all comers.

Tobin, a relic of the horse-and-buggy days of trade unionism, is a small-souled, grasping, selfish old reprobate who thinks the teamsters' union exists for his personal benefit.

In addition to his huge salary he taps the union treasury for heavy expenses and pre-paid vacation trips for himself and family, and makes the union carry his son, whom he is grooming to become his successor, on the payroll at a fancy honorarium. A rich man himself, he fawns on the bosses and the capitalist politicians, but fights the rank-and-file workers with savage fury. In all his long and malodorous career he has never yet been caught in a generous impulse or a gesture of goodwill and solidarity toward the workers who pay his exorbitant salary.

Tobin never knew anything about organizing workers and leading them in struggle to better their conditions. But he is an expert mechanic in the vile trade of breaking strikes, smashing democracy in local unions, working in cahoots with the bosses to keep rebellious workers from making a living at their trade, and spilling blood in gangster raids on the jurisdiction of other unions, and he is getting more proficient as he gets older.

Tobin disposes of a huge treasury—$14,800,000 at the last report—accumulated from the dues payments of the hardworking and underpaid members of the union, and he utilizes a large part of it to maintain what amounts to a private army of murderous thugs, recruited in part from the underworld, many of whom have criminal records. These gangsters, under Tobin's direction, usually operating under the benevolent indifference of the authorities who are "taken care of" in various ways, wage war on the rank and file of the teamster's union, and are at present especially preoccupied with a jurisdictional war to force the brewery workers to quit the union of their choice—the Brewery Workers Union, one of the oldest industrial unions and one well-respected in the labor movement—and to compel them to pay dues into the teamsters' union, whether they desire to or not.

In this campaign, beating, maiming, incendiarism and dynamiting are routine procedures, and murder is not excluded. Announcing a "knockdown drag-out fight" against the brewery workers, Tobin sent his private army of professional thugs into Pittsburgh. They moved in on Pittsburgh to convince the brewery workers that they should give up their own union, now affiliated with the CIO as a result of a free vote of the membership for that preference, and sign up in Tobin's union. And this "convincing" process did not take the form of ideological disquisition or logical elucidation. Tobin's mobsters relied on arguments of another kind learned in their own school, which honors Capone and Dillinger more than Plato and Aristotle.

The usual practice of pulling drivers off their trucks and beating them within an inch of their lives was tried first but did not work very well. The Pittsburgh brewery drivers, with the help of other CIO fellow unionists, proved able to defend themselves on this ground. Tobin's importees then resorted to other techniques. One of their arguments in favor of the AFL as against the CIO was the use of a little homemade gadget known as the fire bomb. These fire bombs, as one reporter described them, "were simple, devilishly destructive little devices consisting usually of a 200 watt electric light bulb, with a hole cut in one end. These were filled with high test gasoline, and the hole then plugged with surgical gauze, providing a fuse to be lighted. Tossed into the cab of a beer truck, they instantly sprayed both truck and driver with flaming gasoline."

These weapons were supplemented later with high-explosive bombs, charged with dynamite, which were recklessly thrown through the windows of distributors handling the CIO beer, regardless of the possible consequences to people living in the building. Testimony before the House Labor Committee, which investigated the

Pittsburgh "beer war," chalked up a score at that time of 10 fire bombings of stores, five explosive bombings and seven trucks bombed and burned. That was over three months ago. The latest scores are not in yet. At present there is a "truce" in Pittsburgh—the publicity about his fire-bombers and dynamiters got too hot for Tobin—but he is still recklessly carrying on his "war" in other parts of the country, spending lavish sums of the union's money to fight another union.

At this time, when the reactionary offensive against the workers on all fronts calls for a labor leadership which would map out the strategy of a counter-offensive and inspire the workers for the struggle, Tobin's hand-picked Executive Board occupies itself primarily with the war against the workers. The three principal items on the agenda of the latest meeting, as reported in the March and April issues of Tobin's official magazine *The International Teamster,* were:

(1) Hearing of appeals from rank and file workers who had been suspended or expelled from various local unions, which were, of course, denied;

(2) Unanimously "approving the acts of the general president and his assistant in the brewery and other matters," and "instructing and empowering the general president to continue financial aid in these matters as long as the general president deems it advisable" and

(3) The adoption of a resolution to take rigorous action against "unauthorized" strikes, i.e., strikes which the general president does not approve, which he nearly always does not, "By unanimous action the Executive Board decided that all unions bringing about unauthorized strikes be censured and condemned and if necessary that the officers be removed."

The published proceedings of the Executive Board dealing with the appeals of suspended and expelled members read like the minutes of an Army court-martial conducted by officers who act from the premise that the private soldier is always wrong. There is the appeal of 13 members of Local No. 549, Kingsport, Tennessee, who had been expelled for unstated reasons, probably for striking or talking out of turn. "Decision sustained and the appeals denied," in the case of 10 of the appellants.

But for all that, the report shows, Tobin's Board will give a worker a nickel's worth of justice if he humbles himself. Tobin, like God, grants mercy to penitent sinners—but not too much. The penalty of three other appellants was modified "in view of their expressions of repentance." Their sentence was commuted to one year of suspension with "probation for a period of two additional years." Whether these three suspended members who "repented" will be permitted to work and make a living at their trade during the suspension was not stated. Probably not.

Tobin's criminal activities in Minneapolis have been rather widely advertised. It is known that he tried to break the great strikes in 1934. He didn't succeed then, and could not prevent a strong union being built up without him and in spite of him. He then tried to get rid of the honest, fighting leaders of the union in 1941 by placing the union in "receivership." When the rank and file revolted against that, he called the federal cops through his friend President Roosevelt, and simply had the leaders thrown into prison.

At the same time, a horde of Tobin's gangsters, armed with blackjacks and baseball bats, were turned loose on the trucking districts with the open connivance of the city police, to force the truck drivers to wear the button of Tobin's "reorganized" local. The State Labor Board, under Governor Stassen, denied the workers the right of an election to register their preference. In return for that favor, the labor-hating Governor, author of the notorious Minnesota "Slave Labor Law," was introduced as the guest of honor and highly praised by Tobin at the subsequent international convention of the IBT.

Having tasted blood in Minneapolis, Tobin has been running wild ever since in his violent campaign against any sign of independence or militancy in the ranks of the International Brotherhood of Teamsters. At the present time approximately 40 percent of the local unions are under "receivership" with appointed officers and no autonomous rights. This simple fact in itself is the most devastating testimony of the extent of the rank-and-file discontent and revolt against the tyranny and treachery of this mean-spirited, vicious old man and the whole gang of well-heeled labor skates and common crooks who make up his unsavory machine.

With this tide of rank-and-file revolt rising all around him, Tobin spits hydrophobic venom in the faces of the union membership and threatens to spend their own money—the money they paid into the treasury of the International Union—to fight them and beat them down. He warns "any foolish group in any district" that they "must get this into their heads now—that if they ever get so cocky and self-important that they think they can defeat this International Union they are making the mistake of their lives. We don't want trouble and disagreement, but when it is forced on us, we will never back down if it costs every dollar in the treasury." You fight me, and I'll hire more gangsters to fight you—that is Tobin's April message to the rebel teamsters. There is no doubt about it, one can buy a lot of professional thugs with $14,800,000.

Daniel J. Tobin employs yet another murderous weapon

in his war against the rank and file of the IBT. He reinforces his brutal dictatorship over the local unions of the Teamsters International by the device of first expelling dissident workers and then taking their bread and butter away from them by "taking them off the job." In the April number of *The International Teamster,* Tobin boasts about breaking up an opposition to the gangster-ridden union machine in St. Louis which culminated in a strike. "The International Union sent in a number of men," he says significantly, meaning a mob of strong-arm men whose assignment was to waylay the strikers and beat them up—"and every business agent and officer of our local unions in this city of St. Louis pledged his full and undivided help." It is known to Tobin that one of these local "business agents," in fact the boss of the whole Tobin set-up in St. Louis, is a gangster with a criminal record.

According to Tobin's account, the leading rank-and-file militants in the strike—truck drivers, not gangsters—also had the bad habit of "continuously finding fault with the union officers." Consequently, "the general president ordered that charges be preferred against them." And, of course, "several of them were expelled from the union."

Next came the deal with the bosses. Says Tobin: "The employers were notified that those men were no longer members of the union and that our union shop agreement must be observed. The employers complied with the agreement, and those individuals were laid off by the employers." By this combination of anti-labor measures the strike was broken. The workers were beaten and forced into line. It was "a famous victory," and Tobin gloats over it. "In a few days," he writes, the men "begged to be allowed to go back to work." Maybe the poor devils had families to support. And maybe the families were hungry. The proudest men have been known to submit under such circumstances.

But proud men who beg through clenched teeth are dangerous animals to provoke. There are many of them in the International Brotherhood of Teamsters at the present time, and their number is steadily growing. One of these days they are going to count noses and come to the conclusion that they are strong enough, if they all act together, to put a stop to the humiliations and defeats imposed upon them by brutal violence and treacherous collusion with the bosses. That will be a bad day for The Mad Dog of the Labor Movement. The dogcatchers will catch up with him.

The treason of the intellectuals

THE MILITANT, MAY 24, 1947

What ever became of the revolutionary intellectuals—and why? What happened to the numerically formidable aggregation of cogitators and problem-solvers who challenged capitalism to a showdown fight in the unforgotten Thirties and appeared to be all set to mount the barricades with fountain pens unsheathed?

Time was when it seemed that a section of the American intelligentsia, quartered in New York, was at long last preparing to emulate that renowned band of educated people in western Europe and old Russia who so bravely revolted against the spiritual stagnation and decay of bourgeois society, abandoned their own class in disgust and contempt, formulated and popularized the socialist doctrines of the proletariat, and placed themselves at the head of its emancipation struggle.

Alas, the hopes aroused by the vociferously uttered challenges of the American intellectuals proved to be immeasurably greater than their capacity to fulfill them. The contrast between their showing and that of the revolutionary intellectuals of Europe and Czarist Russia is appalling to contemplate. The latter went ahead of the workers' movement, organized it, supplied it with ideological weapons and inspired it to strive for great goals.

But here in America the radical intellectuals—with only a very few exceptions—abandoned the mission they had undertaken just at the time when the workers, rising out of nothingness, moved under their own power to create gigantic organizations which boldly engaged in head-on struggle against the most powerful monopolists. Great class battles have taken place, and more momentous ones are in preparation. The workers are on the march. But all is quiet on the intellectual front. The imperialists "pacified" that sector without a fight.

The American intellectuals didn't simply step out for a rest, like tired warriors nursing their wounds after a hard campaign. They quit before the fight got really started. They took it on the lam. They deserted and betrayed. Their well-advertised revolt against capitalism ended "not with a bang but a whimper."

The learned professors such as Hook and Burnham, the writers such as Eastman and Corey, and the journalists whose names are too numerous to mention, did not fall back to an independent middle position after they had deserted the workers whom they had promised to lead and the youth whom they had promised truly to instruct. They went over to the enemy, unconditionally and all the way, with all their bags and such baggage as they had, and helped to lie the youth into the war.

And they lost no time about it. With the most unseemly

haste, without a decent interval for meditation, they began forthwith to ideologize in behalf of American monopoly capitalism as calmly and easily as one changes his shirt. If you draw a line somewhere to the left of the Hearst press and to the right of the *New York Times,* you will identify the present political position of our absconding high-brows. Even Henry Wallace, with his populist-pacifist blather about the "common man" and "peace by understanding," is much too radical, too far to the left, for them. These newly converted servitors of capitalism outshout all others in their zeal, as the man who came to Christ late in life prayed more fervently than the Christians of longer standing and surer conviction.

Professor Sidney Hook, who once expounded the class struggle, declaimed against imperialist war and explained that workers' internationalism alone can lead to peace and socialism, now reveals in the *New York Times Magazine* that the basic conflict of our age is that between "democracy" and "totalitarianism."

Professor James Burnham once informed us, with straight-faced solemnity, that for him "socialism is a moral ideal." Today, with the force-worshipping mentality of a fascist and the irresponsibility of an idiot shouting "fire" in a crowded theater, he incites the power-drunk American imperialists to convince the world of their benevolence by hurling atomic bombs.

Authors like Lewis Corey, who once wrote Marxist books against capitalism in favor of socialism, now writes other books in a directly opposite sense to justify and glorify capitalism. Max Eastman, the original champion of Trotsky and his revolutionary cause, now writes like Herbert Hoover, with the difference only that the style is better.

A fair-sized mob of journalists, who for a while served or aspired to serve the labor movement and the cause of internationalism, have comfortably settled back into editorial spots on the most conservative and reactionary newspapers and magazines and labor there to "slant" the news and poison the wells of public information. A considerable number of the more educated or more sophisticated radicals, ex-Trotskyists or almost-Trotskyists, who fancied themselves to be racehorses, so to speak—and of purest breed at that—now work as harness-broken dray horses hauling loads for Henry Luce, the "American Century" man, and contentedly munch their oats in the editorial stables of *Time-Life-Fortune*.

One and all, these fugitives from the revolution think the late Thomas Wolfe was off base when he said, "You Can't Go Home Again," and refute him with pragmatic proof: "We can and we did." To anyone who values and respects human dignity they present a most unattractive spectacle. Their performance borders on obscenity when they take time out from ballyhooing the "Truman Doctrine" to deliver little homilies about "independence" and to expatiate, like any hypocritical crook, mammon-serving sky pilot or confidence man, on the well-known virtues of "morality." They are just about as independent—and just about as moral—as advertising copy-writers or the authors of radio commercials, including the singing variety.

The dominating fact of present-day society is the struggle between the two great classes, the bourgeoisie and the proletariat, the outcome of which will decide the fate of humanity. No individual and no other class can be "independent" or neutral in this struggle. All must take sides and serve or follow one of the great classes or the other. The powerless, in-between, petty-bourgeois class, which is incapable of maintaining an independent policy, swings from one side to the other, always attracted to the side which displays the greatest power at the moment.

The New York intellectuals, unknown to themselves, are simply verifying this Marxist political law by swinging over to the dominant power of the present day, along with the rest of the petty-bourgeois class to which they belong. At the present time American monopoly capitalism gives the appearance of invincible power. That is what determines the current predilection of the petty-bourgeois class to side with the monopolists against the workers.

To be sure, the present picture of social relations is somewhat deceptive. The "invincibility" of American imperialism is only the temporary and superficial appearance of things and is certain to be exploded in the course of further developments. But the petty-bourgeois intellectuals would not know about that, for they are not much given to analysis, deep thinking and foresight.

No one can be "independent" in the struggle between the great classes. But even in the more limited sense of the term, the independence of character which enables and even requires one to make a free choice of ideas regardless of external circumstances and pressures, and to hold firmly to those which he considers to be right, to see a light and follow it regardless—the quality which most precisely distinguishes the revolutionist from the functionary and the flunkey—even this kind of independence is alien to the palpitating New York intelligentsia who change their ideas according to changes of the weather and the atmospheric pressures of the day.

In the early Thirties, when American capitalism was writhing in the depths of the crisis, while the Soviet Union under Stalin seemed to be going forward from one success to another—and physically annihilating the Trotskyist opposition in the process—the present day professional anti-Stalinists were nearly all fellow-travelers of Stalinism, sponsors of the Stalinist "League Against War and Fascism" and organizers of the "Artists and Writers Committee for Foster and Ford" in 1932.

Later on, when the economic conjuncture in capitalist America began to improve, at the same time that some spots began to show up in the Soviet sun, our doughty fellow-travelers began to travel in another direction, from Stalin and Browder to Roosevelt and Truman, some of them detouring and tipping their hats to Trotsky on the way.

These "independent thinkers" haven't the least idea what it means and what it takes to fight for an idea independently, against any odds whatever. They only know how to serve a power, not to create one of their own. And these professional "moralists" don't bother much about honesty and scrupulousness in practice.

In their apologist propaganda for American "democracy" they systematically throw the Stalinists and the Trotskyists together into one sack which they label alternatively "communist" and "totalitarian"—although they are well aware of the fundamental differences between these mortally antagonistic tendencies. Their venomous hatred of the Trotskyists has the same profound psychological basis as that of the Stalinists. They hate us for the same reason that the Stalinists hate us—because we are witnesses to their treachery. Our existence and our struggle are evidence against them and a reproach to them.

Their desertion, of course, is not evidence of the elimination of the class struggle, which most of them discovered late and soon forgot. It is a sign, rather, of its sharpening and intensification—a process which exerts its pressure everywhere and squeezes people into their proper places.

The working class of America is taking these defections in stride, building up great organizations, tempering them in struggle and looking ever more confidently to a better future. That is the greatest assurance that the present state of affairs, which is not good for the great majority of people, can and will be changed for the better, for the workers have the power to change what needs to be changed and to do what needs to be done.

The terrified rout of the New York professors, writers, journalists and serious thinkers, who didn't stop to think, would be comical—were it not for the sadly disappointed and betrayed hopes of the new generation of students who have been led into a blind alley of pessimism and resignation by these educated Judas goats. It is really too bad that the young generation in the universities, including the veterans who have returned to their studies bitter and disillusioned, have been temporarily disoriented by the circumstance that those ideologists, whom they had a right to look to for enlightenment and guidance, turned rotten before they became ripe, like apples blighted by an untimely frost.

The workers, too, need the forces of enlightenment and progress which a section of the educated classes, as individuals, can supply, and did supply so notably in Europe and old Russia. It will happen here, too. There can be no doubt that the further disintegration of capitalist society in the United States will impel a section of the intelligentsia to revolt. This revolt will acquire great significance when it leads them, as it must, to join forces with the labor movement in the revolutionary struggle for the socialist transformation of society, which alone can save humanity from the abyss.

This union of revolutionary intellectuals with the best representatives of militant labor will open up a perspective of great promise for the leadership of the coming American revolution. But this promise, from the side of the intellectuals, depends entirely and exclusively on the new generation now approaching maturity.

The workers will make the emancipating revolution in

any case, but the task will be easier if the young intellectuals contribute reinforcements to the leadership in time. For that the workers must look forward, not backward. The shameless traitors of the old generation are spiritually dead, and there is no such thing as resurrection. Cross them off. Look to the living and let the dead bury the dead.

A blood transfusion

THE MILITANT, MAY 31, 1947

Things are not exactly what they used to be in South Carolina. The mob of 31 white men who lynched the Negro, Willie Earle, and admitted it with ample detail in signed statements, were put to the inconvenience of a trial in court. That is something new. But it turned out to be a very small point, for the lynchers were all triumphantly acquitted and the dead man is still dead. That's the same old story. Lynch law is still riding high; the courtroom "trial" only added a touch of mockery.

Well, that's one way of handling the race problem and advertising the American way of life to the benighted peoples of the world, who were looking on and listening in through the press and radio, and it may be safely assumed that the lesson will not be lost on them.

But I have seen it done another way—here in America, too—and perhaps it would be timely now to report it as a footnote to the South Carolina affair. This incident occurred at Sandstone prison during our sojourn there in the fall of 1944. I wrote about it at the time in a letter, as fully as I could in the rigidly restricted space of the one sheet of paper allowed for prison correspondence. This left room only for the bare facts, a strictly news report without amplification. But I believe the factual story speaks well enough for itself as then reported, without any additional comment.

Here is the letter:

> I have seen a triumph of medical science which was also a triumph of human solidarity here at Sandstone. When I went up to the hospital at "sick call" one day to have my sore toes dressed, I immediately sensed that something was missing, something was wrong. There were no nurses in evidence; the door of the doctor's office was locked; and the other convicts on sick call were standing in the corridor in oppressive silence. The reason soon became manifest. Through the glass door of the record office, and beyond that through the glass door of the operating room, we could see the masked doctors and nurses moving back and forth around the operating table. Not a sound reached us through the double door. Now a doctor, now a nurse moved in and out of view, only their heads, rather their drawn faces, showing, like figures on a silent movie screen.
>
> The word was passed along the "line" in hushed whispers: a colored man was dying. A desperate emergency operation was failing; the poor black convict's life was slipping out of the doctor's hands like a greased thread. But we could see that the doctors were still working, still trying, and one could sense the unspoken thought of all the men on the line; their concern, their sympathy, and in spite of everything, their hope, for their comrade on the operating table.
>
> After what seemed an endless time, the prison pharmacist who was assisting in the operation came out through the double door into the corridor. His face was the picture of exhaustion, of defeat and despair. There

would be no "sick call" he said; the doctors would not be free for some time. The case of the colored man was apparently hopeless, but the doctors were going to make one final desperate effort. They were sewing up the abdominal wound on the slender, practically non-existent chance that by blood transfusions, they could keep the man alive and then build up his strength for the shock of another stage of the complicated and drawn-out operation.

Then came a new difficulty. The sick man's blood was hard to "type." The blood of the first colored fellow-convicts who volunteered was unsuitable. But the sick Negro got the blood he needed just the same. The white convicts rose up *en masse* to volunteer for transfusions. I think every man in our dormitory offered to give his blood. The sick man hung between life and death for weeks; but the life-giving fluid of the white convicts, steadily transfused into his body, eventually gave the strength for a second, and successful operation.

I saw him line up with the rest of us for the yard count yesterday, this Negro with the blood of white men coursing through his veins, and I thought: The whites, over the centuries, have taken a lot of blood from the blacks; it is no more than right that one of them should get a little of it back.

Farewell to a socialist pioneer

THE MILITANT, JUNE 7, 1947

An old socialist pioneer died in Rosedale, Kansas, the other day, at the age of 89, and I went home to his funeral. I was bound to him personally by many different ties and indebted to him for many things of value beyond computation. He was the first to explain to me that truth and justice are important, and he proved to me, by his lifelong example, that he meant what he said. He really believed in freedom, equality and the brotherhood of man, and thought these things attainable and worth striving for. That was his "principle" and he lived up to it.

It was from him that I first learned about socialism; he took me into the movement 36 years ago, and thus shaped my life in a pattern which has never been changed. Remembering and reliving all that on the long train ride to the old man's funeral, I thought of him not only as a friend and counselor, but also as a true and worthy representative of that noble generation of pioneer socialists who went before us and prepared the way for us. We are here because they were there. We should never forget that.

His socialism—the predominant mid-western American socialism of his time—inspired by the great spirit and burning eloquence of Debs, was broadly humanitarian, more ethical, perhaps, than scientific, and putting more emphasis on the goal than the road to it. But it was right in the essence of the matter, and there was a great driving force of conviction and inspiration behind it. In my opinion, the modern movement, with its more precise analysis and its necessary concentration on the struggle, would do well to infuse its propaganda with more of the old emphasis on the ultimate meaning of the struggle; speak out, as the old pioneers did, for human rights and human dignity, for freedom and equality and abundance for all. That is what we are really fighting for when we fight for socialism.

Ben Hanford, the great socialist agitator of an earlier day, once wrote an encomium of a collective comrade whom he called Jimmy Higgins—the man in the ranks who busies himself without ostentation, recognition or reward to do all the innumerable little and unnoticed things which have to be done to keep the "movement" going and the torch burning. Such was the old man. He was an old-timer from away back—a "labor man" from the days of the Knights of Labor and the eight-hour movement; a Debs' man from the A.R.U. strike of '94 on; and a socialist activist all through the 20-year rise of the Socialist Party after the turn of the century. He ardently sympathized with me in all my work and struggles, and gave all the practical help he could, up to the recent years when he was too old and tired to do any more.

An account of his quiet and sustained activity for socialism could stand, with only a few unimportant changes, as a composite biography of the whole fraternity of anonymous activists whose unrecognized labors and sacrifices, freely given with unfaltering faith, transformed an idea and a hope into a movement which lives after them and will yet prevail.

He was no "leader," but a simple rank-and-file man who "talked socialism" to all who would listen; hustled the subscriptions for the papers; arranged the meetings, rented the hall and drummed up the crowd for the speaker; and always had his hand in his pocket for a contribution he couldn't afford, to help make up the deficit. In addition, he could always be counted on to "put up" a traveling agitator at his home and thus save the party expenses, although his own financial means were all too narrow.

The old man was the friend and partisan of all good causes, always ready to circulate a petition, help out a collection or get up a protest meeting to demand that wrongs be righted. The good causes, then as now, were mostly unpopular ones, and he nearly always found himself in the minority, on the side of the under-dogs who couldn't do him any good in the tough game of making money and getting ahead. He had to pay for that, and his family had to pay, but it couldn't be helped. The old man was made that way, and I don't think it ever once entered his head to do otherwise or live otherwise than he did.

That's just about all there is to tell of him. But I thought, as I looked at him in his coffin for the last time, that's a great deal. Carl Sandburg said it this way: "These are heroes then—among the plain people—Heroes, did you say? And why not? They give all they've got and ask no questions and take what comes and what more do you want?"

That devoted band of pioneer socialists who lived and worked unselfishly for socialism, who did what they could for the "movement" and kept it alive so that a new generation coming along would not have to begin at the beginning, did not live in vain. They were far more important for the future of America and the world than they, with their modesty and their renunciation, could possibly realize. The old man was one of them, and I say farewell to him with gratitude and love. His name was John Cannon. He was my father.

A rift in the iron curtain

THE MILITANT, JUNE 14, 1947

The decay and corruption of present-day society finds its expression in all fields, and not the least in the degradation of the noble art of portraying life through fiction. The novelists, to be sure, are freer and far superior to the professional writers in other fields; but they, too, find it necessary to consider the money angle and keep away from themes which are excluded from honest treatment by an unspoken censorship.

The Catholic Church, for example, with its vast ramifications, and its reactionary power ever more brutally and arrogantly asserted, is virtually unexplored territory. Since James T. Farrell wrote his Chicago novels, I do not know and have not heard of a modern American writer who has touched the Catholic Church without slobbering over it and bending the knee before it. An iron curtain of silence and suppression has shielded the doings and misdoings of this colossal institution from true report, as effectively in fiction as in the press and on the radio and the screen.

All the more welcome and important, therefore, is the publication of a new novel last week which chips open a chink in the iron curtain and throws some light on an underworld of avarice, obscurantism and privilege, dominated by an interlocking directorate of Tammany Hall and the Catholic hierarchy. In *Moon Gaffney* (Henry Holt and Co., $2.75) Harry Sylvester tells the story of a young Irish Catholic made and trained for politics. He was doing well at it before he reached the age of 30, and was scheduled to go higher, much higher, with the assured support and backing of the Church and the "organization," as the Tammany banditti innocently describe their self-serving machine.

The going was all the easier for Moon because he fervently believed in both institutions, and thought politics was the ordained way for a sensible young fellow with the gift of gab and a liking for people to do favors for his friends and make something for himself at the same time. As for the Church, which he also took for granted as God's representative on earth, it not only raised no objections to this somewhat dubious philosophy and practice, but took a big hand in the business and shared in the privileges.

Moon, the son of a deputy fire commissioner who was a power in the "Hall," and well-liked on his own account, was already a favored man in the inner circle of the organization, holding down a sinecure clerkship which gave him plenty of time to get around. He was entrusted with confidential errands for the higher-ups and deferentially treated by the lower orders who were looking for favors; slated for the Party's nomination for the State Assembly at the next election, with higher honors and offices looming ahead; drinking plenty, like all the others in his crowd, and having a good time.

The world looked rosy and the future assured until he stumbled over a cherry stone which he didn't even see and broke his neck. Moon's faults, which eventually disqualified him, were good nature and a strain of conscientiousness which he didn't fully understand and didn't fully believe in, and a glimmering—although only a glimmering—of social consciousness.

One night after a drinking bout he was steered into the office of the *Catholic Worker.* This is a little sheet put out by an unsponsored lay grouping of Catholics who are worried about the sufferings of the poor. It appears that they want, somehow or other, to reconcile institutionalized Catholicism with genuine charity, justice, human brotherhood, etc. This is quite a large order, and the group is not favorably regarded by the well-heeled hierarchs who prefer the flesh pots of Egypt to the locusts and wild honey of the desert. The meek and lowly Jesus stuff is all right for preaching, but these high priests of mammon want no part of it in practice; it smacks of "communism," something they are very allergic to.

Moon slept off his drunk in the *Catholic Worker* office and the next morning, feeling rather heroic, helped the volunteer staff to pass out hot coffee and day-old bread to a line of derelicts who showed up there regularly for handouts. Up to then he had scarcely noticed that there were hungry people around. At the *Catholic Worker* office he was told that a block of slum tenements owned by the Church was about to be torn down to make room for more profitable buildings, and that the poor tenants had been given only 30 days to get out.

This was a double jolt to Moon Gaffney. He didn't know that the Church owned and collected rent from slum properties; and he couldn't believe their story that it was impossible for the poor families, some of whom were Catholic parishioners, to get a hearing at the chancery to plead for a delay in the eviction notice.

On a generous impulse he used his political influence to arrange a meeting with the Monsignor for a spokesman of the tenants, and he went along. That was the beginning of his downfall, although he didn't suspect it at the time. The Monsignor didn't like this sort of interference in the business affairs of the Church. Later, when it was already too late, a priest explained to him: "Oh, I know you didn't do it deliberately, Moon," the priest said, holding up a restraining hand. "It was an impolitic thing to do that was all, the sort of thing that might embarrass the associates of a young politician. That might give them pause as to his future reliability."

Not satisfied with this *faux pas,* Moon—again not realizing what he was doing—secured a friend of his to act as attorney for a struggling union in which the *Catholic Worker* group was interested. Moon felt very good about this gesture. It gave him the double satisfaction of helping out some poor people, and at the same time doing a favor for his young lawyer friend who was badly in need of the fee of $3,000 a year which the job paid. But this good deed also boomeranged. The union was in a fight of some kind with a reactionary and therefore more respectable organization on the docks run by Bernie Brosnan (a thin disguise for Joe Ryan). Brosnan was in solid with the Church, which had written the other union down in its black book as a "communist" front.

The net result was that the young lawyer got in bad with his wife's family for going to work for an outlaw union and had to give it up; her old man was a power in the political machine and he couldn't afford to antagonize him. As for poor Moon, he got tagged definitely as a man whose reliability could not be depended on. Then his father, the influential "commissioner," died and the wolves closed in for the kill. Before Moon Gaffney knew what had struck him, he was out on his ear, his promising career as a politician at an end.

The story part of the novel is integrated with a moving panorama of an upper middle-class Irish Catholic community, with priests and politicians working in cahoots, dominating the scene. Such a job has not been done before in this country to my knowledge. Politics, of course, including the malodorous municipal variety, has been quite adequately treated. The fact that Tammany politicians, like the others, are in politics for what they can get out of it is not a new revelation in American fiction. What is new is the thoroughgoing treatment of the role of the Catholic clergy in politics, and their totalitarian interference in every concern of the daily lives, in the manners, morals and incentives of their parishioners.

The author's account of all this bears all the greater stamp of authenticity because it obviously comes from the inside. The book is not written from an anti-Catholic, but simply from an anti-clerical point of view. The characters whom the author has created to deliver the most blistering philippics against the greedy and materialistic clergy, are all Catholics who aim at the apparently modest but in reality unattainable goal of restoring organized Catholicism, with its huge property interests and uncounted funds, to the simple ideals of Christian charity and justice which inspired the barefooted Christians of ancient days.

But even within this narrow framework, a terrific indictment is brought against the higher ranks of the Catholic clergy of New York in general, and its Irish section in particular. "I'm half Irish" says the Catholic newspaperman Schneider, "and I hate their insane pride of race and of religion and their incredible fatuousness. . . . What I hate is a priesthood that lacks both charity and humility and has misled and confused its people until they mistake black for white, hate for love and darkness for light. A priesthood that has substituted chastity for charity and frequently a chastity so warped and misinformed that its ultimate fruits compare with those of lust."

The author of this book is no Fancy Dan, and he doesn't spar with his antagonists when he gets them into the literary ring. He is strictly a slugger; he hauls off and lets them have it without euphemisms, allusions or indirections of any kind whatever. This man is blazing mad. The pages of the book are scorched with his anger.

In scene after scene he describes and denounces the ignorance, malice, hatred and greed of the Irish clerical bigwigs, and their reactionary hostility to every progressive thought. He exposes their anti-Semitism openly expressed, their vicious prejudice against the Negroes, and their megalomaniac race theory, reminiscent of Hitler's, that the Irish—of all people!—are the chosen ones and the greatest of the earth. Even the Italians who belong to the same church are despised and openly derided as "Ginnies." A well-to-do Irish girl is scolded by a priest for electing to serve as a volunteer in the maternity ward at the hospital, helping out with "Ginny babies," in preference to the more rarefied atmosphere of "the sewing room," where the select circle of Irish Catholic ladies do their charity work in the preparation of bandages and the dissemination of gossip.

Moon Gaffney is a horror story if there ever was one. It depicts a priest-supervised system of marriages for convenience and marriages for money, in which the prospect of bringing more money into the parish of the interested priest is shrewdly calculated. What could be more horrible than that? The book reveals a priesthood obsessed with sex repression, thunderously expounding the hateful dogma that sex is sinful, dirty, unnatural, something to be ashamed of. Overriding all is the devastating picture of the Catholic hierarchy's subservience to wealth and power; their selfish and brutally avaricious participation in the privileges and the callous disregard for the bitter consequences the whole system has for its innumerable victims.

They insanely hate "communism," by which they designate every kind of progressive thought or protest against the most flagrant discrimination and injustice. They tolerate no encroachment on property rights or privileges. Even the pathetic *Catholic Worker* group, with their Christian meekness and their utopian idea that humility and charity can conquer greedy privilege armed to the teeth, is hated and persecuted as a "communist group."

There is a savage irony which the author most probably didn't notice in the circumstances that his Catholic protagonist came to grief, with the consent and connivance of the priests, for doing no more than the mildest liberal or any decent man of good will would do without attaching any great importance to his actions. The bare fact that a man only half consciously performing a few simple humane deeds can be presented as the hero of a novel in an Irish-Catholic setting, bringing the unrestrained wrath of the clergy down on his head, gives a certain measure—perhaps more than the author understood or intended—of the black reactionary mentality of these ecclesiastics who wear the cloak of religion to serve and support a system of exploitation and discrimination.

Moon Gaffney is a warning to all those who strive for social progress that they confront a formidable and uncompromising enemy in the hierarchy of the Catholic Church. There is increasing evidence of this in every field. It is high time to take note of it and to speak out loud about it. It will take more than charity and humility to cope with this monster.

Harry Sylvester deserves praise and his book deserves a wide reading. He has thrown some light on the unpublicized inner workings of a dark and evil institution. And that is what the people need—light and more light.

The two Americas

Keynote speech delivered to the Thirteenth National Convention of the Socialist Workers Party on July 1, 1948 and broadcast at that time over a nation-wide network by the American Broadcasting System

THE MILITANT, JULY 12, 1948

Comrade Chairman, Delegates and Friends:

We meet in National Convention at a time of the gravest world crisis—a crisis which contains the direct threat of a third and more terrible world war. The basic causes of this world crisis are no mystery.

The first cause is the breakdown of capitalism throughout Europe—and Asia—and the colonial lands. The working people want peace and bread, which capitalism cannot give. The colonial slaves don't want to be slaves any more—and capitalism cannot live without colonial slaves. The working people, the poor peasants and the colonial slaves are in revolt against the continued rule of bankers and landlords.

On the other hand, American capitalism—the last solvent stronghold of an outlived and doomed world system—is trying to prop up the hated regimes of capitalists and kings and landlords by economic pressure and military force.

These are the two main elements of the present world crisis.

The Wall Street money-sharks, and the brass hats of Prussian mentality, are riding high in Washington these days. The masters of America, drunk with power, are threatening and terrifying the people of the world—seeking to dominate and enslave them—striving to transform the other countries of the world into colonies of the American empire.

Their program is a program of madness, and it is doomed to failure. The great majority of the peoples of the world do not want to be slaves of America. That is to their credit and we applaud them for it. The attempt to enslave them would be profitable only for the small group of monopolists—and the military caste, who dreams of careers as colonial administrators of conquered peoples.

But the criminal adventure would encounter such ferocious resistance that the American people at home would have to pay an enormous cost in living standards ruined by inflation, in the stamping out of democracy by military rule. And America's young sons would have to pay in misery, blood and death. The American people would be among the first victims of the insane campaign of American imperialism to conquer and enslave the world.

To avoid this calamity it is necessary now to show the people of the world the other America. For there are two Americas—and millions of the people already distinguish between them.

One is the America of the imperialists—of the little clique of capitalists, landlords, and militarists who are threatening and terrifying the world. This is the America the people of the world hate and fear.

There is the other America—the America of the workers and farmers and the "little people." They constitute the great majority of the people. They do the work of the country. They revere its old democratic traditions—its old record of friendship for the people of other lands, in their struggles against Kings and Despots—its generous asylum once freely granted to the oppressed.

This is the America which must and will solve the world crisis—by taking power out of the hands of the little clique of exploiters and parasites, and establishing a government of workers and farmers. The Workers' and Farmers' Government will immediately proceed to change things *fundamentally*—

Throw out the profit and rent hogs, and increase the living standards of the people who do the useful work.

Assure freedom and democratic rights to all, not forgetting those who are denied any semblance of them now.

Call back the truculent admirals from the seven seas—and ground the airplanes with their dangling bombs.

Hold out the hand of friendship and comradely help to the oppressed and hungry people in the world.

These people don't want to fight anybody. They only want to live. There are two billion people in the world—and more than half of them don't get enough to eat. These people should be helped—not threatened, not driven back into slavery, under the social system that has kept half of them hungry all their lives.

It is well to recall now that America was born of revolution in 1776, and secured its unity as a nation through another revolution—the Civil War—which smashed the abomination of chattel slavery in the process. Our great, rich, wonderful country was once the light and the hope of the world. But our America has fallen into the hands of a small, selfish group, who are trying to dominate the world—and to set up a police state at home.

These Wall Street money-sharks are just as foreign to the real America as were the despots who ruled the land before the revolution of 1776. They are just as foreign as were the traffickers in human flesh and blood—the slave owners—whose power was broken by the Civil War—the blessed second American Revolution. These imperialist rulers of America are the worst enemies of the American people.

American democracy, under their rule, is slipping away. The fear that oppressed Mark Twain, the fear that America would lose its democracy, is steadily becoming a reality. The Taft-Hartley Law is but the most recent instance of this ominous trend. The divine right of kings has reappeared in America—disguised as the divine right of judges to issue injunctions and levy fines against labor organizations.

Only three years have passed since the imperialists finished the last slaughter. And now they are drafting the youth for another. Militarism is becoming entrenched in America. Militarism—so long synonymous with goose-stepping Prussianism—is now to be made synonymous with Americanism, if Big Business has its way. A large section of the sturdy immigrants who helped to build this country came here to escape militarism. Now their grandsons face the same brutal regimentation here.

All this is part and parcel of the development of capitalism—the system which puts profits above all other considerations. The capitalist system has long outlived its usefulness. Capitalism offers no future to the people but depressions, imperialist wars, fascism, universal violence and a final plunge into barbarism.

To avoid such a fate, the workers of the United States must go into politics on their own account, independent of all capitalist politics. They must take power, establish a Workers' and Farmers' Government, and reorganize the economy of the country on a socialist basis. Socialist economy in the United States, eliminating capitalist wars, profits and waste, will be so productive as to ensure a rich living for all who are willing and able to work, and provide security and ample means for the aged and infirm.

We should also help the hungry people of the world to improve their standard of life. Socialist America will rapidly make that possible by helping them to secure their own freedom and develop their own economy. Eventually, the economy of the entire world will be united and planned on a socialist basis. This will bring universal peace—and undreamed of abundance for all people everywhere. The real upward march of humanity will begin.

The American working class can open up the way to this new world. They are the majority. They have the power in America. All that is necessary is for the working class to understand it—and to use it.

We firmly believe they will do so. We firmly believe the real America—the America of the workers, the people—will help save the world by saving herself.

We, the American Trotskyists—we, the National Convention of the Socialist Workers Party, summon our America to her great destiny—not as conqueror but as liberator of the world.

Sixtieth birthday speech

Transcribed from wire recording

LOS ANGELES, CALIFORNIA, MARCH 4, 1950

Comrades:

As you know, my sixtieth birthday, which also rounds out my 40 years of activity in the movement, was already celebrated at a dinner in New York. That was three weeks ago, but I haven't grown a day older since then. Time has stood still for me during these three weeks because I was waiting for this second celebration in Los Angeles. I maintained that my sixtieth birthday was not official until it was celebrated here. As you know, I am partial to Los Angeles. Perhaps that is because the Los Angeles comrades have always been partial to me, and have always given me the benefit of their most generous judgment. I like that friendly indulgence; and as a matter of fact, I need it.

In these 40 years of struggle people have been talking about me ever since I started, and most of what was said—at least what I heard—was harsh and critical. Those who might have had other opinions were not so articulate. I never complained about the brickbats tossed in my direction, and perhaps some people thought I was indifferent to the opinions of others. But that wasn't the reason. I had simply learned to recognize hostile criticism as an occupational hazard of the political struggle. If you can't take it you are licked before you start. I learned from Engels that when you go into revolutionary politics you should put on an old pair of pants. And I learned from Marx that you must not let people get you down with pinpricks. So I dressed for battle and developed a tough hide.

But still, I must tell you—although you won't believe me—that when I used to hear people denouncing me and criticizing me, I was hurt and bewildered, for I am by nature friendly and peace-loving. I felt something like Eddie Waitkus, the star first-baseman of the Philadelphia Phillies, who was in the news the other day. He had an unfortunate experience with a deranged woman who was a total stranger to him. She lost her head, and for no reason at all, broke into his hotel room and shot him. They took Eddie to the hospital for an operation, and when he came out of the anesthesia they told him what had happened. His only comment was a question: "Why did she want to go and shoot a nice guy like me?" That is what I have thought all these years about my critics and opponents. They have been shooting the wrong guy all the time.

On the occasion of the celebration in New York, I received letters and telegrams from friends and comrades throughout the country. In several of them there was a recurrent note somewhat as follows: "Celebrating your 40 years in the movement, we expect you to give 40 more." That sounds like a large order, but if, as it is said, longevity is determined by heredity, things might possibly work out that way. I come from a long-lived ancestry. All four of my grandparents lived into their eighties. Two of my aunts lived to be nearly 90. My father lived to be 89. It may be that I still have a long way to go. But I am not making any long-range commitments tonight.

Now I must frankly tell you that I have appreciated in

the highest degree the joint celebration—this prolonged birthday—in New York and in Los Angeles. I wouldn't go for the idea that I should stand in the corner and pretend not to know what was being prepared. I was the biggest promoter of the affair in New York.

I was assigned to be chairman of a public meeting where Vincent Dunne was the speaker, about a week before the birthday celebration. The New York organizer was in a dither as to how to announce my birthday celebration, with me as the chairman of the meeting. He thought it would be too delicate a matter for me to announce myself. When I called him up the afternoon of the meeting and asked him for last instructions about announcements, he said: "You don't have to say anything about the dinner; that will be taken care of by someone else."

I said, "Well, if I am chairman of the meeting, I might as well announce it."

He said, "Would you?"

I said, "Damn right I will. I've been waiting 60 years for this birthday!"

And I used the occasion of Vincent Dunne's lecture to invite everybody down to the birthday party, and to make it very clear that I was as much in favor of it as anybody. I made only one proviso: I said, I want it to be a real party of friends and comrades, and I don't want any enemies of our movement coming around telling me what a good fellow I am. I don't want any Farleys or Baruchs or anybody else who has been opposed to the things I've fought for, coming around to give me some hypocritical personal compliments. I would feel dishonored if those whom I've fought against all my life came around to pay tribute to me on my sixtieth birthday.

I have enjoyed it here tonight, as I did in New York, because there have been no formal compliments, no hypocritical praise—just, maybe, a little exaggeration. I understand that, and I don't take it to be flattery. Flattery means falsehood, deceit. I take all the kind words you have said, rather, as what we Irish call the blarney. The blarney is not falsehood; it is the truth exaggerated and embellished to make it sound better. We always feel that under the husk of exaggeration there is a grain of truth and sincerity in the compliments, and we love the blarney.

After 40 years of experience, of ups and downs and battles and denunciations, criticisms and hardships and rewards—it is nice to sit down at the end of 40 years and hear the friendly words of comrades. Somebody once said: "The sweetest music a man ever heard is the applause of his fellows." And if one can be sure, as I am tonight, that the applause is sincerely meant and freely given, it is doubly sweet.

I also like the fact that this drawn-out celebration, beginning in New York and ending here tonight, has not been isolated and separated from our life and our work. In New York it was simply one of the features of the plenum of our National Committee. We had already been meeting a whole day. We held the celebration in the evening, and then we went back the next morning into another session of the plenum to deal with the problems of today and tomorrow, and not merely to confine ourselves to reminiscences.

I don't want to do that here tonight; but still I think I might be justified to make a brief review or, more correctly, a summary of these 60 years. Rose and I are the same age, with only a few weeks difference, and we have both been in the movement all our lives. This gathering marks her 60 years of life and 40 years of socialist activity too. In all the years we have been together, we never paid much attention to birthdays. The years went by. We were busy and had no time. I don't even remember celebrating birthdays in our house as a rule. Not from year to year at any rate. But when we reached the age of 60, it occurred to both of us, as it has probably occurred to others who have reached that age, to take a little time out to think what has happened, and to make a sort of appraisal of the 60 years.

Speaking for myself, and making a bow to the acquisitive society we live in, I will begin with point one: What have you accumulated? Well, even there it's not so bad. I have a new suit of clothes which was given to me by a friend as a birthday present. I have my weekly allowance from Rose in my pocket. That's more than I had to start with, and it's as much as I ever had. So I feel that in the matter of accumulation, if I haven't gained much ground I haven't lost any. That's a satisfactory inventory.

The second point I ask myself: What have you accomplished? There, I can tell you that I have perhaps made a more objective judgment than you have. I am one man who took seriously the injunction of the Greek philosophers: Man, know thyself. And if I don't know myself, I've come as close to it as a man can. Because I know myself, I don't claim great accomplishments. I am well aware of all the negligences and all the faults. I can't, in good conscience, stand up and say that I did the best I knew; I only did the best I could. That's quite a difference. I only did the best I could, falling short of the best I knew, because I am human and therefore fallible and frail, prone to error and even to folly, like all others. In summing up the answer to that question—what have you accomplished?—I can only say honestly: I did the best I could.

Then I come to the third point of my self-examination: Has your life been consistent with your youth? For me that has always been the most decisive criterion, for one's youth is the gauge to measure by. Youth is the age of wisdom, when our ideals seem to be, as they really are in fact, more important than anything else in the world. Youth is the age of virtue, or more correctly, the age of courage, which is the first virtue. Every man's younger self is his better self.

The struggle for socialism, with all its hazards and penalties, has always been comparatively easy for me, throughout the entire 40 years, because my youth was always with me. My youth was like another person who never forsook me, not even in the darkest hours. It was then that he was always most vividly present as a friend, easy-going and indulgent as a friend should be, with a benign indifference to my faults and my follies which disturbed other people so much. The faults and follies never disturbed my younger self, and I liked that, because I like to have a little leeway in my personal life.

I never promised anybody to be perfect. I only promised to be myself and to be true to myself—that is, to my better self, to my youth. That in itself was a pretty big undertaking, easier to promise than to perform. And this seemed to be the view of my younger self, who followed me everywhere I went. He insisted on that, but on nothing more. He consistently checked me up on that. He was a friend, as I said, but also a censor and a judge—sometimes looking over my shoulder, sometimes looking me straight in the eye, but always confronting me with the one imperious command: Remember, I am your youth, don't betray me!

As long as I didn't do that—and I never did—I felt sure, with never a doubt, that I was on the right road, even though it put me in the minority, and more often than not in the minority of the minority. That wasn't my fault. I have been in the minority, not because I don't like crowds, not because I am sectarian by nature, but because

I couldn't agree with the majority. I couldn't agree with things as they are. I was in favor of things as they ought to be and will be.

That is what put me in the minority and out of step with the others. I found the explanation of that in the writings of Thoreau, and the justification for it too. Thoreau wrote: "If a man does not keep pace with his companions, perhaps it is because he hears a different drummer. Let him step to the music which he hears, however measured or far away."

Have 40 years of activity, of struggle, of life, resulted in defeat or victory? That is a fair question to put on such an occasion as this. And I say the answer depends on how you measure defeat and victory. Our goal is the socialist society, and it is clear that that goal has not yet been attained. But in my youth, when I became a socialist, I associated the ideal of socialism with my own way of life. I decided to be a socialist and to live as a socialist, insofar as physical restrictions would permit, even within the capitalist society. And having that philosophy, I have felt that every little thing I contributed from day to day to the struggle for the socialist goal of the future, was a vindication of my own life that day, and that every day was a victory. If one has that conception of socialism, and lives by it, he does not need to wait for the final victory of socialism. He has his own share of socialism as he goes along.

The prophet Joel, prophesying great things for his people, said: "Your young men shall see visions." In my own youth I saw the vision of a new world, and I have never lost it. I came out of Rosedale, Kansas 40 years ago looking for truth and justice. I'm still looking, and I won't give one percent discount.

I have always agreed with Emerson, who said: "He who has seen the vision of a better future is already a citizen of that future." I take that literally. That was always true in my case. And that was all the reward I needed for anything done or given to the movement. I never found it possible, nor did I ever even think of renouncing my citizenship in the socialist future of humanity. And here with you tonight, in the midst of friends and comrades, I feel like a privileged citizen of the good society of the free and equal, of that future which Jack London so beautifully described as "the golden future when there will be no servants, naught but the service of love."

It is very rarely, and only on the most exceptional occasions, that we revolutionists dare to permit ourselves to express such sentiments, or even to utter such words. In the society which we have been fated to live in, a society divided into classes, deception and hypocrisy rule supreme. The noblest and most fraternal sentiments, which inspire the better selves of the great majority of the people in their relations with each other, are perverted for opposite uses and exploited for the selfish aims of a few.

The most beautiful and holy words that people have articulated to express their deepest feelings and their highest aspirations, have been so prostituted by misuse that they have lost their original values, like coins worn smooth from too much handling. All this perversion of sentiment and prostitution of language makes us cautious and reserved in expressing ourselves, lest we too sound like the hypocrites and the vulgarians who are so glib and free with the use of words which mean nothing to them.

But on this occasion, here among comrades, I will disregard that fear and tell you what I really think and feel, what I have always thought and felt since I became a socialist 40 years ago. I believe in people and in their unlimited capacity for improvement and progress through co-operation and solidarity. I believe in freedom, equality and the brotherhood of man. That is what we really mean when we say socialism. I believe in the power of fraternity and the love of comrades in the struggle for socialism. Walt Whitman said: "I will build great cities with the love of comrades." I would go farther and say: We will build a great new world.

It is not illogical or inconsistent for us soldiers of the revolution to pause in the midst of our labors and our battles, as we do tonight; to rest and relax, to take it easy and have a good time. We are soldiers, that is true and therefore we must be Spartans. We must be able to endure hardship and privation, but we should never inflict it upon ourselves. Soldiers and Spartans, yes but not ascetics. For socialism, the philosophy of the good life and the life more abundant, is alien to all asceticism. Socialism, if you stop to think about it, is the doctrine of the good time coming and "the great gettin' up morning!"

That is how I have thought about it; and it was my good luck that this conception fitted so neatly with my own personal temperament. I just made a small amendment: If socialism means a good time for everybody in the future, why not have a good time in the struggle for socialism? I was always in favor of that. It wasn't always possible. There were some tough times. Forty years of fighting for socialism was not all beer and skittles, as the British would say. But by and large, taking the good with the bad, I had a good time for 40 years and I really have no right to ask for sympathy. I had a good time, and perhaps that is one reason why I lasted longer than some of the others.

And finally, just by having patience, the greatest achievement of all became mine. Just by having patience and waiting around, I reached my sixtieth birthday, which formally ends tonight, and tomorrow morning I will be entering the first day of my sixty-first year. The question then naturally poses itself: What next? Rose and I have to answer that question, as we have answered every important question for 26 years, together.

When we were 40 we took stock of the situation at that time. That was when we had been expelled from the Communist Party for defending the program of Trotsky, and had to start all over again. We were 40—that's older than 20—a little tired. We realized that revolution is rather a young people's occupation, like athletics. But we had to recognize that the movement depended upon us more than ever then, and that we had to make an exception of ourselves. So we said: Well, we'll give 10 more years to the party; after that perhaps they won't need us so much.

Those 10 years passed so quickly, we didn't have a chance to count them. Then we were 50. That was the time of the biggest fight for the existence of the party, in 1940, the fight with the petty-bourgeois opposition. Right in the middle of that fight we celebrated our fiftieth birthday, and we had to admit that we were still needed. There was nothing for us to do but agree to give 10 more years.

Those 10 years went by, busy, active years. We didn't have much time to think about getting old. We were always on the go, both of us, and before we knew what had happened, we reached 60. So here we are, and where do we go from here?

Everybody, I suppose, gives to the movement what he can. It takes all kinds of contributions from all kinds of people to keep the movement going. All we ever had to give was our time, our years. So we sat down, on the eve of our sixtieth birthday, to consider one more donation. We thought: The party is growing, and growing up, and the demands upon us are not as heavy as they used to be. The young recruits of former times have become veterans. A great cadre of leaders has developed. They can do many things that we had to do in the past. We are by no means as much needed as we were 10 and 20 years ago.

But still, we thought, we might be useful if we're there to help a little. So we decided: All right, we'll give the party another 10 years. And then we'll see.

The Korean War

A letter to the President and members of the Congress

THE MILITANT, JULY 31, 1950

To the President and Members of the Congress:
Gentlemen:

I disagree with your actions in Korea, and in my capacity as a private citizen I petition you to change your policy fundamentally, as follows:

Withdraw the American troops and let the Korean people alone.

I am setting forth the reasons for this demand in detail in the following paragraphs. But before opening the argument, I beg your permission, gentlemen, to tell you what I think of you. You are a pack of scoundrels. You are traitors to the human race. I hate your rudeness and your brutality. You make me ashamed of my country, which I have always loved, and ashamed of my race, which I used to think was as good as any.

The American intervention in Korea is a brutal imperialist invasion, no different from the French war on Indo-China or the Dutch assault on Indonesia. American boys are being sent 10,000 miles away to kill and be killed, not in order to liberate the Korean people, but to conquer and subjugate them. It is outrageous. It is monstrous.

The whole of the Korean people—save for the few bought-and-paid-for agents of the Rhee puppet regime—are fighting the imperialist invaders. That is why the press dispatches from Korea complain more and more about "infiltration" tactics, increasing activities of "guerrillas," the "fluid" fighting front, the "sullenness" and "unreliability" of the "natives."

The Korean people have a mortal hatred of the Wall Street "liberator." They despise unto death the bestial, corrupt, U.S.-sponsored Syngman Rhee dictatorship that made South Korea a prison camp of misery, torture and exploitation.

The high morale and fearlessness of the North Koreans and the hostility of the South Koreans toward their U.S. "liberators" alike testify to the unity of the entire Korean people in this unflinching opposition to imperialistic domination.

The explosion in Korea on June 25, as events have proved, expressed the profound desire of the Koreans themselves to unify their country, to rid themselves of foreign domination and to win their complete national independence. It is true that the Kremlin seeks to take advantage of this struggle for its own reactionary ends and would sell it tomorrow if it could get another deal with Washington. But the struggle itself has the overwhelming and wholehearted support of the Korean people. It is part of the mighty uprising of the hundreds of millions of colonial people throughout Asia against western imperialism. This is the real truth, the real issue. The colonial slaves don't want to be slaves any longer.

This is more than a fight for unification and national liberation. It is a civil war. On the one side are the Korean workers, peasants and student youth. On the other are the Korean landlords, usurers, capitalists and their police and political agents. The impoverished and exploited working masses have risen up to drive out the native parasites as well as their foreign protectors.

Whatever the wishes of the Kremlin, a class war has been unfolding in Korea. The North Korean regime, desiring to mobilize popular support, has decreed land reforms and taken nationalization measures in the territories it has won. The establishment of people's committees has been reported. These reforms, these promises of a better economic and social order have attracted the peasants and workers. This prospect of a new life is what has imbued a starving subject people with the will to fight to the death. This is the "secret weapon" that has wrested two-thirds of South Korea from U.S. imperialism and its native agents and withstood the troops and bombing fleets of mighty Wall Street.

American imperialism was quite willing to turn northern Korea over to Stalin in return for control over South Korea, which it ruled through the bloody dictatorship of Syngman Rhee. Now Washington is seeking, against the resistance of the Korean people, to reimpose its imperialist puppet rule, to enforce the division of Korea and to maintain it as a colony and military base for future war on the Soviet Union.

There is not an iota of concern for the wishes and rights of the Korean people in this brutal invasion. The attempt to prop up the Syngman Rhee regime by armed force is part of Wall Street's planned program to dominate and exploit the whole world. Your undeclared war on Korea, Mr. President, is a war of enslavement. That is how the Korean people themselves view it—and no one knows the facts better than they do. They've suffered imperialist domination and degradation for half a century and they can recognize its face even when masked with a UN flag.

The right in this struggle is all on the side of the Korean people. Like the colonial peoples everywhere in Asia, they want no part of U.S. or even UN "liberation." They want the American troops to get out of Korea. They want freedom from all foreign domination. They want to decide their own fate.

The American people well remember the War of Independence that brought this nation its freedom from British tyranny. In the spirit of this revolutionary and democratic tradition of ours, I call upon you to halt the unjust war on Korea. Withdraw all American armed forces so that the Korean people can have full freedom to work out their destiny in their own way. I submit this to the Congress as a motion.

James P. Cannon

Second letter to the President and members of the Congress

THE MILITANT, DECEMBER 4, 1950

To the President and Members of the Congress:
Gentlemen:

Once more, as at the start of your Korean intervention, I take this means to tell you what I believe is the heartfelt sentiment of the overwhelming majority of humanity, including the American people, today:

Stop your criminal aggression against the Asian people.

Your reckless military adventure in Korea has brought this country into a clash with the 500 millions of China and threatens an "entirely new war" that will engulf millions more of our youth and drain our last resources.

You have permitted MacArthur, with his mad ambition to be the conqueror of all Asia, to deliberately provoke a situation that could mean war on a titanic scale. Now he has turned for a "solution" to the "United Nations and chancelleries of the world."

But that is precisely where this grave crisis of humankind has been forged—in the UN and the chancelleries. Can we then entrust the further fate of the world to pin-striped diplomats?

Your proposed solution, Mr. President, is a threat to repeat the atrocities of Hiroshima and Nagasaki by using the atom bomb in Korea.

Take heed, Mr. President, before it is too late! Hear the voice of the people of America and the whole world. They are thundering:

Stop the war NOW! Recall your madly ambitious MacArthur! Withdraw the troops from Korea! Let the peoples of Asia alone to settle their own fate!

Who wants this war?

Not the Koreans, whose cities, towns and villages have been reduced by your bombs to charred rubble, and who mourn hundreds of thousands of the slain.

Not the Chinese people, whose dead in the struggle against imperialism and Chiang Kai-shek's despotism number tens of millions.

Not the peoples of Europe, whose fears are reflected today in the warnings to you by their governments.

The German people, by their votes, have just told you in unmistakable terms that they will not bear your arms in another war.

And if you stop to think about it, Mr. President, the American people are not fools. They are not blind to the price they have paid for your disastrous "police action" in Korea. Their hearts ache for their slaughtered youth. And they dread the hatred that your bombs have generated throughout the vast Asian continent. The American people know that before you can even hope to subjugate the new China, the bleached bones of their boys will be strewn across the desert reaches of Gobi, their frozen corpses will choke the Himalaya passes.

Only your arrogant militarists like MacArthur; only your profits-hungry ruling class of monopolists and international financiers; only the political hirelings of a rapacious imperialism seek this war.

Take heed, Mr. President, I adjure you. You are trifling with the fate of the human race. Stop, look, and listen.

This great and good American people abhor militarism and war. They love the ways of peace and freedom. They are trying to tell you their will:

STOP THE WAR NOW!

James P. Cannon

Third letter to the President and members of the Congress

THE MILITANT, MAY 7, 1951

To the President and Members of the Congress:
Gentlemen:

My purpose in addressing you for the third time since the Korean war began is to present three concrete proposals on foreign policy as an alternative to the policies of the Truman administration on the one hand and MacArthur-Taft on the other.

Your differences are merely tactical. My differences with both sides in your so-called "Great Debate" are fundamental. You are preoccupied with the problem of how to conduct a war the American people do not want and never approved. I propose to end the war at once and let the American people themselves decide the life and death questions of foreign policy.

I submit the following three proposals: (1) Withdraw all American troops from Korea. (2) Recognize the Peking government. (3) Let the people vote by referendum on the issue of war and peace.

I have opposed your Korean war from the start. Twice before in open letters I urged you to heed the peoples' will to stop the war and bring the American soldiers home. American troops have no business in Korea. They are being slaughtered by the tens of thousands for no good purpose. Every day they remain swells the casualties list and inflicts more grief upon parents, wives and children. Every day they remain intensifies the hatred of the Asian people for all things American. Again I urge you: Withdraw the U.S. troops from Korea.

The way to peace in Asia is neither to wage a "limited war," as you are now doing, nor to expand it by bombing Chinese cities and killing the civilian population. The way to peace in Asia is to get out of Asia and let the peoples of Asia run their own affairs. The aroused millions of China have thrown out the corrupt dictator, Chiang Kai-shek, despite all the billions you gave to help him. Cut off all support to the discredited Chiang Kai-shek and recognize the new Chinese government.

The flood of letters to Washington and other expressions of public opinion in the past few months have clearly shown that the people have developed a profound mistrust and suspicion—I might even say, a resentment and hostility—toward you who are in power.

Their mistrust is sharpened by the obvious lack of confidence you have in each other. You, Mr. President, have cashiered MacArthur, the very general assigned to head your Korean "police action." He, in turn, has all but called you a traitor. You, gentlemen of the Congress, charge each other with political infamy and corruption. Your most influential Senate Republican, Mr. Taft, has just voiced complete distrust of the highest military authorities, the Joint Chiefs of Staff.

Your lack of trust in each other is reason enough by itself for the people to place no trust in any of you. But there is another reason: *You have never trusted the people.* You did not ask their consent last June when you sent American troops into Korea, and you have not bothered to consult them since. You have brushed aside their pleas to stop the war and bring the troops home.

Your policies, moreover, have proved you are unfit and unworthy to act in the name of the people on the all-important question of war and peace. Your deeds brand you as betrayers of the hopes of mankind. You have "liberated" the Korean people by bombing and burning their homeland. The victims of your atrocities are already numbered in millions.

All this is against the will of the American people. I challenge you to put it to the test. Submit the question of foreign policy to the people. Let the people themselves decide!

I repeat my three proposals:

(1) Withdraw all American troops from Korea.

(2) Recognize the government of New China.

(3) Let the issue of war and peace be voted on in a national referendum of the entire American people!

James P. Cannon

The Big Wheel

1. The mind molders at work

THE MILITANT, MAY 21, 1951

What would people think about the larger questions of general interest and concern if they were free to make up their own minds; if they got full information and heard all points of view, and were not pressured, badgered, bulldozed and blackjacked into thinking what they are supposed to think? If the reference is to the state of affairs in the police-ruled and regimented domain of Stalinism behind the Iron Curtain, it will be recognized at once that this question is in order. When one source controls all agencies of information and instruction and uses them to serve special interests, it is pretty hard to tell what the people really think, or would think if they had access to all the essential facts and had a fair chance to decide for themselves.

But how do things stand with regard to the shaping of public opinion in the United States, which according to the self-righteous critics of the Stalinist regime, enjoys diametrically opposite conditions of unrestricted democracy? Just what does this free and fair democracy, the necessary premise for which is full information and free criticism from all sides, look like in practice in this marvelous country of ours? From a close-up view it doesn't look so good. People's minds are brutally bludgeoned and one-sidedly manipulated here, too, as can be demonstrated by an examination of the news and information factories of the country and the methods by which they mold public opinion.

Convincing testimony on this point is adduced in an important novel about life and work on the staff of a widely read national news and picture magazine. The book is *The Big Wheel* by John Brooks, first published in 1949 and now brought out in a 25-cent Pocket Book edition. Mr. Brooks brings impressive credentials to his task. He has served on the editorial staffs of several large magazines, including *Time* and the *New Yorker,* and he knows what he is talking about. His book radiates authenticity from every page.

Taking advantage of the greater freedom offered by the novel form in these days of increasing censorship and witch-hunt suppression, the author brings information and depicts reality excluded from expression in other mediums. The truth, nowadays, must disguise itself as fiction. You can come closer to getting honest information about contemporary society in fiction than anywhere else.

The Big Wheel presents a composite picture of the inner workings of such so-called news magazines as *Time* and *Life* and the people who work there. The fictional name of the publication is *Present Day,* "the bright, four-color purveyor of a popular culture that had all the answers, and behind the façade a staff of tortured and doubting men who feel that half of what they did was dishonest," *Present Day,* like all the popular magazines of mass circulation, fat with advertising and expensive illustrations, is engaged in the business of slanting the news by the omission of some essential facts and the exaggeration of others under guise of objective reporting.

The technique of *Present Day* is somewhat different from that of the press in totalitarian countries, but it is no less effective in poisoning the wells of public information. The press behind the Iron Curtain—monopolized by the Stalinist party-state—lies outright, secure against any contradiction by anybody. The technique of the so-called free press of democratic America—in reality the monopoly of a small group of financial interests—is subtler, trickier and more hypocritical. *Present Day,* as the author depicts it, bludgeons the minds of people with the systematic misrepresentation of reality, betrays them with half-truths which are the most treacherous of lies.

One of the central episodes in the book deals with the "editing" of a series of dispatches from Eastern Europe.

They were written by Struther Carson, a noted correspondent who retained the habit of reporting what he saw, while "avoiding responsibility for what happened to his dispatches between the time they came over the transoceanic cable and the time they appeared on the newsstands" under his by-line. Barring this compromise with conscience—a gravely serious one to be sure, but even at that he was 50 percent better than his editors, being only 50 percent crooked—"the instincts of a thorough, honest and fair-minded reporter were still with him." His report was "calm in tone, but let the facts fall where they might; it pandered to nobody's prejudices." But by the time it got into the magazine, it was a different story altogether.

The device by which the dispatches went into the editorial hopper as one thing and came out something else is related in the account of the editorial conference on the matter. "It needs serious work on it, of course," says one of the editors in charge of fouling things up. "Rambles badly, Dick. Got to cut it down. Part about religious freedom in Yugoslavia. Got to go. Dull."

"Isn't that pretty important?"

"No. Now about the trouble with Polish visa. Kind of fascinating. Got to build it up. Elaborate. Set it off so nobody misses. Add a few sentences there."

"Military strength in Russia. Build that up. Get stuff out of files here. Stick it in."

The narrator, who was a green man on the staff, demurred at this butchery of an objective report, but it didn't do him any good. The editor just grinned and said: "Take it easy, will you? You're getting all steamed up about nothing. What the devil, it's only another story. . . . Hell, we're not saints up here. We're in business."

Further: "Listen, it's just routine editing. Mostly cutting things out, not much putting anything in. The piece as it stands is too long, see? It rambles: it needs tightening up. It's not exactly a revolutionary assignment, Dick, asking a man to do some cutting."

That was the way they cut up Struther Carson's unprejudiced report of what he saw in eastern Europe and made it fit *Present Day's* conception of what he should have seen. Hatchet jobs of this kind on every item and article in every department, fashioned *Present Day* into a club to beat public opinion into the desired shape, and gave the editor-in-chief the self-satisfaction of a man of accomplishment, a man with a mission. "It's a good and important job we've got, Dick, molding people's minds, shaking them out of their ruts and putting them onto the path into the future." By the "future" the editor meant more of the present; more of "Our Way of Life" extolled by the magazine, a "way" generally recommended by its beneficiaries to its victims.

It's time here to follow the author of *The Big Wheel* in his clinical examination of the motives and morals of the staff members on *Present Day,* who "mold people's minds" to the acceptance of things as they are by these dirty and dishonorable methods. But space is running out, and the chapter on The Men Who Mold People's Minds will have to hold over for next week.

2. The men who mold people's minds

THE MILITANT, MAY 28, 1951

In last week's review of *The Big Wheel* by John Brooks (Pocket Books, 25¢.) I dealt with the author's exposition of the techniques used by *Present Day,* a national news and picture magazine, in mangling the news and dishing out phony culture for the disorientation and befuddlement of the masses. The trick, in short, is to start out with a predetermined aim to mold people's minds to acceptance and support of the *status quo* and then to slant the news to serve the design.

But *The Big Wheel* does more than describe the mechanics of this devious enterprise. It is a novel and its major theme is people. The author introduces us to the literary craftsmen who work on the assembly line of this misinformation factory, and lets them speak for themselves about the motivations which bind them to their grimy trade. The dialogue reveals their philosophy of life—if you want to call it that.

They are all conventionally educated men, presumably instructed in the basic precept of the Christian doctrine that it's a sin to tell a lie, and the more cogent Yankee supplement that honesty is the best policy from a practical standpoint. But in their case the instruction didn't take. The world-weary cynics on *Present Day* are convinced that the lie runs faster than the truth, and pays better, too.

There was Sturtevant Smith, an all-around journalist who could fill most any post, who was stuck with the job of religious editor. He didn't like it and tried to get transferred, but it was no go; you can't pick your spots on *Present Day.* "I've asked them a hundred times. I've cajoled and I've threatened and I've flatly refused. It's no use. Burnside says I'm *good* at the religious page."

What made him good for this particular job, in the view of Burnside, a sub-editor who liked to badger his underlings, was perhaps the minor circumstance that Smith didn't believe in the religion which *Present Day* heartily recommended to its readers. "His basic assumptions on politics and morality seemed to be at variance with the magazine's." In fact, as he said, he was an agnostic.

Nevertheless he worried over his job and did the best he could. "If he started a piece thinking that he agreed with the magazine, he would change his mind while working on it. The next week the magazine might change *its* mind, and decide to do another piece. . . . In that case Sturtevant would change his mind too."

Why the hell didn't he quit such a disagreeable and degrading job? "How can I? I tell you, I need ten thousand a year to keep the apartment! Besides, where could I go from here? This is the top, Dick. . . . All I could do would be to get some grubby job in newspapers for half the dough I get now." That was the trouble with Sturtevant Smith; he needed—or thought he needed—the extra dough.

"His choice seemed to be between a duplex in the East Eighties with his soul in chains, and a tiny place—say five or six rooms—in some outlandish neighborhood like Riverside Drive, with his soul free. Was his soul worth the difference?" This is an interesting speculation, which as far as I know, has not arisen before in literature. Faust sold his soul to the devil, and that was considered a mistake; but here is a man—and he typifies many—who sold his soul to a God he didn't believe in. The difference, if any, is not clear to me.

There was Herb Katzman, whose department was "critical work, art, music and literature." He was an outspoken fellow of exceptional ability who regarded journalistic integrity as a lot of nonsense. As Herb saw it, his connection with *Present Day* was a business transaction, pure and simple. He tailored his writings and critical judgments to fit *Present Day's* requirements, and they paid him handsomely for his services, and that's all there was to it. No pretensions.

"You know," he said, "that I dislike the magazine's standards from here to Thursday and back again . . . but let me tell you some of the things I like about it. I like the place it lets me live, and lets my wife live, outside town.

I like the meals it lets me buy people in restaurants, the drinks in bars. . . . So they own my talent. Well, Dick, listen to this: I'm proud and lucky to have sold my talent at so high a figure."

But, for all that, Katzman was a queer duck who drew the line at a certain point. He wouldn't pretend to believe in the work he was doing. This got him into trouble with Masterson, the editor-in-chief, who insisted that his staff men must be convinced and have faith in their mission to mold people's minds in the *Present Day* pattern. Katzman's quixotic scruple, which prompted him to insist on his right to recommend a religious book he didn't believe in and said so, eventually cost him his job.

The book in question "was a thin little tract, brought out by an obscure publisher, giving a mystical interpretation of the modern world with special reference to recent political events. The chief point in it was that anything goes in the holy war to the death against the forces of Russian materialism. The author, to cap the climax, had a leftist past—had, in fact, or so the dust cover proclaimed, once been a prominent and active member of the Communist Party."

This was right down *Present Day's* alley. Masterson was delighted with the recommendation, for he was deeply convinced, that in furtherance of the American way of life, the people, especially those who are shy of material things, need religion and plenty of it. "Let's do an illustrated review," he said. "Pictures of the Devil as interpreted by various ages, that sort of thing. And excerpts from the book, boxed off in heavy type. We'll really get our weight behind it."

Katzman's discovery and recommendation of the religious tract which hit the bossman's fancy so hard, might have meant a feather in his cap and—more important from his point of view—a bonus in his pay envelope, if he had only had sense enough to keep his mouth shut and let the ex-radical's spiritual revelations work their own mysterious way. But no, he had to pop off. "Candidly," he had said, "I think it stinks to the skies. It makes me actively ill." That did it.

Masterson, the man with a mission to mold people's minds, had no room on the staff of *Present Day* for a man who could recommend a book he didn't believe in but still hold out his right to say: "It stinks. It makes me ill." Herb Katzman was fired forthwith. This action stirred up a mild revolt among the minor mind molders on the staff—as ridiculous a revolution as ever could be imagined, which brings this remarkable novel to its climax.

A number of the staff writers drew up and signed a petition protesting against the firing of Katzman "because he expressed an opinion indicating that he had submitted to the magazine material in which he does not personally believe." Masterson, the anachronistic romanticist who demanded sincerity from the news-twisting and culture-faking technicians on the staff, blew up over their demand for the right to write what they didn't believe.

"Could they really insist on their right to be whores?" he asked himself indignantly. They did, and they were quite stubborn about it, for it was a matter of principle with them. "What we're trying to do," said their spokesman, "is force you to lower the moral standards you require of your staff."

After somewhat of a ruction, and the intervention of the Board of Directors, Masterson, whose impractical insistence on belief in falsehood caused the trouble, resigned. He was replaced by Jack Johns, who didn't believe in anything himself and didn't give a damn whether others did or not, as long as they kept quiet about it. A tacit compromise was arrived at, and everything remained substantially as before. The staff members won "the right to be whores," but in practice thereafter they kept their private opinions to themselves.

The revolution ended in a draw, and *Present Day* just keeps rolling along.

3. What is a man profited?

THE MILITANT, JUNE 4, 1951

The Big Wheel, by John Brooks, paints a devastating picture of literary work reduced to a mere commodity in the magazine market. Writers are bought and sold like meat on the hoof, and scant consideration is given to the artistically squeamish. The conscience of men and their dignity, the highest things they have attained to in millenniums of upward striving from primeval times, count for no more in the mass magazine market than the hair colorings and markings on a steer bred for beef.

"It is axiomatic that we can replace a writer more cheaply than a typewriter," said the memorandum of the Board of Directors in commenting on the protest petition of staff members over the firing of one of their number, the critic, Herb Katzman, who had been pretentious enough to say openly that he didn't believe in the stuff he wrote or the books he recommended. Burnside, the sub-editor who incidentally bore the burden of no beliefs of any kind, said: "The trouble is, you're a bunch of prima donnas! You think you can indulge your intellectual pretensions up here! You think you can express your asinine, epicene, immortal souls! Hell, we're in business."

The staff members couldn't answer back or dispute the plain talk they were subjected to. As one of them said to another, "You know how easy we all are to replace. They could have an entire new staff up here by tomorrow morning, and a good one. Ever see the lines waiting down on Thirty-Seven, in personnel?"

Where do they get the people to man the staffs of the great magazines where news and culture are processed and squeezed into slick, neat packages for the masses? From what ranges and feed lots are the literary cattle rounded up and shipped to the market? Quite a few of them, especially on such publications as *Present Day,* regarded as "probably the leading force against communism in this country," are graduates of the radical movement which had offered the compensation of working for the truth, but where the pickings otherwise were slim.

"You know," said Masterson—who was an old "ex-radical" himself—"you know we still take some of our best men from the little magazines." Such publications as *Present Day* are crawling with one-time radicals and dissenters who have "learned their lesson" that opposition to the existing social system is tough going, and now devote their talents, and the smattering of knowledge on social questions they picked up in the radical movement, to opposite ends.

I once knew a man, a writer with an exceptional style and considerable reputation, who was better acquainted with Marx than most people who think they have "read" him. He knew all the ins and outs of the labor movement, and even wrote understandingly about the Moscow Trials of the Thirties from the revolutionary standpoint of their victims. It seemed, for a time, that the good cause had found a powerful new champion. He soon tired of that, however—it wasn't getting him anywhere in his profession. When I argued with him that his writings could have a great influence on the younger generation, and urged him to write more on the great theme of socialism—indeed, to devote his whole talent to revolutionary journalism—he answered me wearily: "Where am I going to publish it? No magazine or paper of large circulation will take such writings."

Soon after that conversation, he turned around and began to write on the other side of the social question. He had no trouble finding publishers for that kind of stuff. The more he prospered the more conservative his writing became. He finally ended up as a publicist in the right wing of the Republican Party, and died there not long ago. I knew him well, and sometimes wonder where he went when he died.

Renegacy has become a paying profession in the United States in recent years, especially among the intellectuals. But what do they get for it, after all? According to the testimony of the characters in *The Big Wheel,* they get bigger apartments than they really need, and more money to spend on other superfluous things which a writer with a "mission"—if he really has a mission—would disdain even if he could afford them. Thoreau did all right in a one-room cabin he built himself.

"What is a man profited, if he shall gain the whole world, and lose his own soul?" This is a fair question, but it hardly applies to the minions of the public opinion makers. It is understandable that a man—if he is sick enough—should be willing to exchange his soul to gain the whole world; for the whole world is a great prize and no doubt tempting to ambition grown into megalomania. But even in this exchange we are told there is no profit. It is understandable if millions of ordinary people, hemmed in on every side by pressures and sanctions, feel constrained to keep their opinions to themselves, or even formally to profess contrary opinions, as the price of daily bread for their families. People feel that they must live and bide their time until they get a fair chance to assert themselves and proclaim their own truth.

But what of men of talent and education, such as those *The Big Wheel* portrays—writers, no less—who trade off their souls, if one grants for the sake of argument that they came into the world endowed with such attributes, not for the whole world and not for daily bread—but just for a few extra comforts and trappings which they don't really need and which serve, rather, to complicate their lives and bog them down? The very best you can say for such people is that from a moral standpoint they belong to the lower orders of life, whereas one who has been nominated to the high office of writer should be bound by his calling to the strictest artistic scrupulousness and personal disinterestedness. In other words, to the truth.

Under present conditions in the world a man should disdain material advantages for himself at the expense of others. Superfluous comforts and display, and soft living in general, at this moment in history, are for the slothful, the self-indulgent, the people with a pig-like mentality who have no mission and no purpose in life, and are content to fill their own bellies while others, who make up more than half the world's population, go hungry. Such people are not fit to lead and to shape public opinion.

Yet—and this is the terrible misfortune of America, the curse of America—it is just such people who are today in full charge of the business of forming and shaping, that is, poisoning and corrupting, public opinion. In the service of the privileged few, they monopolize all the great channels of public information, of which *Present Day* is only one example, and use them to serve the special interests of the privileged; while the truth-tellers, deprived of adequate mediums for lack of material means, are voices crying in the wilderness, obliged to restrict their utterances to little, poorly-circulated papers and magazines and small meetings, unnoticed by the great agencies of publicity and advertising.

The people, seeking light and leading, are up against this monstrous monopoly of all the sources and instruments of information and instruction, manipulated in a great coordinated conspiracy for the defense of the present condition of affairs. The "news" and argument issuing from this monopoly are all the people get. The great majority probably don't even know there is another side to the story. But there is another side just the same, and the people are going to find out about it, and then there will be some changes made.

4. The writer and the people

THE MILITANT, JUNE 11, 1951

John Brooks' novel, *The Big Wheel,* tears aside a curtain to reveal the methods by which a big news magazine selects and slants the news, and phonies up its presentations of culture, with the prior aim of molding public opinion in favor of the social system which exploits the many for the profit of a few. And *Present Day,* the magazine of Mr. Brooks' story, is only one wheel in the gigantic mechanism of the American press, all parts of which are coordinated to the same purpose.

In the United States of America, the press is absolutely free. That's what the Constitution says. But there's a catch to it. All the instruments and agencies for the dissemination of news and opinion—the big magazines and newspapers, the motion-picture companies and radio and television stations—are owned and controlled by a small minority of the rich and privileged and used to serve their special interests.

They differ in their methods and techniques. Some are crude and vulgar; others are slick and subtle. Sometimes they argue and quarrel over secondary issues. But on the main questions of social implication they all tell the same story and sing the same song. The world of capitalism is the best of all possible worlds, sacrosanct and unchangeable. Its true name is "Free Enterprise," the national poetic version of which is "The American Way of Life." This way of life has the unique distinction of being good for everybody, for the majority of the exploited as well as the minority of the exploiters.

Of course, you are free to dissent if this contention violates your sense of logic and knowledge of the history and prehistory of man, or contradicts your personal interests as one of the exploited. You can even write an article to this effect if you want to. But you can't publish it in any of the monopolized publications which reach the millions. That's the gimmick in the formal, constitutional freedom of the press in the United States as of today. This kind of free press is 99 percent fraud. There is no honest, objective reporting of all the news. It is all one-sided. There is no real free play of opinion and controversy. No real freedom of choice.

In face of all the systematic misinformation and calculated demagogy with which the people are bombarded by the monopolized press, how will they ever learn the truth and find the means to act on it in their own interest? The struggle between the truth and the lie appears to be an unequal one at this stage of the game, and to some it may appear to be a hopeless struggle. But that is not really so. The truth has great allies. The falsifiers and distorters of social reality overlook one small detail: The reality does not therefore cease to be. Sooner or later the contradiction between the misrepresentations and the reality must lead to an explosion.

Inexorable economic laws, stronger than any specious propaganda, are working to push the masses of the people on the road to struggle for a social transformation as the condition for their own survival. Moreover, the instinctive striving of the great majority for cooperation and equality, inherent in the nature of the human race, as demonstrated in tens of thousands of years of prehistoric society, is working powerfully to counteract, to negate and eventually to conquer the propaganda lie. The truth will break through. And the truth itself is revolutionary.

In their search for the truth and the road to emancipating action, the people will need the help of the writers who are to come from the younger generation of uncorrupted intellectuals. Let them serve the people and scorn all special privileges for themselves. Let them take for their own the affirmation of Whitman: "By God, I will not have anything for myself that others cannot have on even terms."

The writer, the artist and the scientist, the soldier and the revolutionist in this time—they should all be of one order, dedicated to the service of humanity. What need have they of softening luxuries and burdensome impediments? I read somewhere that a famous scientist—I think it was Einstein—early in his life decided to reduce his personal requirements to the essentials—clothing for utility, plain food, one room to work in and one bed to sleep in, no foolish extravagances—so that his time would not be devoured and his life cluttered up with things and the pursuit of things he didn't need, and which might distract him from his scientific work or tempt him to abandon it for a better-paying occupation. I think it was a good decision.

Ours is a time of wars and revolutions, and we should not be alien to our time. Soldiers and revolutionists must travel light. And so, too, must their brothers, the artists and writers, if they want to be free to employ their gifts to serve the people, and not to fool them and mislead them. The world must be transformed. It would be unrealistic to deny the immensity of the task and to discount the heavy odds against us at the moment. But it would be absurd to abandon the battle on that account, for the stakes are great. They are nothing less than the survival and further progress of the human race. That justifies and even necessitates the struggle.

The hazards and penalties for the pioneers can be heavy, but the end in view is worth whatever it may cost. And even under such conditions the compensations of the struggle are not to be despised. They are the satisfaction of devoting one's life to an honest purpose; of identifying one's personal fate with the fate of the whole human family. Those who avow the nobility of this ideal, and serve it—their lives shall not be lived in vain.

The world is in agony, and the great majority of the people everywhere live in poverty, insecurity and fear, because of an outlived social system propped up by lies. The overthrow of this bankrupt system of capitalism is historically necessary and even overdue, and therefore inevitable. By our efforts we will hasten the day. With our help the truth will knock out the lie, and bring freedom and equality to all the people in the socialist society of the future. That's what we believe, and that's what we're fighting for.

To the men who gave their skin

THE MILITANT, APRIL 30, 1951

I woke up this morning and looked over Jordan and what did I see? Stumbling through the morning newspapers, from one report to another—of wars and rumors of wars, and shrieks of danger and threats of calamity, and crime and graft and all-around crookedness in high places, and the hypocrisy of the diplomats and the propaganda lies—I suddenly came across a story on another theme in the *New York Herald Tribune.* This was a factual news report of the human goodness and solidarity of a group of simple, unpretentious men manifested on behalf of a fellow-worker who desperately needed help—and it lit up the paper and the morning and the day like a Christmas tree with all candles burning.

It was the story of "Robert A. Sullivan, 43-year-old boiler-maker with the Consolidated Edison Co., who entered Bellevue Hospital in May with burns covering 70 percent of his body." And after more than 10 months' treatment he was up and about and celebrating his recovery and discharge from the hospital at a party "with ice cream and cookies," with the people who had stood by him, helped him out and seen him through.

The case of Mr. Sullivan was a tough one, the toughest ever, the doctors said. "Doctors who had treated Mr. Sullivan said that his was the most extensive burn case they had ever seen recover. He was given three days to live when he entered Bellevue," says the story written by Frances Poteete, who evidently knows important news when she sees it and knows how to write it up, too. "At first, treatments in shock therapy with whole blood, plasma and chemicals had to be given before any surgery could be done. Even dressings sent the patient into shock, physicians said." How did Mr. Sullivan ever get out of a jam like that and live to celebrate it?

Dr. Currier McEwen, dean of New York University College of Medicine, ascribed the miracle to the cooperation of many people. "Teamwork, modern research, the will to get well and 'the kinds of friends he has' had contributed to Mr. Sullivan's remarkable recovery." Doctors and nurses in "three research teams in the Department of Surgery, groups working on shock treatment, plastic surgery and the physiology of burns—had used 'the collective wisdom that means so much' to give successful treatment," the doctor said.

Modern science, beneficently applied by worthy practitioners, played a mighty role in this case to heal and save, and not to destroy. But the doctors couldn't do it all alone. They had to have some outside help; they had to get some skin, and plenty of it, and that's where "the friends" came in.

"Fifteen skin graft operations were performed. Fourteen fellow workers from the Consolidated Edison, some who had not known Mr. Sullivan before, gave two grafts each of 8-by-4 pieces of skin." This was the skin that made the difference; the skin of co-workers taken off their own bodies twice in 8-by-4 slabs for the benefit of another whom some of them at first didn't even know. They merely knew that he was hurt and needed help, and they gave it.

What better story can a man read these days for the good of his soul and his faith in the future than a true story like this; true as a factual report of something that really happened and no less true as a representation of the deep and indestructible impulse of people, given a fair chance, to cooperate with each other and to help each other unselfishly? All those who hope for a better world are bound to believe that this is the real nature of people, which will assert itself in spite of everything and become a mighty power to change the world and make it a better and fairer place for everybody.

All the great leaders and teachers of our socialist movement have firmly held this faith in people; and we must hold it, too, if we are to be true to their heritage and worthy of the mission we have undertaken. In a time of doubt and fear this faith in people is the light to steer by. William Faulkner spoke with profound insight in his Stockholm speech, when he said: "Man will not only endure; he will prevail." For that utterance alone he deserved the Nobel prize.

The class society of the present day, founded on fraud and deception, puts great emphasis on competition and rivalry and acquisitiveness and brutal disregard of the rights and lives of others—even mass killers are lauded as heroes; and the holy office of science is prostituted to destructive ends. But human nature as it really is at bottom, and as it will finally assert itself and prevail, speaks out for cooperation and solidarity, as the men who helped Mr. Sullivan have demonstrated with the beautiful simplicity of action.

I've been around and seen a lot, and I know very well that this jungle of a class society we live in is full of the tricks and dodges and angles of the self-seeking, and loaded with traps and deadfalls for the trusting. But I know, too, that this is not the whole story, or even half of it. The great majority of people everywhere want to live honestly and help each other. The friendly co-workers of Mr. Sullivan are shining examples of this majority.

When it comes to choosing representatives of the human race as it wants to be and will be, I'll put my chips down on the likes of these people who will give 8-by-4 pieces of their skin for a friend, or for a co-worker who may not be a friend or even an acquaintance, but just a man and therefore a brother.

They are heralds of the future and represent its spirit, the spirit of socialist cooperation, whether they know it or not. They and others like them, harnessing their natural impulses to social goals, will do away with the social system which distorts and cripples human nature. They will change the world and make it fit for all people and all nations to live together in peace and fraternity.

It's coming yet for a' that, as Robert Burns affirmed. "Then Man to Man, the world o'er shall brothers be for a' that." And there's going to be a Great Day.

A welcome to visiting preachers

THE MILITANT, JUNE 18, 1951

I am turning over the soap box today to some visiting divines who have come around, in part, to the position of us heathens and infidels and want to give testimony to their new-found faith. They are reporting straight from the 163rd General Assembly of the Presbyterian Church in the USA, just adjourned at Cincinnati, and they are hot as a pistol with a new zeal for righteousness engendered there. I am going to let them do the talking at today's session, reserving for myself only the office of moderator with the duty of introducing the orators; and reserving the privilege of interspersing the proceedings with a few side remarks and parenthetic reservations, when the visiting men of the cloth, who are only partly reformed, get out of line.

Something struck this General Assembly of the Presbyterian leaders at Cincinnati and moved them profoundly. It may be they woke up in sudden fright, like sleepwalkers on the edge of a precipice. It may be their hearts, for a moment, were touched by a pentecostal flame of repentance and consecration. Whatever the reason, the delegates of Cincinnati didn't talk like the general run of preachers who are whooping it up for war in the name of the Prince of Peace, and blessing the slaughter in Korea with a bland indifference to their own contention that killing is a sin. No, the Presbyterian ministers assembled at Cincinnati talked a different language, as though they had seen for a moment the frightening splendor of the face of truth, and had received the gift of tongues to tell about it.

Listen to this—from preachers, mind you—in the social pronouncement adopted at the closing session, as reported by the *New York Times:*

"Under the stimulus of our fear, we adopt many forms of oppression and terrorism—the very things we despise in communism." (That's Stalinism, Reverend Sirs, not communism, whose ideal is freedom and equality. Outside of this terminological error, you're doing fine. Go right ahead.)

"We countenance character assassination which clearly violates the divine law, 'Thou shalt not bear false witness.' Some forms of loyalty oaths are required which stifle freedom of thought and inquiry. People are afraid to speak their convictions for fear of reprisal. Thus is laid the groundwork for a police society which would destroy the very freedom we seek to save." (That's preaching, brothers! Pour it on!)

In an address preceding the adoption of this social pronouncement, the Rev. Dr. Julian Price Love, professor of Biblical theology at the Louisville Seminary, denounced the "stumbling confusion" of President Truman and the "consistently terrible direction" of General MacArthur. "A plague on both your houses," said the Reverend Love. He denounced militarism as the "greatest enemy of the present age." He called on all Christians "to renounce once and for all the whole militaristic method as a way of trying to solve the modern problems of the world."

Dr. Love condemned the exaltation and glorification of the military caste. "If the nation erects into a privileged class men who wear a uniform, then we shall only repeat what Hitler's Germany did and what the Japanese military did and we shall find, nay, we are already finding, right here in America, that the setting aside of the professional military as a particular class because we feel more secure on that account, is producing a dominance in our own American life of one kind of thinking." (Amen! Thank you, Dr. Love, for your burning words of wisdom and courage, your words of solemn warning, so badly needed by the people and so seldom heard these days.)

Up to this point I have been going right along with the alarmed and burned-up Presbyterian ministers, who have graced our forum today. But in winding up the session, I feel obliged to make one small exception. Dr. Love's intentions are no doubt of the best, but he is away off base in one of his pronouncements. He says: "It were utterly ill to take our soldiers out of Korea unless we put our missionaries in there in tremendous numbers."

I can't follow you there, Doctor. The American soldiers in Korea should be brought home right away, to save the cruel waste of their lives to no good purpose, and to give the Korean people a chance to settle and run their own affairs. They should be let alone in all respects, including matters of religion. Instead of sending more of "our missionaries in there," those who are already in Korea should get the hell out of there. If we are going to stand for freedom and human rights, let's not forget one of the most important rights of all—the right to be let alone.

For all you and I know, Doctor Love, the Koreans may have gods of their own; and they may like them better than the one you want to ship to them. Their gods may be, and probably are, more reasonable and easy-going, and less jealous and vengeful than our harsh Jehovah with his long list of prohibitions and instructions, and his vicious threats of hellfire and damnation for ordinary folk who want a little leeway for fun, sport and amusement. Let the Koreans alone in peace—with their own gods. They will like it better that way. People always prefer their own inventions.

What goes on here?

THE MILITANT, JUNE 25, 1951

Having nothing else to do one day last week, and being in need of diversion, I abstracted myself from reality and took an imaginative journey into the realm of fantasy. In a sort of trance I played the part of a sucker who believes everything he hears from Washington about our cold war propaganda campaign for truth, democracy, freedom and all that sort of thing. In the euphoria of delusion I was feeling as fine as any fool in love with his own ignorance and credulity, until I started to read the testimony and cross-examination of Secretary of State Acheson before the Senate Committee. Then I suddenly woke up with a headache and a hang-over.

In my daydream I had been convinced—because I had been told—that our Seventh Fleet had occupied Formosa in order to defend it against any imperialistic aggression from the Chinese, who for some incomprehensible reason think the island belongs to them, and incidentally because its control is of decisive strategic importance to the defense of our homes and firesides. But the hearing brought out a previously secret document of the State Department, a policy guide sent out to 552 American representatives abroad—dated December 23, 1949—which stated the exact opposite. Referring to Formosa, this 1949 memo deprecated "the mistaken popular conception of its strategic importance to United States defense in the Pacific," and denied that the U.S. was "committed in any way to act to save Formosa."

Now, what goes on here? And which is which? Has our policy changed in its objectives, or has Formosa changed its location, or what? The answer, as it came out in the testimony of Acheson, is that nothing is new. Our policy is just what it was in 1949, and Formosa is still there in the same place. The two different and opposite statements of policy were meant to serve two different purposes. One was a directive to the Navy for *action* to carry out U.S. policy. The other was an instruction to 552 foreign representatives for their guidance in *talking about it* in public statements and radio broadcasts. Just listen to the testimony, reported in the *New York Times,* June 4:

> Senator Knowland, questioning Acheson, said, "This paper (the 1949 memo) clearly enunciated the policy which we were following in regard to Formosa." No, explained Acheson. ". . . this paper is a direction to people making broadcasts how they should deal with these problems in the event that Formosa falls."
>
> Then Senator Sparkman intervened with a question right to the point: "And this paper was issued primarily for the purpose of directing or giving direction to those of our people scattered all over the world who were in charge of what we might call propaganda?"
>
> ACHESON: "That is correct, sir; yes."
>
> SPARKMAN: "And was limited to that?"
>
> ACHESON: "That was the sole purpose."

> SPARKMAN: "And at the very time that was issued, we were actually supplying arms aid to the Nationalists on Formosa?"
>
> ACHESON: "Arms aid, yes, sir."

So! We now have it down in black and white in the sworn testimony of the Secretary of State that the United States Government was *doing* one thing in Formosa all the time and secretly instructing its representatives to *say* the opposite. Did you ever hear such two-faced hypocrites and brazen liars in all your life? For my part, I'll never believe another word they say, even in my sleep.

There are two odd footnotes to this story. The Associated Press reports that Moscow propagandists, who can lie on their own account faster than Count Turf can run, have cited Acheson's testimony as proof that the U.S. Government is "playing a 'dirty game' in Asia" and "'pursuing a false and dishonest policy' toward Formosa, Communist China, and also in Korea." This time even the Moscow liars told the truth.

And the Social Democrats, those unofficial agents of the State Department, who in their own right rank in the order of liars as habituals, first class, also took the occasion to experiment with an honest statement of facts by remarking in the *New Leader* under the by-line of Washington correspondent Robert Dean:

> The Secretary of State had elaborated a necessary distinction between policy and propaganda, but had also put on the record the obvious fact that the U.S. was, at times, doing one thing and saying another—as all countries do. We were minimizing the strategic necessity of Formosa, and denying that we were holding it up, to guard against the possibility of the

island's falling, at the same time that we were, in fact, sending arms.

The moralistic *New Leader* reports these unadorned facts with neither sorrow nor anger. "The U.S.," as it says, "was, at times, doing one thing and saying another." But that's O.K. with the *New Leader.* Why make a fuss about it? After all, we are only doing what "all other countries do." Can you think of any better reason for double-dealing? Hold steady, boys. We'll lie our way to peace and freedom yet.

Barbary Shore

THE MILITANT, JULY 2, 1951

I read Norman Mailer's great war novel, *The Naked and the Dead,* two years ago on a California vacation, when I had plenty of time to work my way slowly through the huge bulk of its realistic detail and to notice, as I went along, that the story of militarized life, with all its episodes skillfully woven together into one tremendous whole, was loaded with symbols and overtones of a wider comprehension which enriched the story without slowing it down. Here is a writer, I thought, who looks with profound insight into the heart of present-day man and his contradiction and sees the central problem which history has dumped into his lap and told him to solve or perish.

War and militarism—the governing theme of this book—is the dominating reality of our time; or rather, half of this reality. The other half is revolution. And the two are joined together as inseparably as the Siamese twins. Implicit in *The Naked and the Dead* was the promise that the author, once he had got the war out of his system, would courageously face this side of social reality too, and report it truthfully. Behind the war novel, powerful in its unflinching realism, the author's aspiring direction toward even wider fields was clear. Here was no mere journalist, however observant and scrupulously honest in his report, but a thinking and feeling man who was already trying to look through and beyond the war to its causes and implications and its ultimate outcome.

Here was a new young writer, fresh and vigorous, untainted by the weary disillusionment and sickly capitulationism which has robbed the older generation of intellectuals of their artistic integrity and turned them into slick propagandists for the *status quo,* which is as out of date as its unbelieving boosters. In this time of turmoil and confusion, the shameful abdication of the older writers has created a vacuum. The people need new writers, above all novelists, for they see deeper and have more freedom to tell the truth than others.

I expected great things from Mailer, and have no doubt this hope was shared by many others who recognized, as I did, that the author of *The Naked and the Dead,* who demonstrated in that book that he is capable of looking fearlessly at all the details of contemporary reality, however ugly and even monstrous, also has something else on the ball. After an interval of three years Mailer's socialist novel, *Barbary Shore* (Rinehart, $3), has now appeared, and the rough hustle it is getting from the critics tells far more about them than it tells about the book itself.

They pretend to judge fiction solely by its stylistic merit and success of character delineation—"art for art's sake." But they are all well aware that the publications they write for have a political line, and their appreciation of literary art usually coincides with it. When a book with a different political slant comes along once in a while they get themselves in an uproar and find all kinds of fault with its style as well as its message.

They have become accustomed to applauding the pessimistic confessional revelations of ex-radicals like Koestler and all that superficial, smart aleck coterie who make a principle of disillusionment and capitulation. When a serious and honest writer like Mailer comes along and picks up the banner of socialist culture abandoned by the apostates, he surprises them like an unannounced and unwelcome intruder. They set upon him like a squad of bouncers in a high-toned saloon. In their fury they forget themselves and their critical manners and attack the political content of his book, disregarding the critical credo that the politics in a novel doesn't count, only the art.

Time magazine, that house of ill-fame where ex-radical literati display their fading charms, derides Mailer as the "Last of the Leftists" in a snotty review which summarizes the political content of his book and finds it entirely out of line with God, country and Henry Luce. The author "has a bad case of moral claustrophobia." *Barbary Shore* is "perched on the stilts of four fallacies." It "is hauled from the literary graveyard of the Thirties, when 'social consciousness' was in vogue." "It tries to pin the blame for human evil on the favorite villain of every park-bench anarchist, 'the system.'" Most of the other reviews I have read follow the same line. But naturally *Time,* the nation's pace-setter in intellectual debauchery, does the dirtiest job.

The Stalinist *Daily Worker,* for its part, joined in the general condemnation of *Barbary Shore*. "It is a bad book," says reviewer Robert Friedman, "so utterly, unbelievably bad, that even the capitalist critics must say so. And they say so regretfully, for Mailer has written a Trotskyite tract. . . ."

I read the reviews before I got a chance to read the book,

and they predisposed me in favor of it. If Mailer had succeeded in telling a good story with the underlying affirmation of the socialist ideal as a faith to live by, so that the ordinary man, for whom novels ought to be written, could read as he runs, I would be only too happy to praise and thank him for his accomplishment, as I do for his effort. But I cannot conscientiously do that. To my great disappointment, I found the book gravely defective in content and difficult in style. It is cast in cryptic, allegorical form that is very hard to follow without a map and compass. And his attempt to depict the revolutionary movement throws no light on the reality, for the reason that the author himself obviously does not see it and therefore cannot tell others what it looks like. Artistically, it seems to me, Mailer is playing around experimentally with uncommunicative literary forms. And politically, I cannot escape the painful conclusion that he doesn't know what he is talking about.

The whole scene of the novel is laid in a run-down Brooklyn rooming house with a cast of characters who, if I read the cryptic script correctly, are supposed to represent various segments of the socialist movement and the hostile forces impinging upon it. Michael Lovett, the narrator, is an ex-soldier who can't remember his past life, except in snatches. He is trying to write a novel in a sun-baked attic room. There is McLeod, an ex-Stalinist functionary who served on the GPU terror squad in Spain and has the blood of honest revolutionists on his hands. He has also switched sides and served the FBI. At the time we catch him in *Barbary Shore* he is dickering with an FBI agent over the surrender of a secret "little object," which he is trying to hold out, and which in the end turns out to be his "socialist conscience." Isn't that a hell of a thing for a GPU murderer to be carrying around in his pocket?

That is not credible, Mr. Mailer.

There is the FBI agent Hollingsworth, who has a room in the house and keeps working on McLeod, trying to third-degree him into the surrender of his "little object"—as if the FBI cares a hoot about anybody's conscience, revolutionary or otherwise, as long as he does their work. Next is a girl roomer, Lannie Madison, who is as crazy as a cuckoo and sexually abnormal. She talks ramblingly of "the man with the beard"—presumably Trotsky—to whom she introduced the assassin sent by "the man with the pipe"—presumably Stalin—and then, after the murder, went off her nut and is that way when we run across her in the book.

In addition, and vitally important to the story, is the landlady, a former burlesque queen, slightly faded, but still equipped with plenty of what the customers used to pay to see, and proud of it. She wants to be called only by her last name. "I was born Beverly Guinevere, but when I was on the stage, I just used to call myself Guinevere, you know one name, like Margo and Zorina." So Guinevere it is. She turns out to be the secret wife of McLeod.

And romping all over the house is their three-year-old daughter Monina—as precocious, shrewdly sophisticated, demanding and charming a little monster as I have ever encountered since my precious granddaughter bit my hand to make me open up and give her the lollypop I was holding out on her. I love that little Monina. And Guinevere is not too bad. Neither Guinevere nor Monina has any abstract ideas. That provides a little needed relief from the ever-lasting talk-talk-talk of the other characters who seem to have nothing else.

As for the revolutionary movement—the real movement—I don't see it here. This movement lives in great surging tides of people throughout the world—in the trade unions, parties, mass meetings, strikes, demonstrations and committees of housewives protesting high prices in the imperialist countries; in the prisons and forced labor camps of the Soviet Union and in the mighty upheavals of the colonial millions in the Orient—a movement often misled, often struggling blindly, but ever struggling and striving toward its destined goal just the same. The revolutionary movement lives in the smaller groups, sometimes in single individuals, who are the carriers of ideas which theorize the struggle and foresee its line of march—"represent the future of the movement in its present"—and aim to unify and coordinate it. All this, the real revolutionary movement, does not appear and is not even reflected in this book.

It looks to me as though Mailer is a good man fallen among screwballs, who have given him a bum steer about the revolutionary movement, what it is, and who represents it. I have been in the movement more than 40 years, man and boy, and I don't recognize it, nor any representation of it, cryptical, mystical, symbolical, or any other way, in the characters who talk in riddles all over Beverly Guinevere's rooming house. If this madhouse described in *Barbary Shore,* and the people who inhabit it and talk through all hours of the night, are the revolutionary movement, I am going to grab my hat and light out for a small community of simple people who work in the daytime and sleep at night, and settle down there for the rest of my natural life.

The supreme falsity of the book is its central character—McLeod. This ex-GPU agent and murderer turned FBI agent and informer—an easy enough transition, often made in real life—nevertheless balks at giving up his secret "little object," namely his "socialist conscience." He hands it over to Lovett, the narrator, on a slip of paper, as his last will and testament, shortly before Hollingsworth, impersonator of the FBI, bumps him off. This is no representative of "the heritage of socialist culture." When socialist culture becomes triumphant, one of the first acts of the victorious revolution will be to round up all such scoundrels as McLeod and try them for their crimes against socialism.

Guinevere, the most solid and real character in the story, is not troubled with any fancy ideas at all—nothing but what comes naturally, nothing but old-fashioned sex appeal without any ideological trimmings, which she flaunts around with an easy sense of power over all the intellectual characters in the house. The space allotted to her and her doings might be thought disproportionate in a novel of ideas. But her attraction which lures all of them—Lovett and Hollingsworth, as well as her dispossessed husband, McLeod, is meant to symbolize, I suppose, that men cannot live by ideas alone. The author may have a point there.

There is no doubt that *Time's* review was right in saying that Mailer's central theme in *Barbary Shore* is the vindication of socialist culture as the hope of mankind. But I do not recognize socialist culture in the character he depicts as its special representative, nor in any of the loquacious crackpots who live and talk their heads off in Guinevere's rooming house.

And finally, in my opinion, Mailer's great theme gets bad service from the cryptic and arty style of its presentation. It is not my intention to be disrespectful toward young artists who find it necessary for their self-expression to experiment with different forms, or to create new ones. But for the life of me I can't see any sense in incommunicativeness. I don't care for writing that has to be explained to me, or that I have to work at like a puzzle. Why can't writing explain itself? Time is fleeting, and the writer who wants to get attention from the general run of people should try to make it simple.

Mailer can do better than this. *The Naked and the Dead* stands as convincing proof. And I am sure he will do better when he recognizes that the defense of socialist culture, which he has undertaken, is a bigger subject than he knew and requires more profound study. Let him get out of the stagnant backwaters on the fringe of the great river and explore the main stream. Let him study and master his theme and return to its representation another time with the necessary equipment. And good luck to him, and thank him for the try.

The incident at Little Rock

THE MILITANT, JULY 9, 1951

When I get to Heaven I'm gonna put on my shoes,
And walk all over God's Heaven.

These words of exultant prophecy from the great Negro spiritual have come down the years from the time of chattel slavery in America. They expressed the longing and hope of the slave for a free and happy time in the hereafter when he would no longer be out of bounds wherever he might choose to go. The slave dreamed of a place of limitless expanse where he would be free to ramble. He called it "Heaven," and put his aspiration for it into the song of his own making. He would have shoes by right, like all the rest of God's children, and he would put them on and walk around wherever he pleased, walk all over God's Heaven.

The heirs of the slave would also like to arrive sometime at a place where there are no signs posted up to inform them that this and that section—always the nicest ones, of course—are reserved for white folks only, and no warning signals in blunter, more explicit terms: "Not for Colored!" or "Colored Keep Out!" Their hearts sick with hope deferred, the grandchildren of the slave still sing the old song of a hoped-for future with some freedom in it.

The worst thing, to my way of thinking, the most intolerable thing, for one who has a little wild blood in his veins, is to have no freedom, to be restricted and fenced in; to have no right to do what others do and to go where others go. I am not a colored man, and haven't begun to suffer a tenth part of the brutal discriminations and indignities which are the daily lot of the Negro people in our America which isn't Heaven yet for them—not by a long shot. But I know what freedom to walk around means to a man who hasn't got it, from my time in prison.

Ask any prisoner, in any jail, what he wants for Christmas, and he will probably tell you in a telescoped phrase: "The bars." By that he means, he wants the bars out of his way, so that he can get up and walk anywhere, and in whatever direction he pleases—"all over," as it says in the yearning spiritual. He will even take it in Heaven, if you can convince him there is such a place, which is doubtful. The poet Swinburne spoke of the "good things" of freedom, the "sweet food" of freedom. I thank the poet for these words and I believe in them. And if you care for the testimony of an ex-convict, the sweetest freedom of all is the freedom to come and go.

I can never be neutral in matters of this kind. My sympathies are with the prisoner, with the man deprived of freedom, every time. So any report of a convict trying to make a get-away, or a Negro claiming about 10 percent of natural rights and freedoms so long denied him and his fathers before him, is apt to attract my attention.

It was this predilection, I suppose, that drew my eye

to a small Associated Press dispatch tucked away among the advertisements on an inside back page of the *New York Post.* A religious colored man passed by a big Baptist revival in Little Rock, Arkansas the other day and heard the sounds of preaching and hymn-singing swelling out of the stadium, which had been properly consecrated and converted into a church for the occasion. Mistaking the stadium-church for the anteroom to the free and equal Heaven of his religious hope, he went in, and walked around, and finally sat down.

As the AP dispatch told the story: "Last night, Joseph Harris, a Negro, entered and took a vacant seat in a section reserved for white persons." And then there was hell to pay in that heavenly revival meeting of the Baptists at Little Rock, Ark. Joseph Harris wasn't in Heaven yet, or anywhere near it, and he soon found it out. "Two white ushers promptly notified him of the presence of Negro sections, but Harris was heard to shout, 'No, that is not my place.'"

The white Christians disagreed with him. "Members of the group dragged Harris from the seat and out an exit to a point under the stadium. There, several persons began choking Harris, said Most Stern, *Arkansas Gazette* reporter."

A couple of Little Rock pastors intervened, according to the AP dispatch. Dr. M. Ray McKay "urged his fellow Baptists to 'be Christians.'" Dr. W.O. Vaught, for his part in the Christianizing business, "led Harris away from the angry group, and escorted him to the speakers' platform. The Negro soon left quietly." This was probably the most sensible thing he could do, because it was beginning to look as though he was not wildly wanted in that white man's personal and exclusive communion with the Lord God Almighty.

I would like to make a few remarks about this incident

at Little Rock. First of all, I would like to say that I don't blame Joseph Harris for thinking he had a right to take any seat he chose in the public revival meeting. And I don't blame him and others for their religion and their aspiration for a Heaven where all are equal, even though I do not share their religious beliefs.

But deeply as I sympathize with Joseph Harris in the trouble he got into at the white men's revival meeting, I have to take exception to his attitude in one respect. The AP report says: "At the gate, he turned and thanked the ministers and said he would pray for the persons at the revival."

Hold on there, Mr. Harris. Aren't you going too far? I have no doubt you are a better Christian than the white Baptists who beat you up and threw you out of the tabernacle. But aren't you just a little bit too much of a Christian? I like some of the things the Carpenter of Nazareth is supposed to have said and done—his angry vigor in denouncing the money-changers and driving them out of the temple; his scorn for the high and mighty hypocrites, and his tolerant friendship and compassionate regard for lowly sinners. I am in favor of neighborly good will toward anyone who is halfway reasonable. I am even willing to agree to the forgiveness of trespasses—up to a certain point.

But I'll be damned if I'll say any prayers for people who are so low-down mean, so corrupt with prejudice, that they will deny a religious man, merely because of the color of his skin, the right to walk into a public revival meeting, and sit down in peace in any seat that is vacant, to listen to a preacher explain how we are all going to be equal in Heaven. I not only will not pray for them, when I see the way they run their church, I won't even believe that their Heaven will be different. Maybe that is Jim Crow too.

Could it be that the Lord God himself, whom the Baptists of Little Rock claimed to represent at their revival, is just another bigoted and prejudiced white man, who has Heaven all staked out, with the best places all reserved for white folks? Could it be that the colored people who get in—if they get in at all—have to keep on their own side of the railroad tracks and do their walking, just like on earth, in the dirty and ugly streets and alleys of a celestial slum? Will they have no right to "walk all over God's Heaven" after they get there?

The whole business looks like a bum deal to me, Mr. Harris. Maybe there is no Heaven, except the one we may create for ourselves. Maybe we had better get together—you and I and the likes of us, the freedom-loving, honest working people of all colors and nationalities—and take hold of the situation in this country and fix it up right. Make conditions fair and square for everybody—so that we can all be free and equal, and put on our shoes and walk all over a Heaven of our own, which we make for ourselves right here on this good green earth.

From Karl Marx to the Fourth of July

THE MILITANT, JULY 16, 1951

I'm a Fourth of July man from away back, and a great believer in fire crackers, picnics and brass bands to go with it. You can stop me any time and get me to listen to the glorious story of the greatness of our country and how and when it all got started. The continent we inhabit has been here longer than anyone knows—but as a nation, as an independent people, the darlings of destiny favored above all others, we date from the Declaration of Independence and the Fourth of July.

The representatives in Congress assembled 175 years ago were the great initiators. When they said: "We hold these truths to be self-evident," they started something that opened up a new era of promise for all mankind. That's what I am ready to celebrate any time the bands begin to play—the start and the promise. But nobody can sell me the Fourth of July speeches which represent the start as the finish and the promise as the fulfilment. I quit believing in them a long time ago. As soon as I grew old enough to look around and see what was going on in this country—all the inequality and injustice still remaining—the beneficiaries of privilege, claiming the heritage of our first revolution, struck me as imposters. I recognized the standard Fourth of July orators as phonies, as desecrators of a noble dream. They didn't look to me like the Liberty Boys of '76.

But that never turned me against the Fourth of July, as was the case with so many American radicals and revolutionists in the past. I thought the Fourth of July belonged to the people. I always regarded its renunciation as one of the biggest mistakes of American radicalism. It is wrong to confuse internationalism with anti-Americanism; to relinquish the revolutionary traditions of our country to the reactionaries; to let the modern workers' revolutionary movement, the legitimate heir of the men of 1776, appear as something foreign to our country.

That is why it did my heart good to see *The Militant* blossom out this year in a special Fourth of July issue, with its front page manifesto greeting the people of Asia, fighting for their national independence, in the name of our own revolution of 1776—and a whole page of special articles devoted to this revolution and its authentic leaders. The articles in this special issue are obviously the result of serious study and historical research. They throw new light on the most important features of the revolution which have long been obscured, and even deliberately hidden, to serve the special interests of the present-day Tories. These revelations put a powerful propaganda weapon into the hands of those who see in the coming revolution of the American workers not a negation, but a continuation and completion of the revolution for national independence of 175 years ago.

The authors of these remarkable articles were guided in their research by a theory which required them to look for the essential facts and to study them in their interrelationship. They sought to uncover the motive force of the class struggle—the key to the real understanding of all history. The theory which inspired the authors of these articles to study the first American revolution, and guided them in their work, is Marxism—which Congress and the courts would outlaw as a "foreign" doctrine, and the teaching of which in the schools is now virtually prohibited.

The procedure through which these articles in the Fourth of July issue of *The Militant* finally took shape is an interesting story in itself. They are the work of students in our party school of Marxism. We are committed to the proposition that the cadres of our party have a historical task to accomplish. That task is to organize and lead the coming revolution of the American working class. How better can one prepare to take effective part in such a colossal enterprise than to study the revolution out of which this nation was born? And how can one study revolutionary history seriously and profitably without the aid of the only revolutionary theory of history there is? That's our point of view anyway. And we are serious enough about it to take a group of our leading people of the younger generation out of everyday activity for six months every year to study the history of their country and this "foreign" doctrine which alone explains it.

You will never find two subjects which fit better together. Marx sketched the whole broad outline of American capitalism as it is today in advance of its development. In return for that, American capitalism in all its main features is the crowning proof of Marxism. Our students go to Marx to study America, and study America to verify Marx.

Marxism is a hundred years old, and has been refuted a thousand times by professorial pundits. Not satisfied with that, its opponents—who have far more than a scientific interest in the matter—continue to refute Marxism daily, weekly and monthly in all their publications and other mediums of misinformation and miseducation. Our students know all about that, and examine all the refutations conscientiously as part of their study of the doctrine itself. In the course of this examination and counter-examination they become real Marxists. They learn their doctrine thoroughly, and in learning they proceed to apply it. Marxism is not a dogma to be studied for its own sake, but a theory of social evolution and a guide to action in the class struggle. It is not a substitute for the knowledge of concrete reality, past and present, but a theoretical tool for its investigation and interpretation. Our students understand it that way. They went to Marx—and discovered America.

And that, in my opinion, is a very important discovery. We have nothing to do with jingoism, or any kind of vulgar national conceit and arrogance. We are internationalists, and we know very well that our fate is bound up with that of the rest of the world. The revolution which will transform society and bring in the socialist order is a world-wide affair, a task requiring international cooperation to which we contribute only a part. But our part in this international cooperation is the revolution here at home. We must attend to that, study it and know it. And we can't do that properly unless we know our country and its history and traditions. They are, for the greater part, good. The country itself is good, and so are the great majority of the people in it. Their achievements are many and great. There is nothing really wrong with the U.S.A. except that the wrong people have usurped control of it and are running it into the ditch.

The cure for that is not to throw away the country and its traditions, but to get rid of the usurpers by the process popularized by our forefathers under the name of revolution. This new revolution will have to complete the work started by the men of 1776. They secured the nation's independence. The Second American Revolution of the Sixties, known as the Civil War, smashed the system of chattel slavery, unified the country and opened the way for its unobstructed industrial development. The task of the Third American Revolution is to take this great industrial machine out of the hands of a parasitical clique who operate it for their own benefit, and operate it for the benefit of all.

That's the general idea. But it is not quite as simple as it sounds. There are complications and complexities. The workers have to make their way through a jungle of traps and deceptions. They need a map and a compass. They need a generalization of the experiences of the past and a theoretical guiding line for the future. That's what Marxism is. The American workers will come to Marx, and with him they will be invincible. "Marx will become the mentor of the advanced American workers," said Trotsky. We have the same opinion, and we are working to realize it.

Karl Marx, the German Jew, who lived and worked out his profound theory in England, is native to all countries.

The supreme analyst of capitalism is most of all at home in the United States where the development of capitalism has reached its apogee. Marx will help the American workers to know their country, and to change it and make it really their own.

The Stalinist ideology

1. Back in the packing house

THE MILITANT, JULY 23, 1951

At hog-killing time in the frosty fall down on the farm, the neighbors gathered from miles around to help in the cooperative labor of converting the live animal into food for humans. Plump hams and lean-streaked slabs of bacon were made ready for the smoke house. Thick sections of flabby fat back were salted down in stout oaken barrels against the time when they would finally come to rest in a simmering pot on a bed of dandelion greens; the two ingredients slowly melting and merging in a liquor of delectable flavor elsewhere unknown this side of paradise. Fresh pork chops, loin roasts and succulent spare ribs were chopped out of the carcass for immediate consumption, all hands present getting a crack at them in a big feast on the spot, and a bundle to take home, while the various odds and ends were ground up for head cheese and sausage. But with all that utilization of diverse parts, quite a bit of the butchered pig was wasted and thrown away.

I was never down on the farm, and this account of

amateur hog-butchering there is based on hear say and imagination. However, I did work in a big Kansas City packing house when I was a boy—in two of them, in fact, Swift's and Armour's. Part of the time I worked on the "hog beds," as they were called, and I remember the process pretty well. It was not a job for the finical—I can tell you that from experience; but it was supremely economical and efficient. There was no waste. They made use of all parts of what once had been a pig, even the bristles, tails and snouts; everything, as they used to say, except the squeal.

I was thinking of this long-gone experience on a tired Friday afternoon last week when I finally got through with the last of eight chapters on the peace campaign of the Stalinists, now running as a separate series on another page of this paper. I finished the messy and most distasteful task which had been assigned to me, with a feeling of relief and satisfaction. But there was a fly in my ointment, or maybe it was a cinder in my eye. Anyhow, I knew there was something amiss. I had to admit to myself, as an old packing-house man, that in confining the pamphlet to the limited theme of the peace campaign, I hadn't been able to use all the stuff I started out to work on. The left-over notes and reference material were piled all over my desk and I didn't know what to do with them. Of course, I might have thrown them away. But then, again, I might have done that with the whole litter of unwholesome reports and speeches in the first place and come out with cleaner hands and a more agreeable smell in my nostrils.

I hadn't done that. I had finished the main job, but there they were—the left-overs. And while my hands were still soiled with the muck and filth of the material I had been working on, I was confronted with a problem. Should I clean up, and report the assignment finished, or should

I go back to work and process the remnants? I solved the problem once, but lapsing into the habit of lackadaisical people who don't know their minds, I didn't solve it for good and had to come back to it. Instead of throwing all the leftover material into the waste basket and forgetting about it, I just dumped it into a drawer and went off for a week end in the fresh, clean country among friends and comrades to match. But I kept thinking of the ugly odds and ends I had left behind.

Conscience, that pestiferous little monster, kept at me with deprecating looks and nagging reminders. "You didn't finish your duty," said the intolerant and uncompromising imp from Satan's domain. "What about Gus Hall's summary speech, with all the repulsive characteristics of a Stalinist functionary sticking out of his answer to a delegate who had ventured to express an opinion? There is an education in the democratic process and the true function of leadership in a dissection of that episode alone. And what about Betty Gannett's 'ideological report' with its unconscious exemplification of what Stalinist ideology really is, and other revealing aspects of the convention proceedings? Are you going to let all that pass and scamp your task now, while you have all the material before you in one mass for the first time in years? Are you a Bolshevik who does a thorough job when it is assigned to him, or a weak-willed Menshevik who does his work as he does everything else—halfway, because that is his nature? In other words, are you a man or a mouse. Think it over." So spoke the voice of conscience.

Well, I thought it over and here I am on Monday morning back in the packing house again. I am sorting out the oozy remnants and scraps of material left over from my pamphlet on the Stalinist peace campaign, resolved to use them, too, in some kind of by-products of the main enterprise before I finally finish up the lousy job for good and go fishing.

One of the leftovers is Betty Gannett's report on "ideology." There is a lot more of the real ideology of Stalinism in this report than she knew. We'll take a look at it next week.

2. The art of lying

THE MILITANT, JULY 30, 1951

The Stalinists didn't invent the art of lying, but they expanded and developed it into a philosophy and a way of life. In that curious lingo of Stalinism, by which they communicate among themselves and with others who are properly conditioned, this philosophy and way of life goes by the name of "ideology." The Stalinists have discovered that the human brain is a delicately sensitive organ, easily affected for good or ill, depending on what hits it first and hardest, and susceptible to befuddlement as well as to enlightenment. The brain may be knocked into malfunctioning by blows of a club; and virtually the same effect can sometimes be achieved by the steady bombardment of propaganda disguised as instruction or indoctrination. The Stalinists know this and work at it.

The main feature of the business is the recourse to assertions and pronouncements which, like the revelations from the papal throne of the Catholic Church, are not subject to doubt or investigation. The believers are supposed to take the stuff as it is dished out without examination, inquiry or demands for proof.

A Stalinist operator, skilled and practiced in this indoctrination technique, is Betty Gannett, who delivered the report on "Ideological Tasks" at the Fifteenth National Convention of the Communist Party, U.S.A.—the proceedings of which, insofar as they relate to the theme of peace, are now under review on another page.* She laid down the line on what it was necessary for the faithful to believe and repeat on other matters also. And like all other reporters to the Fifteenth Convention—or any other Stalinist convention, for that matter—her pronouncements were unanimously approved by the assembled delegates. That's what they were there for.

One of the things the delegates were instructed by the reporter to believe and propagate to the multitude was that democracy is growing and flourishing in the Soviet Union, crowding out everything else, it seems, like crab grass in a lawn. Another instruction was the desirability and necessity of loving and admiring Stalin. There were other commands, but these two in particular leaped out of the report and hit me in the eye. Being a heathen and public sinner, however, with an inquiring mind and a fancy for evidence to support assertions, I am not bound to take her say-so. I want the privilege of asking questions and I want further information, which I suppose I will have to supply myself.

You may have heard whispers to the contrary, but Betty Gannett states categorically that Stalinist party members must believe in and explain "the profound and pervasive democracy in the Soviet Union; the participation of the ordinary man and woman in government; how elections are carried through; how local Soviets function—in order to give the lie to the charge of 'totalitarianism.'"

Just a moment, please. Let's have some detailed amplification on this point. I am interested in democracy, and profoundly believe in it as the mechanism by which the

---

* Published in the pamphlet, *The Road to Peace*. Pioneer Publishers, New York, N.Y.

masses will organize the victorious struggle for their own emancipation from capitalism. I further believe that only by direct participation can the masses work out and solve the many and complex problems of the transition period after the proletarian revolution.

Just how is "the participation of the ordinary man and woman in government" manifested in the Soviet Union to-day? Do they have the right of free speech, free press, and free assembly, the prerequisites of free democratic action? They do not. Betty Gannett knows, what everybody else knows by this time, that all the talking in the Soviet Union is done by the ruling bureaucrats; and that all the newspapers and other mediums of information and communication are controlled by them. She knows, also, that the only time the Russian workers ever get a chance to assemble is when they are called together to vote for resolutions and decisions made in advance and handed down by the same ruling bureaucrats. No, there is not a particle of free speech, free press or free assembly in the Soviet Union. Therefore there is no democracy, "pervasive" or otherwise. Everybody knows this, and anybody who says otherwise is a liar by the clock.

The report of Betty Gannett demanded that people be enlightened on "how elections are carried through in the Soviet Union." That's a hot one. Just how are they carried through? The reporter didn't tell us that, so I'll tell her. Everybody has the right to vote for Stalin and the rest of the slate of bureaucrats selected in advance. But suppose someone wants to vote for another slate. Or better, suppose some group wants to form a separate party and put up its own slate of candidates. How do they go about it?

I have been a friend and supporter of the Russian Revolution since 1917, and still am. I have comrades in the Soviet Union who are formed into an opposition party—the

Russian Section of the Fourth International. It is an honest and revolutionary party, profoundly devoted to the October Revolution and the defender of its heritage. Soviet democracy was one of the first planks in the platform of their long, heroic struggle. But these honest revolutionists are all in prison; that is, those who have not been murdered for demanding some of this "pervasive democracy" which Betty Gannett speaks of with such cynical falsity in her report to the CP convention. All other groups who tried to speak out against the defamation and betrayal of the Revolution and the suppression of democracy suffered the same fate. The martyred victims of Stalin's "profound and pervasive democracy" number millions in the Soviet Union.

The convention reporter on "ideology" instructed the delegates to "give the lie to the charge of 'totalitarianism.'" She said, "analysis and data should be furnished" on this "pervasive democracy" and other subjects. But she neglected to furnish any of the data, or even to suggest what such material would look like and where it could be found. In case any of the delegates, and party members or sympathizers to whom they relayed the convention instructions, are interested in this specific information, there are two ways to discover it. One is to read the numerous volumes of former beneficiaries of everything "pervasive" in Stalin's domain who have escaped and lived to tell the story; the other is to make a personal investigation.

If you doubt the unanimous testimony of all who have escaped from Stalin's torture chambers and forced labor camps, just take a trip to the Soviet Union and see for yourself. If you get in and look around and ask questions, I can guarantee you—on the basis of the experiences of thousands of others who went to the Soviet Union as devoted supporters of the regime, as it had been represented to them by all the Fosters, Gus Halls and Betty Gannetts—you will see all the democracy there is to see; all there is to see, that is, through the bars of prisons or over the gun towers of the forced labor camps, where at least 10 to 15 million work, suffer, starve and die without recourse, without any attention to their cries.

If, by keeping your mouth shut and your eyes closed, you escape prisons and concentration camps and enjoy the life of a free worker in the Soviet Union as it is operated under Stalinism, you will get a good chance to find out through personal experience what is really going on there. You can't miss the ubiquitous police terror penetrating into every corner of the people's lives. You will carry a "work card" on which every tardiness or absence from work or any little dereliction, real or cooked up by the foreman, is noted, marking you for punishment and discrimination in any factory wherever you may work thereafter.

You will learn about passports—not for foreign travel, for that is forbidden to Soviet citizens except bureaucrats on official business—but *internal* passports necessary for the individual worker merely to travel from one town to another, one of the most hated regulations of the old Czarist regime. You will discover "trade unions" whose function is to speed up production, but which have nothing to do with negotiating wage scales and adjusting grievances.

I merely offer this suggestion, that curious Stalinist party members and fellow-travelers make a personal investigation of this "pervasive democracy" which Betty Gannett demanded they should advertize far and wide. But I don't expect any of them to take up the suggestion. They purposely blind themselves to a lot of things, but deep down they know more than they pretend to. They prefer to talk up the glories of the Stalinist regime in the Soviet Union from a distance.

The truth is becoming too well known for anybody in his right senses to take chances on investigating it at close range. The percentage of reckless adventurers who want to verify the facts of the situation by personal observation and experience is decreasing to the vanishing point. The curiosity about "democracy in the Soviet Union" is not as "pervasive" as it used to be. It will take a lot of "ideological campaigns" to change that. You can score this as a victory for truth over Stalinist "ideologists" and their lies.

3. The importance of loving Stalin

THE MILITANT, AUGUST 6, 1951

Reporting on "Ideological Tasks" at the Fifteenth Convention of the American Communist Party, Betty Gannett examined the situation in the party ranks and found it serious, if not dangerous. It seems there are some weak spots through which enemy counter-propaganda is making its way like flood water seeping through the cracks in a dike. She calls for an ideological sandbag brigade to seal up the leaks. She notes that this subversive propaganda is directed not only at the USSR, but also—and this is where undue familiarity becomes intolerable impudence—at "its great leader, Stalin."

"It should be of great concern to us," says the reporter, "that these Trotskyite-Titoite slanders at times find subtle expression even in our own ranks. Thus, a comrade here and there will fall prey to the lying contention about the 'deification' of Stalin, and the slander-propaganda with which the anti-Sovieters seek to conceal the profound love and admiration of the Soviet people for the great leader of the land of socialism."

Such an attitude toward "the brilliant successor of Lenin," who, all party members are required to believe, "is loved and revered by the hundreds of millions of ordinary people throughout the entire world"—to say nothing of the 10 million or more Soviet citizens in forced labor camps, and the rest of the police-ridden working population of the USSR with their "work cards" and internal passports, who are simply nuts about Stalin—this irreverent attitude must be knocked down. And the culprits through whose ignorance or negligence this attitude finds "subtle expression even in our own ranks" must be named and called to order.

Two sleeping sentinels who allowed this deviation to pass through the lines are singled out for special mention as horrible examples. One of them is a writer on *The Daily People's World,* a Stalinist organ published in San Francisco, by the name of Nat Low. And the other culprit—this is self-criticism *in excelsis*—is none other than the reporter herself, Betty Gannett. She admits having been negligent in her duty to admire Stalin in one respect on one particular occasion, and she seeks restoration to Stalinist normality through the catharsis of public confession.

This Nat Low is a dirty dog who had the unspeakable nerve to criticize George Bernard Shaw for once having expressed the opinion that "Stalin is the greatest statesman in the world." That, Low had said, reveals Shaw's "obsession with the Great Man idea." But Low is not going to get away with that kind of "capitulation to this slander" of the Trotskyites-Titoites and other criminal underestimators of the loved and revered Stalin, if Betty Gannett can stop him, and she thinks she can. She goes to work on the errant columnist-capitulator with the favorite instrument of Stalinist surgery—the hatchet. "What place," she demands, "has such an 'evaluation' in a Marxist newspaper?" She formally declares, *ex cathedra,* that "Low the Marxist does not understand what apparently Shaw the Fabian grasped, that there is no antagonism between leadership and the people in a socialist society."

That settled the case of Nat Low, this shameless "evaluater" who obviously doesn't know right from wrong. There is nothing more to be said. The matter has been disposed of by an official pronouncement, and "the rest is silence," to shift the quotation marks from Gannett to Shakespeare. True, there is no real argument advanced. No uncontested facts are adduced, no proofs are offered. No allowance is made for a difference of opinion about Stalin and Shaw's estimate of him. And as a matter of course, nothing is heard from Nat Low in his own defence. His deviation has been outlawed by assertion, by pronouncement. That is the Stalinist method of indoctrination. That is Stalinist ideology rammed down your throat. You can choke on it, but if you want to stay in the Communist Party you can't talk back.

Betty Gannett's own error, which she confesses with the wholehearted abandon of an exhibitionist-convert at a revival meeting, was somewhat different from Low's. It was far less serious, it would appear at first glance, and the ordinary person with a tolerance for human peccadilloes might not even notice it. But the convention reporter couldn't rest until she got it off her chest.

What had Betty Gannett done that impelled her to flop down on the convention floor in grovelling repentance? She hadn't failed to love Stalin—God forbid!—but she had slipped up on another obligation which all well-behaved American flunkeys owe to the Moscow boss. You can believe it or not, but Betty Gannett, a ranking hatchet-woman in the camarilla of Stalinist functionaries, and a convention reporter in charge of ideology at that, failed on one dreadful occasion to pay the required tribute to Stalin's literary style—that special method of putting words together, peculiar and individual to Stalin, which Trotsky once said affected the reader like a mouthful of chopped-up bristles.

She had showed lack of "vigilance," she said, "in an issue of the pre-Convention discussion bulletin, when the editorial committee, and I, a committee member assigned to compile the contributions, allowed to be printed without comment an article on 'simplicity of language' which conspicuously omitted the name of Stalin." Mark that down in your book, if you are thinking of joining the Stalinist party, so you won't forget that your requirement to "love and admire" Stalin includes also his literary productions. For, says Gannett, "Stalin above everyone else has presented the most complex theoretical propositions with a mastery, simplicity, clarity and power." Didn't you know that? Well, you'd better start learning, lest you too become guilty of the fatal omission which Betty Gannett fell into, in a moment of weakness and forgetfulness, under the pressure of "Trotskyite-Titoite slanders" about the "deification" of Stalin.

The merits of Stalin's literary style are at best debatable—a "moot point," as the lawyers say—and I can get you plenty of critics who will take the negative. But that doesn't faze Betty Gannett, who follows one straight line from politics to art. "Who," she asks—"who can ever forget the great lesson of linkage to the people which Stalin presented for us, in the symbol of Antaeus which he drew from Greek mythology?"

Well, to tell you the God's truth, Betty, I not only forgot that Stalin has presented the symbol of Antaeus to us; I didn't even know he had done it in the first place. I have read references to the mythical story of the giant who drew his strength from the earth in the writings of so many others that the symbol has become rather trite. But I'll be a long time forgetting your reminder that Stalin showed the genius of his originality by "presenting" it also.

And every time I think of Stalin I'll think of Antaeus and remember that he was finally finished off by Hercules. Could this victorious Hercules stand as a symbol of the revolutionary working class catching up with Stalin and all his gang of corrupt and crooked functionaries, and dealing out to them the fate of Antaeus? I think so, and I hope with all my heart it will not be long delayed.

4. The bureaucratic mentality

THE MILITANT, AUGUST 13, 1951

Uncontrolled power, the goal to which all bureaucrats and authoritarians instinctively strive, has reached its apogee in the Soviet Union under the Stalin regime, with all the evil consequences inherent in this abnormality. Where there is no freedom of criticism, no free play of idea, the healthy and wholesome process of collective thought is crowded out to make way for the reciprocal corruptions of arbitrariness and subservience. There is inhuman disregard of the rights and opinions of others on the one side, and abdication of the intellect on the other.

The ruling bureaucrats, who are the carriers of this corruption, are also its victims. Their minds become irremediably diseased, and their fatal sickness is infallibly expressed in their mental processes and their manner of expressing them. In the vast domain of Stalinism where all critics and opponents of the regime are in prison or dead, or condemned to silence by police terror, all the ruling bureaucrats have developed a single, uniform method and style of speaking and writing. This official language dispenses with any effort to enlighten, convince and persuade. It rests solely on assertions and pronouncements which settle all questions—from economics and politics to art and linguistics.

When nobody has a chance to answer back, you can get away with anything. That's the way it is in the Soviet Union at present. And this system, along with the method of thinking and the style of expression that goes with it at the Russian springhead, flows down through all the functionary cadres of the national parties of international Stalinism like a polluted stream, turning everything it touches into filth.

In the Soviet Union it is horrible and degrading—all the more so because the power behind it is absolute from one end of the country to another. It is no less horrible and degrading in the Communist Party of the U.S., where the same practices are faithfully imitated. But it is also somewhat ludicrous. Here the will of the feeble functionaries is present, but the power to proscribe is strictly limited to the dwindling ranks of an isolated and demoralized party. Unbelievers, like myself, are free to snicker at their clownish absurdities, and cheerfully do so.

The National Secretary of the American Stalinist party, strutting over the platform in imitation of an all-powerful Soviet bureaucrat laying down the line, resembles a rickety dead-end kid limping around in a marshal's uniform with a sword too heavy for him to lift and a pistol he can't shoot. The will is there, the expressions and the gestures—everything except the power. And if you want my opinion, that's a good thing for this country and its working people.

If you plow through the dreary field of the convention report, as I did in the line of duty, in the hope of turning up some evidence of collective thinking—some contributions, amendments, criticisms or suggestions from the assembled delegates—you will not find it. This so-called report of the Fifteenth Convention Proceedings, bulky in volume as it is, is exclusively a collection of the reports given *to* the convention by the various official functionaries. There is no record of what, if anything, the delegates had to say about the report.

For this kind of information you have to read between the lines of Secretary Gus Hall's summary speech in answer to criticisms. And that's quite a guessing game, for the critics are answered but not quoted. It is not even clear whether the critics were present and spoke at the convention, or had just been running loose in the party, surreptitiously dropping remarks out of the corners of their mouths. The latter was probably the case, for Hall's strictures seem, by internal evidence, to be aimed at absentees from the convention who were destined soon to be absent from the party.

"You know," said Hall, apparently to nobody's surprise, "around the country, in almost all the states, there is a core of comrades around the Party that I will call 'the disgruntled type.'" Obviously something has to be done about that, for there is no provision in Stalinist jurisprudence, as practiced in the Soviet Union, for people to be disgruntled and stay out of prison or a forced labor camp. The means for this healthy corrective being lacking in the United States, Hall reached for the best substitute he could find. He did not suggest that the disgruntled people be invited to formulate their criticisms and have a fair discussion of them in the party ranks. And it never entered his thick bureaucratic skull to point out that a convention where dissatisfied party members had no voice was a mockery of workers' democracy. It never occurred to him to propose a real convention where they would be represented as a minority with full provision to air their grievances. It seems there has been too much tolerance and too much talk already.

Hall's proposal was a short cut to wind up the disagreeable business. "I think," he said, "that we must talk to these comrades in a different vein than we have until now. . . . We must tell these comrades, 'if you are sincere, if you want to help the Party and you have some beefs, come up to the Party leadership and discuss them!'" But what if the "disgruntled" are against "the Party leadership"? Suppose they want to throw them out, not to "come up" to them and talk things over? Hall never even considered that possibility. There is no place for such "beefs" in Stalinist practice. "In this period especially," said Hall in winding up his remarks on this point with the finality of Stalinist wisdom, "we cannot have a liberal approach to such an influence." That ought to satisfy everybody—except the "disgruntled" whose existence was never provided for in the first place.

Reading between the lines of Hall's summary speech, I gather that one disgruntled party member did actually get into the convention and make a speech there. Just how this happened, if it really happened, is not explained. Perhaps there was some slip-up in the apparatus somewhere along the line; with the best will in the world, air-tight perfection is hard to get in these matters. Anyhow, some fellow, whose speech is not printed, seems to have said something which Hall refers to as "the Davidow controversy and the struggle against liquidationism."

Just what Davidow was beefing about we can only surmise from Hall's references to his blasphemous assertion—quoted by Hall—that "the party has watered down the Marxist-Leninist concept of Party membership" and his complaint that "there are loose organizational concepts within the party." Hall's cavalier treatment of this episode doesn't throw much light on the content or merit of Davidow's "controversy," but it can stand as a first class illustration of bureaucratic polemic and pedagogy. "In Comrade Davidow's speech there was a strong element of shadow-boxing." He is wrong because "the party has not lowered or watered down the standards of membership since the 1945 Convention."

As for his beef about "loose organizational concepts," he obviously doesn't know what he is talking about. "Comrade Davidow sets up another straw man." Loose organizational concepts, or loose anything else, simply do not exist outside Davidow's imagination. "Which? Where? . . . I do not think so," says Hall. That ends the argument. All that remains, before passing on to the next point, is a brief, and absolutely unanswerable, suggestion to the critic on proper procedure: "I think it would be much better for Comrade Davidow, in a self-critical manner, to examine his wrong view without rationalization and shadow-boxing, and come to the conclusion that the Party position is correct, and proceed from there."

That's all for Davidow, the lone dissenter obliquely reported as possibly present at the convention by references in Hall's speech. His complaints are answered in exactly the same way as all other questions are dealt with in Hall's speech, and in all the other speeches which roll off the bureaucratic assembly line—by denials, assertions and pronouncements. That is the way the bureaucratic mind works, and they don't even know that there is anything wrong with it. What's wrong with it is everything.

5. The revolutionist and the bureaucrat

THE MILITANT, AUGUST 20, 1954

There is good sense in the old saying that two heads are better than one. The same thought can be profitably extended into the conception that the collective thinking of many, freely expressed, can yield better results in the long run than the arbitrary and capricious decisions of an individual who decides and rules without control or restraint. This is the argument for the practical efficiency of democracy in general, and in the workers' movement in particular.

It is true that democracy is a rather cumbersome process, while bureaucratic short cuts seem to "get things done" without delay. But the trouble is that things done this way are often done wrong. And without the corrective restraint of democracy there is no way of righting them; one error leads to another, and things go from bad to worse, to the detriment of the people whose interests are directly involved. This is the evil story of all uncontrolled bureaucracies—in trade unions, parties or governments.

The great teachers of the working class knew all about this. They were dead set against bureaucratism—every one of them. They were confirmed democrats. I don't mean democrats in the sense of that fraudulent "democracy" by the mechanism of which the masses of the people have the illusion of deciding the conduct of affairs by voting for hand-picked candidates every two or four years; while all the mediums of information and communication which remain in the hands of a small clique of money-sharks, who own all the industries and rule the country behind the parliamentary façade. No, our teachers scornfully exposed and denounced the fraud and deceit and general skulduggery of bourgeois "democratic" politics. They were democrats in the real sense of the word. They maintained that the people should freely discuss and participate in deciding all matters of the general welfare which concerned them—their methods and conditions of work, the affairs of their own organizations, and the government.

Marx and Engels proclaimed that "The emancipation of

the working class must be the act of the workers themselves."

From this profound thought, it necessarily followed that the workers would have to create their own organizations of combat and run them themselves. When the founders of scientific socialism said the workers must emancipate themselves, they meant that nobody would do it for them, and nobody could. The same holds true for their organizations, the instruments of struggle for emancipation. If they are really to serve their purpose, these organizations must belong to the workers and be democratically operated and controlled by them. Nobody can do it for them. So thought the great democrats, Marx and Engels.

The successors of Marx and Engels—Lenin and Trotsky—who executed their testament as leaders of the great Russian Revolution, acted in the spirit of the masters. Lenin outlined the perspective of a really democratic workers' state where "every cook" would learn to take part in the administration of public affairs. Trotsky began his great struggle against the bureaucratic degeneration of the Russian Revolution with the demand for the restoration of Soviet democracy. Genuine democracy is profoundly revolutionary, and all four of our revolutionary teachers—the masters, Marx and Engels and the great disciples, Lenin and Trotsky—were genuine democrats.

Indeed, if you take the trouble to consider the question theoretically and read the history of revolutions in search of what really happened, it becomes clear that the great revolutionists were democrats precisely because they were revolutionists. They had to be democrats in order to organize and lead revolutions. Social revolutions are made by the masses; their independent action is just what social revolution is, in Trotsky's classic definition. When the masses rise up out of passivity and acquiescence, and intervene in events and decide them—that is the time of revolution.

The conception of Marx and Engels, which was shared by their great disciples, that the workers must emancipate themselves, determined their approach to the masses and their attitude toward them. They were in no way disposed to "order" revolutions, as many superficial writers have said and some ignorant people have believed, if for no other reason than that they knew it could not be done that way. Their task, as Marx and Engels explained it, and as Lenin and Trotsky carried it out in practice to a superlative degree, was to bring the element of socialist consciousness into the labor movement; to organize and lead it, but in no case to try to substitute themselves for it. All their writings are permeated with this conception and this practice. They do not give orders to the masses. They inform, they enlighten. They try to explain and persuade. Reading them you can learn. That is why their writings remain ever fresh and new, the greatest treasure of the new revolutionary generation—the heritage of a hundred years of socialist culture.

The bureaucrats are the opposite of all that, and the polar difference sticks out of all their writings and utterances. There is nothing revolutionary about the bureaucrats. They fear the masses and distrust them and are always swept aside during periods of upsurge. Only when the masses quiet down do the bureaucrats have their day—the gray people of the ebb tide. You see this manifested in all workers' organizations in all mutations of the class struggle, from strikes to revolutions, and from trade unions to the organs of state power.

Stalinism, the supreme example in all history of a labor bureaucracy swollen to monstrous proportions, and multiplying in themselves all the negative traits of the ordinary conservative labor skate, who is their blood kin and lacks only their opportunity and their power—Stalinism is the most misunderstood phenomenon of our time. Most ludicrous of all is the widespread impression that these representatives of reaction and stranglers of revolutions are secretly plotting revolution on a world-wide scale. Just mention the word Stalinism to Social Democrats, for example, who fear revolution for their own reasons, and they take to the cyclone cellars on the double, scared out of their livers and their lights. The United States Government recently convicted 11 functionaries of American Stalinism for "advocating" and representing a "clear and present danger" of revolution, and the Supreme Court has upheld the verdict. This is a combination of misunderstanding and frame-up.

The proletarian revolutionist is one thing and the Stalinist functionary is another. They are not only different in their aims and purposes. There is a profound difference in their mentalities and in their methods of expressing them. The revolutionist is a democrat, organizing opposition to the power of the present day, and striving to create a new power of the people. The functionary is merely a bureaucrat, always and everywhere serving an existing power.

The revolutionist is a thoroughgoing radical and is personally disinterested; he wants to change the social order in the interest of all, and considers it beneath his dignity to seek personal advantage. The bureaucrat, in all organizations, and under all conditions, is profoundly conservative and meanly selfish; he strives to preserve the *status quo* in the interest of his privileges.

The revolutionist trusts the masses because they are the makers of revolutions. The bureaucrat fears them for the same reason. The bureaucrat gives orders like a policeman. The revolutionist tries to explain things like a teacher. The bureaucrat lies to the people. The revolutionist believes the truth will make them free, and tells it.

The importance of justice

1. Speaking of trials and confessions

THE MILITANT, AUGUST 27, 1951

American newspapermen, who are known for their capacity to report the troubles of others, however grievous, with objective detachment, are showing more than a casual interest in some troubles of their own that have come up in Czechoslovakia. William N. Oatis, correspondent of the Associated Press in Czechoslovakia, was arrested on a charge of espionage, and after a short imprisonment, was brought into court where he confessed and was sentenced to 10 years' imprisonment.

There have been other cases of this kind, and the imperturbable journalists managed to take them all in their stride. They calmly reported such facts as they found and thought worthy of notice, without intruding any personal opinions. But in their accounts and comments on the case of Oatis, they strike the emotional note of partisans. They are disturbed about the fate of their colleague, and they want something done about it. This, they seem to be saying, is going too far. This trial of Oatis involves us; it involves everybody.

Similarly, a short time ago the case of Cardinal Mindszenty started the Catholic hierarchy in the United States off on a holy crusade for justice and fair play, with Cardinal

Spellman, the bull-necked proconsul of the Roman pope, bellowing in the lead. Their fellow prelate, they said—whenever they caught their breath—had been falsely accused of crimes to which he had falsely confessed. These sons of the Holy Inquisition protested with excited violence against such an outrage, as though they had made a sudden discovery of something that had never happened before. The trial of Mindszenty is our trial, they said; the case of Mindszenty is everybody's case.

In the same way, American businessmen discovered hitherto unsuspected capacities for moral indignation within their own breasts, when William Vogeler had his turn in a Stalinist court in Hungary. They also protested in the name of justice. They contended that the affair of Vogeler is everybody's affair. To be sure, their concern for justice was somewhat belated, and did not occur until a member of their own community was directly involved. But late converts often make up for their tardiness by excessive zeal.

Apparently they all have just discovered the importance of justice. But it has been needing defense for a long time. The right of each and every individual under accusation, whoever he may be, to a fair trial and an honest verdict has been brutally violated many times in many places. Crimes against justice have not been confined to any one country or social regime. For 15 years now the whole world has known that justice has no dwelling place in the domain of Stalin. The Moscow Trials of 1936–1937 revealed for all to see, the main features of the standardized juridical technique of Stalinism—the staged trial, the frame-up and the false confession.

Nobody among the better people got excited about it as long as honest revolutionists or pure and simple scapegoats were the defendants in the dock. Show trials of this sort, usually culminating in the summary execution of the victims, evoked neither surprise nor protest from the editorial and ecclesiastical keepers of morals in the countries of Western civilization. Their concern for justice for its own sake, for any man whatever, was sound asleep in these cases. They didn't bother to inquire whether the victims were innocent or guilty. They didn't care.

The novelty of this monstrous business in the USSR wore off a long time ago. Even the extension of the system of frame-ups and forced confessions to the countries occupied or controlled by the Kremlin, was accepted as a matter of course. But, if one is to judge by the present trend of public opinion, as it is currently being manufactured, things are different now. It seems that even in matters of justice and morals, it makes a difference whose ox is gored. When representatives of Western culture were caught in the steel net of the Stalinist police state, it became Page One news. Pulpits and editorial pages barked like angry guns. Diplomatic intervention by Washington followed right away, and restrictive economic measures have already been taken in retaliation. Even conventions of merchants and manufacturers—for the first time in their existence—put justice on the agenda, and adopted resolutions in favor of it.

The immorality of the Stalinists, it would appear, consists in the fact that they don't know how to put reasonable and proper limits on their perversions of justice. They think frame-ups and fake confessions are good enough for everybody, and are proceeding accordingly. They are now persecuting and framing up the wrong people, and extracting confessions from them. No social category is spared.

Just consider again some of their latest victims. A prince of the Holy Roman Catholic Church is brought into court, after some months of "conditioning" in solitary confinement.

There he confesses to specified offenses, ranging from the high crime of treason to the petty misdemeanor of mean and sordid speculation in the black market for personal gain. Going still higher in the scale of human personality, the Stalinist gang in Hungary dared to lay hands on an American businessman, a vice-president of the American Telephone and Telegraph Company. They got a confession out of him too. And now, worst of all, as this is written, no less a man than the correspondent of the sacrosanct Associated Press of the United States has been arrested on a charge of spying and dragged into court at Prague. He also confessed.

Confessions, all patterned to fit the current political requirements of the ruling Stalinists, are rolling out of the courtrooms in the eastern European countries like identical automobiles from a Detroit assembly line. They are the same kind of confessions as those made by other victims of the Stalinist police system before Mindszenty, Vogeler and Oatis, and the methods of extracting them were very probably the same as those used against the others. Everything is just about the same except the public reaction in the United States. That is what is new and different.

There is no nonchalance in the report and discussion of these new confessions. There is no indifference to the fate of the victims. Far from it. The noble ideal of justice, sadly neglected in the consideration of other cases with other victims, steps forth now in the flesh and blood of a different kind of people. There is a hullabaloo and a hue and cry; and a widespread, excited demand that something be done about it. The protests are all built around three main contentions:

(1) The confessions are false. The prisoners who made the confessions are not to be condemned on any grounds

whatever. On the contrary, they are to be elevated as heroes and martyrs.

(2) Prisoners in the hands of police (in a Stalinist country) can be forced by various means of physical and mental torture, perhaps even by the use of drugs, to make false confessions. This is a new practice invented by the Stalinists.

(3) It is morally wrong and reprehensible to frame-up innocent people and force them to confess to crimes they did not commit. We must protest against this ghastly practice in the name of humanity.

This new campaign for justice invites a discussion in which others can join, and which can be fruitful. Right now, public opinion is concerning itself with these particular trials and confessions. But if moral principles are at stake—and I think they are—the discussion should not be limited to the cases of the Catholic ecclesiastic and the American businessman in Hungary, and the American journalist in Czechoslovakia. Why not include other cases in the discussion? And trials and confessions in general, and the social environment in which they take place? The elemental questions of justice and humanity are at issue in the trial of any man, and so is the social regime under which the trials take place. This is a wide field, well worthy of examination and discussion at this time.

2. The matter of justice

THE MILITANT, SEPTEMBER 3, 1951

The case of William N. Oatis, Associated Press correspondent sentenced to 10 years' imprisonment in Czechoslovakia, after confessing to a charge of spying, has stirred up American newspapers and newspapermen to a partisan interest in justice they never felt before. At any rate, they are expressing themselves about it, volubly and even excitedly, for the first time to my knowledge. Oatis is one of their own. His case also involves them, insofar as it affects the security of foreign correspondents. Oatis has become not simply a case to report but a cause to defend. As with the Catholic hierarchy in the case of Mindszenty, and American businessmen in the case of Vogeler, the individual is represented as the symbol of a principle—the principle of justice and fair play—and the American people are summoned to a moral crusade in its defense.

Our moralistic preceptors have learned to love justice late in life. Justice has been a poor vagabond in the world for a long time, with hardly a place to lay her head, and they never gave her a tumble. I, personally, am in favor of the principle laid down as a basis of this crusade, but I am somewhat mistrustful of late converts—especially those who have an axe of their own to grind.

Please don't misunderstand me. I do regard this awakening to the importance of justice for the individual as ludicrously sudden, and even contemptible in its hypocrisy. But I am making no jokes about the prisoners involved in these cases; or any other prisoners, for that matter. There is nothing funny about a defenseless man—any man—on trial for his life or his liberty, which is practically the same thing. When he is cut off from friends and all means of support, isolated and under pressure in a hostile environment, and deprived of competent legal counsel of his own choosing—it means in effect that he has no defense at all. That's wrong wherever it happens. I believe the world should be concerned about the matter of justice for the individual human being. And this concern is long overdue.

When the friends of Oatis, Vogeler or Mindszenty contend that their cases are the concern of all, they are right to a certain extent. When justice is at stake, all are involved. There is no such thing as the trial of one man; although this is seldom realized until a particular trial strikes home. When one is on trial, all are on trial. The accusers as well as the accused. Not only the victim, but those who impose the punishment. Not only the participants in the trial, but also the observers—the whole community. And they are all subject to judgment—the accused as to the facts in his particular case; the accusers by the manner in which they prosecute; and the observers, the whole community, by their reaction to the proceedings. By this reaction, by this attitude, they also should be judged. It is from this broader, more inclusive standpoint that I wish to discuss here not only the trial of Mr. Oatis, with whom I deeply sympathize, but also the other trials; and trials and confessions in general.

It is not my intention here to debate the merits of the confessions extracted from the cardinal, the businessman, and the correspondent by their Stalinist inquisitors. Espionage, of course, is a business in which the U.S. Government, like all others, is extensively engaged, and on which it expends huge sums of money and uses all kinds of people. Priests, businessmen and journalists are undoubtedly included in their network, like people of any other occupation in ordinary life. The defendants in these particular cases could all be guilty of the offenses charged against them, and such conduct would represent no contradiction to the things they stand for and the interests they represent.

Neither would it be considered wrong by the moralistic phonics who are beating the drums in their defense. The U.S. Intelligence Service, which organizes espionage in foreign countries, is dear to their hearts. And the F.B.I., with its army of domestic spies and stool-pigeons, is the apple of their eye. Even General MacArthur, who sits on the right hand of God, maintained an intelligence service to ferret out those military secrets of the North Koreans and Chinese which the Lord neglected to tip him off to. The only criticism I have heard about this is that the five-star general's spies didn't find out much.

On the other hand, I would be the last person to put any credence whatever in anything coming out of a Stalinist court. I take it for granted, as a matter of course, that all Stalinist trials are designed to serve political purposes. The guilt or innocence of the particular person in the hands of the Stalinist police in a specific case, makes no difference whatever. Guilty or innocent of the specific crime charged against him, he will be convicted just the same. I don't know whether the cardinal, the businessman and the press correspondent are guilty or innocent, and have no way of finding out. Their sponsors have made no attempt to prove their innocence; and the Stalinist proofs of their guilt are worthless. Therefore I am willing to assume, for the purpose of this discussion, what it is always safe to assume about any Stalinist trial—that these particular trials were frame-ups and that the confessions were false.

Assuming this, in order to get extraneous and—in the circumstances—unverifiable questions out of the way, I propose to raise other questions which can be verified. There have been many cases of frame-ups and false confessions right here in the United States. Their victims, being made of flesh and blood, were just as good as Oatis, Vogeler and Mindszenty, and just as much entitled to fair play. What about them? What did our clerical bigwigs, business monopolists and publishing tycoons have to say about the violations of justice in these cases here at home?

An examination of the record, which is wide open for anybody's inspection, will give the answer to this question. It should also throw some light on the worth of their pretensions and protests in the name of justice and morality—in eastern Europe.

3. The dirt on their own doorstep

THE MILITANT, SEPTEMBER 10, 1951

It is a rule of law, often honored in the breach, that a litigant in any lawsuit must come into court with clean hands. The same sentiment, unwritten but more faithfully observed, is expressed in the well-known proverb about the housewife who neglects to sweep the dirt from her own doorstep. She should keep her mouth shut, says the proverb, about the housekeeping habits of her neighbors. What would the leaders of the current moralistic crusade for justice for the individual—in the lands of Stalinism—look like if this rule and proverb were applied to them? They would look, my friend, like what they really are—a gang of cynical hypocrites whose disregard for justice in their own domain disqualifies them from criticism of others. They wouldn't be heard in any honest court, and they would be shamed into silence in any well-ordered neighborhood.

The crimes of Stalinism against the rights and the dignity of the individual human being, cry to heaven for vengeance. But who are the publishers, priests and businessmen of the United States, the leaders of the present hue and cry—who are they to redress these crimes? They and their apologists and camp-followers, such as the social democrats of all grades and breeds, have worked themselves up, all of a sudden into an uproar for justice. They are even ready to start a war for its sake; on the condition, of course, that others do the fighting. I am in favor of justice, and am even willing to fight for it, but not under their leadership. They don't come into court with clean hands. The dirt of their own injustice is piled high on their own doorstep.

I am not speaking now in the broad sense of that social injustice of which they are the bloated beneficiaries. For the purpose of this discussion I limit myself to the narrower terms laid down in their own campaign around the cases of Oatis, Mindszenty and Vogeler—the matter of justice for the individual accused of crime. They have made a record of their own in this respect, and the simple facts of the record disqualify them from any mention of justice.

The Bill of Rights regulates the administration of justice in the United States; and everybody, with only incidental and accidental exceptions, gets a fair trial. That's what they say. And that's probably what the average man, who hasn't yet had his day in court, believes. But it isn't so. The only people who get a square deal from the police and the courts are those who can afford it. Violations of human rights and fair play, brazen disregard of the plain provisions of the Constitution, are not an exception but the rule. If you think I exaggerate, permit me to tell you frankly—that is only because you don't know what goes on in the administration of justice in this country.

The miscarriage of justice in the United States is a wholesale business. Some of it is done by design, at the instigation and with the support of the big moneyed interests who control all departments of the legal machinery without directly operating them. Some of it is done by the police functionaries on their own hook, partly because the system naturally operates that way, and partly because, like the stumbling horse that wasn't blind, they don't give a damn. As a general rule, uncontrolled power and fair play don't go together anywhere. The frame-up and the false confession, now currently advertised as inventions of the Stalinists, are everyday occurrences in the

United States and have been for a long time, longer than anyone can remember.

The world has heard about the famous frame-ups of labor leaders and Negroes, which were thoroughly exposed. But neither the world, nor the general public in this country, knows about the innumerable run-of-the-mill cases of the same kind which were never publicized. This routine business of framing-up obscure and helpless men was rather comically illustrated the other day by a press dispatch, from Sunflower County, Mississippi, as previously reported in *The Militant*. Three Negroes were worked over by a deputy sheriff and a private detective "way up into the night," and then they confessed to the murder of a missing man. By this time the three Negroes would be well on the way to the gallows or the electric chair—or whatever they use in Mississippi for the execution of confessed murderers—if it hadn't been for the accidental circumstance that the "missing man," to whose murder they had confessed, turned up alive and well. It was only this hilarious development that rated a few lines of press publicity for the case.

Far from being a new invention of the Stalinists, false confessions, extorted from helpless prisoners in the hands of police, are an old story. There have been so many instances that it long ago became a rule of law that confessions, unsupported by corroborative evidence, are not admissible in evidence. But this rule doesn't count when a false plea of guilty is entered. Then there is no trial, properly speaking. The prisoner simply enters his plea and gets his sentence, and the judge goes out for lunch, and that's all there is to it.

When, as sometimes happens, the prisoner who signed the false confession gets a lawyer and repudiates it in court, the police who extorted the confession usually have little difficulty in manufacturing some additional evidence to bolster it up. And, if the prisoner is poor and defenseless, judges have been notably liberal in admitting confessions if they are tied to the meagerest scraps of scraped-up corroboration.

This is what happened in the now famous case of the Trenton Six. They were only six poor Negroes without money or influence. Fake confessions they had signed under pressure were received in evidence, and the six prisoners were duly convicted and sent to "death row" to await the day of their execution. They would have been dead long ago if outside people—unknown to the prisoners—hadn't kicked up a fuss, publicized the case and engaged competent lawyers to prepare their appeal. That's what was unusual in the case of the Trenton Six—not the frame-up and the false confessions, but the publicity, the funds, and the entrance into the case of lawyers who knew their business. Clarence Darrow, the famous lawyer, knew as much about American justice as anyone ever did. Out of a lifetime of battling in the courts, he summed up his conclusions in flat assertion that most men in prison were there because they couldn't afford to hire good lawyers.

It is well known among convicts, prison wardens, prosecuting attorneys and policemen that a large percentage of prisoners are doing time for crimes they did not commit. This is not to say they didn't have police records in most cases, and hadn't committed some crime or other—the most important one, the crime of being broke when they were arrested. That's just about the worst fix a man can get himself into in this country—to have a bad record, and no money or influence, and to get picked up by the police when they need some convictions. Many and many a man is doing time in prison for some specific crime to which he falsely confessed under duress; or pleaded guilty to in a deal with the prosecuting attorney and the police who "had something on him;" or for which he was framed.

Every man to his trade. The American police are in the business of arresting people, and they have to make a showing. The prosecuting attorneys have to roll up a large percentage of convictions. "Unsolved crimes" on the record are a scandal and discredit to them both, and bring unfavorable publicity. Every once in a while this record of unsolved crimes is "cleaned up" by the guilty pleas of prisoners who are thought to have committed some crime or other, or who might have done so. Why not make them confess to the unsolved crimes? Lacking the money, influence and legal help to fight their way out, they "cop a plea" and make the best deal they can in the situation. As long as the "record" is cleaned up, the police and prosecutors don't care much whether the scales of justice are evenly balanced or not. What they have to balance are the books which list crimes committed on one page and arrests and convictions on the other.

The famous case of Tom Mooney was completely exposed before the whole world as a frame-up. Even the people who kept him in prison quit pretending that he was guilty of the Preparedness Day dynamiting. But still they wouldn't let him go. "We've got the right man for the wrong crime," they said. That cynical expression sums up the philosophy of the American police system. Formally, and in theory, justice in the United States is administered with scrupulous regard for the rights of the accused and the presumption of his innocence until he is proven guilty—not of some crime, but of the particular crime charged against him. These rules and safeguards operate fairly when a defendant with money, influence and good lawyers is involved. But for the poor and defenseless prisoner it is a different story.

The best he can hope for, as a rule, is a rough hustle. He has a good chance to run into a frame-up. And he is lucky if he isn't beaten and tortured until he signs a fake confession—as thousands of others have done before him. Who cares about him, anyway? Not the organizers of the current moral crusade around the cases of Oatis and the others. They are interested only in justice for high-placed people of their own kind, and in another country. They are the beneficiaries of the social system which breeds injustice in this country, and they never lift a finger against it. The fight for justice, if it is to be real and honest, must begin at home, and against them.

4. Justice in the U.S.A.

THE MILITANT, DECEMBER 24, 1951

A man named Leonard Hankins was freed from the Minnesota State Penitentiary in Stillwater, November 28, by order of the state pardon board, and his name and picture got a big play in the Minneapolis papers. The mere release of a convict, in itself, is not news. Prison traffic in the United States is quite brisk and on the increase; some are going in and others are coming out all the time, and nobody pays any particular attention. But Leonard Hankins got his name in the papers because of special circumstances in his case which impressed the news-minded editors as somewhat out of the ordinary and therefore of public interest. Three points, added together, made a story.

First, Mr. Hankins had been buried alive in prison for nearly 19 years. Second, it was acknowledged that he was not guilty of the crime of which he was convicted on February 6, 1933 and sentenced to a life term. Third—this was the real twist—it was publicly admitted by policemen involved in the case that he had been deliberately framed.

On December 3, said an AP dispatch, another man named Vance Hardy stepped out of Recorders Court at Detroit, a freeman after a directed verdict of acquittal in a new trial. He had been convicted of murder in 1924 and served 27 years in prison. New evidence and a new trial revealed his innocence and finally secured his freedom. His original conviction, it was reported, had been a case of mistaken identity.

In New York, the *Times* of November 15 reported the case of Nathan Kaplan, a 49-year-old salesman. "He was convicted," said the *Times,* "and served seven and a half years for a crime committed by another." Federal Judge Edwards R. Weinfeld, after a new hearing, said that the salesman was innocent and that a "grave miscarriage of justice had taken place." This also was "a case of mistaken identity."

But in the case of Leonard Hankins there had been no mistake whatever. He was convicted of murder after the Third Northwestern Bank robbery in 1932, staged by the Barker-Karpis gang, in which $112,000 was stolen and three people were killed.

The *Minneapolis Star* quotes Sig Couch, a retired Minneapolis detective, as explaining to the state pardon board that "the Police Department was 'getting a lot of heat' then because of unsolved crimes. We needed a goat and Hankins was it." Couch also said that Hankins was beaten by the police after his arrest and that a police showup was "rigged" so that witnesses would point out Hankins from the line-up of men. He added: "Hankins was known as a card sharp, but not as a bank robber."

John Albrecht, former Minneapolis police sergeant, who arrested Hankins two days after the holdup, collected $1,000 reward, but told the pardon board he never did believe Hankins was guilty. Hankin's arrest, Albrecht said, was intended only "to get somebody convicted" in order to quiet public indignation over the holdup and slayings. Albrecht said the prosecution refused to call him as a witness during Hankins' trial "because of my belief that he was innocent." So he just kept the $1,000 reward and kept his mouth shut, and Hankins was railroaded to prison under a life sentence.

Hankins was a made-to-order victim for the frame-up. He was a professional card dealer and thus subject to a pinch at any time; he had a previous police record of several arrests. Worse than that, he was broke when arrested and couldn't even hire a lawyer. The court had to appoint defense counsel. He didn't have a chance.

But after 19 years of imprisonment, accumulated evidence of his innocence, gathered by a number of people who had been induced by his sister, Mrs. Della Lowery, to take an interest in the case, got him a hearing before the pardon board. And there, for some incomprehensible reason, a couple of former cops calmly admitted the frame-up. Under the circumstances there was not much for the pardon board to do but to free Leonard Hankins for whatever may be left of his life.

"I have died ten thousand deaths since I've been here," the former prisoner told a reporter at the prison gate. "A man can't help feeling bitter. But I'm not figuring to get even with anybody." He said he just wanted to get back to his kinfolk in Kentucky. "Right now, I'd just like to sit myself under a big oak tree alongside the Treadwater River down at Dawson Springs, and just laze away."

That seems like a reasonable ambition, all things considered. But just the same, he would probably be well advised to check the situation carefully even after he gets back to Dawson Springs, and make sure he isn't found loafing under any oak tree in the neighborhood of an "unsolved crime." The cops might figure he is just the man they need for a conviction to clear up the case.

There is an interesting footnote to the story of the framing of Leonard Hankins. Sergeant John Albrecht, the Minneapolis police officer who arrested Hankins and got the $1,000 reward, was the same sergeant who organized the police ambush of pickets on Third Street North in the July truck drivers' strike of 1934. The cops opened fire on the unarmed strikers at close range. Henry Ness and John Belor were killed in the ambush and 48 other pickets were wounded, including Harry DeBoer, who served time with us in Sandstone Prison after our conviction in the Minneapolis Trial of 1941.

Naturally, nobody was punished for these atrocious crimes. Police in this country have a license to shoot strikers as well as to frame victims when they need convictions.

The prize fighters

1. Murder in the Garden

THE MILITANT, SEPTEMBER 17, 1951

This begins as a straight news story with the who, what, where and when right up at the front. The why and the wherefore come later, after the bare facts are set down in proper order. The who in this story is, or rather was, Georgie Flores, 20-year-old Brooklyn welterweight. He was knocked out in the semi-final bout with Roger Donoghue at Madison Square Garden August 29. He collapsed in his dressing room a few minutes after the knockout and died in the hospital five days later without ever recovering consciousness. Georgie leaves a wife, Elaine, 18 years old, who was at his bedside when he died, and a month-old baby son who hasn't heard about it yet.

Other technical information, as reported by the experts at the ringside: The fatal blow was a sharp left hook which floored the young boxer just 46 seconds after the opening of the eighth and final round of the bout. His head hit the canvas hard and he was counted out by the referee as he lay flat. Cause of death, as reported by the medical experts at the hospital, was a brain hemorrhage resulting from a torn blood vessel. Two operations were unsuccessful. His last hours were spent in an iron lung.

Georgie Flores didn't die of old age or incurable illness, and there was no suspicion of suicide. He was killed. Murdered, if you want the truth unvarnished. And he was not the first to die that way. Sudden death is an occupational hazard in the prize-fight business. Six boxers have been killed in the U.S. already this year, if you count only those who died more or less immediately, as a result of blows in the ring. The score would be much higher if you include those who were badly hurt and had their life expectancy sharply cut down in this grisly business, which is sometimes described by fools or cynics as "the sport" or "the game." This sort of thing goes on all the time. As a rule, the killing of a prize fighter doesn't rate more than a few paragraphs in the news, a few floral offerings from the fight mob, and a small purse scraped up for the widow.

But some exceptional circumstances in the killing of Georgie Flores have caused a sort of an uproar and a public demand for some kind of an investigation. The State Athletic Commission, which is responsible for the supervision of boxing in New York, has solemnly announced an "investigation." The District Attorney is "looking into the matter." Even Governor Dewey, who is a hard man to move, has stated—officially—that the young boxer's death is "a tragedy." The Athletic Commission's investigation, he said, should tell whether any precautions could have been taken to prevent it.

This investigation will undoubtedly find that no required precautions were neglected and that all the rules were observed. They will find that the killing of Georgie Flores was, unfortunately, just one of those things, and—after one minute of respectful silence in his memory, and maybe one official crocodile tear from each member of the Commission—they will proceed to business and approve the arrangements for the next bout. The "game" must go on—the game in which human heads are the baseballs and lightly-padded fists are the bats.

Things were not quite so formal and official with Elaine Flores, the young widow of the slain boxer. According to all the reports—and there were many of them, for the sports writers really went to town on this story—the kid took it hard. It seems she loved this guy Georgie and had plans for the future. She stayed at his bedside for the whole five days that he laid there in a coma, refusing to leave until the final verdict came in. I'm afraid she made a bit of a nuisance of herself at the hospital, hanging around and getting in the way of people who had routine work to do. But there are no reports that anybody complained. She didn't kick up a fuss, according to the reports. She just sat there and kept quiet and waited.

Elaine didn't see the fight where Georgie got hit. She didn't like him fighting and was always afraid he would get hurt. She had been trying to get him to give up the fight business. "I never liked fighting," she told the reporters. "After every fight I told him to quit." Georgie would promise, but after a few days he would start training again. He said it was the quickest way to get the money they needed. "George was going to buy a home so that we could live by ourselves," Elaine told the reporters. "Just a few more fights, he said, and he'd be able to make a down payment on a house." Her father, Alexander Rosenweig, said Flores had promised her he would really quit after the Donoghue fight.

Elaine and Georgie met at Coney Island. They had gone out there to see what they could see, and found each other. They went together a year before they were married. She has the baby to show for their brief time together; that and the purse from Georgie's last fight. "He's a good baby," she told the reporters. "I want him to be a doctor when he grows up. That's a good profession."

Well, it beats boxing; that's for sure. In fact, you would have a hard time naming any profession or good-paying trade that doesn't beat boxing. Nobody knows that better than the fighters who take the punches. Then why do they go into it? That's a fair question and it deserves a fair answer. But it can't be answered in a short sentence. The boxer, taking punches in the ring, is put there by many things and circumstances beyond his control; some of them even beyond his knowledge. Georgie Flores, the poor kid who roamed the slums in his early adolescence, without a home or even a regular place to sleep, was not the master of his own destiny.

The fight mob turned out for the funeral. There were some floral offerings. Roger Donoghue, Georgie's opponent in the fatal bout, sadly recited the Rosary, led by a member of the fighter's family. The Rosary and the Lord's prayer, intoned by the funeral director, were the only religious notes in the service. Georgie didn't belong to any church, or at any rate, wasn't in good enough standing to get a sermon from a practising clergyman. A crowd of about 300 stood silently outside the funeral home during the brief service and remained to watch as the funeral cortege left for the cemetery. That's all for Georgie Flores.

2. A dead man's decision

THE MILITANT, SEPTEMBER 24, 1951

Dead men tell no tales; but sometimes, as is well known, the memory of what they did, or the way they died, exerts an authority over the living and affects their actions and decisions. The continuing influence of great men needs no argument. And once in a while, in exceptional circumstances, the lowly, too, speak from the grave. Even the lowliest of the lowly. Georgie Flores, the young boxer who was killed in the ring at Madison Square Garden just recently, cast a long shadow over the Turpin-Robinson fight for the middleweight championship at the Polo Grounds last Wednesday, and most probably determined the outcome of this million-dollar affair.

Turpin was on the ropes, but not out, when the referee stopped the fight with only eight seconds to go in the tenth round of the scheduled 15-round bout, and gave the decision to Robinson on a technical knockout. But it is highly doubtful if Robinson was the winner on actual merit. The fight was scored even up to the tenth round. Robinson was bleeding like a stuck pig from an eye cut; and Turpin, with the stamina of youth in his favor, figured to recuperate during the intermission between rounds and take charge from there on. Turpin and his manager protested the referee's action on these grounds, and subsequent evidence seemed to bear out their contention. Turpin, according to all reports, was fresher and stronger than Robinson in the immediate aftermath of the fight.

Then why was the fight stopped so precipitously, with

only eight seconds to go in the round—a very unusual procedure in a championship fight? The answer, as everybody knows, is the death of Georgie Flores on the eve of the battle for the middleweight title. Flores was in the minds of all concerned. They were all thinking: What happened once can happen again. This nervous apprehension was reflected in the action of Ruby Goldstein, the referee. The sports writers, the U.S. fight mob, the fight fans, and the distinguished people who turned out to view this modern gladiatorial spectacle, unanimously applauded the referee's action. They all gave the same reason: Turpin, they said, might have been badly hurt if the fight had not been stopped at the precise moment in history of two minutes, 52 seconds of the tenth round. This time the sportsmen in the arena put thumbs up, not down; they didn't say "kill him!" but "let him live!"

You can attribute this gesture to a sudden rush of mercy to the head, or to the fear of another scandal in the full glare of world publicity—but there it is, any way you want to explain it. Robinson is champion again, the beneficiary in this instance of the guilty conscience of the boxing business. This is probably the first time the still small voice of conscience ever made itself heard in these strange precincts; and certainly the first time a boxer ever got the benefit of it.

Georgie Flores' tragic and most untimely death was just another nine-day sensation. That's all. It lasted just about long enough to influence the decision in the Turpin-Robinson bout. The echoes of the uproar are already fading away. The jitters have yielded to the sedative of time—it didn't take long—and the boxing business is just about back to normal, back to business as usual. All that the hullabaloo produced, while it lasted, were a few proposals for better supervision of boxing bouts in the future; for some more elaborate rules and regulations; for what Governor Dewey, in his humane wisdom, called "precautions" which might keep boxers from getting hurt when they get hit.

It is a commentary on the times, and the social environment out of which the boxing business rises like a poisonous flower from a dunghill, that nobody came forward with the simple demand to outlaw prize fighting, as it was outlawed in most of the states of this country up till the turn of the century. Cock-fighting is illegal; it is considered inhumane to put a couple of roosters into the pit and incite them to spur each other until one of them keels over. It is also against the law to put bulldogs into the pit to fight for a side bet. But our civilisation—which is on the march, to be sure—has not yet advanced to the point where law and public opinion forbid men, who have nothing against each other, to fight for money and the amusement of paying spectators. Such spectacles are a part of our highly touted way of life.

The "precautions," advocated during the brief excitement over the killing of Georgie Flores, simmered down to a few piddling suggestions that fighters not be over-matched; that they be required to train properly and enter the ring in good condition; that the boxers' gloves and the ring canvas be padded a little more; and that each boxer's head be thoroughly examined by X-ray before each bout to see if he had suffered a previous brain injury. "Boxing can be made a safe sport," said Dr. Frank R. Ferlaino to Milton Gross, sports writer for the *New York Post*, "if these regulations are observed." The doctor, of course, is talking through his hat.

The precautions, which are supposed to take care of everything, in reality take care of nothing. When you get inside those ropes your head is a target for self-propelled missiles known as fists, and there is no way of making that safe. As the soldier said, when he was asked why he ran away from the front lines: "You can get hurt up there." Blows over the head never did anybody any good. And if anybody ever got any fun out of it, he hasn't been heard from yet. The "sport" in prize fighting is strictly for the spectators and the managers and promoters.

The incomparable Joe Louis himself testified to this in a notable statement at a newsreeled press conference, when he renounced his title to turn promoter. A reporter asked: "Which do you think you like best, Joe, fighting or promoting?"

Joe, a man of few words, answered: "I like promotin'."

"Why is that, can you explain it?"

"Sure," said Joe. "They can't hit you when you're promotin'."

Those words belong in the Book of Proverbs.

Crime and criminals

1. A petition for Harry Gross

THE MILITANT, OCTOBER 1, 1951

You have to be careful what you sign these days; it can get you into all kinds of trouble, and first thing you know you are pegged as subversive and put on the blacklist. But if they come around to me with a petition for the unconditional pardon of Harry Gross, the fall guy in the Brooklyn cops and bookies scandal, I'll make it a matter of principle and sign it. And if the petition adds another point calling for Judge Leibowitz to be put in jail in place of Gross, I'll sign it twice.

I would sign the first part of the petition—for the pardon

of Gross—not because I am a sentimental admirer or sympathizer of crooks, big or little. I don't see anything glamorous or admirable about racketeers; and I care still less for the cops who are in cahoots with them and without whom they could not operate. Their incentive is money and material advantages for themselves at the expense of others. That is not my idea of a hero; and ordinarily I wouldn't go out of my way to do them any favors, not even so much as signing my name to a petition. But I do believe in a sense of proportion. And I don't care for hypocritical talk about justice when the whole thing is lopsided and discriminatory, and the punishment is dealt out to minor offenders while the big criminals come out unscathed.

Gross, by all accounts, is a crook. But he isn't the biggest or the worst crook in the town or the country. Compared to others who have not been punished or indicted, he is a piker. Why should he take the rap? Gross is obviously the fall guy for the whole gang of thieves, official and unofficial, including higher-ups in the O'Dwyer administration; going right up to the City Hall, to the highest officials who sit in the seats of power there. They haven't been indicted or even mentioned in this whole judicial fiasco, to say nothing of the still bigger crooks behind them who rob and bleed the people of this country. They all go scot-free while one uneducated bookie, who learned all he knows in the crap-game joints and pool halls of the Brooklyn slums, where the quick dollar is regarded as the highest value, gets the business. What's fair about that?

Gross has already been sentenced to 1,500 days in jail and a fine of $10,000 for contempt of court in refusing to testify against himself and the cops and politicians who shook him down for "protection" money; and he faces another long prison sentence on his previous plea of guilty to paying off these same cops and politicians when he goes into court this Thursday. Specifically, he admitted paying out over $1,000,000 a year in graft to New York cops for protection in operating his bookie business. That is a crime under the law, no doubt; and $1,000,000 out of the pockets of suckers who tried to beat the odds weighted against them in horse races, which were probably rigged in the bargain, is a lot of money. But compared to the take of organized exploitation in this country, it is mere chicken feed. And compared to the crimes of others involved in these proceedings, including those who shout loudest about law and justice, the offense of Gross is a mere peccadillo.

Take the crimes of Judge Samuel S. Leibowitz, who presided over the trial in Kings County Court, for example. This scoundrel acted not as an impartial judge, but as a prosecutor against the helpless bookie who was unlucky enough to get caught in the toils of what they euphemistically call "the law." Leibowitz certainly made a hash of the law, and the Constitution too, when it came to dealing with little Harry Gross. He held him in bail of $250,000—just think of it!—in brutal violation of the constitutional provision which expressly prohibits the exaction of unreasonable bail. He kept him in solitary confinement for six months, which again violates the law and the Constitution by inflicting punishment before trial. More—as Gross brought out on the witness stand—he knowingly sanctioned third-degree methods to make Gross talk before he was tried, under threat of a heavier sentence if he stood on his rights and refused to incriminate himself. The Bill of Rights prohibits "cruel and unusual punishment" in the case of convicted criminals in the country's prisons. Leibowitz sanctioned such punishment of a man before he was even tried.

On top of all that, by his hypocritical posturing on the bench and his abusive threats to a helpless prisoner on the witness stand, this unjust judge, this modern Jeffreys, compounded his crimes. "I will chain you to the stand with handcuffs," he shouted at the bookie. "If you have to rot in jail for 100 years, you will get it." This is what is known in Brooklyn as judicial poise and impartiality.

Under his goading and threats, Gross told the story of what had been done to him: "Why don't you explain to the court that you held me as a material witness in solitary confinement in the civil prison? Why don't you explain that, heh? Why did you have me assigned to a chair in solitary the whole 24 hours with the light twitching in my eye? . . . Did you ever try to spend 23 out of 24 hours in your cell with the light on there over your cell? . . . You took 20 years off my life with the condition you had me kept in. When I asked the sheriff over in the civil prison, all they give you was, 'Orders of Honorable Judge Leibowitz'. . . . You have ruined my eyesight; no glasses, no radio, no newspaper, no visitors. You are a very honorable man." (*New York Herald Tribune*, Sept. 20.)

I say that Judge Leibowitz, the author of these crimes, is worse than Gross. I say the bookie, for his comparatively piddling offenses, has already suffered too much. I am not a believer in jails as a cure for human defects, as a way of making people better. In the communist society of the future there will be no jails. But in the meantime if there must be jails, and if it is strictly understood that they are for punishment, not reform—then they ought to be inhabited by those who deserve them most. If justice were done in this case, it would mean turning the bookie loose and putting Leibowitz in jail in his place.

Of all the characters directly or indirectly involved in this whole unsavory spectacle, little Harry Gross comes out best as a man, as a plain human being. He at least was loyal to something. That's more than can be said, on the record, for the others. As far as can be seen with the naked eye, the others were loyal to nothing; nothing important, that is. O'Dwyer, the political kingpin of all the rackets, took it on the lam to Mexico and picked up an ambassadorship en route. The crooked cops had no motive but to keep their swag and keep their jobs so they could collect more. The District Attorney wanted to build himself up as a candidate for Governor in the pattern of the notorious Dewey. Leibowitz wanted to outshine Medina, the Federal Judge who had copped the glory by kangarooing the 11 Stalinist leaders. But when all the chips were down, and threats of 100 years of imprisonment were hurled at Gross from the bench, the little bookie took a stand for some kind of principle, even if it isn't the highest principle in the world, and they couldn't budge him from it.

"I am thinking of my family," he said. "My family, my wife and children, are more important to me than anything." There he stood and there he stands. Little in size as he is, and little and tawdry as his whole career has been, he's bigger than the others. Bigger, and better.

I had intended, in connection with this case, to pay my respects also to Rudolph Halley, the "crime-busting" phoney, who is running on a white horse for president of New York City Council with "socialist" support. But space has already run out, and that will have to hold over until next time.

2. Crime and politics

THE MILITANT, OCTOBER 22, 1951

The working people of New York City, caught in the squeeze play between rising prices and the wage freeze, with the shadow of another war in the making darkening every home, are being offered a slick package of entertainment to take their minds off their fears and troubles. The promoter of this diversionary circus is Dubinsky's Liberal Party, and the attraction they offer is the new "crime-buster," Rudolph Halley, candidate for president of City Council. You can catch him on television most any night between the wrestlers and the so-called comedians.

Halley is running on a one-point program. He calls it "the fight against crime." He and his political sponsors promise to put a stop to that sort of thing; and to that end Halley, writing appropriately in the *New Leader,* calls for "a movement of reform, a New Reformism." The first step in this all-saving crusade, of course, is to elect Halley to the office of Council president.

Unless my ears are playing me false, I've heard all that before—and so have you if you aren't deaf or recently arrived in this country. The crime-busting racket is as old and familiar as the calliope and the shell game when the carnival comes to town. It has been played so often for the special benefit of new crops of suckers, that one more exhibition, even with a brand new performer, would hardly be worth notice if it were not for a new gimmick in the act. This white-haired television boy, who boils all the great political issues of the day down to the one issue of crime; this Fearless Fosdick who is going to straighten out New York City and solve all problems by stopping the bookmakers in their tracks and pinching a few crapshooters—this preposterous phony is running for the top city office, next to mayor, with the endorsement and support of people who call themselves "socialists."

The Socialist Party has withdrawn its own candidate and formally endorsed Halley "as their contribution to the movement to end the alliance between crime and politics." That's new. And that's a crime against principle and the interests of the working people—a defamation and betrayal of the name of socialism—beside which the offenses of all the Costellos, reprehensible as they are in themselves, shrink into trifles.

The Socialist Party, organized 50 years ago, has come to this shameful and treacherous end under the leadership of Norman Thomas. Viewed retrospectively, in the light of world experience of the half century, the Party, even in its early days, its best days, was never free from grave defects and contradictions. But all things considered, the work of the Party in the time of Debs, with Debs himself in the forefront, will occupy a place in the history of America not without honor. Debs, and the Party with him, never thought of political action as a means of electing some shyster to office on his mere promise to clean up the town and put a stop to minor crimes. On the contrary, Debs, in his great campaigns, used the elections as a forum to discuss the real issues, the real crimes, of capitalist exploitation. He scorned and denounced piddling "reformers" who dealt only with minor excesses of the capitalist system while supporting the system itself.

Debs laid his axe at the root of the tree. His election campaigns were the occasion every time for intensified agitation and propaganda for the abolition of capitalism. Young workers were educated in these campaigns; they became staunch anti-capitalists, and were inspired in their work by a vision of the socialist future which Debs held out to them. What education will the youth of today acquire from the ignoble position of the Socialist Party in this present campaign? And what inspiration, what goal of the future, does it hold out to the youth?

This action of the Socialist Party was not unexpected. Rather, it was somewhat overdue. The fact of the matter is that the Party, in withdrawing its own candidate and supporting the Democrat Halley in this local campaign, is only formalizing a political position long ago arrived at in essence. When the Socialist Party, under the direction of Norman Thomas, betrayed its tradition and its specific pledge and promise by supporting American imperialism in World War II, it surrendered its basic position as an anti-capitalist party and therewith the right to an independent existence. When these misnamed "socialists" lined up in support of the cold war program of the Truman administration, endorsed the massacre in Korea and gave lackey support to obvious preparations for another war to conquer and enslave the world, they compounded the crime. The half-hearted campaign of Thomas in 1948 was already anomalous; his program was basically no different from Truman's.

The final capitulation, the renunciation of an independent Socialist Party ticket in favor of supporting "good men" or "liberals" or "reformers and crime-busters" on other party tickets, had to follow as a matter of logic and necessity. The withdrawal of their candidate in the New York City election only sets the pattern. It presages the withdrawal in all elections all along the line. The Socialist Party of Norman Thomas has become a miserable appendage of the two-party capitalist political system, which it started out so bravely to fight under Debs 50 years ago.

In the meantime, the greatest crime against humanity remains the outlived capitalist system itself, with its exploitation and its wars; and the need for a party that speaks out in every election with an honest socialist voice is more imperative than ever. The American underworld is a vicious and ugly social manifestation; but it did not fall from the skies. Graft and crime and extortions and rackets are the symptomatic products of a diseased social system and its false values. These dark and evil symptoms can't be eliminated, or even seriously curbed, until they are tackled at the source. A party which says this, a party which tells the truth as Debs told it, is not excusing crime and criminals or evading the issue; it is, rather, dealing with the issue realistically and fundamentally.

The members of Local New York of the Socialist Workers Party have a right to be proud of their accomplishment in putting their own candidate on the ballot for president of City Council. It was not easy to gather 15,000 signatures on the petitions in the face of the witch-hunt and the public fears it has engendered. But they did it. They stood their ground when others capitulated. They worked when others lagged and quit, and they accomplished their task. They could do this because they have the courage and driving energy that comes from genuine socialist conviction.

In the person of Michael Bartell they have a candidate who is worthy of them and their party. He is a worker, a trade unionist, an activist in the fight for human rights. Most important of all, he is a revolutionary socialist who campaigns against capitalism and its war program. That's the real issue in the New York election, and every other election. Let the traitor socialists have Halley and his popgun shots at "crime." But I believe the real socialists will agree with Bartell and vote for him.

3. They strain at a gnat

THE MILITANT, OCTOBER 29, 1951

"Politics makes strange bedfellows," and the issue of "crime in politics," Rudolph Halley's one-point program in the race for president of New York City Council, is a big enough blanket to cover a wide assortment of sleepers. Staking out a place for itself on the same bunk with the *Socialist Call* and the *New Leader,* the *New York Times* says positively: "There is one overriding issue in the election of Nov. 6." That issue "is corruption, graft, bribery, political favoritism, the Tammany-Costello type of government."

The *ADA World,* organ of Americans for Democratic Action, has an article on the same theme by Gus Tyler, one of the bright young left-wing socialists of the Thirties, who made the remarkable discovery that socialism doesn't pay but crime does, and something ought to be done about it. Crime, that is, not socialism. "Sin," he says, is "THE dominant issue in the many municipal elections across our country this November." Halley, for his part, avows in the *New Leader* that "the fight against crime is my personal war." And Tyler comes right back with a new synonym for sin and crime and a false definition: "The BIG FIX is the selection and election of public officials who know that they owe their elevated position in government to the underworld."

I don't believe a word of it. Even on their own level—the level of crime, graft and corruption—the campaign of Halley and his Liberal Party sponsors and his Republican, Democratic and "Socialist" supporters is a fake and a diversion from the real, big-scale political shake-down racket. They "strain at a gnat and swallow a camel."

There is no doubt whatever, as numerous investigations and exposures have already revealed, that the American governmental structure is rotten with corruption from top to bottom. But the operations of the local gamblers and gangsters are only a small part of it. The real big steals and swindles take place in Washington under the protecting umbrella of the Truman Administration. Nobody knows that better than Rudolph Halley. Why doesn't he tell the people the truth about the high-class grafters and influence-peddlers down there? Why does he nibble at the fringes of the question and concentrate all attention on the comparatively minor grafts and rackets of the local criminals who have to operate in the shadows outside the law?

Perhaps a speech of Halley's, reported in the *New York Post,* gives the explanation. Speaking at the local convention of Americans for Democratic Action—those daredevil liberals who have the bookies scared to death—Halley said that as a Democrat it was not a pleasant thing to have to fight his own party. But, he added, the organization had to be purged of gangsters and self-seekers. He meant the local organization of his party, Tammany, which has always been fair game for any two-bit reformer. He didn't mean the national organization in the saddle at Washington where the big thievery goes on. He didn't tell us anything about that. So I'll tell him a few things; just a few—it would take a big book to tell only a small part of what informed people already know.

I'll skip over the well-publicized deep-freezers, mink coats, free hotel accommodations, big cameras and medium-sized hams, and similar trifles and trinkets which mysteriously accrued to practically every government official of Mr. Halley's "own party" who has been investigated yet. This small stuff is interesting only as "atmosphere." National Democratic Party Chairman Boyle's "legal fees" come under the same general heading. After all, he only collected a hundred thousand dollars or so—as far as the investigation has revealed up to date. That's still peanuts. The appropriation of other people's money in the form of more or less "legitimate" graft runs into billions and tens of billions. Part of the story is already known, but Halley, hot on the trail of gamblers and gangsters, hasn't said anything about it yet.

Take the "tax amortization" racket, for example. That is really fantastic. Tom Conlan explained in *The Militant* a few weeks ago how it works:

> "Tax amortization" is a slick scheme whereby the big corporations may evade paying taxes altogether. Here is how it works. A corporation files notice that it proposes to construct and equip such and such a plant and then gets it certified as "vital for defense." Thereupon it is issued special certificates enabling it to deduct from its taxes the full cost of such a plant in five yearly instalments. The plant thus costs the corporation exactly nothing. The total of such "amortized" plants already amounts to *almost* 10 *billion dollars.*

Whose money is that? Well, pal, some of it used to be yours before the government put the withholding tax bite on your pay envelope. You could lose a lot of two-dollar bets to the bookies and still feel no pain if you had that tax money back.

Take one more example of the big and still slightly legal graft revealed by Joseph Alsop in the *New York Herald Tribune,* October 10. Truman appointed his "poker crony, former Gov. Mon C. Wallgren of Washington" as chairman of the Federal Power Commission, and Wallgren, "turned the Power Commission over to the industries it is supposed to regulate."

There was big dough in this deal. Alsop continues:

> As soon as Wallgren was named chairman of the Federal Power Commission, he enacted by simple administrative ruling Sen. Kerr's bill to free natural gas producers from Commission regulation, which the President had just vetoed. The first beneficiary was the

giant Phillips Petroleum Company in which Senator Kerr had a vital interest.

Says Alsop:

> The effect of the Wallgren ruling, of course, was to permit the increased gas prices being demanded by Phillips. In his minority opinion, Power Commissioner Thomas Buchanan estimated that these gas price increases would cost the customers of just one pipeline company, the Michigan-Wisconsin, a total of $3,500,000 annually, or $125,000,000 for the life of the contract. For the people of Detroit alone, the bill was put at $1,770,000 a year. Former Power Commission Chairman, Leland Olds, has also estimated that the price increases raised the value of the natural gas reserves of the Phillips Company alone by no less than $700,000,000. And, of course, the Power Commission ruling in the Phillips case means similar golden results for all other gas-producing companies like Phillips.

Senator Kerr, who is not on the list of criminals against whom Halley is waging a "personal war," did pretty well for himself in the deal. Alsop writes:

> Under the circumstances, it is hardly surprising that Phillips should have shown friendship to Sen. Kerr, proponent of the Kerr bill, worker for the Wallgren appointment, and large owner of gas and oil properties in his own right. And in fact, at the time when the Kerr bill was expected to become law, Phillips transferred 100 sections of proven gas acreage to the Tascosa Corporation, a specially organized subsidiary of Sen. Kerr's company, Kerr-McGee. Phillips also entered into

> a most unusual contract with Tascosa for exploitation of this acreage.
>
> According to an official memorandum from the Phillips Company files, this transfer and contract will result in a long-run profit to Tascosa, also chiefly owned by Sen. Kerr, of at least $1,297,000 and more, probably upwards of $2,000,000.

What Truman's "poker crony," Mon C. Wallgren, got out of it is not stated. But at the risk of getting pinched for gambling in the current anti-crime crusade I'll lay you 6 to 5 he didn't lose anything.

Alsop is worried about the chain reaction from the Phillips case:

> The "integrated" pipeline companies, including Panhandle Eastern, employing as counsel John Scott, an ex-law office associate of Democratic National Chairman William Boyle, have now come before the Federal Power Commission. These companies own their own gas wells as well as pipelines. They say, "If Phillips can charge whatever the traffic will bear for gas at the wellhead, why can't we?"

Why not, indeed? Especially if they have an ex-law office Associate of ex-Chairman Boyle to front for them. "If this happens," says the indignant Joseph Alsop, "the process that began with Mon C. Wallgren can end, not with a mere additional annual bill of a couple of hundred millions for natural gas consumers, but an additional bill of maybe $1,000,000,000 or more for electricity users."

It begins to run into money, doesn't it? But even these huge sums are only the spill-over from the main shake down of capitalist exploitation. That works automatically to make a few drones and parasites fabulously rich and keep the workers poor from working.

Richard Croker, the unabashed Tammany leader of an earlier day, put his finger on it when he told Lincoln Steffens, "There is graft in Wall Street, of course. . . . Like a businessman in business, I work for my own pocket all the time." And then he added for the benefit of charlatan reformers and their dupes who promise to solve social problems by fighting petty crime:

> If we get big graft, and the cops and small-fry politicians know it, we can't decently kick at their petty stuff. Can we, now? We can't be hypocrites like the reformers who sometimes seem to me not to know that they live on graft.

4. The big swindle

THE MILITANT, NOVEMBER 5, 1951

For the past two weeks this space has been devoted to a critical review of the Biggest Show in Town. That's not "Guys and Dolls" or Judy Garland at the Palace, but Rudolph Halley's campaign for City Council presidency, under the auspices of Dubinsky's Liberal Party with the endorsement of Norman Thomas' Socialist Party, on the single issue of local crime and graft. And the fantastic spectacle has not been fully covered yet.

Halley himself, of course, would be no more attractive than any other political shyster trying to make hay for himself on his reputation as a "crime-buster"—one of the oldest and most familiar dodges in the American political game—if the International Ladies Garment Workers' Union hadn't been dragooned into sponsoring him by Dubinsky, and if the Socialist Party had not been betrayed into endorsing him by Norman Thomas.

It is this aspect of the Halley campaign which justifies extended treatment, for it leads straight up to questions of transcendent importance, to wit: What is labor and socialist politics all about; and what should workers and socialists go into politics for? If the Halley catastrophe jolts some workers into a thoughtful consideration of these questions it may have, indirectly, a beneficial result never intended by its authors.

I personally am not in favor of crime and graft, and would like to see it stopped by removing its basic cause. But when I hear anybody say or even imply that gambling is the main source of the trouble, and that the cure is to pass some more laws and shake up the police department, and thus fix things so that a man can't make a two-dollar bet with the bookmaker's runner on the corner, while betting at the race tracks is perfectly legal—when I hear anyone make that pitch I know right away that he is a liar and a faker and therefore a crook himself.

You can't even stop off-track gambling that way. The only result of such measures and the general clatter and uproar around them always has been, and always will be, that the bookies have to pay more for protection while the heat's on. Or, perhaps, you are going to get "honest cops" this time? When you get them let me know. But don't expect me to live that long.

Fred Jaffe, an experienced reporter who has covered politics and crime from the City Hall and Albany to the Kefauver hearings and knows the real score, takes a dim view of the current hue and cry.

In a round-up report for the *New York Compass* he refers disdainfully to "the inordinate emphasis placed on gambling in recent investigations," and the shake-down graft of the cops inseparable from it, even though this graft has been shown to run into millions of dollars a year in New York City alone. He says flatly that "the big graft is located" in Washington where "they've stopped counting the billions being spent by the Federal Government, especially for armaments."

The concentration of the crime crusaders on relatively minor items in the national aggregate of crime and graft is only a means of covering up and distracting attention from the bigger steals engineered down in Washington under the Truman administration which Halley supports. Washington is the place where the gravy train is really high-balling down the line. It's "a long train with a big red caboose." But it isn't hauling your troubles away, like the train in the popular song. It's hauling your money.

Last week I cited a few facts and figures on only two rackets—"tax amortization" (more than 10 billion dollars) and Federal Power Commission handouts to the big oil and public utility companies (a couple of billion more). Here's another item—"tax cheating." Not much of this is done by the little fellow. He is overtaxed to start with and then watched like a convict on parole. The real cheating is done by the rich who can pay for a fix.

Sylvia F. Porter, financial editor of the *New York Post,* says: "Tax cheating is the No. One racket in America today." She's wrong about that, but it's quite a racket just the same. "A conservative estimate," she says, "is that as a result of tax evasion, graft, downright fraud, the Treasury is losing at least $2 billion annually and the tax crooks have accumulated at least a $7 billion to $10 billion kitty just since World War II."

But even these huge sums, which begin to add up to more money than you can count unless you went to college and studied astronomy, don't tell the whole story of graft in this country. They represent only the illegal or slightly irregular forms of getting something for nothing. If all this shady business were to be miraculously stopped by a morally regenerated public administration, and if all these thieves were put in jail by a staff of fearless prosecutors and incorruptible cops under some super-Halley—are you laughing or crying?—it wouldn't change things fundamentally.

It still wouldn't touch the heart of the question of graft—if you will just broaden out the definition a little to mean by graft the appropriation of other people's money, or its equivalent, without rendering any productive service in return.

The Big Swindle in this country is the capitalist system of exploitation which, under the euphemistic title of "free enterprise," robs the worker of the bulk of the fruits of his labor and makes the rich richer all the time. And it's all perfectly legal. Its operators are ornaments of society and pillars of the church. They don't have to dodge the law and the cops. The law and the cops are working for them, to protect their loot. Profits for 1951 are running at the rate of $50 billion a year for which no useful or productive services whatever are rendered.

That's the racket that keeps the workers poor. Things work out so that even the fully employed and better-paid workers, in these times of artificial boom, barely manage to keep their heads above water; while "one-third of the nation," now, as in Roosevelt's time, still live in direst poverty with incomes far below what it takes to maintain a "modest but adequate" standard of living.

This disproportion has been operating for a long, long time. We have now reached the point where 2 or 3 percent of the population own 40 or 50 percent of the private property of the United States. They dominate the whole banking, industrial and commercial system of the country.

They run the government to suit themselves, in their own interests. This government has appropriated $60 billion this year for military purposes. Every dollar of this astronomical sum represents values produced by the workers.

They have to give up this money without being consulted and have no say in how it is to be spent. It is to be spent for the armaments of war which the workers will be called upon to fight. They got your money, and now they want your life. That's the way things are working out under American capitalism on the strictly legal plane.

How do you like that? Don't you think these things should be talked about in election campaigns when all the people are listening? Rudolph Halley, who is in the spotlight as candidate for president of City Council, doesn't think so. On the contrary, he supports this system and thinks it's fine. In supporting Halley in this election campaign, the so-called "socialists," with Norman Thomas as their bellwether, are, in the strict and literal sense of the word, supporting capitalism and war.

Debs didn't conduct election campaigns that way. In his acceptance speech opening his 1904 campaign, he said: "The Socialist Party . . . throws down the gage of battle and declares that there is but one solution of what is called the labor question, and that is by the complete overthrow of the capitalist system." In his 1908 campaign he wrote: "The Socialist Party is the political expression of what is known as 'the class struggle.'" These are not isolated expressions; Gene talked that way all the time. Labor and socialist politics made sense when Debs campaigned.

The Socialist Party of Norman Thomas has abandoned the class-struggle politics of Debs in favor of a Democratic Party careerist who advocates a "new reformism," which he translates into a "fight against crime." But they still incongruously remember Debs' birthday. They held another

"Annual Debs' Day Dinner" last week at Schwarz' Restaurant, with Norman Thomas, of course, as one of the speakers.

They pushed the date ahead a little—Gene's birthday comes on November 5—in order, I suppose, to utilize the occasion for the benefit of Halley's campaign. If the diners felt a slight tremor of the building, accompanied by a rumbling sound, it wasn't caused by the subway train rolling by. That was probably Debs turning over in his grave.

The Catholic church

1. From Hollywood to Rome

THE MILITANT, NOVEMBER 12, 1951

Taking advantage of what is left of my rights, I hereby serve notice of intention to join in the public discussions stirred up by President Truman's decision to send a United States ambassador to the Vatican. And if you expect me to be calm and politely restrained in my utterances, you're in for a disappointment. I was burned up about the encroachments of authoritarian clericalism long before the President's decision was announced. His latest stroke of statesmanship just added a little fuel to the flames which have been searing my tender flesh.

This is not a debate, properly speaking. From the looks of things, it is turning into a free-for-all fight. I am glad to see that, and I want a hand in it. My intellectual convictions on this issue, which are quite firm and definite, are reinforced by personal grievances which cry for redress. Grover Cleveland once remarked: "It is a condition which confronts us—not a theory." In this case there is a theory too, and a very simple one. But the thing that hurts right now is a condition which is already infringing on my right to live as a free man in a free society.

The Roman Catholic hierarchy in this country is getting pretty bold and taking in a lot of territory. They not only want to regulate the morals of their communicants; they also want to regulate mine and yours according to their own perverted conceptions of morality. That's where my grievance begins. It may seem like a long way from a couple of movies to the highest affairs of state. But there is a direct connection as I see it; and they merge together, along with a lot of other related questions, into a menacing shadow of clerical thought-control over America.

Experience has made me leery of Hollywood and taught me to be choosey about what movies I see. This caution and discrimination pays off. When something good comes along on the screen, some artistic creation which holds the mirror up to human nature, I appreciate it all the more. And I treasure my right to see and admire and pay for the privilege, like any other free-born citizen. I saw "Open City" and "The Bicycle Thief," and bowed in reverence before the uncontaminated art of the Italians. When I read the reviews and heard the comments of friends about Rossellini's picture called "The Miracle," I decided to see that, too, at the first opportunity.

But before I got around to it, the right to see this picture was brutally taken away from me and others who wanted to see it. Cardinal Spellman, the ecclesiastical hoodlum who broke the strike of the cemetery workers and splattered Mrs. Roosevelt with mud in a gutter brawl, denounced "The Miracle" as immoral. And forthwith the subservient public officials in New York banned the picture and took it off the screen.

I won't stop here to argue the worth or worthlessness of Spellman's moral standards. I am concerned with more important questions. What about the right of Rossellini and his company to produce their work of art according to their own lights and insights? And what about my right and the right of other citizens to see the production and judge it for ourselves?

When I read the announcement that the movie version of "A Streetcar Named Desire" would be shown in New York, I said right away, without waiting for reviews or recommendations from anybody: This is a picture I must see. The reason for my recklessness in this case was that I had seen the original play on the stage, as played by a good company of actors on the summer theater circuit. I don't care much for decay and degeneration as themes of art. But that, it seems, is all you can get in a serious novel or play about people in the land lost in darkness south of the Mason-Dixon line. The artists paint what they see, and will not lie. It's terrible, but it's true and therefore beautiful.

That is the profound impression I took away from the theater when the final curtain fell on Tennessee Williams' powerful, mercilessly realistic, and yet compassionate play. I wondered what Hollywood would do with it, and made arrangements of my time in advance to go and see for myself.

I am happy to report that Hollywood didn't foul up this job. The picture faithfully follows the stage play and brings all its characters to life as the author conceived them. For this we owe our thanks to Elia Kazan, who produced the original play on Broadway, and then went along to Hollywood to direct the picture. Warner Brothers had sense enough to provide him with the best possible cast, headed by the incomparable Vivien Leigh, and let him alone.

But then, after the picture was finished to the satisfaction of all concerned, some mutilating cuts were made without the director's knowledge or consent. Elia Kazan told about it with cold fury in the *New York Times* a couple of weeks ago. Between the time the picture was finished and its release in New York, the Legion of Decency went to work. This is a special organization set up by the Catholic hierarchy to police and censor works of art, and to decide what can't be shown under threat of boycott. They preach Christian charity, but they rely on brute force. They let Warners know that they were going to give the picture a "C" or "Condemned" rating. "This," says the angry director, "would mean that people of the Roman Catholic faith would be instructed not to see it."

You might think that this doesn't concern you, since you pay no attention to such "instructions." But you are mistaken. Warner Brothers didn't doubt for a minute that it concerned them in the center of their most vital and sensitive interest—the box office.

Says Elia Kazan: "The studio's reaction was one of panic. They had a sizable investment in the picture, and they at once assumed that no Catholic would buy a ticket. They feared further that theaters showing the picture would be picketed, might be threatened with boycotts of as long as a year's duration if they dared to show it, that priests would be stationed in the lobbies to take down the names of parishioners who attended. I was told that all these things had happened in Philadelphia when a picture with a 'C' rating was shown there, and, further, that the rating was an invitation for every local censor board in the country to snipe at a picture, to require cuts or to ban it altogether."

So, without consulting or even informing the distinguished director of the picture, they made 12 cuts in the finished film to satisfy the demand of the clerical censors, and delayed the planned showing of the picture until the mutilated version finally secured their "B" rating.

It is just the good luck of the movie-going public that the cuts were minor and do not seriously affect the flow and tremendous drive of the picture. That may be because Tennessee Williams' play, directed by Elia Kazan, is too powerful and subtle a thing for the ignorant Legion of Decency really to understand. We can't hope for such good luck every time. If this gang gets a little more power in this country, it will tell the people what they can see, and hear, and read, and what their children shall be taught in schools, and back up their regulations with force, as they do everywhere they can get away with it.

I, for my part, can get along without the movies, if necessary, but I can't get along without freedom. One of the greatest threats to our freedom in America comes precisely from the totalitarian enemy of enlightenment and freedom known as the Roman Catholic hierarchy, which President Truman has greatly strengthened and encouraged by his monstrous decision to send an official ambassador to the Vatican.

I am looking for allies in this fight, and it begins to look now as though we're going to have plenty of them. Some of them are good allies, and fighting mad, which is just exactly the mood this great discussion needs.

2. Church and state

THE MILITANT, NOVEMBER 19, 1951

It's a fairly safe bet that President Truman didn't know exactly what he was doing when he announced his decision to send a U.S. ambassador to the Vatican, nominating General Mark W. Clark to the post. Inhibited by training and constitutional disposition from seeing anything more important or farther in the future than the next election, he probably thought he was just firing off a cap pistol to attract the Catholic vote in 1952. He didn't know it was loaded.

But the recoil of the gun and the noise of the explosion leave no doubt about it. The shot heard 'round the country has had results undreamt of in the philosophy of the Pendergastian politico in the White House. A bitter controversy, long smoldering, has burst into a flame that brings both heat and light into American politics. Sides are being chosen for a fight. In my opinion, it's a good fight worth joining in.

"Congress shall make no law respecting an establishment of religion, or prohibiting the free exercise thereof." So reads the first clause of the First Amendment to the U.S. Constitution, adopted under the pressure of the people to protect their rights and freedoms. The meaning of this constitutional provision is quite clear to all who have no special interest in muddling it. It is the doctrine of "the separation of church and state."

It means that all religions must operate on their own; that no church is entitled to a privileged position so far as the state is concerned, and has no right to financial support from public funds. Congress is specifically enjoined from "making any law" which infringes this principle. That is how the people of this country have understood the first article of the Bill of Rights; and that is how the highest courts have interpreted it up to now.

All religions claim to operate under the sanction of the Almighty; and with this unlimited power on their side they should have no need of material reinforcement from human institutions, such as the state, in their business of saving souls. The authors of the First Amendment, however, clearly indicated that the people could not trust any church to limit itself to spiritual pursuits and rely entirely on supernatural favor. They all had to be restrained by constitutional fiat from seeking mundane advantages at the expense of rival claimants to the divine certificate of authority. Hence the amendment requiring the separation of church and state.

This doctrine has been subject to persistent encroachment in recent years by the one religious institution in this country which doesn't believe a word of it. The Roman Catholic Church, here and now, as everywhere and always, wants temporal as well as spiritual power. They claim the exclusive reservation of all places in heaven, but they want the real estate and money of this world too. By various devices and subterfuges they have been trying, with unwavering persistence and increasing boldness, to get into a preferred position to regulate public morals by police methods and to dip into public funds to support their religious schools.

Their campaign for special privileges has received a tremendous impetus from the President's decision. The constitutional doctrine of the separation of church and state is directly under attack in this proposal. Some protest by the Protestant clergy was no doubt expected by Truman and his advisors. But the unanimity, the fervor, and even the fury of this Protestant counter-attack has upset the apple cart. Frozen with fear over the political implications of the Catholic aggression and the Protestant uproar, Congress adjourned without acting on the appointment of General Clark as America's ambassador to the Pope. The issue remains in doubt as the controversy rages from one end of the country to the other.

In some respects the conflict has the aspects of a religious war which can have profound consequences for good and evil. But it is more than that. All the people of this country who cherish the freedoms they have inherited have a stake in the controversy. The leadership of this fight belongs by right to the labor movement, for the trade unions cannot live and breathe without freedom from the control of both church and state. They will not escape eventual involvement, although the entire leadership is trying to evade the issue in craven silence. The simple truth is that the labor skates are afraid of the Catholic Church, whose cardinals and bishops are already reaching out for control of the unions. Woe to the American labor movement if they succeed!

We Marxists are by definition alien and hostile to each and every form of religious superstition. We believe with Marx that religion is the opium of the people; and we are not Marxists, not genuine socialists, if we do not say so openly, regardless of whether our opinion is popular or not. Our business is not to save souls for another world, but to tell the truth about this one. What, then, have revolutionary socialists to do with this controversy between the churches? Plenty.

The U.S. Constitution in some of its sections sanctifies private property in the means of production. This must be abolished for the good and welfare of the people, and the future Workers' Government will make the necessary constitutional changes. But in my opinion, one part of the present Constitution will stand; that is, the first ten amendments (the Bill of Rights) in general, and the First Amendment in particular. The revolutionary people will have no reason to strike out or alter that. On the contrary, believing in and needing democracy and freedom, they will treasure it and guard it.

The First Amendment to the Constitution is our amendment; and we must defend it tooth and nail against all aggressions, whether secular or religious. It seems to me not accidental at all that the authors of the Amendment linked freedom of worship with free speech and free press in the same sentence. Thereby they clearly indicated that religion is to be considered a matter of opinion, in which each individual is free to choose, and by no means a revelation binding upon everybody. Moreover, "freedom of worship" implies also freedom of non-worship. That's the freedom I am exercising and I would surely hate to lose it.

Under this interpretation of the First Amendment, free thinkers and atheists, heathens and public sinners, who are very numerous in this country, have had a chance to breathe and spread enlightenment without fear of the dungeon and the rack. The First Amendment has been a protecting shield for the Children of Light and has enabled them to make their great contributions to literature, art and science. A breach in this provision of the Constitution, leading to its eventual repeal, would be an unspeakable calamity aiding and strengthening the forces of reaction and obscurantism here and all over the world.

The Protestant clergymen are "on the side of the angels" in this dispute, and all friends of enlightenment and progress owe them unstinting support.

3. The Protestant counter-attack

THE MILITANT, NOVEMBER 26, 1951

In the present cold war, which is getting hotter all the time, those who rely on what they hear and read must believe that the United States Government is the champion of freedom and democracy. That's what the leaders of the people—the statesmen, the big press and the labor leaders—say all the time. They can't all be liars. Or can they?

To be sure, the aggressions of our government against China—just to take one example—would seem to contradict the noble pretensions of our leaders. But to this skeptical suggestion they have a handy answer: That's in another country; and, besides, the Chinese, as Secretary Acheson put it so felicitously at the United Nations in Paris last week, are some sort of sub-humans, below "the general level of barbarism."

But now we have a red-hot issue of democracy and freedom right here in our own country. This issue has been hurled into the political arena by President Truman's nomination of a United States ambassador to the Vatican. What have our leaders got to say about this concession to reactionary clericalism? Nothing very direct and straightforward; instead, a chorus of silence and evasion.

The politicians and the labor leaders have stood mute, as the lawyers say, or dummied up as some other people would put it, as though they didn't hear the question. The metropolitan press on the whole, led by the *New York Times,* cautiously supports the appointment as "an experiment worth trying" without stating the real issue. With that unctuous hypocrisy and specious reasoning which are the trademarks of the *Times'* editorial page, it is represented that "our envoy will be the Ambassador to the State of Vatican City," and not "to the Roman Catholic Church." This distinction without a difference is a rather untimely joke, serving only to irritate people who take a serious issue seriously.

In this situation the Protestant clergymen have stepped forward as the defenders of the democratic tradition so crudely violated by Truman's decision. No doubt religious animosities will be inflamed at some of the lower levels of the fight; and no good can come of that. But the most authoritative and influential spokesmen of American Protestantism are putting the issue squarely on political grounds. They are speaking out fearlessly like real statesmen, putting the cowering politicians and labor skates to shame. And they are being heard.

On Reformation Sunday, October 28, commemorating the day in 1517 that Luther "nailed his theses to the door," the congregations of 8,000 Protestant churches across the country were rallied in a demonstration against the President's action. Petitions to be sent to Washington were signed on church steps. The preachers have their fighting clothes on. They know what the fight is about, and they are pulling no punches.

The Rev. Dr. Robert J. McCracken, minister of the Riverside Church in New York, in his Reformation Sunday sermon, said the Catholic Church is making an "open bid for power and dominance in this country," of which the Truman nomination of an ambassador to Rome was "only the latest example." He called on the Protestant churches in this country to "build up a resistance movement against the encroachments" of the Catholic hierarchy. "There will have to be some plain speaking," said the Rev. Doc., and he proceeded to speak, plainly and truthfully as follows:

> With the tide running against it in Europe, its stronghold for centuries, Roman Catholicism is engaged in ceaseless surreptitious pressure to obtain a position of preference and control in the New World. Nor can there be any doubt as to the success attending its efforts.
>
> It has an astonishing hold over the machinery of American life—the press, the radio, the films, the whole field of public relations. It is constantly bringing its weight to bear on local, state and national officials, on the political machines which rule many of our cities, on labor unions, welfare agencies, teachers' organizations. . . . It is high time Protestants realized that Rome has established itself as an independent empire in the United States.

Other preachers, from one end of the country to the other, have spoken out in the same tone of "God's angry men." But the clearest, sharpest and most political argument and denunciation came, as was to be expected, from Dr. G. Bromley Oxnam, Methodist Bishop of New York.

This man is a tough fighter, full of roast beef and the love of Jesus, and no respecter of persons. He practically challenges Truman to take off his coat and grab his best hold for a rough-and-tumble. In his blistering declaration there is no tone of subservience, or even of respect, for the present occupant of Blair House. Truman may be President of the United States by accident, but Oxnam is Bishop of the Methodist Church by the grace of God, and he speaks from a superior position.

He starts out by flatly accusing Truman of lying and breaking his promises to Protestant leaders. Writing in *The Nation,* November 3, the Bishop says:

> He told one of the most influential religious leaders of the nation in the early summer that the issue of an ambassadorship to the Vatican was dead. He told another leader that as long as he was President there would never be an ambassador to the Vatican.

The implication is obvious. Powerful pressure must have been put on Truman by the Vatican and the Catholic hierarchy in this country. But this overbold aggression of abhorrent clericalism brought an unexpected reaction. The Protestant clergymen are hot under their ministerial collars and up and jumping, with the great Bromley out in front. He calls for a *political* fight without compromise. Says the Bishop: "The American people will not be led down the road to Rome. . . . Protestants will fight the confirmation of General Clark and, if needs be, will carry this issue to the American people for final decision."

Leaving theological differences entirely aside he puts the issue where it belongs on political and democratic grounds:

> The road to Rome leads to clericalism. Hierarchies are characterized by lust for power, property and prestige. Clericalism is "the pursuit of power, especially political power, by a religious hierarchy, carried on by secular methods and for purposes of social domination." Protestants are resolved that clericalism shall not take root in this land and that their own freedom shall not be placed in jeopardy.

Bishop Bromley is not taken in for a minute by the pretense that General Clark has been nominated to the "State of Vatican City," and not to the Vatican as church, as the *Times'* editorial writer sophistically explains with tongue in cheek. "No amount of casuistical camouflage can conceal the fact that when the United States government sends an ambassador to the Vatican, it is actually sending a representative to the Roman Catholic church."

Again on the same point:

> The Roman Catholic hierarchy is not content with spiritual power. It demands temporal power. The present Pope bargained with Mussolini and got a few acres of land and sovereign right thereto. The so-called state is a subterfuge. It is the church in politics. It is the repudiation of the American conception of separation of church and state.

From start to finish of his militant manifesto, the political-minded Bishop is in there crowding his opponent and forcing the fight all the way. He winds up with a wallop:

> The road to Rome leads to an alliance with a church that is itself, as a vast landholder, allied with the reaction

in Europe that has often stood against the reform necessary to establish the free society.

That thesis will be hard to counter, for it states the simple truth—as far as it goes. The Bishop could have added that the U.S. government is already allied on the international field with the "vast landholder" and powerhouse of reaction centered in the Vatican. That's one of the main reasons why the million-masses of exploited workers and land hungry peasants throughout the world are against America.

When the working people of this country realize the full implications of the move to extend this reactionary alliance to our own soil, and thus to strengthen the trend to reactionary clericalism here, they will have no choice but to join Bishop Oxnam and the rest of the Protestant clergy in the fight against it. If the workers want to know what clerical domination means, let them take one good look at Spain.

The Protestant leaders don't go all the way, but as far as they go it is in the right direction and their fight on this issue is the people's fight too.

Stalinists and unionists

1. Some chickens come home to roost

THE MILITANT, DECEMBER 3, 1951

In the heyday of the Communist Party in this country, when they were the most frenzied of all the patriots, supporting the no-strike pledge in World War II and receiving governmental favor in return, the number of Stalinist-controlled unions and central labor bodies of the CIO reached an imposing figure.

They controlled the CIO Industrial Union Council of New York City, for example, and manipulated it at will in support of the current slogans of the Party. The executive bodies of such powerful organizations as the National Maritime Union and the United Electrical Workers were in their hands, along with a dozen or more other important unions. "Local 65," the big organization of Wholesale and Retail Workers in New York, was tightly controlled by the CP and operated like a dairy full of milk cows for the benefit and sustenance of the Communist Party and its various enterprises.

With this line-up, the Stalinists appeared to have a position of great strength in the trade-union movement which would be very hard to break. The appearance, however, was somewhat illusory, as subsequent developments, following the break-up of the American-Soviet war alliance and the beginning of the "cold war," soon revealed.

The methods of unscrupulous demagogy, bureaucratic manipulation and deals with careerists, by which the Stalinists had gained control of the unions and central labor bodies from the top, were the very same methods employed by Murray and Co. to "decontrol" them, and proved even more efficacious. The Stalinists in most instances lacked the "secret weapon" of support by an ardent and educated rank-and-file. The dizzying speed with which they were unhorsed in one union and industrial council after another, when the government which they had supported so enthusiastically during the war turned against them, was one of the amazing wonders of recent labor history.

Years ago the Communist Party embarked on its course of expelling revolutionary militants, who can't be had at a price, and turning toward opportunists and careerists whose single principle is self-interest. For a time, in a favorable conjuncture, this method of operation brought quick, if deceptive results. As long as things went well, with the government and even some of the biggest employers taking an attitude of benevolence or neutrality toward the Stalinists, their manipulations and deals with trade union careerists at the top and their brutal bureaucratic suppression of the ranks at the bottom paid off like a slot machine rigged to beat the sucker.

This policy can work miracles in the service of a dominant power, but it is absolutely no good to create a new and independent power from scratch. That requires the principled politics of the class struggle. Everything changed almost over night with the change in the international situation, when the power the Stalinists had been serving turned against them. All the clever tricks turned into disastrous fumbles. The top careerists upon whom they relied and ostensibly "controlled" simply weren't there any more.

Following their noses in the direction of personal interest, as this tribe always does, the careerists promptly swung over to the stronger side and became the most virulent "red-baiters" in the business. Conspicuous examples are Quill and Curran, long regarded, with good reason, as CP labor stooges. But they are only two of scores and hundreds of major and minor functionaries who deserted the Communist Party ship as soon as it sprung a leak.

After the big purge carried out by the Murray leadership, with the open support and even at the instigation of the government, the Stalinists were left with a few "independent" unions, such as the West Coast Longshoremen, Local 65 in New York, the Fur and Leather Workers, a minority of the United Electrical Workers, and the rumps and tag ends of other unions. When the "shake down" was apparently completed and a certain new equilibrium established, it was generally assumed that these expelled independent unions which had resisted the purge were Stalinist-controlled, for sure and for good.

That is not necessarily so. For the most part, the top bureaucrats in these unions are substantially no different in character from the others who had switched allegiance under pressure. The only real difference was in the circumstances which made the switch of allegiance easier for some, like Quill and Curran, and more difficult for others.

Curran, for example, was the lucky beneficiary of a split in the CP maritime fraction, which brought him the support of its strongest section and gave him the necessary elbow room. Quill had only to renounce and denounce the Communist Party in super-patriotic terms to demonstrate that the Stalinists had no real support in the ranks of the Transport Workers Union and were absolutely powerless in the show down. Some of the leaders in other unions were more closely surrounded by strong fractions and could not follow the example of Quill and Curran. Murray made their position all the more difficult by rejecting all compromise and forcing an immediate decision.

However, I suspected from the start that the process of disintegration would continue even in these independent unions. I thought it quite possible that many of the careerist bureaucrats in the expelled unions, having interests of their own to serve, which are not always identical with the interests of the Stalinist Party bureaucrats, would eventually follow the example of their former colleagues; only, perforce, at a slower pace and by a more devious route.

This trend was already indicated by the policy of the leaders of the independent UE from the first moment of the split. They left the CIO Convention, where the expulsions were to take place, before the floor fight was finished, leaving the other Stalinist labor skates at the convention in the lurch. Their first concern was to get back in the field and mend their own fences for the coming split. This was the first ominous sign of things to come.

It was further to be noticed that the UE, which had once stood out in front as a political instrument of Stalinism, promoting all the political slogans of the party, changed its tactical line radically. In their organizational struggle against the rival CIO union in the same field, the UE leaders began to overlook, leave out and forget many of the political slogans—which were of primary interest to the Party bureaucrats—and to concentrate on purely trade-union issues—which were of primary interest to them. This was another sign.

Further and more definite indication of this trend of some of the independent unions toward independence of the Communist Party, apparently leading to an outright break, is clearly revealed now in the latest developments in the Distributive, Processing and Office Workers Union, formerly known as "Local 65." The bureaucratic chickens of the CP are coming home to roost here too. In a major shake-up, four vice-presidents have been "reorganized" out of their posts. And from the way the *Daily Worker* is complaining about it, one must definitely conclude that the "reorganization" was not planned that way by the political bureau of the CP.

This red-hot development is what I started out to write about today, but the introduction has already used up my space. An examination of the heads that rolled in the palace revolution in "65" will have to wait till next time.

2. A trade-union episode

THE MILITANT, DECEMBER 10, 1951

After the top bureaucracy of the CIO had carried through its great purge, two of the weaker Stalinist unions, decimated by the raiding and wrecking assaults of both the CIO and AFL, sought shelter from the storm in a hasty merger with a stronger organization. Last year the hard-hit and groggy Food, Tobacco and Agricultural Workers and the United Office and Professional Workers effected a fusion with the former "Local 65" of the CIO Wholesale and Retail Union. This local has a membership of about 30,000 centered in big New York department stores and dry-goods concerns. The amalgamated body took the name of the Distributive, Processing and Office Workers' Union, the original "Local 65" of the CIO becoming District 65 of the new set-up.

This merger of convenience of three unions in unrelated fields appeared, on the surface at least, to consolidate the defensive position of the Stalinists against the fury of the government-CIO-AFL attack. Latest reports, however, indicate that things didn't turn out this way, as mentioned last week.

The Food and Tobacco Workers and the Office and Professional Workers, which were weaker and more dependent on the Communist Party and, therefore, more firmly controlled by it, were originally given equal representation in the executive body and staff of the new organization. That arrangement is out the window now. A few weeks ago the heads of District 65, which represents the real numerical and organizational power in the national body, carried through a major internal reorganization. Four of the vice-presidents from the other unions suddenly found themselves out of office and presumably out of jobs. At the same time the list of vice-presidents was reshuffled to give the Distributive section a mechanical majority in the future.

The meaning of the shake-up is quite clear, and so are the reasons for it. It is sufficient to read the comments of George Morris, labor editor of the *Daily Worker,* to get the pitch. He refers to the "alarm and bewilderment" of many people over the "recent trend" in the union, and leaves no doubt that he shares in the alarm if not in the bewilderment. He laments the unceremonious ousting of such old reliable Stalinist hacks as James Durkin, former president of the old Office and Professional Workers' Union, later secretary-treasurer of the merged union, and now divested of all official titles and emoluments.

Naturally, Morris says, "It is the DPO's democracy that has suffered." But Arthur Osman and David Livingston, the top bosses of District 65, who learned the tricks of demagogy from the Stalinists, didn't fail to give the same "democracy" a verbal workout in their press release. They justified their move in the name of "more democratic organization" and "equal representation in the leadership."

What really happened here is the same thing that has happened before and will happen again before the skein is finally unwound. Opportunist labor leaders, whom the Stalinists helped to put in power and protected against the pressure of rank-and-file militants, turned against the party at the moment when their allegiance was most needed. Osman and Livingston, like all the rest of their breed, have their own axes to grind. They are obviously taking advantage of the difficulties of the Communist Party to shake loose from its control and get themselves into a position for maneuvers and deals with the CIO, which has something to give them.

To be sure, this ingratitude, not to say cynicism of these white-haired boys who so long enjoyed the favor, support and publicity boosts of the Communist Party, is not a very admirable trait. But that's the way it is with careerists; you can buy them but they won't stay bought.

Morris' comments on the new developments are all couched in a hypocritical tone of regret and friendly admonition. The curses and brutal denunciation, which the Stalinists usually bestow upon their friends and favorites of yesterday, are withheld. This could indicate that the fight is still going on in the ranks and that the issue is not finally decided. The trend, however, is clear.

Morris refers to the recent anniversary festival of District 65 in Madison Square Garden, where the union's 18-year history was told in skits, pantomimes and speeches. "What struck me," he says, "was the omission of any reference to the union's origin and history as a left-wing organization, and the fact that throughout its history it drew its spirit, program and strength from the left stream of America's labor. This couldn't have been an oversight."

No, it was not an oversight. It is obvious that Osman and Livingston are engineering a swing to the right in line with the American labor bureaucracy as a whole. And it doesn't take a prophet or the son of a prophet to foretell that the majority of the job holders in the union, most if not all of whom belonged to the CP when it had something to give them, will go along with Osman and Livingston in the show down. It is possible, of course, for an honest revolutionary party to raise and educate a cadre of trade-union militants, including officials, who will stand up under pressure. We proved that in the Minneapolis fight. But human material of this kind can't be bought, as the new experiences in District 65 illustrate once again.

Such incidents as the shake-up of functionaries in the DPO are primarily of interest for the future. Nothing now taking place in the trade unions settles anything definitively. All the expulsions, raids and wrecking operations of the conservative bureaucrats are, after all, mere episodes in the evolution of the American labor movement. They are the product, in the main, of the present atmosphere of reaction and are favored by it. This atmosphere will change, and with it, the situation and relation of forces in the unions.

The radical labor movement will rise again, stronger than before and wiser for the rich and varied experiences of the past 20 years. The Stalinists perverted and betrayed the last uprising of militant labor and thus made possible the present domination of the unions by the government. Will they get a chance to repeat that performance next time? Not if the revolutionary workers know their business and stick to it. That is the most important conclusion to be drawn from current events in the trade unions.

3. The tragic story

THE MILITANT, DECEMBER 17, 1951

For the past two weeks this space has been devoted to report and comment on the continuing misfortunes of the Stalinists in the trade unions. The right-wing bureaucrats haven't been doing so well in the protection of the workers against the twin scourges of speed-up and inflation. But in the internal fight against the remnants of Stalinist influence and control they are still shooting fish in a barrel.

The patriotic labor skates have all the advantages in an unequal struggle. They enjoy the solid backing of the government, and are also supported by all the monopolized agencies for the manufacture of public opinion. The general atmosphere of reaction favors them. And they have been aided in no small degree by the witch-hunt and the brutal persecution of the Communist Party leaders, which the CIO Convention formally—but only formally—decried. For the moment, at least, the right-wing, pro-government faction of Murray and Reuther are the victors. Moreover, they continue to gain, directly or indirectly, from new betrayals and defections which afflict the Stalinists, even in their "independent" unions, like active hemophilia.

If one can contemplate the trade-union troubles of the Stalinist fakers with equanimity it is not because of indifference to the present trend of events. The over-all result is the consolidation of a conservative, pro-government bureaucracy which smothers the militancy of the unions created in struggle and harnesses them to the imperialist war machine. Revolutionary militants are bound to struggle against this course. It would be a fatal error, however, to identify this struggle with the Stalinists and to regard them as its banner bearers. The Stalinists are losing positions they never earned and never used to good purpose. Why shed tears for them? Sympathy should be reserved for their victims.

The chief victim of Stalinism in this country was the magnificent left-wing movement, which rose up on the yeast of the economic crisis in the early Thirties and eventually took form in the CIO through a series of veritable labor uprisings. Such a movement, instinctively aimed against American capitalism, was bound to find a political leadership. Conditioned by their frightful experiences, the workers in the vanguard of the great mass movement were ready for the most radical solutions. The Stalinists, who appeared to represent the Russian Revolution and the Soviet Union, almost automatically gained the dominating position in the movement; while thousands of young militants—not the worst, but in many cases the very best—were recruited into the Communist Party.

The story of what happened to these young militants; what was done to them, how their faith was abused and their confidence betrayed by the cynical American agents of the Kremlin gang—that is just about the most tragic story in the long history of the American labor movement. The promising young movement was manipulated, twisted and distorted to serve the current aims of Russian foreign policy. The young militants seeking education from the Communist Party, were dosed with demagogy and double talk. They were taught that bureaucratic tricks and manipulations, and horse trades with careerist labor officials, were more important than the politics of the class struggle.

The best young militants with independent minds, who wanted to think and learn and act consistently according to principle, were ruthlessly expelled. Others were cowed into silence and acquiescence, befuddled into the sadly mistaken belief that by all the lies and treachery they were somehow or other serving a good cause.

By their whole policy and conduct; by their unprincipled opportunism, their unscrupulous demagogy, systematic lying and calculated treachery—the Stalinists demoralized the left-wing labor movement. They squandered its militancy and robbed it of the moral resources to resist the reactionary witch-hunt instituted in the unions with the beginning of the "cold war." Murray and Reuther only appear to be the conquerors of the left-wing workers. It was really the Stalinists who beat them.

Losses and defeats can't be avoided in times of reaction, when the relationship of forces is unfavorable. This is true in all stages and phases of the class struggle, from trade-union activity to revolution. But there are defeats and defeats. Those which come in battle under honest leadership leave a tradition upon which the movement lives and later rises to victory. Other defeats which derive from cowardice and treachery bring demoralization and yield no moral capital for the future. Such is the defeat engineered by the Stalinists in the present internal struggle in the trade unions.

The great majority of the young militants attracted

to the Communist Party in the past 20 years have fallen away in disillusionment and disgust. A very large percentage of those who remained in the party have been hopelessly miseducated and corrupted. But for all that, some of the present members of the Communist Party no doubt retain their revolutionary aspirations and faith. We encounter such individuals quite often and we sympathize with them, and try to find a basis for cooperation. We don't blame them for all the crimes of the Communist Party leadership. They are the fall guys in a stupendous frame-up and confidence game. Any time they take a single step toward a break with perfidious Stalinism, toward the politics of the class struggle, they will find us ready to help, to discuss the great questions of principle, and to cooperate in the struggle against American capitalism.

Some material for an honest revolutionary party will yet be salvaged out of the mass of people attracted to the Communist Party in the past and miseducated by it. But on this score one should have no illusions. The main mass of American militant workers poisoned by Stalinism are a used-up generation, morally spent. It is tragic, for they were good material, the kind of material out of which a revolutionary party can be made; but it can't be helped.

American labor radicalism has a great future, and its next upsurge very probably will not be long delayed. We should make no mistake as to where the troops are coming from. The next drive will be spearheaded by the young militants of the new generation who are soon to enter the arena with all the courage and ardor of the generation of the Thirties; and very likely in even more imposing numbers. They will avoid the fate of the preceding generation if those who have learned from the tragic experiences do their duty. The first element of that duty is to inoculate the new generation of militants against the deadly virus of Stalinism.

Whittaker Chambers' revelation

1. The informer as hero

THE MILITANT, JUNE 2, 1952

By their heroes ye shall know them—if an infidel may paraphrase the gospel of St. Matthew—for in the individuals whom they exalt and glorify and hold up to the youth as examples, every class and every movement unfailingly reveals its standards of worth, its morality, its very soul.

Thus, the communist workers of Germany glorified the name of the courageous and incorruptible Liebknecht who sacrificed his life in battle for a great cause. The degenerate Nazis countered with the dedication of their official hymn to Horst Wessel, the pimp who was killed in a brawl. The Liberty Boys of '76 celebrated Patrick Henry and his stand for "Liberty or death." The British oppressors took Benedict Arnold, the traitor, to their bosom. The southern slave-holders hanged John Brown. But the feet of the slave-liberating soldiers of the Union were quickened on the march by the song about "John Brown's Body," for his soul marched with them.

The vanguard of the modern labor movement, with its grandiose perspectives of the future, lives on the memory of Parsons and Debs who put the freedom and welfare of the working people above personal concerns. American capitalism, turning rotten before it got fully ripe, acclaims the stool pigeons and informers, who squeal and enrich themselves, as the embodiments of the highest good they know. By their heroes ye shall know them.

The latest hero and beneficiary of the build-up is Whittaker Chambers. He is the darling as well as the envy of all the renegade intellectuals, for he has made the biggest splash and drawn down the biggest "take" of all the professional witnesses who have ingeniously tied together in a package deal their twin talents for testifying against others and writing about themselves. Chambers, who put the finger on Alger Hiss and got immunity for himself, is currently offering a lengthy apologia for an unadmirable life in a scrubbed-up autobiography (*Witness,* Random House, $5), and at latest reports is doing pretty good for himself.

The height of philistine aspiration is reached when moral complacency is happily combined with material success. That is the prescription for the good life lived in the American way. And if the agencies which monopolize publicity and the manufacture of public opinion in this country don't succeed in putting Chambers over as a man who had attained these highest values, it will not be for lack of trying.

Witness is the bonanza of the publishing business and the sensation of the literary racket. It has been a long time since any book got such a send-off. Random House, it is reported, is spending $30,000 to advertise the Chambers' revelation. But this extraordinary allotment of the publishers, who stand to profit, is only a small part of the build-up. Eight chapters of the book were previously serialized in the *Saturday Evening Post* in extra editions, promoted by full-page ads in the daily papers, reaching nearly five million readers. In addition, the publication of the book made news in every newspaper and literary journal in the country, and it is getting top billing and extensive space in all the reviews.

Time Magazine, whose publisher is devoutly dedicated to the proposition that there is no such thing as a piece of news that can't be slanted and angled until the fact is lost in the interpretation, spreads its laudatory review over six pages and concludes that Chambers "speaks, like the Publican, with the tremendous eloquence of humility," although it fails to explain what Henry Luce and Co. would know about such things.

Saturday Review, the top-drawer weekly of the New York literati, abandoned all its customary restraint to spread five separate reviews of *Witness* over nine pages. And all the other publications I have seen, from the *New York Post* to the *Christian Science Monitor,* give this literary event of the year the full treatment in their review columns.

There is a motive behind this stupendous ballyhoo. The insecure and frightened reactionaries sense that they are losing ground in the "propaganda war." Chambers has a "message" for them and offers them a program. He claims he has had a "religious experience" and has come to Christ with a bang. He has heard voices, and the voices have told him that the struggle for the *status quo* against social revolution must be explained as a war of God versus human reason. There is nothing that an unreasonable and outlived social system needs more than that formula.

In my time as a hobo, I have known mission stiffs to confess Christ for a bowl of soup and a flop. Chambers has done better than that. His resounding literary fame is being supplemented—incidentally, of course—by material rewards. *Time Magazine,* which has no motive for lying about its distinguished alumnus, says "*Witness* has already earned him more than $100,000. It may well earn over $200,000 (before taxes) by 1953 or 1954." And even this not untidy sum leaves out of account prospective fees for lectures before audiences of believing McCarthyites, radio serialization and movie rights.

Chambers, in fact and by his own report, never got very far in the scramble for prominence in the Communist Party. And in the spy apparatus of the GPU, to which he claims he belonged, he never rose above the lowly role of courier, with the special privilege of developing microfilms in an improvised darkroom. But there's no denying that he is now a literary lion, in the chips, and in a fair way to be built up and passed off as a shining exemplar of the All-American Boy. As such he and his book deserve notice; and, after I get these introductory remarks out of the way, I intend to offer my contribution, from my own point of view, which is different from that of the other reviewers, and for my own peculiar reasons, as follows:

First, I have had no love for informers since, at an early age, I heard the story of the struggles of my Irish ancestors and learned the verse of the poet who longed for "a tongue to curse the slave" who betrayed them. Chambers, on the record, only strengthens my original prejudice in this respect.

Second, I know something about Chambers and know that he is a sanctimonious liar by commission and omission. I don't know whether he lied about Alger Hiss or not; the spy business is outside the field of my experience. Competent legal authorities, however, have expressed grave doubts about the guilt of Hiss. Charles Alan Wright, Assistant Professor of Law at the University of Minnesota, writing in the *Saturday Review,* says flatly that he thinks Hiss is innocent; and he characterizes Chambers' book as "one of the longest works of fiction of the year." Besides that, new evidence assembled by Hiss' attorneys is widely held to indicate an elaborate frame-up of the unfortunate

Hiss and to justify a new trial.

I don't know about that. But I do know that Chambers is an impostor. He was never a Communist as he pretends, but merely a Stalinist who consciously practiced the Stalinist methods of double-dealing and betrayal. He is traveling as an ex-Communist on a false passport.

2. False witness

THE MILITANT, JUNE 9, 1952

Experience over the ages has taught most people that it is imprudent to trust the unsupported word of a police informer against another person or persons who may have been associated with him. There is always a suspicion that he may be lying to save his own skin, or otherwise to benefit at the expense of others. So far as criminal cases are concerned, this well-grounded skepticism has been crystallized into the legal maxim that the testimony of an accomplice is inadmissible as evidence without independent corroboration. This principle of law should be extended to impose a double caution with regard to the testimony of an informer who switches sides in a social conflict and stands to benefit from his apostasy.

The many perjuries admitted by Whittaker Chambers under cross-examination in the Hiss case raised an uneasy doubt in the public mind over the value of any of his testimony. Is his evidence against communism any more trustworthy? There seem to be widespread doubts about this too; and Chambers has now offered a book of 800 pages in an effort to dispel them. This book, *Witness,* is being highly touted by the beneficiaries of privilege and their literary apologists who badly need a believable witness against communism. The unprecedented advertising and publicity campaign behind it is designed to make an impression by sheer volume. Chambers is recommended as a "sincere" witness whose numerous admitted lies in the past should not be held against him, and as an authentic ex-Communist who has finally seen the light and now recognizes that the present social system, being designed by God, shouldn't be tampered with.

Chambers' record, however, does not justify such a recommendation. He does not tell the truth about his time in the Communist Party, nor about the reasons for his long delay in breaking with it, nor about the motivation for the break when it occurred in 1938. *Witness* is an attempt to rewrite the actual record in terms more suitable to his role of convert touched, as he claims, by the finger of God and, by special dispensation, getting his reward without waiting for the next world.

I wrote last week that Chambers "was never a Communist as he pretends, but merely a Stalinist who consciously practiced the Stalinist methods of double-dealing and betrayal." Formally speaking, the first half of that sentence was a slight exaggeration. The second half, however, needs no amendment. Chambers joined the Communist Party in 1925 when the process of Stalinization was far from completed, and a party member had a right to think he was a Communist, or wanted to become one. But American communism was then already in the grip of an internal crisis which had its source in the creeping degeneration of the Soviet Union. As in all political organizations, the principal issues at stake, first latent but eventually clearly defined, could not be resolved otherwise than by factional struggle.

Every party member worth his salt took a position and took part in these factional conflicts. Chambers piously explains that he stood aloof from all the factions and stayed away from unit meetings in order to avoid involvement. That says a lot about the seriousness of his membership in the Party, but somewhat discredits his present claim to give an accurate report of what happened there. He took no risks and accepted no consequences. When American communism was fighting for its life in the factional struggle of those years, he was a bystander. Chambers does not write about the experiences of those times with the authority of a participant.

He took no part; but as the factional struggles came to climax and split, he had an interest and sympathy which he lacked the moral courage to act upon. Even worse, he befouled his sympathy with a petty betrayal. Shortly after we were expelled from the Party in 1928 because of our support of Trotsky and the Russian Opposition, Chambers furtively expressed interest and sympathy with our cause. We had an important document in German—Trotsky's appeal to the Sixth Congress of the Comintern—which we wanted to publish. Shachtman showed Chambers the document. He read it, expressed interest and offered to translate it for us so that we could publish it in *The Militant*.

Shachtman gave him the copy, the only copy we had, and that's the last we ever saw of it. We waited impatiently for the translation to be completed, but heard nothing from Chambers. Finally Shachtman called him up and asked when the translation would be ready. Chambers answered that he had turned it over to the Central Committee of the CP. A small incident, perhaps, but more revealing for the judgment of a man's character than 800 pages of self-serving apologia.

In the fateful years 1936–1937, the years of the Moscow Trials and Purges, when the old guard Bolsheviks, who had really borne witness for communism, were being framed and slaughtered because they were Communists, Chambers held his peace and continued to serve the dominant power—the Stalinist murderers and their GPU. Now that he has gone whole hog in his "conversion" to another power, he tries to wash out the truth about that awful time and to exculpate himself in the process. He dumps the Stalinists and the Trotskyists, the traitors and the revolutionists, the murderers and the victims, into one sack. The issues between them, drawn by a great river of blood, were "merely quarrels over a road map." Going beyond the boundaries of shame, this "witness" for God's justice even excuses the slaughter of the irreproachable Old Bolsheviks. "Acting as a Communist, Stalin had acted rightly." That's what Chambers says now.

But that's not the way I heard it the first time. Chambers knew the truth about the Moscow Trials. And that is what bothered him, as it was bound to bother anyone with a glimmer of communist conscience. This is clear even from his own back-written, doctored-up account of his first reaction to the trials. Listing the names of the most prominent victims, he inadvertently remarks: "The charge, on which they were one and all destroyed, the charge that they had betrayed their handiwork, was incredible. They *were* the Communist Party." The Moscow Trials, not the afterthoughts about God and the FBI, are what moved Chambers finally, after two years of intellectualistic mulling and moping, to break with the Stalinist apparatus in 1938.

We knew about it first for the simple reason that, after his break with the GPU, he came to us first—to us and to others who had cooperated to expose and discredit the Moscow Trials, those who had spoken out against that infamy when he had remained silent in the service of its monstrous authors. He didn't go to the Church, or the Quaker Meeting House, or the FBI; he came to us. He expressed, and no doubt felt, a great admiration for Trotsky as the incorruptible representative of the communist faith which Chambers imagined that he also professed. The question was: What to do about it?

We did not represent a power of the present—only a program by means of which a future power can and will be created through struggle against any odds whatever. We didn't have much to offer him but a part in the struggle for ideas as a member of an isolated and persecuted minority. Chambers didn't have what it takes for that. That would have meant, in deed and not in pretentious rhetoric, to be a *witness,* to "testify for his faith, disregarding all risks, accepting all consequences," as Chambers wrote in his book without understanding what it really means.

Chambers had spent the best years of his life as a functionary in the service of a power of the present represented by the Stalinist GPU. A struggle to create a new power of the future was beyond his capacity, perhaps even beyond his comprehension. He really didn't know what it meant to be a genuine Communist in this country, with the corruption of Stalinism on one side and the power of bourgeois society on the other. When the showdown came at the turning point of his life, after a couple of years of mawkish indecision, he switched his allegiance to another power of the present represented by the FBI, with God rung in for moral support.

There, in a nutshell, is the life story of Whittaker Chambers. All that is left out of his autobiography which purports to be a full and true confession. That is why the whole book is a lie. It is not a "witness" against communism, but against Chambers and all his ilk, and against a social system in decay which can find no better heroes.

3. The informer's message

THE MILITANT, JUNE 23, 1952

In these days of wholesale renegacy under witch-hunt pressure, one more convert to the side of the ruling powers, laying one more bone of information at their feet, couldn't expect to cause a sensation or rate more than a small stick of type in the daily press. Such news has grown stale by too much repetition of the same thing.

If Whittaker Chambers had done nothing more than that he could not have attained his present status as a modern oracle. His services as an informer, of course, would have been appreciated; and like the less-favored of his dreary brethren, he would have been paid off, dismissed and told to wait on call for possible use in another case.

But Chambers is an exception who has been blown up into a celebrity because he went beyond the familiar routine of peddling information for immunity and bearing false witness against communism. Chambers has written a book (*Witness,* Random House) with a message to the effect that, to his personal knowledge, God has taken a definite position against communism and all revolutions past, present and future. That is a message which the instigators and beneficiaries of the current hysteria want to hear and have proclaimed far and wide.

Powerful agencies, monopolizing the mediums of information and publicity, consciously strive to mold public opinion in a reactionary pattern. Chambers' revelation, wrapped up in 800 pages of *Time*-style literary trimmings, fits perfectly into this design and fills a special need. It puts an intellectual and spiritual gloss upon the crude and brutal operations of the Congressional Un-American Activities Committee, the loyalty boards, and all the various McCarthys, McCarrans and other vigilantes, national and local. The extraordinary build-up of the book and the author is well motivated.

Our country is not what it used to be. Within the space of a single generation, a remarkable transformation has taken place in America's position in the world. Political thinking has changed correspondingly. For more than a century the United States, with a whole continent of its own to exploit, developed into a mighty industrial power in comparative self-sufficiency behind ocean barriers and tariff walls. This geographical security found its political expression in the doctrine of isolationism. Washington's warning against foreign entanglements was the popular creed.

All that is changed for good. The material basis for the doctrine of isolationism has long been outlived, and the doctrine itself has of necessity been relegated to the past. American capitalism is involved in the world, and there it is running up against all kinds of economic dislocations and the rising tide of social revolution and colonial insurgence. Bourgeois America is in a jam which its deepest thinkers never foresaw or bargained for. Even the thickest heads on the shoulders of our lords and masters have begun to ache from worry and apprehension over the problem.

They are confronted with the alternative: dominate the world or perish. This dilemma is pretty well recognized by all the factions in the ruling circles. Counsels are divided only about the policies and means whereby American capitalism can survive and establish its world domination. The division, however, is not really serious. The necessary decision has already been made.

There is still a faction, more articulate than effective, which talks piously about maintaining all the material benefits of a Welfare State in the United States and, at the same time, scattering these peculiarly American blessings among the hungry and benighted people of other lands. This program expresses itself in the New Deal within the country and the blather about Point Four abroad. The proponents of this paper program say we can outbid communism and win people's minds to a better faith, a faith in democracy and universal prosperity as exemplified in the USA.

The other, more realistic, faction—the faction that is in the saddle whether in office or not—recognizes that this program, as a program for American capitalism, is impractical. They have no further use for the New Deal or other welfare measures. And they don't intend to build any TVA's on foreign rivers either. American capitalism, they are convinced, can save itself and conquer the world only with force and not with largesse, which anyway it can't afford. This is precisely the program that American capitalism needs—if it is to remain what it is. Moreover, it is the program that is actually being put into effect.

Domestic and foreign policy in practise are of one piece. At home there is the progressive destruction of civil rights; the thickening atmosphere of police-state terror and suppression of dissenting thought; the increasingly vicious anti-labor laws and the preparation for an all-out assault on the trade-union movement. The aim of this domestic policy, bluntly put, is to beat down the standards of the American working people and make them pay for the impending war. From the standpoint of capitalism this is a simple necessity. The costs of a total war, high wages and a Welfare State don't go together; any bookkeeper can tell you that. Those who say otherwise are liars or muddleheads.

Abroad, despite all the tongue-in-cheek palaver about democracy, national independence, Point Four, etc., the same policy is extended. The world sees America everywhere in alliance with the most reactionary elements—capitalists, landlords and usurers—who exploit and oppress the people. Imperialist America's foreign policy has, and can have, only one counter-revolutionary aim—to support capitalism wherever it is threatened and to restore it wherever it has been overthrown.

But such a program and practice, frankly declared, couldn't be very attractive to its present and intended victims. It has to be dressed up and disguised. Even the most stupid reactionaries realize that a war for world conquest, necessitating the mobilization of tens of millions, requires some kind of ideological justification, some sort of "faith"—all the better if it doesn't cost anything. That is why they are inclining more and more to the promotion of a revival of religion; a religion, that is, of a special kind, a religion which fits the needs of the trend toward a police state and eventual fascism—which will surely be America's fate if the workers' revolution doesn't arrive in time.

The religion they want is none of the easy-going, love-thy-neighbor Christianity which many humble rank-and-file followers of the gospels believe and practise to the best of their ability; none of the Protestant liberality which allows a person—more or less—to form his own idea of religion as a code of ethics and worship God in his own way; and certainly none of the freedom of thought and inquiry and reliance on human reason bequeathed by the Enlightenment of the eighteenth century. No, the rulers of America who want to rule the world want an *authoritarian* religion with an iron-fisted God who *decides* what's good for people and has a temporal power to *enforce* his decisions.

That is why the Catholic hierarchy, which aims at totalitarian rule over the minds of men, gets more and more favor and support and thrives accordingly. That is also the reason why Chambers' book, with its formula of God standing above human reason and against it—God against revolution and even against New Deal social reform—has met such an enthusiastic response in reactionary circles as a literary weapon in their fight.

Where do the New Dealers, the liberals, the literate

ex-radicals and the rest of the literary gentry who want to support an unreasonable social system without renouncing human reason—where do they come in? Chambers' book upsets them—they like it and they don't like it. They support twentieth century American imperialism just as he does. But they want to dress it up in the ideological clothes of the eighteenth century.

They are out of date. The clothes they offer don't fit any more. That's why their reviews of Chambers' book produce such a comic effect. Chambers is a far more authentic ideologist for imperialists trending toward fascism, because he offers a spiritual justification of the only program they can have, the program they are already carrying out—at home and abroad.

Tentative action on the civil rights front

THE MILITANT, DECEMBER 31, 1951

All who are informed on world affairs know that the United States today is the most undemocratic country still maintaining the outward democratic forms of government. There is far more freedom in Britain and France today than in Lincoln's "new nation conceived in liberty;" not only in the formal legal sense but also in the general atmosphere; not only more freedom of discussion but also more freedom of thought. Even in Italy, whose people almost lost the memory of freedom in more than two decades of fascism, there is more respect for the right of opinion and free discussion than here.

The United States has enacted the most barbarous legislation and is brutally enforcing it—mainly, at first, against the Communist Party. But reaction is not confined to the legal field. The dominant powers are waging a psychological war against free thought and dissenting opinion on a scale that goes far beyond the legal suppression—and prepares the ground for its intensification and expansion.

Ever since the beginning of the cold war, brutal and ignorant reaction has been on the offensive. The raging witch-hunt has invaded the schools and the trade unions, and so far has met little or no opposition. Indeed, the labor leaders who could easily be the next victims of a mounting reaction, as the tragic experience of Germany in the 'thirties so clearly demonstrated, gave at least left-handed support to the witch-hunt and rode on it in their internal fight with the Stalinists. Even the voice of American liberalism, when it has been heard at all, has been frightened, timid and weak. Opposition to the witch-hunt has been paralyzed.

The basic factor, paralyzing the traditional defenders of constitutional rights, has been their support of the administration's foreign policy, which is a policy of war and world conquest. Civil rights can hardly prosper under the domination of such a policy. The Truman domestic implementation—the "loyalty" oaths and purges and prosecutions—has had at least the virtue of greater consistency. Politicians never see any reason to pay for votes they can get for nothing. Support for the main line, pledged in advance, has robbed the advocates of civil liberty of their bargaining power.

Nevertheless, a considerable and growing concern about the increasing invasion of constitutional rights is to be noted among wide circles of people. Various reasons motivate this concern. Some, who have nothing to do with radicalism, or any thought of it, consider it unwise to scrap the Constitution all at once. They fear excesses which could cause a revolutionary rebound and deal damaging blows to the social system which they support. Some of the sharpest and clearest expressions have been heard on the right.

Federal judges are counted, with good reason, among the most conservative representatives of the existing social order. It is rather ironical, therefore, that the first serious note of opposition to the unbridled disregard of constitutional rights and regulations came from a number of them. This has been particularly demonstrated in decisions overruling the lower courts in the matter of bail. In the general hysteria, these lower courts yielded to the demands of Truman's prosecutors and fixed the bail of the indicted Communist Party leaders at unreasonable figures which they couldn't possibly meet. The honorable judges of the higher courts have stated that exorbitant bail means, in effect, imprisonment without trial. And that, of course, is precisely what Truman's prosecutors intended it to mean. We are glad to see the federal judges take this position, whatever their reasons may be.

All the more to be welcomed are the recent signs of uneasiness and concern in circles which have traditionally stood for free speech and fair trial. The first good sign of a new awareness and intention to do something was the announcement of the formation, a short while ago, of the Emergency Civil Liberties Committee, headed by Professor Paul Lehman, acting chairman, and James Imbrie, acting secretary. Their declared intention to give active defense to all groups and individuals whose rights are violated by the mad dogs of reaction, regardless of their political opinions, was certainly an important step forward.

Following that, the thirteenth CIO Convention condemned the Smith and McCarran Acts. The adopted resolution deplored the decision of the Supreme Court upholding the conviction of the Communist Party leaders under the Smith Act as "a grave blow to America's precious heritage of freedom of speech." I wouldn't give much for the enthusiasm and energy of the CIO leaders in implementing this resolution by an earnest fight in the next stage of developments. They left out the main thing: a demand for the release of the imprisoned Stalinists and an end to prosecutions under the Smith Act. But the adopted resolution has its own logic, and may prepare the way to more important action.

Now comes a welcome, if belated, declaration of Americans for Democratic Action that they will fight for the repeal of the Smith Act "because it proposes to prosecute people for what they think and say rather than what they do." The ADA further says that it proposes, "together with the American Civil Liberties Union, the CIO, and other non-Communist organizations which have condemned the Smith Act, to fight for its repeal and for the reaffirmation by Congress of our basic freedoms." They also neglected to mention the most important point: the release of the imprisoned Stalinists.

All these moves are timid and tentative, but they go in the right direction. The ADA, like the others, would limit its cooperation to "non-Communist organizations." That's up to them, I suppose. We can't object to people choosing their associates and working for a good cause in their own way and in their own field. But they will not get very far, or do very much for civil rights, until they face the real issue of the witch-hunt as it stands today.

That is open and active defense of Stalinists who—in the given circumstances of the cold war—are the first and main victims. The Emergency Civil Liberties Committee, to its credit, has taken a clear position on this crucial point. There is not much value in talking about defending civil rights unless one is willing to defend the victims of their violation. The truth is always concrete, and so are civil rights.

The battle of Koje Island

THE MILITANT, JUNE 16, 1952

The whole story of Koje Island is not yet known, but from the few scraps of information which have been blown out of the prisoners' compounds, like hot rocks from a heaving volcano, the world is becoming uneasily aware of awful and fateful events transpiring there, with the premonition of more to come.

Through a breach in the military censorship the world is catching glimpses of a conflict of gigantic proportions in which ordinary men, as often before in history, play big parts because of the things they represent. In the great crises of history some men always rise above themselves and attain the stature of heroes. That happened in our own history—in 1776 and again in 1861. In the men who made these two revolutions young America saw the magnified image of itself.

The same thing appears to be happening now once again in a far-off land, and we are witness to it. The transcendent issues of our century are being dramatized on Koje Island in human terms, as in a heroic epic which has for its theme the death agony of an old social order and the birth pangs of a new one. Colonial oppression and struggle for national independence; western supremacy and Asian self-assertion; war and revolution—these are the colossal issues involved in the confrontation of white and yellow men across a barbed-wire barricade.

Outwardly it would appear that the struggle is unequal, with the outcome foreordained. The American army, which never lost a war, goes into the battle of Koje Island with much better equipment than the "Ragged Continentals" of 1776, who defended their land and their homes with an odd assortment of old muskets and sticks and stones, and a more impetuous policy than the patient General Washington's strategy of attack and retreat to wear out the enemy and keep his own army in being.

For the battle of Koje Island we needed a different kind of general and we found him. To the atta-boy applause of the editorial writers, who unfortunately can't leave their desks to take part, General Boatner has proclaimed a crack-down and he has the stuff to make good with it. Press dispatches bristle with accounts of the formidable array of armament he has brought up for use against the prisoners of war who persist in waving their own banners within the compounds. There are daily reports of prisoners being killed and wounded since Boatner took charge and announced a "get tough" policy.

Things are moving to some kind of a show-down in this battle of Koje Island; and the American people, with the historic memory of Bunker Hill not yet entirely obliterated, would do well to ask for a little more information about what we are fighting for there. We have heard the explanations of the brass hats. The captured "gooks," it seems, are "surly" and "fanatical." They "don't know who's boss" and they have to be shown. The compounds have to be split up into smaller units so that the prisoners can be "screened" more effectively. The improvised banners, waved from sticks inside the compounds, must come down. These are our declared war aims at Koje.

The prisoners' side of the story didn't come through

yet, although a UP dispatch of May 21 reports that they made a strenuous effort to tell correspondents what it is. "When the prisoners inside saw newsmen arrive they set up a clamor to be allowed to talk to them," says the report. "One shouted in English: 'Let us talk to these war correspondents!' Authorities refused." Could this incident, buried in a long dispatch, have been a correspondent's indirect way of telling the world that the whole truth is not coming out because he and his colleagues are not allowed to send it?

As the climax approaches, the papers are full of information about the battle plans of the forces outside the barbed wire. The *New York Times,* June 9, reports: "General Boatner has shaped up a full-scale offensive with all the troops under his command. . . . The plans call for battalions of infantrymen with fixed bayonets to crash through the barbed-wire barricades into the compounds, supported by several Patton tanks and under the protective range of machine guns."

That ought to do it. Military doctrine says that, other things being equal, superior fire-power prevails and decides. What chance, then, remains for the Koje prisoners who have no fire-power whatever? They have no chance at all—if other things are equal. But could it be that the prisoners keep their morale unshaken in the face of superior force because they think that the other things are not equal? That they have on their side some intangibles not comprehended by the military mind—some secret weapon more powerful than a bomb, some moral force generated by the things their banners represent and symbolize to them?

If that is the case, history tells us that such men will not be easy to conquer. History also tells us that men so inspired can lose a battle and still win the war. The most dangerous animal on earth is the man who has nothing to lose and is convinced that he has everything to gain. That's the trouble with the ill-starred American adventure in Korea—it is up against men like that, who are convinced that their historic hour has come; that they have great allies; that hundreds of millions of their kindred are behind them because they are in the same fix.

Such a conviction can make all things possible. From such a conviction comes the fanatical courage of the Koje prisoners—you can even call it heroism and you won't go wrong—to face all the military power of America unarmed and defiant. Yesterday they were nothing, with no rights that a white man was bound to respect. But a mighty revolution, coming up like thunder out of China and echoing throughout the entire Orient, has changed all that. Revolution has made new men out of them, lifted them to their feet and inspired them to sing and firmly believe: "We have been naught, we shall be all!"

That may be the secret weapon of the prisoners of Koje Island.

The doctor's dilemma

THE MILITANT, JUNE 30, 1952

American medicine, its personality split by the contradictory social conditions under which it must operate and the dual functions they impose upon the doctors, seems to be running a race with itself toward the opposite goals of public homage and opprobrium. Like Dr. Jekyll and Mr. Hyde, the modern doctor has two souls and doesn't know which one to call his own. The American people are not getting any benefit from this schizophrenia of the medicine men.

Medicine as a science is progressive and revolutionary, constantly sharpening its theoretical tools, bold and thoroughgoing in its increasingly successful search for new techniques. Medical science is benign, by its very nature social-minded, humane and out-giving, committed to the most ennobling ideal—the service of others. Who can be more deserving of the grateful acclaim of the people than those who heal the sick and make human life more livable? The doctors—as doctors—belong to the Order of the Friends of Man.

But the way things are, the doctor, who shouldn't have to bother with anything but his profession, must also be a businessman who has to make a living, charge all the traffic will bear and try to get rich in competition with others. This side of the picture is not so attractive. Medicine as a business, self-centeredly working for its own pocket, is no better than any other business. In some respects it is even worse, for the unnatural mixing up of a profession designed for service with the business of making money entails a special corruption of its own, which merits nobody's veneration.

Commercialized medicine leads to discrimination against those who need medical service most in favor of those who can pay best. The number of doctors is artificially restricted in order to reduce competition. Well-heeled hypochondriacs are over-attended while a large segment of the population goes without any proper medical attention at all. There is no justice in this lopsided distribution of service. The business side of the medical profession is ugly and abominable.

The doctor as a businessman has no claim to recognition as a public benefactor. And when he goes into politics in the interest of his business he is even less attractive. The people, if they had a free choice in the matter, would gladly furnish the necessary public funds to educate enough doctors to serve the whole population and to provide a good living for the doctors. That ought to be done as a matter of course. But the American Medical Association, dominated by the richest doctors, doesn't want it that way.

This medical trust fights every step and every legislative proposal to broaden medical coverage and base eligibility on need rather than on ability to pay. The rank-and-file doctor is terrorized into silence or acquiescence in this monstrous policy, and is even black-jacked into paying for the publicity campaign and lobby to support it. The lobby of the American Medical Association in Washington spends more money than any other to influence legislation in an exclusively reactionary and anti-social direction.

There are signs, however, that they may be overplaying their hand. The average layman, who appreciates the scientific achievements and services of the medical profession, is already pretty well fed up with the attempt to protect its nefarious business aspects by political propaganda and pressure. Some doctors themselves, big enough to speak out without fear of reprisals, are taking note of the angry drift of public opinion and making a timely bow to it. Thus Dr. Paul B. Magnuson, Chairman of President Truman's Commission on the Health Needs of the Nation, has got his dander up over what he aptly calls the "public be damned" attitude of the American Medical Association.

Dr. Magnuson, a noted orthopedic surgeon of Chicago and former medical director of the Veterans Administration, sounded off at the AMA meeting in Chicago against the hired publicity experts of the AMA, whose slick misrepresentation and high-pressure campaigns are bringing the medical profession into disrepute and making "the health and well-being of the American people" a "football for an obscene and vulgar battle between highly paid publicists."

Responding to the action of the AMA brass in denouncing the mere proposal for a government commission to investigate the people's health needs, Dr. Magnuson let them have both barrels. "My conscience is clear," he said. "They can all go to hell. I am doing a doctor's job, and in my book, the patient comes first."

That is good advice for the medical profession in general, and they would do well to heed it voluntarily before the people make it compulsory. Dr. Magnuson's words sound like the Hippocratic Oath which every young doctor takes on graduation, and then is expected to forget when his profession becomes a business and a political machine rigged out with publicity sharpers and Washington lobbyists. The Oath of Hippocrates obligates the doctor to visit the sick wherever they may be and to serve anyone whatever, on the sole condition that he needs medical care.

That ideal of the legendary founder of the medical profession must govern its future too. But that can be fully realized only when the practise of medicine as a social service—its justification and its glory—is completely separated from sordid business considerations and shabby politics—its degradation and disgrace.

That will require a change and reorganization of our social system, as revolutionary as any changes that have been made in the practice of medicine. The doctors have been bold enough to make such changes in their own profession, when scientific analysis demonstrated their necessity. They need a similar attitude toward the social problem. Socialism will be good medicine for the doctors who just want to be doctors. It will free them from the contradiction between their functions as physicians and businessmen, and cure them of the split personality which is caused by this contradiction.

Labor and foreign policy

THE MILITANT, JULY 7, 1952

Politics, properly so called, is an expression of the struggle of classes for control of government in order to use it to advance their interests. The class positions, in turn, are defined by contrasting programs. Within that basic framework the trifling squabbles and struggles of individuals and cliques over place and preferment, which mistakenly go by the name of "politics," have only a superficial and transient significance.

Nevertheless, such secondary manifestations often claim the popular attention and overshadow the deeper realities of the struggle. This is happening again as the 1952 presidential election campaign gets under way. As far as public attention at the moment is concerned, the show will be stolen by the frenzied struggle between factions of the ruling capitalist class—represented by the Republican and Democratic parties—for power to execute policies which are basically identical.

From a historical point of view, however, the presidential campaign of the Socialist Workers Party is far more important because it alone presents a class program of the workers against the class program of the parties of the monopolists. In the real sense of the word, this is the only political struggle going on this year. Despite all attempts to relegate it, our campaign foreshadows the line along which American politics must develop as class lines become more sharply drawn. The side show of the present will become the main event of the future.

Frankly defending the interests of the working people, our campaign will revolve around an idea which, as we see it, is the necessary premise for a correct orientation in American politics. This is the simple proposition that class interests can no longer be served on national grounds unless they are approached from an international point of view.

The nominal leaders of the two capitalist parties, and even more so the financial magnates who control and manipulate them, already know this. That is why foreign policy is their first concern. In this respect, their approach to national politics in 1952 is the same as ours. The theme is the same—but the class interest and the point of view are different. The political thinkers and ideologists of the ruling capitalists recognized long ago that American "isolationism" has no place in modern politics. We have the same opinion. They are involved in the world as it exists today, and concerned about things transpiring in other lands. So are we—but again for different reasons.

An increasing number of the organized workers are interested in foreign policy and recognize, to one degree or another, that it is the Number One political question, but they have yet to work out a logical foreign policy of their own. The foreign policy recommended by such global thinkers as Green and Reuther is not the product of their own independent thought. It is nothing but a mimeographed handout from the State Department, which in turn gets it from the New York bankers who are also the directing powers behind the anti-union drive. This policy doesn't make much sense for a steelworker on the picket line. The imposition of this Wall Street foreign policy on the trade-union movement is one of the main reasons why the instinctive striving of the organized workers to participate effectively in American politics is bedeviled and frustrated at the outset.

The official labor leaders support every move of American foreign policy even before they hear about it. Being in agreement with the "principle," they don't quibble about the details. They have their reasons, which have nothing to do with what they say. Many workers may be taken in by the propaganda about America's mission to bring democracy, prosperity and peace to the benighted heathens and strangers who have been overtaken by darkness in other parts of the world. The motivation of the labor statesmen is less altruistic. They toss this grandiloquent verbiage around with pitchforks, but they consider it strictly hay. They support imperialist America's foreign policy for practical reasons of self-interest, which they deem to be good and sufficient—although they happen to be wrong even on this ignoble score.

These mystics are believers in the myth of the "American Century," which might better be called the American pipe dream. They think the United States can conquer and dominate the world and prosper on the exploitation of other peoples, leaving a margin to maintain high living standards at home for trade unionists and government recognition for compliant labor leaders. The narrow-minded and meanly selfish bureaucrats think this would be fine and dandy. But it can't be done.

Besides being dishonorable and anti-human, this calculation is dead wrong from a practical standpoint. It misjudges the direction of the drift of history. American imperialism arrived at the top of the world too late to keep its balance there. It cannot conquer and subjugate the peoples of this planet and force them back into the framework of an outlived economic and social system, and will break its own neck trying. If you want a small, preliminary indication of the prospects just take one good look at Korea, where America's imperialist adventure is turning into a debacle.

The American workers need a foreign policy which will put them on their own side of the world conflict—which also is the winning side. For this, they have to push their blind leaders out of their sight and see for themselves what the real situation in the world is, and what is really going on.

The over-all determining fact of the present day is the manifest inability of capitalism, as a world social system, to regulate and control the world any longer. That is one-half of the present reality. The other half is the tumultuous advance of anti-capitalist and anti-imperialist revolutions in large parts of the world. The great events which the statesmen cannot regulate, but are rather regulated by, are all the product of these central dominating features of the present moment in history.

The world is changing. We live in the most revolutionary and warlike epoch in all history. It is a time of the breaking of nations and the creation of new ones on new economic foundations. Wars and revolutions now in progress, and more to come—world-wide in scope—are yet to be fought out before the issue is finally decided. But the general drift of history is absolutely clear. The American workers have nothing to fear from this. On the contrary, they have everything to gain. They need international allies to help them in their struggle at home. They need a foreign policy which expresses this self-interest of their own class.

Such a foreign policy cannot be the policy of the financial magnates who own this country and want to own the world. They fear the revolutionary events happening outside our borders and strive to halt them. The workers should welcome these events and help them along with their sympathy and support. The American capitalists feel in their bones that every blow at capitalist private property in any country whatever, every uprising of colonial slaves, helps to undermine their own international position and eventually their control of this country. And they are right about that.

When the American workers come to believe just as firmly that every revolutionary advance, anywhere in the world, brings up new allies of the American workers—they will be just as right. And, in the field of foreign policy, they will begin to fight on their own side.

How we won Grace Carlson and how we lost her

THE MILITANT, JULY 7, 1952

Grace Carlson is a victim of the reactionary atmosphere in general and the witch-hunt in particular. Her sudden action in resigning from the numerically small and persecuted Socialist Workers Party for sanctuary in the rich and powerful Catholic Church, is only the final effect of the many successive blows of persecution, poverty and discrimination which had been inflicted upon her during the long time she fought on the side of the poor for the great ideals of socialism.

There had been no previous intimation of this sudden decision. Within the past month she spoke and debated on the campuses of New York University and the University of Minnesota in defense of Marxism against political opponents. The reason she now gives for her precipitate resignation from the party—"a difference in basic philosophy"—is not the real reason.

When Grace Carlson came to the Socialist Workers Party in 1936 she held a good position in the Minnesota State Department of Education, received a good salary and was honored and respected in the Twin City circles of the rich and powerful as a Doctor of Philosophy. Her decision at that time to join with us in the service of the great ideal of socialism was a happy decision, as she stated at the time and repeated many times thereafter. We won her by our ideas and ideals and kept her for 16 years. We won her by persuasion, by arguments and by the example of comrades putting service to a great cause above personal interest.

The forces of reaction have finally broken her away from the socialist movement by a different method. They made Grace Carlson pay for her idealistic and self-sacrificing work for socialism. She had to give up her position with the Minnesota State Department of Education and drastically cut her standard of living. She had to sacrifice her honored position in the community. In 1943 she had to go to Federal prison along with 17 other members of the party. On her return from prison in 1945, she had to register with the Police Department of St. Paul as an ex-convict. She was blacklisted from all employment in the Twin Cities. Sacrifice after sacrifice was imposed upon her.

For 16 years the powerful forces of reaction hammered and pounded at this woman until they finally beat her down, broke her spirit of resistance and compelled her to leave the party which she had served so long and so honorably. That's how the Catholic Church won a shabby victory against the Socialist Workers Party over the body of Grace Carlson. The question of "philosophy" had nothing to do with it. That's merely the explanation, not the reason.

In her statement to the press, Grace emphasized what she had told us at parting, that she was not going to join the ranks of the contemptible informers. "I want it understood I am not becoming an informer on my friends of many years. Neither am I going to write any books like Budenz." That does her credit, as do the 16 years of service she gave to the good cause in comradely association with these same friends. But it really doesn't make much difference to us. The Socialist Workers Party is not a conspiracy but a political movement which reports all its activities and says everything it has to say in its press. All the "information" anyone can find against us is printed there.

In her press interview, reported in the *Minneapolis Star,* June 30, Grace refers to her last meeting with me in Minneapolis on Friday, June 20. The reporter quotes her as saying: "It was one of the saddest meetings I have ever attended." I don't doubt that, but the reason for her sadness should be explained.

She did not make any arguments to sustain her action. She did not express any differences with the party program nor any grievances against its people. On the contrary, she affirmed her love and respect for the comrades with whom she had worked so long.

I spoke to her about the Catholic Church which exploits the religious sentiments of its communicants to support reaction and oppression everywhere.

I reminded her that the policies of the Catholic Church are not determined by the parishioners nor by the parish priests, but by the Catholic hierarchy, which is first of all a political power, the most reactionary and obscurantist force in the entire world. I reminded her of Cardinal Spellman, who broke the strike of the cemetery workers in New York, and who has just recently been to Spain, where he paid homage to the bloody dictator Franco. I reminded her that her socialist comrades in Spain are in Franco's prisons and torture chambers, if they are not in their graves.

Grace Carlson knows all that as well as I do, and has said it many times. She didn't answer my reminders with any argument or justification, but with the bitter tears of a defeated and broken woman. She does well to say that it was a sad meeting for her. It was a sad meeting for me too, but for different reasons.

Socialists have deserted the movement before under pressure. But still the movement grew. There are more socialists in the world today than ever before. The worldwide cause is growing and will continue to grow. That will be the case in this country too. Individuals, broken by too many blows, may fall by the wayside. But the great movement for the socialist emancipation of mankind will march on and conquer. Grace Carlson's desertion will not affect this course. The party will draw its ranks closer together in defense against the raging reaction which has reached inside our ranks to strike down one of our women comrades.

The forthcoming convention of the Socialist Workers Party in New York, called to nominate its presidential candidates for the 1952 campaign, will demonstrate this. The convention will demonstrate the determination of the members to do a little more and give a little more to make up any losses suffered by this defection.

The convention will reaffirm again, what Grace Carlson said many times before her defection, that the place to fight against the threatening war, and all the evils of this diseased capitalist society and for a better life on earth, is not in the Catholic Church but in the socialist movement.

5

Los Angeles 1954

Introductory note

Cannon moved to Los Angeles in 1953. Sen. Joseph McCarthy, an anti-communist demagogue with the backing of a section of the ruling class, was then still at the height of his influence.

Along with other militant workers, a number of SWP members faced victimization for their political views during these years. One prominent case involved James Kutcher, an SWP member fired from a civil service job for belonging to a "subversive" organization. A World War II veteran, Kutcher had lost both legs in combat; his fight became known as the "case of the legless veteran," which was also the title of Kutcher's book describing the history of the case (*The Case of the Legless Veteran*, Pathfinder, 1973).

The articles in this section are devoted to analyzing McCarthyism as an incipient fascist movement, indicating the stakes involved for the working class, and why countermobilization and political action by the labor movement is necessary to combat such movements.

The case of the legless veteran

A letter to James Kutcher

THE MILITANT, JANUARY 11, 1954

Dear Jim:

Your book moved me profoundly, and I would like to tell you why. In my opinion the story you tell about yourself in *The Case of the Legless Veteran* is even more important than the case itself. The dramatic incident of your war injuries in Italy and the shabby pay off from the Veterans Administration in America are well worth a book for their own sake. But they are only a part—one might almost say an incidental part—of the book you have written about your life as a whole.

When you started to write the story of your case, I suppose it never occurred to you that your life, being very little different from that of millions of others, would have any special interest except as background material. In your opening chapters you seem to be hesitant about introducing personal matter into the account of a celebrated political case, in which you just happened to be the man in the middle.

You begin with the remark, "I am an ordinary man"—as though ordinary men are not supposed to talk about themselves, which as a rule, they don't. But as I see it, just because your life has been one of many; because you have seen and felt and lived pretty much the same things as the others—in speaking of yourself you have spoken for the others too, with their own thoughts and feelings and

James Kutcher, fired from his Veterans Administration job for membership in Socialist Workers Party, successfully challenged thought-control laws in one of the most dramatic and widely supported defense cases of the Joe McCarthy era.

in their own language.

In this book, which is so completely American, and yet so purely free from national pride and arrogance, so personal and yet so objective, you have unknowingly given the movement a model example of the right way to explain socialism to those who need the information most. The socialist revolution is a world-wide affair, but the man who will make it in this country does not live all over the globe. He lives right here; he is the American worker as he is, and as he will change, without ceasing to be what he is. He is the man who will decide everything, and for that reason he is the one we have to talk to. Those who don't understand that, who talk "over his head," are in reality talking only to themselves. Nobody is listening, and they might as well shut up.

I read your book with great satisfaction; not only for its own interest and merits as such, but also because I found in it a certain justification and support of my own conception of the tasks of the American socialist movement, and what I personally have tried to do about it.

The international outlook, which takes the modern world as a unit and proceeds from that, is the necessary starting point for the orientation of a revolutionary party in national affairs. But the international outlook is only that—the starting point and means of orientation; it is not a substitute for the building of an indigenous national party, rooted in the soil of its own country and articulating the instinctive striving of its own working class. I have always wanted our party to be the most internationalist and at the same time the most American, the most theoretical and also the most practical, of all the political tendencies in the labor movement.

We were animated by this unified conception from the first, in the pioneer days of American communism, when the idea of internationalism, with our help, brought the main core of the radical American workers' movement to the Russian Revolution and the Communist Party. We clung to the same conception during the first decade of American communism, when we fought to Americanize the party; to connect it with the living movement of the American workers, and to resist the tendency which later succumbed to the fatal theory of "socialism in one country," i.e., in Russia alone.

Again, in the early days after our expulsion from the Communist Party, when we were condemned by the circumstances to preoccupy ourselves in isolation with international and theoretical questions, we never lost our aspiration to find contact again with the mass movement. We regarded our theoretical work as the preparation for a more fruitful activity in the mass movement later on. It worked out that way when the revival of labor radicalism opened the doors of opportunity for us after five years of isolation.

Now we have a new situation, in which our work must be guided by a plan. The combined weight of the artificially prolonged prosperity and the raging witch-hunt again submits the vanguard of the vanguard to the cruel test of isolation. We have to theorize the new situation in order to find a way out. At the same time, a revisionist current in our world movement again obliges us, whether we like it or not, to concentrate our attention on international questions. In these circumstances, once more, we need an occasional sharp reminder of our old unified conception—that theoretical preoccupation is not a substitute for mass work but a means of developing it more effectively; that international ideas and associations are not a substitute for work on the national field.

More than that, the two sides of these combined tasks should not be separated from each other, either in theory or in daily activity. The moment a party begins to neglect its external propaganda, the moment it ceases to search for new people to talk to and to recruit, it begins to die. The national and international, the practical and the theoretical, ought to be united and carried on at the same time. This, of course, is easier said than done. It requires a conscious effort on the part of some to start the work that may be neglected on one side or the other, and set the example. From that point of view I am especially grateful and inspired by the appearance of your work of socialist propaganda at the present time.

For more than a year our movement has been up to its neck in an internal factional fight, and now has to turn its attention to an international extension of the same thing. This has been the signal for wiseacres, who never do anything themselves, to begin once again to cackle: "Oh, those Trotskyists, they're at it again; they spend all their time on factional squabbles." At such a time, it is most refreshing and inspiring to see an unpretentious man named Jim Kutcher, who takes a firm stand in the faction fight himself, come forward with a simple and powerful work of socialist propaganda, which shows that he has not forgotten the ordinary American worker and knows how to talk to him about the problems of his life and his socialist future.

Anyone who can do that, Jim, and who likes to do it and thinks it is important, is my brother. Of all the different kinds of work I have done in my time in the movement, that which I have enjoyed most, which gave me the most complete personal satisfaction, was the writing of propaganda pieces in my "Notebook of an Agitator." I would have been content to stay in a corner of the party, doing that kind of work, and let others take care of other tasks. I deeply regretted that the exigencies of the internal factional struggle interfered with the realization of this modest ambition.

But after all, the party is what counts and the party line comes first. None of us can do much by himself if the party line is not straight. If the party's policy is wrong and the leadership is inadequate, the work of individuals comes to naught. We can work effectively only in and through the party. Sometimes that requires a factional struggle to straighten out the party.

But at the same time, we should never get so lost in the faction fight that we neglect the broad constructive work of propaganda; forget to talk to the ordinary worker; still worse, forget even how to talk to him. For my part, I am glad that I didn't forget. Despite my preoccupation with the internal struggle against a crude revisionist and capitulatory current in our party during the past year, I still managed to sandwich in my six lectures on "America's Road to Socialism," which now take their place, in pamphlet form, beside your book in the propaganda arsenal of the party. I feel good about that.

That party will win in the United States which keeps its revolutionary political line straight, and takes time to straighten it out when the line deviates, and yet never ceases to believe in the American workers, and never stops talking to them in their own language. Sometimes this two-sided task requires a division of labor among the people who make up the party. Our National Committee is giving the party an example of this combination of tasks and division of labor.

It has done its full duty on the front of the internal struggle during the past year, and is now doing all it can do to help orthodox Trotskyists on the international field to combat the revisionist tendency. At the same time, the party is bound to note with approval that the National Committee—without neglecting its international duties—is also sounding the alarm, and leading and organizing a struggle on the domestic field against the manifest emergence of a native fascist movement.

The secret of success for a revolutionary party, I repeat

again, is the unified conception of its tasks and the division of labor. Your life story, which you have told so effectively in *The Case of the Legless Veteran,* is a great contribution on your part to the division of labor. You can, and no doubt will, say: "Why, I did nothing but tell what I saw and experienced and felt and thought as the son of a working-class family in high school, in the long depression, in the war, and then in the witch-hunt. I'm not much different from the others. I just happened to come into contact with the socialist movement—that made all the difference and changed my whole life."

But that's just the point, Jim. In your book you speak, in anticipation, for millions of others like yourself, who will also come into contact with socialist ideas. That will make all the difference for them too, and with that little difference they will change this country and change the world. Anyone who helps to disseminate these change-making ideas, in a form and language accessible to the American worker as he is, is helping thereby to change this country and the world.

With warm personal regards and thanks from one agitator to another.

James P. Cannon
LOS ANGELES, CALIFORNIA

'The irrepressible conflict'

A speech at Los Angeles

THE MILITANT, MARCH 1, 1954

We meet on Lincoln's birthday. A very important date in the history of our country, and one which the American people rightly hold in reverence. Lincoln, as President of the United States, was the executive leader of the forces of the Union in the great Civil War, which smashed the abominable system of chattel slavery and formally emancipated the slaves, unified the country, and created the conditions for its industrial development and expansion.

The great Civil War under Lincoln's executive leadership was a glorious victory for the American people and for all humanity. It is rightly regarded as the Second American Revolution. This Second American Revolution prepared the way for a third revolution which, in its turn, will emancipate the working class and finally put an end to all forms of discrimination in society. We do well to honor Lincoln and the glorious war he led to victory.

Lincoln's birthday may seem like a most inappropriate occasion to talk about Senator McCarthy; but I think there is a Freudian law known as the "association of opposites." Perhaps we can speak of Lincoln and McCarthy together under this head. Where the name of Lincoln symbolizes progress, McCarthy is the outstanding demagogue of reaction. Where Lincoln symbolizes the emancipation of the chattel slaves, McCarthy is the representative of those dark forces in America whose ultimate objective is to fasten the chains of fascist slavery on the American working class.

Before the Civil War of the Sixties broke out in full fury in 1861, there was a long period of preparation for it, when both sides fought with ideas and arguments and mobilized their forces around these ideas. In these preparatory days, William H. Seward described the debate as an "irrepressible conflict" which could not be resolved by argument alone. That would be a proper way to describe the present situation in this country. We are witnessing a clash of ideas and arguments, and the preliminary mobilization of forces, for a coming show down in what is indeed another "irrepressible conflict." It also will not be decided by argument alone.

In the year prior to the Civil War, the Abolitionists, of reverential memory, conducted a great agitational activity to alarm the people to the dangers of the time and to clarify their ideas as to what was really involved in the irrepressible conflict. The modern heirs of the heroic Abolitionists of a hundred years ago, the advocates of the abolition of the capitalist system of wage slavery, are conducting a similar campaign of agitation and explanation, of clarification of ideas as to what is now involved in the new irrepressible conflict. The clearer we see the picture as it really is, the better we will be prepared for things to come.

There are differences of opinion as to what the shape of things to come will be; but there is almost universal recognition that the present state of affairs has no permanence. We are now coming toward the end of the long prosperity artificially promoted by huge government expenditures for war and preparations for war. A serious recession is already under way; and the prospect of a deep economic crisis, paralyzing industry and depriving many millions of workers of the opportunity to work and to live, looms directly before us. At the same time we are nearing the end of the stalemate in the cold war, and stand face to face with the prospect of an atomic war on a world scale.

Which will strike first—the depression or the war? The present situation may be described as a race between war and depression, with the winner not yet decided.

Parallel to this race between war and depression, and as a result of it, there is an impending conflict between two different forms of governmental rule and a race between them. The winner in this race is also not yet decided. In order to wage an atomic world war, and to provide the incalculable expenditures which it will entail, more than military preparation is needed. The monopolists who own this country and control its government are both required and determined to reduce the living standards of the workers and make them pay the expenses of the contemplated war.

The barrier standing in the way of this program is the great trade-union movement, 17 million strong. Before an all-out wage-cutting program could be put into effect, this trade-union movement would have to be smashed or, at the very least, intimidated and domesticated to such an extent that it would lose its powers of resistance. A large section of the ruling capitalists are playing with the idea that a depression would facilitate this program. They see in a prospective depression not the untold misery of tens of millions of people, but a golden opportunity to smash the unions and to deprive them of their combative power.

This ambitious program is easier said than done. It requires among other things, a mobilization of reactionary forces by a tremendous campaign of demagogy, incitement and intimidation. This campaign is already under way. Although it is first ostensibly directed against "reds" and "subversives," its real target is the organized labor movement of the United States. That is the real meaning of the incipient fascist movement in this country, spearheaded at the present time by McCarthy, the senatorial demagogue from Wisconsin. McCarthyism is a dagger pointed at the heart of the trade union movement, and at all the civil rights and freedoms of the American working class.

On the other hand, if the labor movement is to survive it cannot stand still. It must go forward or perish. And the only road forward is the road, first toward recognition of the mortal danger that confronts the labor movement, and then toward the mobilization of its own forces for an offensive struggle to change the relation of social forces in favor of the workers. That is the road of militant struggle, of radicalization and, in the ultimate show down, of social revolution—a Third American Revolution which will complete the work of the First and Second and put the working class in power.

The present period of the new "irrepressible conflict" can be properly described as the period of the clarification of ideas and of the preliminary mobilization of forces, similar to the preparatory period of the irrepressible conflict a hundred years ago. We are in the preliminary stages of a race between fascism and workers' revolution.

The issue is not yet decided. Power is on the side of the workers. They will win if they see the issue clearly, and begin their counter-mobilization in time. To help them to see, to warn them of the danger of waiting too long with a counter-attack, is the purpose of the agitational campaign against McCarthyism which is now being conducted by the Socialist Workers Party.

In honor of Laura Gray

A letter to Local New York

THE MILITANT, MARCH 8, 1954

People who never talk themselves up don't always escape the encomiastic comments of others. This is happening right now in the case of Laura Gray, in whose honor the New York Local of the SWP is throwing a party on the occasion of her tenth anniversary as staff cartoonist of *The Militant*. This is really a nation-wide affair. The New York Local is staging the celebration, but all the members of the Party and all the readers of *The Militant* are present with you in spirit. And we are all saying, "Thank you, Laura;

Laura, you're wonderful."

The proletarian movement takes great pride in its intellectuals and artists; all the more so, since under the present conditions of the struggle in this country it can boast so few of them. There is a reason for this scarcity, but there is also a reason why we count on its remedy. The revolutionary workers and the artists need each other, and their union will be a certain consequence of new developments in the coming stages of our struggle for Socialist America.

In our present class society, the intellectuals and the artists don't get a fair chance. By themselves, they are weak. They are not a self-sufficient class, but rather a selection of exceptional people, who in seeking to realize themselves—which means, first of all, to *be* themselves—require the support of a class which represents a power.

Nearly all of them, at the present time, are consciously or unconsciously servants of the ruling power of the dominant class of exploiters, and depend on its patronage. But they pay a price for this allegiance which strikes at their very reason for being. Their inner compulsion is to portray reality, to tell the truth as they see it. But this inner compulsion runs up against the contradiction that the class society, which is founded on lies, has no use for the truth and savagely persecutes those who portray it.

This places the artist before a cruel dilemma. He needs freedom above everything—the freedom "to draw the thing as he sees it." That is the artist's bread of life. The denial of this right turns the artist's bread into a stone. But there is nothing he can do about it by himself. The so-called "ivory tower" is not a place of refuge but of exile from the real world. The salvation of the artist is to ally himself with a power which will permit him to do his work—that is, to live and be his real self—and to protect and sustain him in its performance.

Cartoonist Laura Gray views U.S. role in Korean War in *The Militant*, June 15, 1953; see p. 443 for Cannon's tribute to Laura Gray.

There is such a power, and the artist should recognize it and seek alliance with it. That is the modern working class, represented by its conscious vanguard, whose cause is served only by truth. By that fact, it is the natural ally and protector of all truth-seekers, among whom the artist stands in first place. The alliance of the true artist with the labor movement is the condition for his own emancipation.

If the artist needs the labor movement, no less does the labor movement need the artist. The workers need not only the crude truth which is the ugly reality of their daily existence. They need also the truth that illuminates and inspires, the truth that shines, as only the artist can reveal it. It is a lucky day when our movement finds such a person. And it is the part of wisdom, as well as of gratitude, to cherish the alliance and to celebrate it, as you are doing tonight at the party for Laura Gray.

I don't doubt that Laura made her first appearance in the office of *The Militant* so quietly and unobtrusively—as is her manner—that scarcely anyone noticed her in the busy hubbub in which a paper always goes to press. But she came into Sandstone prison, where some of us were residing at the time, with a clatter and a bang. Her first cartoon scattered the gray shadows of the prison like the powerful headlight of a locomotive rolling down the right of way. Every week thereafter we looked for her cartoons, and they brightened the prison day each time they came.

The readers of *The Militant* everywhere, immersed in the prosaic details of everyday life and the routine tasks of the struggle for a better world, have greeted her weekly drawings with the same gratitude and enthusiasm. And they have derived from them the same inspiration, the same anticipatory glimpse of a better world wherein all people will express themselves better, more completely, in more effective communion with others; that is to say, more artistically.

I speak of this as an anticipation. For in the socialist society of the free and equal, all will be artists; all will have the means and the opportunity, and the favorable social environment, to tap their springs of talent and their instincts for self-expression in artistic form, which are today hidden, suppressed and denied. The true artists, who feel impelled to draw the true picture of life as they see it, not only as it is, but as it ought to be and will be, can find the fullest freedom for the exercise of this impulse today only in alliance with the great labor movement, which is forcing its way, through the blood and filth of capitalist society, to the new world of truth and beauty. In particular, the revolutionary party, which represents the conscious elements of this great movement, is the natural ally of the aspiring artist.

Many of them will come to us in the future, and if we are wise we will receive them gladly. Our Laura, cartoonist for *The Militant,* is the advance guard, the harbinger of the poets and artists to come. In honoring her, on the occasion of her tenth anniversary on the staff of *The Militant,* we are honoring the paper, the party and ourselves. And we are honoring, at the same time, the coming grand alliance of revolutionists and artists in the great battle wherein no one can fail.

James P. Cannon
LOS ANGELES, CALIFORNIA

Notes for a historian

THE MILITANT, MARCH 22, 1954

Dear Sir:

I received your letter stating that you are working on a history of the American communist movement, I am interested in your project and am willing to give you all the help I can.

Your task will not be easy, for you will be travelling in an undiscovered country where most of the visible road signs are painted upside down and point in the wrong directions. All the reports that I have come across, both from the renegades and from the official apologists, are slanted and falsified. The objective historian will have to keep up a double guard in searching for the truth among all the conflicting reports.

The Stalinists are not only the most systematic and dedicated liars that history has yet produced; they have also won the flattering compliment of imitation from the professional anti-Stalinists. The history of American communism is one subject on which different liars, for different reasons in each case, have had a field day.

However, most of the essential facts are matters of record. The trouble begins with the interpretation: and I doubt very much whether a historian, even with the best will in the world, could render a true report and make the facts understandable without a correct explanation of what happened and why.

As you already know, I have touched on the pioneer days of American communism in my book, *The History of American Trotskyism*. During the past year I have made other references to this period in connection with the current discussion in our movement. The party resolution on "American Stalinism and Our Attitude Toward It," which appears in the May-June issue of the *Fourth International* magazine, was written by me.

I speak there also of the early period of the Communist Party, and have made other references in other articles and letters published in the course of our discussion. All this material can be made available to you. I intend to return to the subject again at greater length later on, for I am of the definite opinion that an understanding of the pioneer days of American communism is essential to the education of the new generation of American revolutionists.

My writings on the early history of American communism are mainly designed to illustrate my basic thesis, which as far as I know, has not been expounded by anyone else. This thesis can be briefly stated as follows:

The Communist Party originally was a revolutionary organization. All the original leaders of the early Communist Party, who later split into three permanent factions within the Party, *began* as American revolutionists with a perspective of revolution in this country. Otherwise, they wouldn't have been in the movement in the first place and wouldn't have split with the reformist socialists to organize the Communist Party.

Even if it is maintained that some of these leaders were careerists—a contention their later evolution tends to support—it still remains to be explained why they sought careers in the communist movement and not in the business or professional worlds, or in bourgeois politics, or in the trade-union officialdom. Opportunities in these fields were open to at least some of them, and were deliberately cast aside at the time.

In my opinion, the course of the leaders of American communism in its pioneer days, a course which entailed deprivations, hazards and penalties, can be explained only by the assumption that they were revolutionists to begin with; and that even the careerists among them believed in the future of the workers' revolution in America and wished to ally themselves with this future.

It is needless to add that the rank and file of the Party, who had no personal interests to serve, were animated by revolutionary convictions. By that I mean, they were believers in the perspective of revolution in this country, for I do not know any other kind of revolutionists.

The American Communist Party did not begin with Stalinism. The Stalinization of the Party was rather the end result of a process of degeneration which began during the long boom of the Twenties. The protracted prosperity of that period, which came to be taken for permanence by the great mass of American people of all classes, did not fail to affect the Communist Party itself. It softened up the leading cadres of that party, and undermined their original confidence in the perspectives of a revolution in this country. This prepared them, eventually, for an easy acceptance of the Stalinist theory of "socialism in one country."

For those who accepted this theory, Russia, as the "one country" of the victorious revolution, became a substitute for the American revolution. Thereafter, the Communist Party in this country adopted as its primary task the "defense of the Soviet Union" by pressure methods of one kind or another on American foreign policy, without any perspective of a revolution of their own. All the subsequent twists and turns of Communist Party policy in the United States, which appear so irrational to others, had this central motivation—the subordination of the struggle for a revolution in the United States to the "defense" of a revolution in another country.

That explains the frenzied radicalism of the Party in the first years of the economic crisis of the Thirties, when American foreign policy was hostile to the Soviet diplomacy; the reconciliation with Roosevelt after he recognized the Soviet Union and oriented toward a diplomatic rapprochement with the Kremlin; the split with Roosevelt during the Stalin-Hitler Pact, and the later fervent reconciliation and the unrestrained jingoism of the American

Stalinists when Washington allied itself with the Kremlin in the war.

The present policy of the Communist Party, its subordination of the class struggle to a pacifistic "peace" campaign, and its decision to ally itself at all costs with the Democratic Party, has the same consistent motivation as all the previous turns of policy.

The degeneration of the Communist Party began when it abandoned the perspective of revolution in this country, and converted itself into a pressure group and cheering squad for the Stalinist bureaucracy in Russia—which it mistakenly took to be the custodian of a revolution "in another country."

I shouldn't neglect to add the final point of my thesis: The degeneration of the Communist Party is not to be explained by the summary conclusion that the leaders were a pack of scoundrels to begin with; although a considerable percentage of them—those who became Stalinists as well as those who became renegades—turned out eventually to be scoundrels of championship caliber; but by the circumstance that they fell victim to a false theory and a false perspective.

What happened to the Communist Party would happen without fail to any other party, including our own, if it should abandon its struggle for a social revolution in this country, as the realistic perspective of our epoch, and degrade itself to the role of sympathizer of revolutions in other countries.

I firmly believe that American revolutionists should indeed sympathize with revolutions in other lands, and try to help them in every way they can. But the best way to do that is to build a party with a confident perspective of a revolution in this country. Without that perspective, a communist or socialist party belies its name. It ceases to be a help and becomes a hindrance to the revolutionary workers' cause in its own country. And its sympathy for other revolutions isn't worth much either.

That, in my opinion, is the true and correct explanation of the Rise and Fall of the American Communist Party.

Yours truly,

James P. Cannon
LOS ANGELES, CALIFORNIA

Fascism and the workers' movement

1. Notes on American fascism

A letter to the Militant

THE MILITANT, MARCH 15, 1954

Editor:

I haven't been able to disentangle myself from other preoccupations to send you any connected thoughts on McCarthyism and the probable character and perspectives of American fascism in general. The articles of Breitman are very effective arguments against people who will not recognize incipient American fascism until it obliges them by assuming the "classic" European form. What will they do if American fascism neglects or refuses to accommodate them in this respect, right up to the eve of the show down—which it may well do?

I will have something to say about the question of American fascism a little later when I get free from some other commitments. Meantime, I am in basic agreement with the campaign you are conducting and the arguments for it, especially those given in Breitman's articles. I believe these articles would make a good follow-up pamphlet to the first one.

Those who would judge specific American forms of fascism too formalistically by the European pattern, arbitrarily limit capitalist aggression against the workers' movement in two forms:

They see the democratic form by which the workers are suppressed through strictly legal measures in accordance with the law and the Constitution—such as the Taft-Hartley Law, formal indictments and prosecutions for specific violations of existing statutes, etc. All this, despite its obvious "inconvenience" to the workers' movement, is characterized as democratic.

On the other side they see the illegal, unofficial forms of violence practiced by "storm troopers" and similar shirted hooligans outside the forms of law, as in Italy and Germany. This is characterized as fascist.

But what about violence which is technically illegal and unconstitutional, but carried out nevertheless by duly constituted officials clothed with legal authority? What about such things as the breaking up of meetings and picket lines by official police and special deputies; wire tapping; inquisitions; screening and blacklisting of "subversives"; and all the rest of the intimidation and terror of the witchhunt? These procedures don't fit very well into the "democratic" formula, although their chief instruments are legally-constituted officials, supported and incited by press campaigns, radio demagogues, etc.

This kind of illegal violence under the outward forms of law has a distinctive American flavor; and it is especially favored by a section of the ruling class which has very little respect for its own laws, and cares more for practical action than for theories as to how it is to be carried out.

This is, in fact, an important element of the specific form which American fascism will take, as has already been indicated quite convincingly.

The depredations of Mayor Hague, who announced that "I am the law," were a manifestation of this tendency back in the late Thirties. Trotsky, by the way, considered Hague an American fascist. He described his unconstitutional assaults on free speech and free assembly, through the medium of *official police,* as a manifestation of incipient American fascism. I think he was right about that. If the workers stand around and wait until the labor movement is attacked directly by unofficial shirted hooligans, before they recognize the approach of American fascism, they may find their organizations broken up "legally" while they are waiting.

The truth of the matter is that American fascism, *in its own specific form,* has already a considerable army of *storm troopers* at its disposal in the persons of lawless prosecuting attorneys and official policemen who don't give a damn what the Constitution says. Incipient American fascism—already, right now—has a press and radio-television power which makes Hitler's *Angriff* look like a throwaway sheet. It has political demagogues, like McCarthy, who are different from Hitler mainly in the fact that they are clothed with official legal powers and immunity, while Hitler had to build up an independent, unofficial and at times persecuted movement without any direct support from the established press, etc.

"McCarthy is different," say the formalistic wiseacres, as if that were a help and a consolation. He is indeed different in several ways. But the most important difference is that *he starts* with a great power behind him, and operates with formal legal sanction and immunity. The right comparison to make is not of the McCarthy of today with Hitler on the verge of taking power in 1932, but rather with Hitler in the middle Twenties. The main difference we find in this comparison is that McCarthy is way ahead of Hitler.

Another point: the German-American Bund of the Thirties was not a characteristic manifestation of American fascism, but rather a foreign agency of Hitler's German movement. Neither is it correct to look now for the appearance of genuine American fascism in lunatic fringe outfits such as the Silver Shirts, Gerald Smith, etc. A powerful section of the American bourgeoisie, with unlimited means at their disposal are *already fascist-minded;* and they have a big foot in the Government, national and local. They feel no need at present of unofficial movements.

To the extent that such outfits will appear here or there, with the development of the social crisis, they will probably be subsumed in a broader, more powerful, adequately financed and press-supported general movement, which operates under more or less legal forms. It is far more correct, far more realistic, to see the incipient stage of American fascism in the conglomeration of "official" marauders represented by McCarthy than outside it.

James P. Cannon
LOS ANGELES, CALIFORNIA

2. Perspectives of American fascism

THE MILITANT, MARCH 29, 1954

The campaign of the Socialist Workers Party against the ominous upsurge of McCarthyism, and its characterization of the McCarthy movement as American fascism in incipient form, has been misunderstood by some people who don't want to think, as well as by others who prefer to misunderstand us in order to misrepresent us.

Up till now we have not heard any cogent arguments against our campaign and its motivation. The most we can make out so far are some mutters and murmurs of dissent, to which we will give a preliminary answer while our critics and opponents are getting up the nerve to speak more distinctly.

One of these muted criticisms appears in a clouded statement in one of the documents of the Pablo faction which Joe Hansen is taking apart in serial articles on another page of *The Militant.* Remarking that the Socialist Workers Party has "sounded the alarm on the fascist danger in the United States"—an accusation which cannot be denied—this document represents the campaign as a sign of our "pessimism," a conclusion which at the very best can be characterized only as a misunderstanding.

There is an obvious contradiction in this recognition of our campaign and the conclusion drawn from it. The woods are full of pessimists about the future of America in general, and about the prospects of American fascism in particular, but they are not organizing any campaigns. It is not in the nature of pessimists to do anything of that sort. Pessimism is not merely a gloomy view of evils to come, but a capitulatory reconciliation to them in advance. The real pessimists are simply keeping quiet—concerned to prolong their own grub-like existence, and hoping to adapt themselves to whatever comes by acquiescence and conformity.

The attitude of the SWP is the opposite of all that. The character of a party is not indicated by what it sees and points out but rather by what it does about it. To accuse the SWP of "sounding the alarm on the fascist danger in the U.S." is only to pay to the Party the indirect and unintended compliment of saying that it calls for a struggle against the danger. Pessimists don't sound any alarms or organize any struggles. They just run for cover. Pessimist is just another name for quitter and capitulator.

Some other critical murmurs we have heard, which have not yet found their way into print, represent our campaign as an "exaggeration" of the fascist danger and an apprehension of its imminent victory. That is another misunderstanding. To sound the alarm against the danger of fascism in the United States—and to state frankly that its victory is possible—is by no means to be taken as an admission that fascism is already in power, or close to it. Neither is it to be taken as a prophecy that fascism is destined to conquer eventually.

That will be decided in the struggle. The aim of our campaign is to "alarm" the labor movement to the reality of the danger and, from that, to the necessity of organizing the struggle on the right basis while there is yet time. The workers still have time to organize the counter-movement, but they don't have forever; and the sooner they recognize the central reality of the whole problem—that the issue will be decided in struggle—the better chance they will have to be the victors.

A fascist movement does not arise from the bad will of malicious demagogues. Neither is a radicalized labor movement created by the propaganda of revolutionists. Both are products of the incurable crisis of capitalism, which renders it unable to maintain a stable rule through the old bourgeois democratic forms. One way or another—these forms will be changed. The latent crisis, which has been artificially suppressed and disguised by war and military expenditures, promises to break out with redoubled fury in the coming period. This will spell impoverishment and misery for tens of millions of people, and it will generate an enormous discontent with the hopeless state of affairs. The unfailing result will be a widespread desire for a radical change.

This mass discontent and desire for a change can take one of two forms, or both of them at the same time.

The workers are the strongest power in modern society. If they show a resolute will to take hold of the situation and effect the necessary revolutionary change, the millions of desperate middle-class people—impoverished farmers, bankrupt small businessmen and white-collar elements—who have no independent power of their own, will follow the workers and support them in their struggle for power. This was demonstrated in the Russian Revolution of November 1917.

On the other hand, if the workers, as a result of inadequate or pusillanimous leadership, falter before their historical task, the allegiance of the middle classes will rapidly shift to the support of the fascists and lift them into power. This alternative outcome of the social crisis was demonstrated in Italy and Germany.

How will things go in this country? The most "optimistic" way to answer that question is to tell the truth and to say once again: It will be decided in a struggle. Experience of other countries has already shown that a fascist movement and a movement of labor radicalization, which arise in the first place from the same cause, make their appearance at approximately the same time. But they don't develop at the same rate of speed. The "subjective" factor, the factor of leadership, plays a big role here.

In Italy, and later in Germany, the movement of labor radicalization had a big jump on fascism at the start. In these two countries fascism began to become a mass movement and a formidable power only after the workers had failed to carry through their revolution when they had the chance—in 1919–1921 in Italy, and in Germany from 1918 to 1923. The tumultuous rise of the fascist movement in those two cases, and its eventual victory, were the answer to the workers' default and the penalty for it.

Here in the United States we see a somewhat different development of the two antagonistic forces—fascism and workers' radicalization—and a different rate of speed in their development. But these are only tentative manifestations which are not yet by any means decisive. The extraordinary thick-headedness of the labour bureaucracy in this country, and the lack of a revolutionary party with a base of mass support, have given incipient fascism the jump on the labor movement. A form of preventive fascism, of which McCarthy is indubitably the chief representative, has already got a head start and has widespread ramifications of support, inside the governmental apparatus as well as outside it. To recognize that fact is not to conjure up imaginary dangers but simply to recognize the obvious reality of the situation.

And this recognition of reality is the first prerequisite for the organization of an effective counter-movement. McCarthyism, as it appears today, is undoubtedly an *incipient* fascist movement, but that's all it is. The beginnings of a fascist movement aiming to take power in this country, and fascism already in power, are not the same thing. Between the one and the other lies a protracted period of struggle in which the issue will be finally decided. Whoever recognizes that and "sounds the alarm," and thus helps to prepare the struggle of the workers is doing what most needs to be done at the present time. Such a campaign is by no means a manifestation of pessimism, but the best antidote for it.

Power is on the side of the workers, and all the chances of victory are in their favor. But they will never gain the victory without the most resolute struggle. The first prerequisite for that is an understanding of the irreconcilable nature of the struggle and what it's all about. The fate of America, and thereby of all mankind—that's what it's all about.

3. First principles in the struggle against fascism

THE MILITANT, APRIL 5, 1954

The honorable Joseph McCarthy is not much of a thinker himself, but he has certainly stimulated a lot of thought, or what passes for it, in the minds of others. His unbridled aggressiveness in recent months has stirred up quite a fluttering in the dovecotes of so-called liberalism. The pontifical pundits, who yesterday thought the specter could be exorcised by ridicule, or by pretending not to notice it, are now deep-thinking second thoughts about the Wisconsin demagogue and what he stands for.

Some apprehension of the deadly seriousness of McCarthyism has even begun to dawn in the thick skulls of the official labor leaders, and that alone is testimony to its penetrating power. It is now widely recognized that if the Wisconsin demagogue is crazy, he is crazy like a fox, and has to be taken seriously. It would also seem that the liberals, and the labor leaders who farm out their thinking to the liberals, are catching up with the SWP, as far as the definition of McCarthyism is concerned. Lately we see more and more references to McCarthy as an American Hitler. For example, Adlai Stevenson, who cannot justly be called an extremist, referred to McCarthy in his Miami speech as the apostle of a "malign totalitarianism."

But we are still poles apart from the liberals and the labor skates on the main question; that is, the analysis of the causes of this preliminary manifestation of a "malign totalitarianism"—the Stevensonian euphemism for fascism—and the program for struggle against it. They all regard our revolutionary approach to the question as extreme and unrealistic. The unrealism, however, is on their side, because they separate McCarthyism from the social causes which have generated it, and which in fact, make such manifestations inevitable. If McCarthy did not exist American capitalism would have to invent him, or a reasonable facsimile.

In every great social struggle, those who understand its laws and foresee how it must develop according to those laws, have a big advantage over those who deal with surface manifestations. If the Socialist Workers Party has been the first and only group in American political life to state categorically that the rise of a fascist movement in the United States is an absolute certainty; and likewise the first to recognize McCarthyism as the preliminary manifestation of American fascism, and to call it by its right name—this was not guesswork in either case.

Our approach to the question of American fascism, as to every other political issue, begins with and proceeds from a basic theory of American perspectives which is different from that of all other political parties and tendencies. That is not because we deny America's exceptional position in the world today. It is known, and has been said often enough, that American capitalism is in a different position from other sectors of the same world in other countries. I am even willing to repeat it once again if such reassurance will do anybody any good. But there are points of similarity as well as of difference, and the former are more important than the latter. That is the main point.

The American capitalists are richer and stronger than their counterparts in other lands. They are also younger and more ignorant, and therefore more inclined to seek a rough settlement of difficulties without diplomatic subtlety and finesse. All that does not change the fact that

American capitalism operates according to the same laws as the others, is confronted with the same fundamental problems, and is headed toward the same catastrophe.

Of all the mistakes that can be made in judging the nature and prospects of the present social system in this country—and it is safe to predict that the American labor leaders, being what they are, will exhaust every possibility in this respect—the worst and most disorienting mistake is to regard American capitalism as *fundamentally* different; as immune from the operation of the same laws which determine the evolution and development of the same social system—through crisis, revolution and counter-revolution—in other countries.

This pernicious theory of "American exceptionalism," which seized the leadership of the American Communist Party in the latter days of the great boom of the Twenties, disoriented the party in the great crisis which exploded soon afterward. This same theory, which is today held by the entire labor officialdom, is what disarms the American workers at the present time more than anything else, and gives the preliminary movement of American fascism such an easy advantage in the beginning.

We Trotskyists never belonged to this school of "exceptionalism." In 1946, right at the time when the editorial spokesmen of American capitalism were proclaiming the advent of "The American Century," and the American labor leaders were adjusting their so-called thinking to this illusory prospect, the Socialist Workers Party outlined a different and more realistic perspective for this country. The "Theses on the American Revolution," adopted by the party convention in that year, expressed its conception in the very first paragraph, as follows:

"The United States, the most powerful capitalist country in history, is a component part of the world capitalist system and is subject to the same general laws. It suffers from the same incurable diseases and is destined to share the same fate. The overwhelming preponderance of American imperialism does not exempt it from the decay of world capitalism, but, on the contrary, acts to involve it ever more deeply, inextricably and hopelessly. U.S. capitalism can no more escape from the revolutionary consequences of world capitalist decay than the older European capitalist powers. The blind alley in which world capitalism has arrived, and the U.S. with it, excludes a new organic era of capitalist stabilization. The dominant world position of American imperialism now accentuates and aggravates the death agony of capitalism as a whole."

This formulation of American perspectives, which governs all the work of the Party, determines its analysis of McCarthyism as the incipient stage of American fascism; its categorical assertion that this movement will grow bigger, stronger and more cohesive with the development of the oncoming crisis; and its program for the struggle against it.

Some such manifestation as the present McCarthy movement was foreseen; and it needed only to make its appearance and score some initial successes, as it has manifestly done since the Brownell-Truman affair, for the Party to react with its counter-campaign of agitation. The fact that the party members have recognized the necessity of the campaign, and responded to it with unanimous participation, is a sign that they were prepared for it by a long previous period of doctrinal education.

I speak of our view of American fascism as a doctrine; for we consider it a matter of principle that the war prosperity of U.S. capitalism has been sick with a latent crisis from the start; and that this crisis is bound, sooner or later, to explode with devastating fury. This exploding crisis is certain to produce two antagonistic phenomena; a fascist movement on the one side, and a radicalized labor movement on the other.

The same social crisis which poses the threat of revolution in each and every capitalist country without exception, likewise generates the attempt to head off such a revolution by means which ruthlessly break down all the old forms of democratic rule. An organized fascist movement is an imperative necessity to the ruling class in every modern capitalist state threatened with social revolution; and is, in fact, a reflexive answer to it. In this view, the fascist movement is not something arbitrarily created by demagogues, to be talked-down by appeal to reason and an alliance of all men of good will. Fascism is organized counter-revolution.

There is no law which forbids such a counter-revolutionary movement to get under way before the prospect and threat of revolution is clearly evident to all. A social revolution is immanent in the present position of American capitalism, and so is the counter-revolution. McCarthyism, as the first definite preliminary manifestation of the counter-revolutionary movement, does not lose this basic characteristic simply because it is a preventive mobilization against a revolution which has not yet taken visible form.

McCarthyite fascism has its cause and origin in the crisis of a social system which is pregnant with a revolution; and is in fact, the preliminary form of a preventive counter-revolution. A general hue and cry against McCarthyism won't amount to much until this is recognized.

4. A new Declaration of Independence

THE MILITANT, APRIL 12, 1954

Fascism is a product of the crisis of capitalism and can be definitively disposed of only by a solution of this crisis. The fascist movement can make advances or be pushed back at one time or another in the course of this crisis; but it will always be there, in latent or active form, as long as the social causes which produce it have not been eradicated.

Looked at from this standpoint, the threat of American fascism is not a short-term problem, and by no means can it be eliminated at the next election—or, for that matter, at any other election. The American fascist movement, and the workers' struggle against it, will be a long drawn-out affair, from now to the final show down, which in the end can be nothing less than a show down between fascist capitalism and the workers' revolution.

If the default of the labor movement has given American fascism, in the incipient and preventive form represented by the McCarthy movement, an advantage at the start, it still represents nothing more than an episode in a long struggle which will have many ups and downs. The real movement of American fascism is now only in its preliminary stages of formation, and the counter-movement of the workers against it is not even started yet.

At any rate, American fascism, in its McCarthyite form or under some other aegis, is bound to provoke a militant resistance from the workers as soon as it passes over from its present preoccupation with a hunt for spies and "subversives" to a direct assault on the labor movement. Thereafter, the fascist movement will not develop on a straight ascending line. There will be zigzags on one side and the other, advances and set backs and periods of stalemate. In this protracted conflict the labor movement will have time to get a clearer picture of the real nature of the problem, and to mobilize its forces for an all-out struggle.

At the present time, the myopic policy of the liberals and the labor leaders is concentrated on the congressional elections next fall, and the presidential election to follow in 1956. A Democratic victory is counted on to deal a death blow to the McCarthy aberration. "McCarthyism is becoming a danger all right, and it begins to look like a fascist movement; but all we need is a general mobilization at the polls to put the Democrats back in power." Such are the arguments we already hear from the Democratic high command, the literary liberals, the labor leaders and—skulking in the rear of the caravan, with their tails between their legs—the Stalinists.

This would really be laughable if humor were in place where deadly serious matters are concerned. The Roosevelt New Deal, under far more favorable conditions, couldn't find a way to hold back the economic crisis without a war. A Stevensonian version of the same policy, under worse conditions, could only be expected to fail more miserably. A Democratic victory might arrest the hitherto unobstructed march of McCarthyism while it re-forms its ranks. It might even bring a temporary moderation of the fury of the witch-hunt. But that's all.

The fascist movement would begin to grow again with the growth of the crisis. It would probably take on an even more militant character, if it is pushed out of the administration and compelled to develop as an unofficial movement. Under conditions of a serious crisis, an unofficial fascist movement would grow all the more stormily, to the extent that the labor movement would support the Democratic administration, and depend on it to restrain the fascists by police measures.

Such a policy, as the experience of Italy and Germany has already shown, would only paralyze the active resistance of the workers themselves, while giving the fascist gangs a virtually free rein. Moreover, by remaining tied to the Democratic administration, the labor movement would take upon itself a large part of the responsibility for the economic crisis and feed the flames of fascist demagogy around the question.

That would be something to see: The fascists howling about the crisis, and stirring up the hungry and desperate people with the most extravagant promises, while the labor leaders defend the administration. The official labor leaders are fully capable of such idiocy, as they demonstrated in the last presidential election. But with the best will in the world to help the Democratic administration, they couldn't maintain such a position very long.

The workers will most probably accept the recommendation of the labor leaders to seek escape from the crisis by replacing Republican rascals by Democratic scoundrels in the next election. But when the latter become officially responsible for the administration, and prove powerless to cope with the crisis, the workers will certainly draw some conclusions from their unfortunate experiences. The deeper the crisis, and the more brutal the fascist aggression fed by the crisis, the more insistent will be the demand for a radical change of policy and a more adequate leadership.

From all indications, the workers' discontent will be concentrated, at first, in the demand for a labor party of their own. This will most probably be realized. It will not yet signify the victory over fascism—not by a long shot—but it will represent the beginning of a counter-movement which will have every chance to end in victory.

The break with the Democratic Party will be an implicit recognition that the fight against fascism is fundamentally a fight against capitalism in the period of its agonizing crisis of disintegration and decay; and that there is no hope of victory for the workers in alliance with one of the parties of this same capitalism, and still less under its leadership, as at present. The formation of a labor party, based on the trade unions, will represent the American workers' Declaration of Independence. It will be a great turning point in American history. All developments will be speeded up after that.

It would be a great mistake, however, to speak of a prospective labor party as the solution of the problem of fascism. As in 1776, the new Declaration of Independence will signify not the end, but the beginning of the real struggle. The final outcome will depend on the program and the leadership. These will become the burning issues of an internal struggle for which the labor party will provide the main arena. It is from this point of view—clearly stated at all times—that we advocate the formation of a labor party and do all we can to hasten the day of its appearance.

5. Fascism and the labor party

THE MILITANT, APRIL 19, 1954

Our campaign against McCarthyite fascism is an agitational campaign to arouse the labor movement to the advancing danger, and to stimulate a counter-mobilization of the workers. Along this road we participate wholeheartedly in every practical action regardless of its official auspices. Such actions have a logic of their own and can lead, in a step-by-step process, to a final settlement of accounts with fascism and the social system which turns to fascism as a last resort.

The struggle against fascism is an affair of the working class, and the revolutionists would only defeat their own purpose by sectarian abstention from anti-fascist mobilization of the class. *The Militant* is certainly correct in calling for a general congress of labor, to consider the question of a united anti-fascist struggle of the entire labor movement; and in advancing the slogan of a labor party as the general formula for the political independence of the workers in this struggle.

But even while advancing and popularizing these slogans, which sooner or later will be accepted and supported by millions, we ought to explain their limitations as well as their advantages. The assertion that the labor party "will stop McCarthyism," which makes its way into our agitation now and then, is an oversimplification which ought to be guarded against. A labor party would represent a gigantic step forward in the struggle against fascism, but is not in itself a panacea for victory.

A fascist movement is an inherent necessity to the capitalist system at a given stage of its disintegration. Nothing will "stop fascism" short of the overthrow of capitalism. This is the simple truth of the matter; and if our party doesn't tell this truth constantly it would have no reason to exist. There are plenty of others to sow confusion and foster illusions, and they are not entitled to any direct or indirect help from us. There is good ground for confidence that the workers will prevail in the final showdown, and that fascism will never come to power in America. But there is no ground for the assumption that the workers' victory will be quick and easy, or that a mere demonstration of organized labor's opposition would scare the fascist menace off the map.

The workers of Germany were politically organized in two great mass parties. Moreover, the Communist and Social Democratic parties of Germany, who shared the allegiance of almost the entire working class between them, were at least formally committed to a socialist program. They collapsed under the blows of fascism just the same, precisely because they hoped for the miracle of victory without a real struggle. That would surely happen in this country too, even with a labor party supported by the entire trade-union movement, if it should offer no more resistance to fascism than plaintive objections and parliamentary opposition.

I believe it is correct to say that a real first step toward a serious struggle against American fascism could hardly be anything less than the formation of a labor party. As long as the trade unions are allied to the Democratic Party and thereby, in effect, dependent on capitalist politicians to protect them against the onslaughts of a fascist party dedicated to a capitalist counter-revolution—they have not even begun to fight.

For that reason, it is perfectly correct to put the slogan of a labor party in the center of our agitation and to concentrate all agitation around it. But in doing so, we have no need to oversimplify the fundamental problems posed by the beginnings of a fascist movement, and to think that we are doing our full duty if we stop at that. We must look far ahead—from the beginning of the struggle to the end—and keep the goal in mind in all that we do and say. We have to be with the workers in all their practical actions and in all their struggles. But we will be no help to them if we simply follow along, keep quiet about the workers' present illusions and thereby foster them.

If we see the impending struggle in its true shape as a drawn-out affair, we must recognize that coming developments will work powerfully to realize the slogans of the present. After that, new events will prepare the conditions for a widespread acceptance of the more advanced slogans required at a later stage of development. As a revolutionary party, we ought to foresee these developments and formulate the necessary slogans in advance.

Looking to the future, as measured now only in years rather than in decades or generations, it can be expected that a labor party will take shape and command the allegiance of millions of workers from the start. This will represent a real beginning of the anti-fascist mobilization of the American working class, which will just be another name for the mobilization against capitalism, of which fascism is the final resort. But our agitation, and our participation in practical actions leading to this preliminary mobilization, will have real importance and significance only to the extent that we keep the whole line of future developments in mind and prepare ourselves and others to meet them.

If the slogan of a labor party based on the trade unions is the most correct and necessary general slogan of agitation at the present time, the simultaneous explanation of the inescapable trend of developments toward a revolutionary show down, and the building of a party of conscious revolutionists based on this perspective, cannot be put aside in the meantime. The two tasks go together; and taken together, they constitute the most important work of preparation for things to come.

6. Implications of the labor party

THE MILITANT, APRIL 26, 1954

The formal launching of an Independent Labor Party, the indicated next step in the preliminary mobilization of the American working class against a rising fascist movement, will hit this country like a bomb exploding in all directions. It will not only blow up the traditional two-party system in this country and bring about a basic realignment in the general field of American politics. It will also mark the beginning of a great shake-up in the labor movement itself. The second result will be no less important than the first, and it should be counted on.

Under the present system the political stage is occupied by two rival capitalist parties, which in reality represent two different factions of the ruling class. The workers play merely the part of a chorus in the wings and have no speaking part on the stage. The formation of a labor party will change all that at one stroke. The struggle of capitalist factions for control of the government will be subordinated to the struggle of classes, represented by class parties. That is the real meaning of politics anyway.

The political realignment, brought about by the appearance of a labor party on the scene, cannot fail to have profound repercussions inside the labor movement. There will be a great change there too. The break of the trade-union movement with capitalist politics will coincide with the rise of the big opposition to the present official leadership. This rank-and-file opposition movement will most likely take shape in the struggle for a labor party, and be identified with it.

To imagine that the present official leaders can make the great shift from the Democratic Party to independent labor politics, and maintain their leadership smoothly in an entirely new and different situation, requires one to overlook the basic causes which will force them to make this shift. That is, the radicalization of the rank and file and their revolt against the old policy. No matter how it is formally brought about, a labor party will be the product of a radical upsurge in the ranks of the trade unionists. The more the officialdom resists the great change, the stronger will grow the sentiment for a different leadership. Even if the present leaders sponsor the labor party at the start, they will be under strong criticism for their tardiness. The real movement for a labor party, which will come from below, will begin to throw up an alternative leadership in the course of its development.

The demand for a labor party implies the demand for a more adequate leadership; and the actual formation of a labor party, under the auspices of the present official leadership, would only accelerate the struggle under more favorable conditions. As revolutionists, we advocate the formation of a labor party with this perspective also in mind.

It is true that the simple fact of the formation of a labor party, by itself, would have a profound influence in speeding up radical and even revolutionary developments. But those who are satisfied with that might as well retire from the field and let the automatic process take care of everything. The automatic process will not take care of anything except to guarantee defeats. The conscious revolutionists, however few their numbers may be in the beginning, are a part of the process. Their part is to help the process along by telling the whole truth. The fight for a labor party is bound up with the fight to cleanse the labor movement of a crooked and treacherous leadership, and cannot be separated from it. Those radicals and ex-radicals who are willing to settle for a labor party, leaving the question of program and leadership unmentioned, are simply inventing a formula for their own betrayal.

It is not permissible for revolutionists to pass themselves off as mere advocates of a labor party, pure and simple, like any labor faker who devotes Sunday sermons to this idea. A labor party headed by the present official labor skates, without a program of class struggle, would be a sitting duck for American fascism. That's the truth of the matter, and advocacy of a labor party isn't worth much if it leaves this truth unsaid. Large numbers of trade-union militants know this as well as we do. They know that the present official leaders are no good for a real fight on any front, and that they have to be thrown out before there can be any serious thought of a show down with American fascism.

Those militants who know the score on this ought to

organize themselves in order to conduct their struggle more effectively. This organization of the class conscious workers can only take the form of a revolutionary party. There is no substitute for that. And since the SWP is the only revolutionary party in the field, there is no substitute for the SWP. Those workers who today already recognize the necessity of a labor party ought to take the next step and unite with the SWP in its effort to direct the struggle toward a revolutionary goal.

Joseph Vanzler

THE MILITANT, JULY 9, 1956

To comrades throughout the world who are familiar with his writings and translations of Trotsky's works, he was known as John G. Wright. His real name was Joseph Vanzler. His friends never called him anything but "Usick." The obituary articles by other comrades will, I am sure, give an account of the essential facts of his life and the many contributions he made to our movement over the past quarter of a century. It is an imposing record.

Here I wish only to say a few words in memory of Usick as a friend. I first remember meeting him 23 years ago at a party forum on the German crisis, in the days when Hitler was coming to power. He was obviously deeply disturbed by the German events and spoke excitedly at the forum. Soon afterward he joined our organization, and I gradually came to know him. It took time to know him as he really was, however, because the real man didn't reveal himself very well in branch debates.

It took personal association, over a long time, to know

the real Usick. Our association during the first year or so was dominated by conflict over one question of party policy and another. In 1934 we came to agreement on party policy and perspectives for the long pull and were reconciled in an unbroken union that lasted 21 years. We became more than comrades in the political struggle. We became friends.

Over that long stretch of time, without a break at any point, Usick gave me what everyone needs—I, perhaps, most of all—and that is simple friendship. It is the hardest thing to find, but it can't be got in any other way except by finding it. In present day business and politics people tend to think of "friendship" as a relation based on the exchange of favors. It implies calculation and dependence of one kind or another. But friendship, as I understand it, is no good unless it is disinterested, free from any taint of self-concern.

The friendship that gives freely without counting, is the only friendship worth talking about. That, I imagine, will be the normal, taken-for-granted relation of congenial people in their communion with each other in the future. But in the class society of the present, with its lack of freedom and its artificial values, such friendship is exceptional. When such a person as Usick comes along, with his simple, almost child-like trust, his appeal to the best in others and his readiness to believe the best about them, it is hard at first to believe that it is real.

Usick lived for more than 50 years in a transition period of the history of humanity. It is a mere interlude in the long evolution of the human race, but it has encompassed all our lives, and the lives of many generations. In this historical interlude, mankind, losing even the memory of its communal solidarity of earlier millenniums, has descended into the underworld of competitive class society in order to forge there the weapons for its liberation from helpless dependence on nature, and to create the material conditions for its re-emergence in the communal solidarity of classless society in the future.

The present world of class society, wherein all human relationships are tainted by conflicts of interests, was a world Usick never made and he was not made for it.

He was our most learned man. Indeed, in the many broad fields which were the subject of his thought and study—the whole range of Marxism, history, philosophy and world literature—it is doubtful that the workers' movement anywhere in the world possessed a comrade so roundly learned as Usick was. He was an intellectual. If there is such a thing as a pure intellectual, one concerned with theoretical ideas as a primary interest, Usick was one. He was also a pure idealist, in that his whole life was devoted to the socialist ideal, but he knew and taught that the ideal must rest on material foundations and can be realized only in the struggle of classes.

Usick's learning and his idealism were his strength—and also his weakness. At home in the broad ocean of theoretical concepts, Usick floundered helplessly in the narrow creeks of practical affairs in the workaday world; and that included the political and party struggle, which, unfortunately, is not always free from the malignant influences of the class society it strives to change. Usick, the scholar and idealist, didn't know how to take care of himself in the rough-and-tumble business of the political fight, which others handle by reflex action, almost without thinking about it. He needed help there, lest he be taken advantage of.

It was here that a few of us, who had learned how to fight for our place under the banner without forgetting the larger aims of our struggle; how to survive in the political alley-fights and protect ourselves and others against the groin-kickers and eye-gougers—came to Usick's aid. We valued him for his learning, for his real and solid contributions to the cause, and we would not allow him to be thrust aside. I am proud of that, and it is my consolation in sorrow today.

Usick gave a lot to the Party and thereby to the great cause it represents. His contributions of steady daily work—his articles, lectures and translations—added considerably to the sum total of the Party's capital, and all those who have inherited this capital are his debtors.

To his friends he has left the memory of uncounted acts of generosity and kindness, of simple service simply given, which helped to take the rough edges off many a tough personal situation. The grief is too deep for tears, but we hope and believe that the memory of Usick, as he was in life, will be stronger than the grief. Usick helped the cause he believed in, and helped his friends to persevere. He helped to build our faith in men by showing us the example of a communist man. None of us can hope to do more. His life was not lived in vain.

James P. Cannon
LOS ANGELES, CALIFORNIA

Glossary

Baker, Charles – Socialist Party member sentenced to one-year term in Canton, Ohio, workhouse for encouraging draft resistance during World War I.

Barbusse, Henri (1873–1935) – prominent French writer; later became supporter and apologist for Stalin.

Barnett, Eugene (1891–1973) – member of IWW; framed up and imprisoned 1919 in Centralia case; released in early 1930s; later became CIO organizer.

Baruch, Bernard (1870–1965) – U.S. stock and bond speculator and presidential adviser; head of War Industries Board during World War I.

Belor, John (1885–1934) – unemployed worker and supporter of Minneapolis Teamster strikes; killed in "Bloody Friday" police massacre.

Benson, Allan (1871–1940) – right-wing leader of Socialist Party; SP presidential candidate 1916; supported U.S. entry in World War I and resigned from party.

Berger, Victor (1860–1929) – right-wing leader of Socialist Party from Milwaukee; first Socialist member of Congress 1911–13; reelected 1918, 1919, 1922, 1924, 1926.

Billings, Warren K. (1894–1972) – militant trade unionist; framed up with Tom Mooney in 1916 on charges of planting bomb at 1916 "Preparedness Day" parade in San Francisco; released from prison in 1939.

Breitscheid, Rudolf (1874–1944) – member of German Social Democratic Party; Prussian interior minister 1918–19.

Bridges, Harry (1901–1990) – born in Australia; leader of 1934 San Francisco longshore strike; longtime president of International Longshoreman's and Warehouseman's Union; strongly promoted by Communist Party.

Browder, Earl (1891–1973) – general secretary of U.S. Communist Party 1930–45; expelled 1946 as scapegoat for CP's openly pro-imperialist policy dictated by Stalin in World War II.

Brown, Bill (1897–1938) – president of Minneapolis Teamster Local 574, 1921–38; collaborated closely with Communist League members in leadership of 1934 strikes.

Budenz, Louis (1891–1972) – former leader of Communist Party and editor of *Daily Worker;* left CP in 1945; wrote anticommunist autobiography in 1947; later became informant for Sen. Joseph McCarthy.

Burnham, James (1905–1987) – prominent philosophy professor at New York University; member of SWP in 1930s; split from SWP in 1940; later worked for Central Intelligence Agency; subsequently editor of right-wing *National Review.*

Carlson, Grace (1906–1992) – joined SWP 1936 in Minneapolis; one of 18 SWP leaders convicted and imprisoned under Smith Act during World War II; SWP candidate for vice president 1948; left party in 1952.

Centralia case – originated from November 11, 1919, attack on Centralia, Washington, IWW headquarters by members of American Legion; IWW member Wesley Everest was castrated and lynched in the attack; eight IWW members were convicted on frame-up murder charges for defending themselves; most were released in early 1930s; last defendant freed in 1939.

Chambers, Whittaker (1901–1961) – member of Communist Party in 1920s and 1930s; in 1948 accused Alger Hiss of passing State Department documents to USSR; author of autobiography entitled *Witness,* published 1952; became senior editor of *Time* magazine.

Chaplin, Ralph (1887–1961) – IWW organizer; artist and songwriter; sentenced to five-year prison term under Espionage Act during World War I.

Chiang Kai-shek (1887–1975) – military dictator of China from 1927 until toppled in 1949 revolution; subsequently dictator of Taiwan.

Citizens' Alliance – antiunion, strikebreaking organization of Minneapolis employers; mobilized against workers during Teamsters strikes of 1934.

Cline, Charles – IWW member framed up in 1913 along with other supporters of Mexican revolution, charged with murder of police officer in El Paso, Texas; convicted and sentenced to 25-years-to-life; pardoned in 1926.

Corey, Lewis (1894–1953) – writer and professor; founding leader of U.S. Communist movement as Louis Fraina; left CP in early 1920s; supporter of Lovestone organization in 1930s; repudiated Marxism in 1940.

Curran, Joseph (1906–1981) – president of National Maritime Union 1937–73; worked closely with Communist Party in 1930s and early 1940s; broke with CP in 1948.

Darrow, Clarence (1857–1938) – noted civil liberties attorney; defended a number of fighters jailed in the fight for workers' rights.

DeBoer, Harry (1907–1992) – a leader of 1934 Minneapolis Teamsters strike; imprisoned with Cannon and other SWP leaders during World War II under Smith Act; member of Socialist Workers Party until 1982.

Debs, Eugene V. (1855–1926) – leading left-wing member of Socialist Party; five-time SP presidential candidate; attended 1905 founding convention of IWW; imprisoned 1918–21 for antiwar speech at Canton, Ohio; sympathetic to Russian Revolution, but remained in SP after 1919 split that formed Communist Party; prominent supporter of ILD until his death.

De Leon, Daniel (1852–1914) – principal leader of Socialist Labor Party from early 1890s until his death; participant in founding convention of IWW in 1905.

Dewey, John (1859–1952) – liberal U.S. philosopher and educator; chairman of 1937–38 Commission of Inquiry into the Charges Made Against Leon Trotsky in the Moscow Trials, which rejected Stalin's frame-up charges.

Dubinsky, David (1892–1982) – president of International Ladies' Garment Workers' Union 1932–66.

Dunne, Vincent R. (1890–1970) – founding member of U.S. Communist movement; longtime leader of SWP and its forerunners; a central leader of 1934 Minneapolis Teamsters strikes; imprisoned with other SWP leaders under Smith Act during World War II.

Dunnigan, E.H. – U.S. Department of Labor mediator in 1934 Minneapolis strikes.

Durkin, James (1912–) – president of United Office and Professional Workers of America (CIO).

Eastman, Max (1883–1969) – early sympathizer of Trotsky in 1920s and translator of several of his works; later became anticommunist and editor of *Reader's Digest.*

Engels, Frederick (1820–1895) – lifelong collaborator of Karl Marx and cofounder with him of modern communist workers' movement.

Everest, Wesley (1890–1919) – IWW member and World War I veteran; castrated and lynched by right-wing mob November 1919 in Centralia, Washington.

Farley, James A. (1888–1976) – prominent capitalist politician; chairman of Democratic Party National Committee under Roosevelt.

Farrell, James T. (1904–1979) – noted novelist; sympathizer of SWP in 1930s and early 1940s; national chairman of Civil Rights Defense Committee, which organized support for Minneapolis Smith Act defendants; later became supporter of social democracy.

Fitzpatrick, John (1871–1946) – became president of Chicago Federation of Labor in 1901, holding that post for over 40 years; a leader of labor party movement 1919–23.

Ford, James W. (1893–1957) – Communist Party vice-presidential candidate 1932, 1936, 1940.

Ford, Richard – California farm workers' leader framed up for murder in 1913 during police attack; convicted and sentenced to life imprisonment; released on parole 1925; rearrested immediately but acquitted.

Foster, William Z. (1881–1961) – Communist Party presidential candidate 1924, 1928, 1932; CP national chairman 1945–57.

France, Anatole (1844–1924) – prominent French writer.

Franco, Francisco (1892–1975) – leader of fascist forces in Spanish civil war; dictator of Spain from 1939 until his death.

Frankfurter, Felix (1882–1965) – liberal jurist; author of 1927 book opposing Sacco-Vanzetti conviction; member of U.S. Supreme Court 1939–62.

Gannett, Betty (1906–1970) – longtime member of Communist Party; became CP national education director 1950; editor of *Political Affairs* 1963–70.

German-American Bund – organized 1936 by U.S. supporters of Hitler; campaigned against unions, communism, and Jews.

Gompers, Samuel (1850–1924) – founder and president of American Federation of Labor 1886–1924 (except 1895); supporter of U.S. entry into World War I.

Gorky, Maxim (1868–1936) – prominent Russian writer and novelist; sympathizer of Bolsheviks and Russian workers' movement before 1917; critical of Soviet regime in its early years; later publicly supported Stalin.

Gray, Laura (1909–1958) – member of SWP; cartoonist for *Militant* 1944–58.

Green, William (1873–1952) – president of American Federation of Labor 1924–52.

Haas, Francis J. (1889–1953) – Catholic priest; federal mediator in 1934 Minneapolis Teamster strikes.

Hague, Frank (1876–1956) – Democratic Party mayor of Jersey City, New Jersey, 1917–47; gained national notoriety during 1930s for use of fascist methods to drive labor organizers out of city; mobilized police, special deputies, war veterans, and city employees to smash union meetings.

Hall, Gus (1910–2000) – national leader of Communist Party since 1940s; CP general secretary from 1959.

Hanford, Ben (1861–1910) – Socialist Party leader; SP candidate for vice president 1904, 1908.

Hansen, Joseph (1910–1979) – joined Communist League of America 1934; secretary to Leon Trotsky 1937–40; longtime leader of SWP until his death; served as editor of the *Militant, International Socialist Review,* and *Intercontinental Press.*

Harden, Maximilian (1861–1927) – German journalist.

Haymarket martyrs – eight anarchists framed up following 1886 bombing at Haymarket Square in Chicago in which seven policemen were killed; four defendants were hanged and one committed suicide in 1887; remaining prisoners were pardoned in 1893.

Haywood, William D. ("Big Bill") (1869–1928) – leader of Western Federation of Miners 1901–07; founding leader of IWW 1905; arrested in 1906 with Moyer and Pettibone on frame-up charges of plotting murder of former Idaho governor; acquitted 1907 after international defense campaign; arrested 1917 for opposing U.S. participation in World War I and convicted in 1918; joined Communist Party 1921; left country while out on bail in 1921 and lived thereafter in Soviet Union.

Hill, Joe (1879–1915) – IWW member and composer of labor songs; framed up and convicted of murder in Utah; executed by firing squad.

Hillman, Sidney (1887–1946) – president of Amalgamated Clothing Workers 1915–46; vice president of CIO 1935–40.

Hillquit, Morris (1869–1933) – founding member of Socialist Party; leading reformist; central SP leader at time of death.

Hiss, Alger (1904–96) – U.S. State Department official; charged in 1948 by Whittaker Chambers with passing government secrets to USSR; convicted of perjury in 1950; sentenced to five years' imprisonment.

Hook, Sidney (1902–1989) – professor of philosophy at New York University; sympathizer of communist movement in 1930s; became vocal anticommunist in 1940s.

Hunter, Ivan – head of International Seamen's Union during 1930s.

Industrial Workers of the World (IWW) – founded 1905 as revolutionary industrial union movement; anarcho-syndicalist in orientation; rejected participation in political struggle, work in AFL; opposed U.S. participation in World War I and suffered severe repression.

International Labor Defense (ILD) – united front defense organization initiated by Communist Party in 1925 to defend political prisoners on nonpartisan basis; published *Labor Defender;* had 20,000 members and 156 branches at its height; Cannon was national secretary from its founding until his expulsion from CP in 1928; subsequently became sectarian appendage of CP; merged into Civil Rights Congress in 1946.

Johannes, Michael J. – Minneapolis police chief during 1934 Teamsters strikes; organized "Bloody Friday" massacre of strikers.

Karsner, Rose (1889–1968) – joined Socialist Party 1908; a founder of communist movement and SWP; business manager of *Militant* during 1930s; companion of James P. Cannon.

Koestler, Arthur (1905–1983) – novelist born in Hungary; member of Communist Party in 1930s; broke with CP over Moscow trials; author of *Darkness at Noon,* published 1941.

Koje Island – island off coast of South Korea; site of camps for 80,000 Chinese and North Korean prisoners of war;

scene of several POW rebellions in 1952 repressed by U.S. troops, with over 100 killed.

Kutcher, James (1912–1989) – member of SWP who lost both legs in combat in World War II; fired from civil service job in 1948 for membership in a "subversive" organization; defense campaign on his behalf won case in 1956; author of *The Case of the Legless Veteran.*

Labor Defender – monthly magazine of International Labor Defense.

Lansbury, George (1859–1940) – prominent British Labour Party member of Parliament.

Lenin, V.I. (1870–1924) – founder of Russian Bolshevik Party; chair of Council of People's Commissars (Russian Soviet government) 1917–24; central leader of Communist International until his death.

Lewis, John L. (1880–1969) – president of United Mine Workers union 1919–60; president of CIO 1935–40.

Little, Frank (1879–1917) – IWW organizer; lynched in Butte, Montana, by company-hired vigilantes during copper miners' strike.

Livingston, David – longtime leader of District 65 of Retail, Wholesale, and Department Store Workers union (later of UAW); became union president in 1952.

Loebe, Paul (1875–1967) – president of German Reichstag 1924–32; member of Social Democratic Party.

Lundeberg, Harry (1901–1957) – head of Sailors' Union of the Pacific from mid-1930s and of Seafarers International Union from its chartering in 1938; leader of syndicalist tendency.

MacArthur, Douglas (1880–1964) – commander of U.S. armed forces in Korean War; advocated expanding war into China; relieved from command by Truman in 1951.

Macdonald, Dwight (1906–1982) – author and journalist; joined SWP 1939; broke with party 1940; editor of *Politics* during 1940s; later wrote for *New Yorker.*

Mannerheim, Karl von (1867–1951) – head of counterrevolutionary forces in Finnish civil war and White Terror; president of Finland 1944–46.

Marx, Karl (1818–1883) – founder with Frederick Engels of modern communist workers' movement.

McCarthy, Joseph (1908–1957) – Republican senator from Wisconsin; most prominent spokesman of anticommunist witch-hunt during early 1950s.

McInerney, James (d. 1930) – member of IWW; framed up and imprisoned in 1919 in Centralia case; died in prison.

Meany, George (1894–1980) – became secretary-treasurer of AFL in 1939; AFL president 1952–55; president of AFL-CIO 1955–79.

Merrick, John – union militant framed up in 1923, charged with planting bomb at shoe factory in Haverhill, Massachusetts; sentenced to 3–6 years imprisonment.

Metaxas, Joannes (1871–1941) – dictator of Greece 1936–40.

Militant – socialist weekly newspaper; founded 1928 by expelled members of Communist Party with James P. Cannon as founding editor; known as *New Militant* 1935–36, *Socialist Appeal* 1937–41.

Mindszenty, Josef (1892–1975) – cardinal in Catholic Church; imprisoned by Hungarian Stalinist government 1948–55; lived in U.S. embassy 1956–71; subsequently allowed to emigrate.

Minor, Robert (1884–1952) – radical cartoonist and anarchist before World War I; joined CP 1920; later became leading Stalinist functionary.

Minority Movement – left-wing caucus in British Trades Union Congress initiated by Communist Party in 1924.

Mooney, Thomas J. (1882–1942) – left-wing labor leader in San Francisco; opposed U.S. entry in World War I; framed up in 1916 with Warren K. Billings, charged with planting bomb at 1916 "Preparedness Day" parade in San Francisco; sentenced to death but sentence commuted in 1918 due to international defense campaign; pardoned in 1939.

Morris, George (1903–1997) – leading member of Communist Party; correspondent for *Daily Worker.*

Moyer, Charles H. (1865–1929) – president of Western Federation of Miners 1902–12; arrested in 1906 with Haywood and Pettibone on frame-up charges of plotting murder of former Idaho governor; following international defense effort, charges were dropped after acquittal of other defendants in 1907.

Murray, Philip (1886–1952) – leader of Steel Workers Organizing Committee from 1936; international president United Steelworkers of America 1942–52; president of CIO from 1940–52.

Mussolini, Benito (1883–1945) – former Italian Socialist Party member expelled 1914; founded fascist movement 1919; Italian dictator 1922–43.

Ness, Henry (1894–1934) – member of Teamsters General Drivers Local 574 in Minneapolis; killed in "Bloody Friday" police massacre.

Olson, Floyd (1891–1936) – Farmer-Labor Party governor of Minnesota 1931–36.

Osman, Arthur – president of District 65 of Retail, Wholesale, and Department Store Workers union from its founding in 1933 until 1952.

Pablo, Michel (1911–96) – Greek communist; leader of Fourth International after World War II; engineered a split in that organization in 1953.

Palmer, A. Mitchell (1872–1936) – U.S. attorney general 1919–21; ordered nationwide raids arresting thousands of alleged Communists in December 1919 and January 1920, known as the "Palmer raids"; over 700 were eventually deported.

Papcun, George – organizer of mine workers in Pennsylvania and leader of Young Workers League; convicted in

1926 under state anti-sedition law after making speech at miners' meeting.

Parsons, Albert (1848–1887) – workers' leader and anarchist framed up and executed in Chicago Haymarket case.

Petrillo, James (1892–1984) – president of American Federation of Musicians 1940–58.

Pettibone, George A. (d. 1908) – supporter of Western Federation of Miners; arrested in 1906 with Haywood and Moyer on frame-up charges of plotting murder of former Idaho governor; acquitted 1907 after international defense campaign.

Quill, Michael (1905–1966) – president of Transport Workers Union 1935–66; aligned with Stalinists until late 1940s; then became outspoken anticommunist.

Rákosi, Mátyás (1892–1971) – leader of Hungarian Communist Party; imprisoned by Hungarian military dictatorship 1925–40; premier in Stalinist-led Hungarian government until August 1956.

Rangel, José – IWW member framed up in 1913 along with other supporters of Mexican revolution, charged with murder of police officer in El Paso, Texas; convicted and sentenced to 25-years-to-life; pardoned in 1926.

Reuther, Walter (1907–1970) – president of United Auto Workers 1946–70; president of CIO 1952–55.

Rhee, Syngman (1875–1965) – president and dictator of South Korea 1948–60; installed in office under U.S. occupation; ousted after popular rebellion in 1960.

Ruthenberg, Charles E. (1882–1927) – a leader of Socialist Party left wing during World War I; national secretary of Communist Party 1919–27.

Ryan, Joseph (1884–1963) – elected president of International Longshoremen's Association 1927; made president for life 1943; retired 1953.

Sacco, Nicola (1891–1927) – immigrant worker active in working-class struggles; framed up with Bartolomeo

Vanzetti on charges of robbery and murder 1920; executed after long appeals and mass international defense campaign.

St. John, Vincent (1873–1929) – general secretary of IWW 1908–14.

Shachtman, Max (1904–1972) – editor of *Labor Defender,* 1926–28; expelled with Cannon from CP 1928; a founding leader of Communist League of America; led 1940 split from SWP; fused with SP in 1958.

Shaw, George Bernard (1856–1950) – playwright; member of British Fabian Society.

Silver Shirts of America – U.S. fascist organization founded 1932 by William Dudley Pelley; carried out vigilante actions against labor movement during 1930s.

Smillie, Robert (1859–1940) – president of British Miners' Federation 1912–21.

Smith, Elmer – member of IWW; tried in 1919 Centralia frame-up case but acquitted.

Smith, Gerald L.K. (1898–1976) – a leader of U.S. fascist movement in 1930s; headed Christian Nationalist Crusade, directed against unions and communism.

Socialist Party of America – founded 1901; left-wing majority split in 1919 to form Communist Party; in 1936 communist forces entered SP to win new radicalizing forces; revolutionaries were expelled in late 1937 and formed Socialist Workers Party.

Socialist Workers Party – formed 1938; traces its continuity to the founding of the communist movement in 1919 and the fight for a communist perspective led by Cannon and other cadres expelled from the CP in 1928, forming the Communist League of America.

Spargo, John (1876–1966) – prominent Socialist Party member; resigned from party in 1917 as supporter of U.S. entry in World War I.

Spellman, Francis (1889–1967) – Catholic cardinal in New York; defender of Sen. Joseph McCarthy and vigorous opponent of labor movement.

Spies, August (1855–1887) – working-class militant framed up and executed in Haymarket case.

Suhr, Herman D. – California farm workers' leader framed up for murder in 1913 during police attack; convicted and sentenced to life imprisonment; released on parole 1926.

Sullivan, Joseph (1866–1935) – a leader of British mine workers union; Labour Party member of Parliament 1922–24, 1926–31.

Thomas, Norman (1884–1968) – leader of Socialist Party from late 1920s until his death; six-time SP presidential candidate.

Tobin, Daniel J. (1875–1955) – president of International Brotherhood of Teamsters 1907–52; joined in government-employer attack on Minneapolis Teamsters movement.

Trimble, Glen – joined Socialist Party in 1930s; leader of California SP left wing; member of SWP 1938–40.

Trotsky, Leon (1879–1940) – a leader of 1917 Bolshevik revolution; head of Red Army during 1918–20 civil war; a central leader of Communist International; in 1923 became principal leader of communist opposition to Stalin-led bureaucracy; expelled from Soviet Union 1929; founding leader of Fourth International; assassinated by agent of Stalin.

Tyler, Gus (1911–2011) – leader of Socialist Party; editor of *Socialist Call;* later left SP and became assistant president of International Ladies' Garment Workers' Union.

Vanzetti, Bartolomeo (1888–1927) – immigrant worker framed up on charges of murder in 1920 together with Nicola Sacco; executed after long appeals and mass international defense campaign.

Vanzler, Joseph (John G. Wright, Usick) (1902–1956) – member and leader of Socialist Workers Party from 1933 until his death; translator of many books by Leon Trotsky.

Wagenknecht, Alfred (1881–1956) – leader of Socialist Party left wing; served one-year prison sentence for opposing U.S. entry in World War I; a founding leader of Communist Party.

Wallace, Henry (1888–1965) – U.S. vice president 1941–45 under Roosevelt; broke with Truman in 1946 over cold war policy toward Soviet Union; ran for president in 1948 on Progressive Party ticket, backed by Communist Party.

Walling, William (1877–1936) – leader of Socialist Party; resigned from SP as supporter of U.S. entry in World War I.

Whitney, Charlotte Anita (1867–1955) – Communist Party member convicted in 1920 under California criminal syndicalist law; conviction upheld by Supreme Court in 1926; subsequently pardoned.

Wilkinson, Ellen (1891–1947) – socialist and suffrage leader; later became Labour Party member of British Parliament.

Woll, Matthew (1880–1956) – supporter of U.S. entry in World War I; became AFL vice president in 1919.

Workers Defense League – nonpartisan defense organization founded 1936 by members of Socialist Party.

Young People's Socialist League (YPSL) – Socialist Party youth organization; majority were expelled in 1937 as supporters of communist left wing; became fraternal organization of SWP in 1938; disaffiliated from SWP following 1940 party split.

Index

ALSO BY JAMES P. CANNON

The History of American Trotskyism, 1928–38

Report of a Participant

"Trotskyism is not a new movement, a new doctrine," Cannon says, "but the restoration, the revival of genuine Marxism as it was expounded and practiced in the Russian Revolution and in the early days of the Communist International." Talks by a founding leader of American communism on building a proletarian party in the United States. $17. Also in Spanish and French.

The Struggle for a Proletarian Party

"The workers of America have power enough to topple the structure of capitalism at home and to lift the whole world with them when they rise," Cannon asserts. On the eve of World War II, a founder of the communist movement in the US and a leader of the Communist International in Lenin's time defends the program and party-building norms of Bolshevism. $20. Also in Spanish and Farsi.

Socialism on Trial

Testimony at Minneapolis Sedition Trial

The revolutionary program of the working class presented in federal court in 1941 on the eve of US entry into World War II. The frame-up charges of "seditious conspiracy" targeted leaders of the Socialist Workers Party. $15. Also in Spanish, French, Farsi.

The First Ten Years of American Communism

Report of a Participant

"Stalinism has worked mightily to obliterate the honorable record of American communism in its pioneer days. Yet the Communist Party wrote such a chapter, and the young militants of the new generation ought to know about it and claim it for their own. It belongs to them."
—*James P. Cannon*, 1962. $17

PROGRAM AND COMMUNIST CONTINUITY

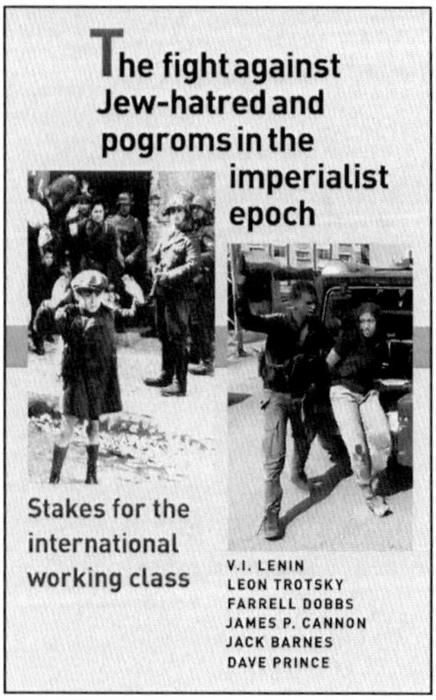

The Fight Against Jew-Hatred and Pogroms in the Imperialist Epoch

Stakes for the International Working Class

V.I. LENIN, LEON TROTSKY
FARRELL DOBBS, JAMES P. CANNON
JACK BARNES, DAVE PRINCE

Jew-hatred and pogroms—such as Hamas carried out on October 7, 2023—are part of the social convulsions and wars of the imperialist epoch. The authors explain why fighting Jew-hatred is decisive to the working class and oppressed nations of the world—and *what is to be done to end it*. $10. Also in Spanish, French, Greek.

The Communist Manifesto

KARL MARX AND FREDERICK ENGELS

Communism, say the founding leaders of the revolutionary workers movement, is not a set of ideas or preconceived "principles" but workers' line of march to power. It springs from a "movement going on under our very eyes." $5. Also in Spanish, French, Farsi, Arabic.

Lenin's Final Fight

Speeches and Writings, 1922–23

V.I. LENIN

In 1922 and 1923, V.I. Lenin, central leader of the world's first socialist revolution, waged what was to be his last political battle—one that was lost after his death. At stake was whether that revolutionary government and the world communist movement it led would remain on the revolutionary proletarian course that brought workers and peasants to power in Russia in 1917. $17. Also in Spanish, Farsi, Greek.

The Low Point of Labor Resistance Is Behind Us

The Socialist Workers Party Looks Forward

JACK BARNES, MARY-ALICE WATERS
STEVE CLARK

The global order imposed by Washington is shattering. A long retreat by the working class and unions has come to an end. The bosses and their government are stepping up attacks on our wages, conditions, and constitutional rights. This book highlights opportunities for building a mass proletarian party able to lead the struggle to end capitalist rule, opening a socialist future for humanity. $10. Also in Spanish, French, Greek.

Tribunes of the People and the Trade Unions

KARL MARX, V.I. LENIN, LEON TROTSKY
FARRELL DOBBS, JACK BARNES

A tribune of the people uses every manifestation of capitalist oppression to explain why working people, in class battles, will break from the bosses' parties, organize a revolutionary fight for state power, and lay the foundations of a socialist world of human solidarity. $12. Also in Spanish, French, Farsi, Greek.

In Defense of Marxism

Against the Petty-Bourgeois Opposition in the Socialist Workers Party

LEON TROTSKY

A reply to those in the revolutionary workers movement in the late 1930s who buckled to bourgeois patriotism during Washington's buildup to enter World War II. Trotsky explains why only a party fighting to bring workers into its ranks and leadership can steer a communist course. In the process, he defends the materialist and dialectical foundations of Marxism. $17. Also in Spanish, French, Farsi.

CUBA'S SOCIALIST REVOLUTION

New!
Revolution and the Road to Peace in Colombia

The Example of the Cuban Revolution

FIDEL CASTRO

"No crime can be committed in the name of revolution," Fidel Castro declares, drawing from the example set by working people of Cuba as they took state power out of the hands of its capitalist rulers. In 2008, as part of efforts to end six decades of armed conflict in Colombia, he shared the exemplary record of Cuba's revolutionary struggle with the Revolutionary Armed Forces of Colombia (FARC) and the world. $10. Also in Spanish and French.

The First and Second Declarations of Havana

Nowhere are the questions of revolutionary strategy that today confront men and women on the front lines of struggles in the Americas addressed with greater truthfulness and clarity than in these uncompromising indictments of imperialist plunder and "the exploitation of man by man." Adopted by million-strong assemblies of the Cuban people in 1960 and 1962. $10. Also in Spanish, French, Farsi, Arabic, Greek.

Playa Girón/Bay of Pigs

Washington's First Military Defeat in the Americas

FIDEL CASTRO, JOSÉ RAMÓN FERNÁNDEZ

In less than 72 hours of combat in April 1961, Cuba's revolutionary armed forces defeated a US-organized invasion by 1,500 mercenaries. The Cuban people set an example for workers, farmers, and youth the world over that with political consciousness, class solidarity, courage, and revolutionary leadership, we can stand up to seemingly insurmountable odds—*and win*. $17. Also in Spanish.

New!

Cuba and the Independence War in Guinea-Bissau and Cape Verde

The Fall of the Last Colonial Empire in Africa

VÍCTOR DREKE

In 1974–75 the people of two West African countries, Guinea-Bissau and Cape Verde, put an end to 500 years of Portuguese colonial exploitation. Led by a popular movement forged by Amílcar Cabral, their struggle triggered the collapse of Portugal's entire colonial empire and brought down the 40-year fascist dictatorship in Portugal itself. Víctor Dreke's firsthand account brings to life this decisive victory. $12. Also in Spanish and French.

October 1962

The 'Missile' Crisis as Seen from Cuba

TOMÁS DIEZ ACOSTA

In October 1962 Washington pushed the world to the edge of nuclear war. Here the full story of that historic moment is told from the perspective of the Cuban people, whose determination to defend their sovereignty and their socialist revolution blocked US plans for a devastating military assault. $17

Cuba and the Coming American Revolution

JACK BARNES

This is a book about the example set by the Cuban people that socialist revolution is not only necessary—it can be made. A book about the struggles of workers and other exploited producers in the imperialist heartland, and the youth attracted to them. About the class struggle in the US, where the revolutionary capacities of working people are as utterly discounted by the ruling powers as were those of the Cuban toilers. $10. Also in Spanish, French, Farsi.

FROM PATHFINDER

Malcolm X, Black Liberation, and the Road to Workers Power

JACK BARNES

"The conquest of state power by a class-conscious vanguard of the working class is the mightiest weapon possible in the fight against Black oppression, the subjugation of women, Jew-hatred, and every form of human degradation inherited from class society." $20. Also in Spanish, French, Farsi, Arabic, Greek.

Is Socialist Revolution in the US Possible?

A Necessary Debate Among Working People

MARY-ALICE WATERS

An unhesitating "Yes"—that's the answer given here. Possible—but not inevitable. That depends on what working people do. $7. Also in Spanish, French, Farsi.

The Case of the Legless Veteran

JAMES KUTCHER

James Kutcher, a worker who lost both legs in World War II, was fired from his federal government job in 1948. The stated reason was that he was a member of the Socialist Workers Party, which had been declared "subversive." With support from thousands of unionists and other supporters of democratic rights, Kutcher won back his job in 1956. This is the story of that eight-year battle. $17

The Teamster Series

FARRELL DOBBS

Four books on the 1930s strikes, organizing drives, and political campaigns that transformed the Teamsters into a militant industrial union movement. Written by the organizer of these battles and leader of the Socialist Workers Party. A tool for workers seeking to use union power and advance the fight for a party of labor. $16 each, series $50. Also in Spanish. *Teamster Rebellion* is also available in French, Farsi, Greek.

Are They Rich Because They're Smart?

Class, Privilege, and Learning Under Capitalism

JACK BARNES

Exposes growing class inequalities in the US and the self-serving rationalizations of well-paid professionals who think their "brilliance" equips them to "regulate" working people, who don't know what's in our own best interest. $10. Also in Spanish, French, Farsi, Arabic, Greek.

The Turn to Industry

Forging a Proletarian Party

JACK BARNES

A book about the working-class program, composition, and course of the only kind of party in the imperialist epoch worthy of the name "revolutionary." A party that can recognize the most revolutionary fact of this epoch—the worth of working people, and our capacity to change society when we organize and act to win power from the capitalist class. $15. Also in Spanish, French, Farsi, Greek.

New International

A MAGAZINE OF MARXIST POLITICS AND THEORY

NEW INTERNATIONAL NO. 7

Opening Guns of World War III: Washington's Assault on Iraq

JACK BARNES

The murderous assault on Iraq in 1990–91 heralded increasingly sharp conflicts among imperialist powers, growing instability of capitalism, and more wars. Also includes:

1945: When US Troops Said 'No!'
by Mary-Alice Waters
Lessons from the Iran-Iraq War
by Samad Sharif

$14. Also in Spanish, French, Farsi.

NEW INTERNATIONAL NO. 10

Imperialism's March Toward Fascism and War

JACK BARNES

"There will be new Hitlers, new Mussolinis. That is inevitable. What is not inevitable is that they will triumph. The working-class vanguard will organize our class to fight back against the devastating toll we are made to pay for the capitalist crisis. The future of humanity will be decided in the contest between these contending class forces." $14. Also in Spanish, French, Farsi, Greek.

NEW INTERNATIONAL NO. 12

Capitalism's Long Hot Winter Has Begun

JACK BARNES

Today's global capitalist crisis is but the opening stage of decades of economic, financial, and social convulsions and class battles. Class-conscious workers confront this historic turning point for imperialism with confidence, Jack Barnes writes, drawing satisfaction from being "in their face" as we chart a revolutionary course to take power. $14. Also in Spanish, French, Farsi, Arabic, Greek.

THE ROAD TO WOMEN'S EMANCIPATION

New Expanded Edition!

Cosmetics, Fashion, and the Exploitation of Women

MARY-ALICE WATERS
JOSEPH HANSEN, EVELYN REED

"Norms of beauty and fashion are inseparable from the class struggle." That's the title of the opening chapter of this new expanded edition of a lively 1950s debate in the *Militant*, a socialist newsweekly. How cosmetics and fashion monopolies rake in profits from social insecurities of women and adolescents. Why women's integration into the workforce and unions is a major advance in the fight for emancipation. A Marxist classic on the origins of women's oppression and the working-class road forward.

$15. Also in Spanish, French, Farsi, Greek.

Women in Cuba: The Making of a Revolution Within the Revolution

VILMA ESPÍN, ASELA DE LOS SANTOS, YOLANDA FERRER

The integration of women in the ranks and leadership of the Cuban Revolution was intertwined with the proletarian course led by Fidel Castro from the start. This is the story of that revolution and how it transformed the women and men who made it.

$17. Also in Spanish, Farsi, Greek.

PATHFINDERPRESS.COM

EXPAND YOUR REVOLUTIONARY LIBRARY

Thomas Sankara Speaks

The Burkina Faso Revolution, 1983–87

Under Sankara's guidance, Burkina Faso's revolutionary government led peasants, workers, women, and youth to expand literacy; to sink wells, plant trees, erect housing; to combat women's oppression; to carry out land reform; to join others worldwide to free themselves from the imperialist yoke. $20. Also in French.

The Jewish Question

A Marxist Interpretation

ABRAM LEON

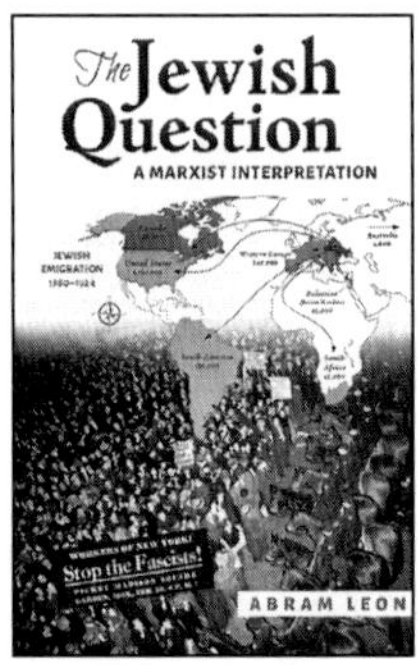

The battle against reactionary forces aiming to exterminate the Jews remains central to world politics, as shown by the genocidal October 2023 pogrom in Israel. Why is Jew-hatred still raising its ugly head? What are its class roots? Why, as Abram Leon explains, is there no solution "independent of the world proletarian revolution"? Revised translation, new introduction, 40 pages of illustrations and maps. $17. Also in Spanish, French, Greek.

Capitalism's World Disorder

Working-Class Politics at the Millennium

JACK BARNES

The social devastation and financial panic, coarsening of politics, cop brutality, and imperialist aggression—all are products not of something gone wrong with capitalism but of its lawful workings. Yet the future can be changed by the united struggle of workers and farmers increasingly conscious of their capacity to wage revolutionary struggles for state power and to transform the world. $20. Also in Spanish and French.

Malcolm X Talks to Young People

"The young generation of whites, Blacks, browns, whatever else—you're living at a time of revolution," said Malcolm in 1964. "And I for one will join with anyone, I don't care what color you are, as long as you want to change this miserable condition that exists on this earth." Four talks and an interview in the last months of Malcolm's life. $12. Also in Spanish, French, Farsi, Greek.

Women's Liberation and the African Freedom Struggle

THOMAS SANKARA

"There is no true social revolution without the liberation of women," explains the leader of the 1983–87 revolution in the West African country of Burkina Faso. $5. Also in Spanish, French, Farsi, Arabic.

Pathfinder Press **accessible e-books** for the blind, those with low vision, or other challenges reading print books

For a list of current accessible titles, go to: pathfinderpress.com/collections/books-for-the-blind.

Visit bookshare.org for information on how to sign up.

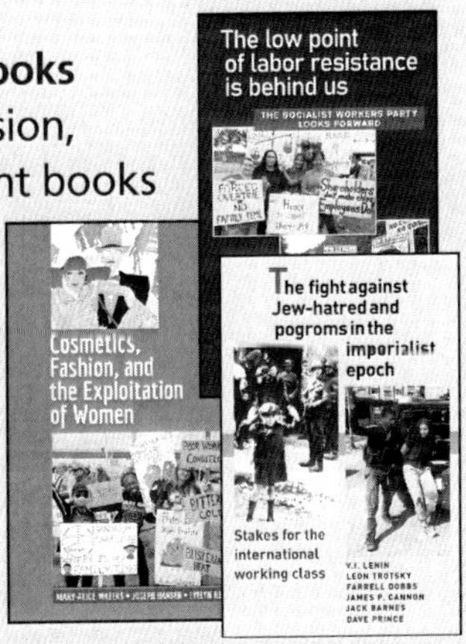

PATHFINDER AROUND THE WORLD

UNITED STATES
(and Caribbean, Latin America, and East Asia)

Pathfinder Books, 306 W. 37th St., 13th Floor
New York, NY 10018

CANADA

Pathfinder Books, 7107 St. Denis, Suite 204
Montreal, QC H2S 2S5

UNITED KINGDOM
(and Europe, Africa, Middle East, and South Asia)

Pathfinder Books, 5 Norman Rd.
Seven Sisters, London N15 4ND

AUSTRALIA
(and New Zealand, Southeast Asia, and the Pacific)

Pathfinder Books, Suite 2, First floor, 275 George St.
Liverpool, Sydney, NSW 2170
Postal address: P.O. Box 73, Campsie, NSW 2194

BUILD YOUR LIBRARY!
JOIN THE PATHFINDER READERS CLUB

$10 / YEAR
25% DISCOUNT ON ALL PATHFINDER TITLES
30% OFF BOOKS OF THE MONTH
Valid at pathfinderpress.com and local Pathfinder book centers

Go to: pathfinderpress.com/products/pathfinder-readers-club

Pathfinder
pathfinderpress.com